THE GLORY THAT WAS GREECE

Odysseus bound to the mast of his ship listens to the sirens.

THE GLORY THAT WAS
GREECE
by J. C. STOBART

4th edition, edited and revised by

R. J. HOPPER

SIDGWICK AND JACKSON
LONDON

ST. MARTIN'S PRESS
NEW YORK

COPYRIGHT © 1961 BY
SIDGWICK AND JACKSON LTD

ALL RIGHTS RESERVED. FOR INFORMATION IN THE
UNITED STATES WRITE: SCHOLARLY AND REFERENCE
DIVISION. ST. MARTIN'S PRESS, INC.,
175 FIFTH AVENUE, NEW YORK, NY 10010

LIBRARY OF CONGRESS CATALOGING-IN-PUBLICATION
DATA APPLIED FOR

First Edition	*1912*
Second Edition, revised	*1920*
Reprinted	*1925*
Third Edition, revised and reset	*1934*
Reprinted	*1938*
Reprinted	*1946*
Reprinted	*1948*
Reprinted	*1949*
Reprinted	*1951*
Reprinted	*1955*
Fourth Edition, entirely reset and revised	*1961*
Soft Cover Edition	*1971*
Reprinted	*1976*
Reprinted	*1978*
Reprinted	*1984*
Joint Imprint Edition	*1987*

ISBN 0-283-48455-1 (Sidgwick and Jackson, Softback)
ISBN 0-283-35320-1 (Sidgwick and Jackson, Cased)
ISBN 0-312-03102-5 (St. Martin's Press)

Printed in Hong Kong

PREFACE

TO THE ORIGINAL EDITION

With the progress of research, classical scholarship tends more and more towards narrower fields of specialisation. Real students are now like miners working underground each in his own shaft, buried far away from sight or earshot of the public, so that they even begin to lose touch with one another. This makes an occasional survey of the whole field of operations not only necessary for interested onlookers, whether they happen to be shareholders or not, but also serviceable to the scholars themselves. The task of furnishing it, however, is not an easy one. No man nowadays can be as fully equipped in archaeology, history, and literary criticism as were great writers of general history in the last century like George Grote and Theodor Mommsen. We are driven, therefore, to one of two courses : either to compile encyclopaedic works by various writers under slight editorial control, or else to sacrifice detail and attempt in a much less ambitious spirit to present a panorama of the whole territory from an individual point of view. The former plan is constantly producing valuable storehouses of information to be used for purposes of reference. But they tend to grow in bulk and compression, until, like the monumental "Pauly-Wissowa", they are nothing but colossal dictionaries.

The writer who attempts the second plan will, of course, be inviting criticism at a thousand points. He is compelled to deal in large generalisations, and to tread upon innumerable toes with every step he takes. Every fact he chronicles is the subject of a monograph, every opinion he hazards may run counter to somebody's life-work. He will often have to neglect the latest theory and sometimes he is unaware of the latest discovery. The best that he can hope for is that his archaeology may satisfy the historians and his history the archaeologists. My only claim to the right of undertaking such a task is that circumstances have so

v

directed my studies that they have been almost equally divided between the three main branches—archaeology, history and literature. I have experienced the extraordinary sense of illumination which one feels on turning from linguistic study to the examination of objective antiquity on the actual soil of the classical countries, and then the added interest with which realities are invested by the literary records of history.

It is by another title that the writer of a book like this makes his appeal to the general reading public. He must feel such a love of Greece and of things Hellenic that he is led by it into missionary enthusiasm. The Greek language has now, probably for ever, lost its place in the curriculum of secondary education for the greater part of our people. Whether this is to be deplored is beyond the question: it is, at any rate, inevitable. But there has always been a genuinely cultivated public to whom Greek was unknown, and it is undoubtedly very much larger in this generation. To them, though Greek is unknown, Greece need not be wholly sealed. But their point of view will be different from that of the professional philologist. They will not care for the details of the siege of Plataea merely because Thucydides described it; they will be much less likely to overrate the importance of that narrow strip of time which scholars select out of Greek history as the "classical period". Greek art will make the strongest appeal to them, and Greek thought, so far as it can be communicated by description. They will be interested in social life and private antiquities rather than in diplomatic intrigues and constitutional subtleties. My object is to present a general and vivid picture of ancient Greek culture. I recognise that the brush and camera will tell of the glory of Greece far more eloquently than I can. My text is intended to explain the pictures by showing the sort of people and the state of mind that produced them. Some history, some politics, some religion and philosophy must be included for that purpose. The result will be a history of Greece with statues and poems taking the place of wars and treaties.

J.C.S.

1911

PREFACE

TO THE THIRD EDITION

A REVISION of the text for the purpose of a third edition had been commenced before his death by Mr. J. C. Stobart. The completion of this task had of necessity to be left to other hands; but the reviser's first care has been to interfere with the text as little as possible, and it is hoped that the book is substantially what it would have been had Mr. Stobart completed the revision. Points of detail have been checked throughout, and a very few paragraphs have been modified or rewritten where the trend of modern research seemed to lead away from the conclusions adopted by Mr. Stobart. Such cases occur most frequently in the opening chapters, as is inevitable in view of the great advance made of recent years in the study of the prehistoric civilisations of Greece. Lastly, the opportunity has been taken of renewing the illustrations throughout, improving on the old blocks and adding fresh material.

F.N.P.

1933

PREFACE

TO THE FOURTH EDITION

THE fifty-odd years which have gone by since this book was first written have seen great additions to our knowledge of the Greeks, in terms both of material remains and of general appreciation. There have also been changes in points of view, and horizons have widened. On the other hand a reviser of Stobart's book cannot but be impressed both by his acute assessment of new material even when it was but recently discovered, and by the modernity of some of his observations. More than this. Some of the views expressed in the original version rest on attitudes and values different from those of the present day, and it is therefore in itself a valuable document of a past age, and evidence of something growing rarer in our times: the influence of Greek studies seriously pursued on a man of education, an amateur in the best sense of the word rather than a professional scholar. The eternal and universal character of the appeal made by the ancient Greeks is thereby demonstrated as it should be. An effort has therefore been made to preserve as much of the original work and its arrangement as possible, not least its racy and vigorous style. This applies to the illustrations as well as to the text, and it should be pointed out that the plates are therefore not arranged in anything like the logical and chronological order; but they illustrate well enough the development of the narrative.

While so much of the text has been retained, an effort has also been made in the Notes to the Plates, and in the Bibliography, to provide up-to-date information, and to introduce material new since Stobart's day. Some account has also been taken, in the choice of material to be illustrated, of the shift of taste, which may only be temporary, from the art of the fifth and fourth centuries B.C. to the Archaic period in one direction and to the Hellenistic in the other. A few outmoded ideas, especially on racial origins, have been omitted.

I would like to thank all those who have aided in procuring photographs.

R. J. HOPPER

CONTENTS

NOTES TO THE PLATES

Plate

Frontispiece

Odysseus bound to the mast of his ship listens to the Sirens. Copyright photograph, British Museum. From an Attic red-figured stamnes in the British Museum, B.M.E. 440 from Vulci in ancient Etruria. By the Siren Painter of the Late Archaic period.

1 Copyright Hirmer, Munich. The sanctuary at Olympia; the line of treasuries on the right, and the temple of Hera, under the slope of the Hill of Kronos. Under the trees there are also some traces of prehistoric houses. In the distance the column-drums of the temple of Zeus. See pages 72-75, 141.

2 Copyright Hirmer, Munich. Temple D (the so-called "Juno Lacinia") at Agrigento (anc. Akragas, Roman Agrigentum) in Sicily. A modest Doric structure of c. 450 B.C., one of a number which stand on a ridge between the mediaeval and modern town and the sea. One of them was of great size and unusual construction (see page 126). They are indicated in modern times by letters.

3 Copyright Hirmer, Munich. Columns of the temple of Athena incorporated in Syracuse Cathedral, Sicily. It was erected in the Doric style by the Syracusan tyrants Gelo and Hiero, c. 480-470 B.C. The columns are built into the outer wall of the Cathedral, and the ancient *cella* wall is pierced to form divisions between aisle and nave.

4 Copyright Hirmer, Munich. Olympia and the Alpheios valley. View from the north-west (from the hill above the SPAP Hotel), looking east and south-east over to the Hill of Kronos (left centre), the Altis or sacred enclosure,

Plate

the Kladeos bed (below the trees of the Altis), and the Alpheios flowing west from Arcadia.

5 Copyright Hirmer, Munich. The Temple of Apollo and the Pleistos valley at Delphi, seen from the Theatre. In the centre is the Temple of Apollo, its platform and substructures. Some of the columns (Doric) are re-erected at the eastern end. Beyond, on the slope, the Sacred Way and the Treasury of Athens (re-erected in the nineteenth century). On the upper left the "Flashing Rocks", the cleft of the Castalian Spring and the road to modern Arachova. Below the road, the lower Delphic site (Marmariá), with gymnasia, baths and temples, and the valley of the Pleistos flowing into the Gulf of Corinth.

6 Copyright Elsevier, Amsterdam, and The Royal Hellenic Airforce. The land-scape of Arcadia around the temple of Apollo Epikourios at Bassai ("The Glades") near Phigalia, on a slope descending to the River Neda. Note the stony denuded land-surface and thin scrub. On the Doric temple by Iktinos, architect of the Parthenon, the earliest Corinthian capital which it contained, and the internal frieze (now in the British Museum), see page 160. The temple is to be dated to the late fifth century, perhaps c. 420 B.C. See also PLATE 82.

7 Copyright Elsevier, Amsterdam, and The Royal Hellenic Airforce. Aerial view of Sparta and the Eurotas Valley looking approximately west to Taygetos, a water-course from which descends through the fields and olive-groves to join the river. At top middle of the photograph the entrance of the Langadha, a pass over westwards into Messenia and modern Kalamai (Kala-mata).

8 Copyright Hirmer, Munich. View over the theatre at Epidauros, from the higher ranges of seats above the *diazoma*. The rest of the sanctuary is beyond the trees to the left. This, the finest of Greek theatres, is ascribed by Pausanias to the Younger Polyclitus, but its date must be later, the beginning of the third century B.C. It shows several features of late date, especially in the stage buildings. It was extended in the second century B.C.; to the original 34 rows 24 more were added above the *diazoma* to seat 14,000 spectators in all.

9 Copyright (a) and (b), The American School of Archaeology at Corinth. (a) The Acrocorinth and the archaic temple of Apollo in the lower city.

Plate

Looking approximately south-west from the direction of the North Market. The Lechaion Road and the Basilica of the Roman town lie to the left behind the spectator, and the Market before him to the left. For the temple (550–540 B.C.; note the flat *echinus* of the capital and the very obvious *entasis* of the column shaft) see page 102. The Acrocorinth is 564 metres (1,886 ft) high; there are remains of fortifications from ancient times, but the main part is Frankish, Venetian and Turkish.

(b) View of the Isthmus of Corinth and the Corinthian Gulf, looking north from the summit of the Acrocorinth. In the foreground fragments of the wall of the Frankish-Turkish-Venetian fortress. Beyond: New Corinth, the end of the Corinthian Gulf, the Isthmus, Megavid, and Mount Geraneia. The coast of the Saronic Gulf is just off the photograph to the right.

10 Copyright Hirmer, Munich. The Acropolis of Athens (156.2 metres) from the south-west. From left to right: (above): the Propylaia and the temple of Athena Nike, Erechtheum (west end) with North and Caryatid Porches, the Parthenon; (middle): the Theatre of Herodes Atticus, the Stoa of Eumenes; above the Stoa, various shrines. The South (Cimonian) wall of the Acropolis (under a later outer covering). The isolated columns are former choregic monuments (see page 171). The Theatre of Dionysos is just off the photograph to the right.

11 Copyright Agora Excavations, American School of Classical Studies, Athens. Scene from the Hill of the Nymphs (Observatory Hill) behind the Church of Ayia Marina. Left to right: the so-called Theseum, in fact a temple of Hephaistos and Athena, the patron deities of arts and crafts, located in a district given up in ancient times to industrial establishments. The market-place with the rebuilt Stoa of Attalos facing. Slope and summit of the Areapagus Hill, and behind it the Acropolis showing the west end and north slope.

12 Copyright Agora Excavations, American School of Classical Studies, Athens. (a) The western side of the Athenian market-place (Agora) as excavated, with the temple of Hephaistos above. Mount Aigaleos behind to the north. On the west slope of the market-place in order from the bottom of the photograph: fountain-house, Tholos, Metroon (behind, the Bouleuterion) in front of which were the statues of the Eponyms, then a group of small temples and the Stoa of Zeus. See pages 157-158. This area was repeatedly restored, and systematised only in the Hellenistic period.

(b) A plaster model by Mr John Travlos, which shows the state and organisa-

Plate

tion of the western side in the second century A.D., in the period, therefore, between two great disasters, the destruction by Sulla in 86 B.C. and the Herulian sack of A.D. 267.

13   Copyright (a) Professor J. D. Evans and the British School of Archaeology at Athens. (b) Agora Excavations, American School of Classical Studies, Athens.
(a) Traces of the Early Neolithic habitation beneath the Central Court of the Minoan Palace at Cnossus, Crete. The earliest settlement on bedrock, showing the numerous pits and postholes; probably the camp site of the first settlers at Cnossus. Carbon 14 dating 6100 ± 180 B.C.
(b) Neolithic pottery from the earliest recorded graves in the Agora of Athens, from a shaft-grave two metres east of the façade of the Metroon. The pottery is grey (1) and reddish-orange (2), and of coarse fabric, to be dated to the close of the Neolithic culture early in the third millenium B.C.

14   Copyright National Museum, Athens. Cycladic marble "sculpture" (in fact abraided with corundum or emery stone fron Naxos).
(a) Harp-player from Keros near Amorgos. Ht. 21.5 cm.
(b) Stylised head from Amorgos. Ht. 29 cm. Stone vessels were made in the same technique. Most common are very stylised angular and relatively flat standing figures. The figures are of marble and belong to the second half of the third millenium B.C.

15   Copyright Professor C. W. Blegen and the University of Cincinnati, Ohio.
(a) from *Troy* IV 2 fig. 24; (b) from *Troy* III fig. 1. Views of the citadel of Troy.
(a) In the foreground remains of Troy VII a; above (middle), street of Troy VII a-VII b. The pillar belongs to the "Pillar House" (Troy VI). The complexity of the site is very apparent from this photograph.
(b) Tower VI h and the east fortification wall of Troy VI in 1938 at the time of the re-excavation of the site. Troy VI was probably destroyed by an earthquake *c.* 1275 B.C., Troy VII a 1 by external attack (the closest approach to Homer's Troy) in the first half of the thirteenth century also. Troy VII b shows the appearance of a new people shortly afterwards.

16   Copyright Miss Alison Frantz, Agora Excavations, Athens. The Mycenaean "Palace of Nestor" at "Pylos" near the Bay of Navarino in the western Peloponnese. The view looks south-west or south. The palace stands on something of an eminence, but is not fortified as are Mycenae and Tiryns. The history of the palace as revealed by excavation *could* fit in with the coming of Neleus from Thessaly to the Peloponnese before the Trojan War.

Plate

There are beehive (*tholos*) tombs in the vicinity, but not everyone is convinced that this is the palace of the Neleids, that is of Neleus and his son Nestor. There are tombs also at Kakovatos, and another palace may remain to be discovered. The present "Palace of Nestor" lies between the village of Chora and the north end of the Bay of Navarino (Koryphasion). In order from the bottom of the photograph: store chamber with jars; *megaron* with hearth; *prodomos*, *aithousa* and court. On the left, the "Queen's Megaron" and bathroom; at the top right, the building set diagonally is the find-spot of the Linear B tablets.

17   Copyright Professor J. L. Caskey and Miss Alison Frantz. Neolithic clay statuette (18.5 cm. (7.5 inches) high as preserved) from Lerna in the Argolid. "It is a figure of youthful maturity, full without heaviness, gracefully natural in its pose . . . waist and hips and, most particularly, the planes and curves and transitions of the lower back, are rendered with skill and sensitivity. The legs, in contrast, are schematised as solid tapering pedestals without articulation." (J. L. Caskey, in *ILN* 12.1.57).

18   Copyright Hirmer, Munich.
(a) Ht. of largest figure 23 cm. Votaries in clay (giving examples of male and female dress), from the Petsofa sanctuary and a house at Chamaizi in East Crete. Middle Minoan I, 1950–1850 B.C.
(b) Ht. 14.5 cm. "Teapot" with fire-mottled decoration. Vasiliki style, from Vasiliki near Gournia in East Crete. Early Minoan II, 2400–2100 B.C.

19   Copyright (a) and (b) Hirmer, Munich. (c) John Chadwick, Cambridge.
(a) Fragment of steatite vase with Linear A inscription. From Apodhoulou, South Crete, c. 1550 B.C.
(b) Fragment of pot with Linear B inscription from the Palace, Cnossus. After 1400 B.C. Import ?
(c) Tablet with Linear B script from the Palace, Cnossus. Late Minoan II, 1450–1400/1375 B.C.

20   Copyright Hirmer, Munich. Phaistos, a group of Middle Minoan I houses from the period before the construction of the Old Palace (1950–1850 B.C.). Geometric and Hellenistic houses were later built over them.

21   Copyright Hirmer, Munich.
(a) Spouted vase with painted flowers in the Kamares style. Ht. 12 cm. From the Kamares Cave on Mount Ida. Middle Minoan II, c. 1800–1750 B.C.

Plate

(b) Wine mixing bowl with polychrome (white, red, yellow and black) decoration in the Kamares style, and flowers and chains modelled in clay. Ht. 45.5 cm. Middle Minoan II; perhaps an imitation of stone or metal. From the Old Palace at Phaistos.
(c) A cup in the same style, but more stylised.

22   Copyright Hirmer, Munich. "Snake Goddess" in coloured faience. Ht. 34.2 cm. Middle Minoan III, c. 1700-1600 B.C. From the underground treasury of the central sanctuary in the Palace at Cnossus.

23   Copyright Hirmer, Munich.
(a) Funnel-rhyton of black steatite. Ht. 46.5 cm. Four friezes, with boxing, bull-leaping and wrestling. Some of the boxers wear helmets. The pillars, tapering upwards and supporting a panel, are odd and unexplained. From the Palace of Ayia Triadha, Late Minoan I, c. 1500 B.C.
(b) The "Chieftain Vase" in black steatite. Greatest diameter 9.9. cm. In low relief on the front, an officer with parade sword, and a prince or young dignitary; on the back, three soldiers behind huge shields (?). The scene has been variously described in general (some have suggested children at play) and in detail. The "shields" may be animal skins; the "officer" may carry a "crook" on his left shoulder, or this may be the crest of his helmet. From the Palace of Ayia Triadha. Late Minoan I, c. 1500 B.C.
(c) Faience relief plaque (19 cm. wide), of uncertain decorative use (inlay ?), with a wild goat and two kids. From the underground treasury of the central sanctuary in the Palace of Cnossus. Middle Minoan III, c. 1700-1600 B.C.

24   Copyright Hirmer, Munich.
(a) Mace-head in the form of a battle-axe of schist or slate with the back end in the form of a leopard or panther. Length 14.8 cm. Found at Mallia in the west wing of the Palace with other fine objects including a dagger with a gold hilt and a sword with gold hilt and amethyst pommel. Dated variously Middle Minoan I A (c. 1850 B.C.) or Middle Minoan III (c. 1700-1600 B.C.). The question naturally arises how this ceremonial object might be related to the "Battle Axes" of Northern Europe, South Russia and Troy II.
(b) Ceremonial vessel in white limestone in the form of the head of a lioness. Diameter at rear, 16.6 cm. Eyes probably inlaid originally with red jasper and rock-crystal. The stone and the manufacture might be either Cretan or Greek. From the sanctuary in the west wing of the Palace at Cnossus. Late Minoan I, c. 1550-1500 B.C.

25   Copyright Hirmer, Munich. Ovoid vase of black steatite, made in three pieces the lowest of which is missing. Greatest diameter 11.5 cm. From the Palace

Plate

of Ayia Triadha. The significance of this most brilliant work of Cretan art is uncertain; it must be some form of harvest-home procession, but what harvest? The implements carried have been variously identified; are they for olive-gathering? There is a strange leader to the procession with a bell-shaped garment decorated with up-turned scales and a fringe. Late Minoan I, c. 1550–1500 B.C.

26 Copyright Hirmer, Munich.
(a) Beaked jug. Ht. 29 cm. A fine example of decorative naturalism. From the New Palace of Phaistos. Late Minoan I, c. 1550–1500 B.C.
(b) Lentoid flask. Ht. 28 cm. In the Marine Style, with octopods. From Palaikastro. Late Minoan I, c. 1550–1500 B.C.

27 Copyright (a) Hirmer, Munich. (b) British Museum.
(a) Clay rhyton (libation vase). Vase ht. 33 cm. Marine decoration of starfish, sea shells and sea weed. From Zakro, East Crete. Late Minoan I, c. 1550–1500 B.C.
(b) Restored fresco-fragment of the so-called "Cup-bearer", processing and carrying a large funnel rhyton. He is clad in a loin-cloth, and wears an arm-band and belt, and a seal-stone on his wrist. The background is stylised (clouds ?); the colours used are red for flesh, blue and yellow. From the Procession Fresco (with two registers) in the South Propylon of the Palace of Cnossus. Late Minoan I, c. 1550–1500 B.C.

28 Copyright Hirmer, Munich.
(a) The Western Court at Phaistos with the "sanctuary" of the Old Palace, the stepped (theatral) area on the north side, and the grand staircase of the New Palace; before it, the processional way. The Old Palace was destroyed c. 1650 B.C.
(b) The West Magazines of the Minoan Palace at Cnossus. Note the pithoi of various Late Minoan forms, and the stone-lined pits (*kaselles*). See also FIG. 2.

29 Copyright Hirmer, Munich. The Minoan town of Gournia on the Gulf of Mirobello. The local ruler's palace was at the top of the hill, and the narrow steep streets of houses below it. View from the east. Late Minoan I, c. 1550–1500 B.C.

30 Copyright Professor J. D. Caskey and Miss Alison Frantz. The Early Bronze Age "House of Tiles" at Lerna in the Argolid, on the Gulf of Argos. The

Plate

famous spring of Lerna lies to the right, off the picture. This building is large, and was of at least two storeys. It was roofed with rectangular terra-cotta tiles. It may have been a centre of government or of cult; the only comparable building is the circular structure under the megaron of Tiryns. The "House of Tiles" was destroyed in a conflagration, and afterwards covered with a low mound. At Lerna there is a cultural break within the Early Helladic period, and then a gradual transition from Early Helladic to Middle Helladic; it is therefore different from other sites. There are evidences of connections with Crete, Troy and the central Balkans. See also PLATE 17.

31 Copyright Hirmer, Munich. The "casemate" of the Mycenaean fortress of Tiryns (see also FIG. 2) in the "Cyclopean" style. The so-called Great Casemate on the south is of Late Mycenaean (thirteenth century) date. Similar structures have recently been found at Mycenae; and at Tiryns has been discovered a fortified spring similar to those at Mycenae and Athens: all evidence of an expectation of external attack at this same period in the late thirteenth century B.C.

32 Copyright Hirmer, Munich.
(a) The "Lion Gate" at Mycenae, of the late thirteenth century, *i.e.* of the latest stage of the fortifications. The relief, which has lost the feline heads, may have been some sort of coat-of-arms.
(b) The interior of the "Treasury of Atreus" at Mycenae, in "corbelled" masonry smoothed within. This was the largest and probably the latest of the *tholoi* or beehive tombs, finished in the late thirteenth century, and empty since antiquity. There are smaller tholoi, which preserved at least part of their contents, at nearby Dendra (Berbati).

33 Copyright Hirmer, Munich. Inlaid daggers from Shaft Grave Circle A (excavated by Schliemann) at Mycenae. The blades are of bronze inlaid (perhaps in a technique connected with Egypt) with gold, silver and niello.
(a) Length 16.3 cm. From Grave V. Leopard among wild duck, and fish in a stream.
(b) Length 23.8 cm. From Grave IV. Lion hunt. Note the shield-types: figure 8, covered with oxhide, carried back and front, and the "tower" shield. Late Helladic I.

34 Copyright Hirmer, Munich.
(a) Gold death-mask from Shaft Grave Circle A, Grave V. Schliemann called the deceased "Agamemnon". Ht. 26 cm. It has been pointed out that some of these masks seem to represent strong and vivid personalities.
(b) Ivory group of two women and a child. The women are sometimes

Plate

called nurses, or princesses, or goddesses, and the child a "divine" child, or prince. In effect all this is quite uncertain. Found on the citadel of Mycenae. Dated to the fifteenth century B.C. and regarded as showing strong Minoan influence.

35   Copyright Hirmer, Munich.
(a) Fresco fragment from Mycenae, with Cretan-Mycenaean Ta-urt "demons", in white (reserved ?), black outline, and blue background; the back crest or "loose skin" is blue, yellow-brown and dark red. From a private house. The creatures look more ass-headed than the jug-holding "crocodile" demons of Crete, but they clearly represent a take-over of ideas from Crete.
(b) Beazel of a gold ring from Mycenae, approximately three-and-one-third times actual size (width 3.4 cm.). From the treasure found south of Grave Circle A, a grave-robbers' hoard buried in Mycenaean times. It contains many elements of Minoan-Mycenaean religion: a goddess underneath a tree with poppies; female attendants with lilies; lion masks; double axe; sun and moon; descending "warrior god".

36   Copyright (a) National Museum, Athens; (b) Agora Excavations, American School of Classical Studies, Athens.
(a) Gold cup with wild bulls found in the Vaphio *tholos* tomb in Laconia, perhaps a royal tomb connected with the Mycenaean rulers of Laconia. Upper diameter 10.8 cm. Late Minoan I, c. 1500 B.C.
(b) Ivory pyxis or jewel box from the grave of a Mycenaean "princess" on the side of the Areopagus Hill at Athens. There were other ivory objects: large ivory bars, a smaller ivory pyxis, and ivory pins. The pyxis illustrated was made from a large tusk; its diameter is 11.2 cm. The interior was lined with strips of tin. The exterior decoration consists of two griffins attacking four stags.

37   Copyright (a) M. Chuzeville, Paris; (b) Hirmer, Munich.
(a) Late Mycenaean Cypriote mixing bowl, from Aradhippo, Cyprus, in the Louvre, Paris (AM 876). The scene, in the curious Late Mycenaean figure style, is difficult to explain; it represents *either* men and a seated goddess *or* a "divine king" and a goddess. Fourteenth century B.C.
(b) Late Mycenaean mixing bowl from the House of the Warrior Vase at Mycenae. Ht. 41 cm. A departure of warriors with late-type helmets and shields; a woman makes a gesture of grief. A rare figure scene of about 1200 B.C., appropriate to the disturbed times.

38   Copyright The German Institute of Archaeology, Athens. Pottery from the Potters' Quarter (Kerameikos) of Athens, showing the transition from Late

Plate

Mycenaean to Protogeometric (end of the Bronze Age and beginning of the Iron Age). All these vases come from the section of the cemetery by the Eridanos watercourse.

(a) Submycenaean amphora. Ht. 24.5 cm.

(b) One-handled jug, ht. 16 cm. and stirrup-jar (in the Mycenaean tradition), ht. 21 cm.

(c) Clay model tripod-cauldron. Ht. c. 16.5 cm.

39   Copyright (a) National Museum, Athens; (b) Museum of Fine Arts, Boston, Mass., U.S.A.; (c) Royal Ontario Museum, Toronto, Canada.

(a) Geometric style ivory "goddess" (the description is uncertain) from a grave in the Dipylon Cemetery; one of several figures of the same sort in the grave-group. Ht. 24 cm. The nudity suggests an oriental model, and the material is a link with the Near East.

(b) Miniature bronze stag group in the Geometric style, in Boston. It is a good example of a large group of small cast bronzes of animals (some of which, like human figures also, may have decorated tripod-cauldrons), some in groups and fairly elaborate (like the Centaur fighting with a man), others quite simple and paralleled by figures in clay which often decorate clay pyxis lids.

(c) Corinthian Geometric mixing bowl in Toronto, of the last quater of the eighth century B.C. Ht. 22.6 cm. The picture is probably intended to represent a forty-oared "longship" steered by two large oars. Following a Geometric convention the rowers are shown in full view with their oars passed over the gunwhale, but it may be suggested that in fact they were protected by the high sides of the ship, while the oars were passed through the ports. These may have been the improvements made by Ameinokles, and in such "longships" Corinthians made some of their voyages in the eighth century and later.

40   Copyright (a) German Institute in Rome; (b) Metropolitan Museum of Art, New York, U.S.A. (Accession Number 14.130.15; Rogers Fund 1914).

(a) Local (?) geometrically-decorated clay cup (imitating a common East Greek type) found in the Austrian excavations on Ischia (Pithekoussai), a forerunner settlement to Cumae on the mainland opposite. The cup is probably not later than 700 B.C. and might well be earlier. An inscription scratched on it makes (in addition to a reference to Aphrodite) the statement: "I am the fair cup of Nestor" (the name can be picked out in the illustration). It is written, as in the Phoenician script, from right to left. It appears to be a joking reference to the great "cup" of Nestor in *Iliad* xi 632, though this latter would have been very different, and in effect one of the "mixed" concepts of the epic—a mixture, it might be suggested, of the Mycenaean *di-pa* of the Linear B tablets and perhaps an Urartian cauldron with human-headed bird attachments.

(b) A scene of "lying-in-state" from an Attic (clay) standed mixing-bowl in New York, also decorated with a chariot procession and shielded warriors.

Plate

The "conceptual" characteristics of the Geometric style are clearly seen, and also the *horror vacui*. The scenes could be epic or contemporary. The complete vessel, 1.305 metres high, is a fine example of the monumental "Dipylon" style.

41 Copyright (a) German Institute of Archaeology, Athens; (b) The University of Pennsylvania and Professor Rodney S. Young; (c) Dr. L. H. Jeffrey, Oxford.
(a) Bronze bowl from the Kerameikos Cemetery, Athens. Diameter c. 17.5 cm. From Geometric grave 42 on the south bank of the Eridanos. Possibly North Syrian or Cypriote in origin. 850–830 B.C.
(b) A bronze libation bowl from a great tomb at Gordion (Phrygia) in west-central Asia Minor. It has an inscription in the Phrygian alphabet, which may have been acquired from the east by the Phrygians independently of the Greeks, scratched in beeswax. The Gordion royal tombs have yielded remarkable Phrygian and other metalwork, and objects in inlaid wood and ivory, the metalwork in particular showing affinities with regions farther east.
(c) Athenian Geometric jug from the Dipylon Cemetery given as a prize (? for dancing). It is probably to be dated in the second half of the eighth century, and the inscription is the earliest known from Attica, showing very early characteristics. It has been suggested that it was not necessarily written by a native of Attica, but possibly by someone from the East Mediterranean, who was then imitated, in a second inscription, by another less skilled writer.

42 (a) Photograph by E. N. Androulakis, Heraklion, Crete, with permission of the Director of the Heraklion Museum. Copyright (b) Soprintendenza alle Antichità dell' Etruria Meridionale, Rome (c) Soprintendenza alle Antichità di Etruria, Florence.
(a) Bronze gong decorated in relief with Gilgamesh rending a lion (bull below) flanked by two genii. Diameter 55 cm. Assyrianising style of North Syria or Urartu, of c. 700 B.C. Possibly made in Crete by immigrant oriental craftsmen. From the Idaean Cave.
(b) "Phoenician" silver-gilt bowl from an Etruscan tomb at Palestrina (ancient Praeneste) near Rome, in the Villa Giulia Museum, Rome. Diameter 20 cm. The mixed style of "Assyrian" and "Egyptian" elements is well illustrated in it, and also the concentric band decoration which suggested the arrangement of the Shield of Achilles in the *Iliad*. Early seventh century.
(c) Alphabet incised on an ivory writing-tablet from Marsigliana (in Tuscany) in the National Museum, Florence, of the first half of the seventh century. It is written retrograde (from right to left), and is an early indication of the arrival of the Euboic alphabet among the Etruscans from Cumae, the Euboic Greek colony north of Naples.

43 Copyright (a) German Institute of Archaeology, Athens. (b) The French School of Archaeology, Athens. (c) The British School of Archaeology, Athens. (d) The British Museum, London.

Plate

(a) Bronze relief plaque with bearded and long-robed man, found at Olympia, Ht. 15.7 cm. Date c. 700 B.C. Later Hittite (Assyrianising), or perhaps from Urartu (kingdom of Lake Van).

(b) Ivory figure, "The Lion Tamer", found at Delphi. Ht. without base, 19 cm. Oriental (Phoenician, Assyrian, North Syrian) subject and style, but probably of Greek manufacture, perhaps from Ionia or Rhodes. Date, mid-seventh century.

(c) Free-standing ivory sphinx (not, apparently, a furniture attachment). Ht. 7.5 cm. From Perachora on the Corinthian Gulf north of Corinth. Date, early seventh century.

(d) Ivory plaque (an attachment to furniture?) from a deposit on the site of the archaic temple of Artemis at Ephesus. About 4.5 cm. long. Stylised ibex, of sixth century date, showing in its rendering something of the contortion of nomad (Scythian) art, which is also represented by a plaque in the form of a wolf from the same site.

44 (a) and (d) Photographs by E. M. Androulakis, Heraklion, with the permission of Professor S. Marinatos. Copyright (b) of the Museum of Fine Arts, Boston, and (c) of the German Institute of Archaeology, Athens.

(a) and (d) Figures of bronze plate (*sphyrelata*) over a wooden core, found at Dreros in Crete. Ht., the warrior, 0.80 m., the female figure, 0.45 m. Date, 650 B.C. or somewhat earlier.

(b) The statuette dedicated by Mantiklos to Apollo, as the inscription indicates. In Boston (03.997). From Thebes? Ht. 20 cm. The figure originally had a helmet and probably shield and spear. Date 700–675 B.C.

(c) Bronze statuette of a youth found at Delphi. Ht. 19.7 cm. Perhaps of Cretan manufacture in the so-called "Daedalic" style of "Dorian" art. In the National Museum at Athens (NM 2134). Date 640–635 B.C.

45 Copyright (a) Hirmer, Munich; (b) The British Museum, London.

(a) The statuette (Ht. 0.75 m.) in limestone (originally coloured) once in Auxerre, France and now in the Louvre, Paris, It is in the so-called "Daedalic" style; cf. PLATE 44 (c). Date, c. 645 B.C.

(b) Ivory figure of a priestess from the site of the archaic temple of Artemis at Ephesus. In the National Museum, Istanbul, Turkey. The figure is in fact intended to be surmounted by a pole topped with a hawk, which survives and is to be placed in a hole in the top of the figure's head. Ht. of figure, 10.7 cm.; of pole and hawk, 15.6 cm. She carries a jug and a libation bowl of Phrygian type. Note the rendering of the fine drapery folds, characteristic of some Ionian work even in stone (cf. PLATE 53 (a)), and the moon face, plump and satisfied. Early sixth century East Greek work.

Plate

46   Copyright (a) and (b) The British Museum; (c) Hirmer, Munich.
(a) The Macmillan aryballos (or perfume vase) in the British Museum. Ht.
6.7 cm. Decorated with four tiny friezes: floral chain, hoplite battle, horse-
race and hare-hunt, in reddened black glaze paint, and added yellow-brown
and red, with very fine incised detail. Finest miniature style of between 650
and 640 B.C. By the same painter as the Chigi Jug (c). The plastic mouth in
the form of a lion's head shows the imitation of the late Hittite and North
Syrian lion type; it is paralleled in contemporary Crete. Corinthian.
(b) Corinthian jug (olpe) of c. 625 B.C., transitional from the so-called "Late
Protocorinthian" to "Early Corinthian", with characteristic neat animal
frieze decoration in black silhouette with incised inner detail and red enhancement. Later the animal frieze style becomes less careful, and the filling ornament thicker and less neat. In the British Museum (B.M.60 20-1 18). Ht.
30.5 cm.
(c) A portion of the main frieze of the Chigi Jug (olpe) in the Villa Giulia,
Rome. Found at Formello near Veii in Etruscan Italy, but made in Corinth.
Ht. c. 26 cm. (whole vase). Date, c. 640 B.C., by the same painter as (a). Two
techniques of decoration: white outline floral ornament on the black glaze
background of the jug, and silhouette and outline drawing in black, yellow-
brown, red and incision on a pale buff clay surface. A hoplite battle, horsemen, chariots, goat hunt, lion hunt, the Judgement of Paris, and a hare hunt
are the subjects which fill the friezes as elaborately as those of (a) but in what
may be called a more monumental style, which may in fact have been
influenced by such major painting as the painted clay metope slabs from
Thermon in Aetolia west of the Pindos. The portion illustrated is a fine example of a hoplite battle, with two opposed ranks of heavily-armed infantry-
men with emblazoned shields and a piper between; a common theme on
vases in this century which saw the development of the hoplite army.

47   Copyright (a) The British Museum; (b) Hirmer, Munich.
(a) Jug from one of the Cyclades islands in characteristic rather loose orientalising style, having affinities with Asia Minor, and with a mouthpiece in the
form of the head of a griffin, a favourite seventh century monster used very
frequently as an attachment to bronze cauldrons. It may have been a Greek
invention, not from the Orient. In the British Museum (B.M. 73 8-20 385).
Ht. 41.5 cm. Date, c. 640-630 B.C.
(b) An "Island" style amphora in the National Museum, Athens. Ht. 90 cm.
Decorated in a closer orientalising style than (a), of the later seventh century,
elaborate but uninspired. On both sides riders and curvilinear patterns in
brown-black glaze paint and violet-red. The style is often called "Melian"
because of the finds of this style on that island, but it seems likely that it was
made on one of the islands not too far from Delos; recently Paros has been
suggested.

Plate

48 Copyright Max Hirmer, Munich. The site of Olympia (in the western Peloponnese), the Altis enclosure, and the foundations and one or two columns
of the temple of Hera. The temple erected about 600 B.C. had cella walls
of sundried brick with stone foundations and orthostates, wooden columns
gradually replaced (one survived into Roman times), and a terracotta entablature gaily painted; "a veritable museum". Under it were the remains of a
simple temple with a front porch (*prodomos*) but no back porch (*opisthodomos*),
and without a peristyle, and perhaps with a flat roof. This belonged to the
middle of the seventh century. The side walls of the later temple were
sustained by short walls at right-angles, forming niches, one of which later
housed the Hermes "of Praxiteles". See also PLATE 4.

49 Copyright (a) British School of Archaeology, Athens and Mr. R. W.
Hutchinson; (b)-(k) British Museum, Department of Coins and Medals.
Dumps and coins showing the early development of Greek coinage.
(a) Gold ingots and silver "dumps" from the Khaniale Tekke tomb, Knossos,
Crete. c. 700 B.C.
(b) Electrum stater of earliest type, 10.81 gr.
(c) Electrum stater; stag feeding. 14.02 gr. Possibly of Ephesus. The inscription
is variously interpreted: "I am the badge of Phanes", or "I am the sign of
the Bright One". It seems clear from a 1¼3 stater obviously of the same mint
(and found at Ephesus, while the stater was found at Halicarnassus) that the
inscription means "I am the badge of Phanes". Date c. 600 B.C.
(d) Aegina, silver stater with sea turtle. 12.44 gr.
(e) Electrum stater of Phokaia, with a canting device (a seal, i.e. *phoke*) and
phi. 16.52 gr.
(f) Electrum. ? Lydia. 16.09 gr. Lion's head.
(g) Gold stater. Lydia. Foreparts of lion and bull facing each other. 8.04 gr.
(h) Athens. Silver tetradrachm of archaic style. Helmeted head of Athena
on obverse; owl, olive sprig and inscription ATHE on reverse. 17.16 gr.
The date of the earliest of these coins is much disputed, as is also the question
of what went before them. Some think Solon (594 B.C.) commenced their
issue; others the tyrant Pisistratus, between 547 and 527 B.C.; others his son
Hippias (527-510 B.C.), causing them to follow on after the so-called
"Heraldic" coins which may belong to Athens.
(i) Corinth. Silver stater of the earliest type, with Pegasus and *koppa* on the
obverse, and a mill-sail incuse on the reverse. 8.31 gr.
(j) Thebes. Silver stater with Boeotian shield on the obverse, and *theta* in
the centre of a mill-sail incuse on the reverse. 8.91 gr.
(k) Gold daric of Darius I. King holding a bow and spear. 8.27 gr.

50 Copyright (a) Alinari, Florence (No. 3455); (b) British Museum.
(a) The François Vase (so called from its finder) in the National Museum at
Florence, found at Chiusi in Etruria, but of Attic manufacture. A volute-
handled mixing-bowl decorated with multiple friezes of figures in the

Plate

"black-figure" style of c. 570 B.C. Ht. 66 cm. The painter was Kleitias and the potter Ergotimos. The style is a miniature one, very different from the monumental style of Lydos, for instance. It is a remarkable picture-book of mythology, showing some of the adventures and experiences of Peleus, his son Achilles, and Theseus, together with the Return of Hephaistos, zones of wild animals, the Battle of the Pygmies with the Cranes, the Gorgon, and Artemis as Lady of the Animals. Sir John Beazley describes it: "Small figures, precise, angular, keen, nearly all identified by inscriptions."
(b) The Burgon Panathenaic amphora (so called from its former owner) in the British Museum (B 130). Ht. 63.5 cm. The earliest known example of the special type of amphora given as a prize at the Panathenaic festival, in a heavy style contemporary with the black-figure painter Lydos. Date 566 B.C. or slightly earlier. It bears on one side the figure of the Armed Athena and the inscription "I am a prize from the Games at Athens", and on the other a *synoris*, a curious type of race-team of two horses drawing a light cart. In later examples Athena is flanked by columns surmounted by cocks.

51 Copyright British Museum.
(a) One side of the exterior of a black-figured lip cup signed by Phrynos as potter, in the British Museum (B.M.B 424). The Introduction of Herakles to Zeus by Athena. On the other side the Birth of Athena from the head of Zeus. Date c. 550 B.C. in the so-called Little Master Cup style, of remarkable charm and liveliness.
(b) Black-figured amphora from Vulci (Etruria) in the British Museum (B.M.B 210). Signed by Exekias as potter and inscribed *Onetorides Kalos*, a salute to a boy of that name and his youthful charm. Sometimes such aristocratic youths became famous men, and such references help in the dating of vase-paintings. The subject is the Slaying of Penthesileia, Queen of the Amazons, by Achilles. On the other side Dionysus holds a wine-cup into which Oinopion pours wine. The flesh of Penthesileia was rendered in over-painted white, and this has largely disappeared. Date, third quarter of the sixth century.
(c) Black-figured amphora in the British Museum (B.M.B 226). Olive-gathering; on the other side, Herakles and the Centaur Pholos. Late sixth century. Assigned to the Antimenes Painter.

52 Copyright (a) Metropolitan Museum of Art, New York. (b) British Museum. (c) Hirmer, Munich.
(a) Statue of a youth (*kouros*), said to be from Attica (and probably a grave-monument), in the Metropolitan Museum, New York, No. 32.11.1. Purchased by the Fletcher Fund (1932). Ht. 1.843 m. It belongs to the earliest group of this type of figure (except for a few fragments), which is to be associated with the gigantic Sounion Kouros in the National Museum, Athens. Date c. 615-590 B.C.
(b) The so-called "Strangford Apollo" in the British Museum (B 475). So-called after its former owner Viscount Strangford. Possibly from the Aegean island of Anaphe. Ht. 1.01 m. Late sixth century.

Plate

(c) The so-called "Apollo" of Tenea, No. 168 in the Antikensammlungen, Munich. Ht. 1.53 m. Found at Tenea near Corinth, associated with a tomb. Its advance over (a) is to be noted, and its elasticity of limb and youthful vigour. It is probably of Corinthian origin, and to be dated c. 560–550 B.C. (a), (b) and (c) represent with many others the striving for ideal naturalism only fully attained in the earlier fifth century: this was the first of several stages which should be noted: the body rendered with an equal stance, then with weight on one leg, then in motion, and finally its relation to others and to drapery explored. Thereafter came the rendering of spiritual and emotional content, and realism.

53 Copyright (a) Hirmer, Munich. (b) Staatl. Museen, Antikenabteilungen, Berlin (East).
(a) Standing female figure in the Louvre, Paris (No. 686). Ht. 1.92 m. The missing head would resemble PLATE 54 (a), and the whole scheme of the figure is also represented in a common type of East Greek perfume vase in clay. It was dedicated to Hera at Samos by one Cheramyes (hence the name "Hera of Cheramyes"), one example of a large body of sculpture found at the Samian sanctuary of the goddess, and in the East Greek style. The figure is clad in clearly differentiated chiton, cloak and veil. Noteworthy are the fine folds, and delicate rendering of contours despite the apparent treetrunk-like lower part of the figure. Samian. Date, c. 560 B.C.
(b) Standing female figure in Berlin, Inv. 71, the so-called Berlin Standing "Goddess". From Attica (Keratea), and made of Attic marble. Ht. with plinth, 1.93 m. She holds a pomegranate, and may be the figure of a goddess; the statue is said to have been found carefully wrapped in lead and intentionally buried. On the other hand the figure might be an aristocratic grave memorial. It still retains considerable traces of original colour on the garments, viz. blue, red and yellow. Date, c. 570 B.C.

54 Copyright (a) British Museum. (b) Staatl. Museen, Antikenabteilungen, Berlin (East).
(a) Fragment (Ht. 19 cm.) of a female head from either a statue or a relief, found at Ephesus, now in the British Museum (B 89). The eyes were originally painted in. Note the soft loose contours. Milesian? Date, c. 550 B.C.
(b) Fragment (Ht. 55.5 cm.) of a female figure from a relief-decorated plinth (?) of a column from the temple of Apollo at Didyma, the site of an oracle of Apollo, south of Miletus in western Asia Minor. In East Berlin, PM 1571. The temple was destroyed by the Persians in 494 B.C. Date, c. 550–525 B.C.

55 Copyright (a) and (b) Hirmer, Munich.
(a) The so-called "Calf-Bearer" (Moschophoros) in the Acropolis Museum

Plate

Athens. Ht. 1.65 m. Of Hymettus marble. Found on the Acropolis. A dedication by one Rhombos, of himself and the calf he brought as an offering, though there are, and especially from Arcadia, numerous small bronzes representing shepherds carrying animals. The eyes were probably inset in coloured stone. Date, c. 570 B.C.

(b) The head of a horseman, the "Rampin Head" so-called from its former owner, now in the Louvre, Paris. The fragments of a horse and the body of its rider found on the Acropolis and now in the Acropolis Museum (Acrop. 590) were found by the late H. G. G. Payne to belong to the head, the latter making a clear join with the body of the rider. This was obviously the dedication of an elegant and horse-loving aristocrat. Ht. of the head, 29 cm. Its date is somewhat earlier than 550 B.C., and it is thus the earliest statue of its kind in Greece. It has been suggested that a later work by the same sculptor is the "Peplos Kore" (PLATE 56 (b)); the simplicity of detail of the latter is an interesting contrast. They both belong to the period of the tyranny at Athens, but the elegance of the Horseman is matched by that of his younger "sister" the *kore* of Lyons (just after 550 B.C.), the young gentleman of the early red-figure (PLATE 58 (a)), and *his* younger sister the *kore* from Chios PLATE 56(a)). Under the tyrants Athens was clearly a smart place.

56 Copyright (a) and (b) Hirmer, Munich.
(a) Statuette (Ht. 55.5 cm.) of a young woman, found on the Acropolis and now in the Acropolis Museum, in a delicate and elaborate style contrasting with (b). It is carved in marble from Chios (?) and is in an East Greek style associated with that island. It bears considerable traces of colour, including blue (now turned green) and red. Date, c. 510 B.C.
(b) Statue of a young woman (*kore*), the so-called "Peplos Kore", since she wears this Dorian woollen garment, the *peplos*, and a linen *chiton* beneath it. Ht. 1.21 m. Found on the Acropolis, and now in the Acropolis Museum. Her arm was carved separately and attached. She wore a metal wreath and earrings, and colour was used (green, blue, red and black) for patterns of garments, hair, lips and eyes. Date, c. 530 B.C.

57 Copyright (a) and (b), Hirmer, Munich. Slabs from the sculptured frieze of the Treasury of Siphnos at Delphi, in the Delphi Museum. Ht. about 66 cm. It comes from a small building of great architectural elaboration (including two maiden figures as supporting members in its porch) set up by the Siphnians of the Cycladic island in the days of the prosperity of their silver mines. The slabs illustrated come from the North frieze with the battle of the Gods and Giants: Herakles, Cybele, Apollo, Artemis and Dionysus (surely not a Giant as sometimes suggested?). There are traces of blue and red paint, and an indecipherable inscription on one of the shields. The North and East friezes showed the battle of the Gods and Giants, and possibly the Greeks and Trojans in the presence of the Gods, by what may have been a Parian artist; the West and South friezes showed the Judgement of Paris and the Rape of the Daughters of Leukippos (or Pelops and Hippodameia), possibly by a

Plate

North Ionian artist. Certainly two artists seem to have been concerned. Date c. 525 B.C.

58   Copyright (a) Max Hirmer, Munich. (b) Metropolitan Museum of Art, New York. Accession No. 45.11.17. Rogers Fund 1945. (c) British Museum.
(a) From the back of a pot in Berlin (F 2159), an amphora from Vulci (Etruria). An elegant young man acts as judge at a wrestling contest. On the front Apollo and Herakles strive for the Tripod. It is signed by Andokides as potter, and stands at the transition from black-figure to red-figure at Athens. Date c. 520 B.C. See above on PLATE 55 (b).
(b) Fragment (Length 15 cm.) in basalt of a large shod foot, in the Metropolitan Museum, New York, from a relief of Darius at Persepolis. It bears incised sketches in a manifest Greek style, which seem to indicate the presence of Ionians (?) in Persia, perhaps serving there as craftsmen either voluntarily, or carried away captive.
(c) From a red-figured plate in the British Museum (E 136). A helmeted youth and a horse. Signed by Epiktetos as painter; an artist admirably skilled in fitting groups into such a tondo. Date, c. 520 B.C. or somewhat later

59   Copyright (a) American School of Classical Studies, Agora Excavations, Athens. (b) Hirmer, Munich.
(a) Exterior of a fragmentary red-figured drinking cup found in the Agora excavations at Athens (P24913), and signed by the potter Gorgos. The whole decoration of the cup, it has recently been pointed out, is a "compendium of the main themes of Attic vase painting", that is, everyday life, war and wine. The portion illustrated represents Thetis, Achilles, Memnon and Eos, not infrequent symbols of the tragic mothers of doomed heroes. Date, c. 500 B.C.; perhaps a very early work of the Berlin Painter.
(b) Base of a statue (the latter now lost), 32 cm. by 81 cm., found built into a wall at the Dipylon Cemetery, Athens, and now in the National Museum. It is decorated with reliefs on the front and two sides; the reliefs had a background painted red. On the front: runner, wrestlers and spear-thrower (?); on the sides, a ball-game and young men at a cat-and-dog fight. Very close in detail of garments and bodies to red-figure vase-painting of the last decade of the sixth century.

60   Copyright (a) Metropolitan Museum of Art, New York. Accession No. 11.185.185 a–d. Hewitt (1911), Rogers (1921), Mounsey (1936 and 1938) Funds, Anonymous Gift 1951. (b) National Museum, Athens.
(a) Funeral monument of youth and girl from Attica. Total reconstructed height including the sphinx, 4.234 m. Fragments of the little girl's figure are in Berlin (A 7), replaced in New York by a cast. The youth holds a pomegranate and an aryballos, and the girl a flower. The panels above and below may have been painted; paint was also used elsewhere: on the relief, including

Plate

red for the background, red and black on the capital, and red, black and blue on the sphinx. A splendid monument raised by a great family c. 540-535 B.C. But it is doubtful if the family was that of the Alkmeonidai, as has been suggested.

(b) The funeral slab (*stele*) of Aristion, the work of Aristokles, from East Attica (Velanideza), in the National Museum, Athens. Ht. without base 2.40 m. Traces of red and blue paint still remain, and the former presence of painted ornament can be detected on the surface of the stone. Date, c. 510 B.C.

61 Copyright, Hirmer, Munich.
A view at Delphi down the Sacred Way below the terrace of the temple of Apollo, looking along the Stoa of the Athenians to the Treasury of the Athenians. The terrace wall is in polygonal masonry, built between 548 and 510 B.C. after the destruction of the previous temple. The earlier classical temple was started some short time before 510 B.C., and destroyed in 375 B.C., to be replaced (369-329 B.C.) by the temple of which the substructures and platform survive (see PLATE 5). The Stoa is of disputed date, varying between 506 B.C. and post-480 B.C. The same is true of the Treasury, which has been dated 510-505 B.C., and also 489 B.C. It is important for the sculptured metopes with Athenians and Amazons, and the Exploits of Theseus and Herakles.

62 Copyright (a), (b) and (c), British Museum.
(a) Female head from a relief decorating a column base of the archaic temple of Artemis at Ephesus, in the British Museum (B 91). Ht. 30.5 cm. An approximate date is available since Herodotus associates Croesus (c. 560-546 B.C.) the king of Lydia with these columns, but there is probably a fair spread of time covering all the fragments, say c. 550-530 B.C.
(b) One of the reliefs (length 2.45 m.) in the British Museum from the so-called "Harpy Tomb", a tall rectangular pillar tomb at Xanthos in Lycia, South Asia Minor, which takes its name from the spirits, half woman and half bird, which carry off the souls of the dead. The subject of the frieze illustrated is the making of offerings to the heroised dead rather than "a warrior yielding up his armour to Pluto". It shows that Greek styles (here heavy East Greek) penetrated to some of the native peoples of western Asia Minor. Opinions vary as to the date, from 500 B.C. to 480 B.C.
(c) Seated figure in the British Museum (B 271), one of an avenue of such leading to the oracular shrine of Apollo at Didyma south of Miletus. The series of seated figures represented members of the family of the Branchidai, a sacerdotal family which had charge of the oracle. They are all plump, but as time passes become more obviously able to rise from their chairs. Ht. 1.55 m. Date, c. 570 B.C.

Plate

63 Copyright (a) Staatl. Museen, Antikenabteilungen, Berlin (East). (b) Alinari, Florence (29195).
(a) Seated goddess in Berlin (A 17), said to have been found at Taranto. Ht. 1.51 m. Parian marble. Paint was used on it, and also metal adjuncts. Connections of style have been suggested with Aegina. It is characterised by high technical skill in some respects, but by inferior skill or experience in others. It may represent Persephone, Hera or Aphrodite. Date, c. 480 B.C.?
(b) Metope from the temple of Hera at Selinunte (Temple E), in the National Museum, Palermo. Ht. 1.7 m. It is carved of limestone tufa, but the head, arms and feet of the goddess are inserted in marble identified as Parian. Rather old-fashioned and probably local work. Date, c. 470-460 B.C. The subject is the Unveiling of Hera by Zeus, or what is often called a *Hieros Gamos*.

64 Copyright Hirmer, Munich.
Metope from Temple C at Selinunte (ancient Selinus) in Sicily, in the National Museum, Palermo. Perseus, in company with Athena, slaying the Gorgon Medusa. Old-fashioned work (note the primitive frontality and large heads) some fifty years behind the times. Of local stone, and probably local workmanship. Date, c. 550-540 B.C.

65 Copyright, Hirmer, Munich. "Back" panel of the so-called Ludovisi Throne in the Museo Nazionale delle Terme, Rome. Ht. 1.04; breadth 1.44. The marble is identified as being from the Aegean. It was found in the grounds of the Palazzo Ludovisi in Rome, in antiquity part of the Gardens of Sallust. It is obviously cut about, and the volute ornaments at the bottom of back and sides have been chiselled away. It is difficult to discuss its purpose without reference to the similar Boston Throne, which came to light later (without any clear information as to its find spot, through if it is genuine it is most likely that it was found in the same region as the piece in Rome). Great doubt reigns on the association of the two, and their purpose: altar wind-break, part of the enclosure of a ritual area, wings of a monumental altar and the like; they are certainly not "thrones". The subject: in the Ludovisi Throne a female figure rising from the pebbly ground, aided by two other female figures (heads lost), with a young nude female flute player, and an older draped woman offering incense, on the sides; in the Boston Throne a winged boy holds a balance which inclines down to a draped and veiled woman seated at one side who raises her hand (in joy?), while opposite her another draped woman bows (in dejection?), with a youthful nude male lyre player (seated on a wine-skin?) and an old draped but unveiled woman (a slave?) on the sides. The Birth of Aphrodite has been suggested, or the Return of Kore, or a ritual baptism; and for the Boston Throne a Weighing of Souls. It is best to suggest in general some mystic theme, perhaps associated with Aphrodite. A leading authority has regarded the Ludovisi Throne as imported or by an immigrant from the Aegean "with a feeling for the expert

Plate

handling of marble", and the Boston Throne as being by a South Italian (in view of the similarity to the terracotta Locrian plaques from South Italy) who had little such experience. This hypothesis explains the outstanding archaic charm of the Ludovisi Throne and the clumsiness particularly of the back panel of the Boston Throne. The latter might be a Roman archaistic production, scarcely a modern forgery despite the obscurities of its modern history. Date of the Ludovisi Throne c. 470 B.C.

66   Copyright (a) and (b), Antikensammlungen, Munich.
(a) Warrior (restored) from the (earlier) western pediment of the temple of Athena Aphaia in Aegina, now in Munich.
(b) Head of a dying warrior (restored) from the (later) eastern pediment of the same temple. The bulk of the sculptures were found in 1811 near the temple, and some fragments later. The restorations by Thorvaldsen are to be regretted. The older eastern pediment, damaged c. 487-485 B.C. in the war between Athens and Aegina, was replaced later by a new one, showing freer movement of the figures. Older and newer may be placed in the period 500-480 B.C.

67   Copyright (a) and (b) The German Archaeological Institute, Athens (Olympia Excavations).
(a) Persian helmet, Olympia B 5100. Ht. 23.1 cm. Thickness 1.5-2.5 mm. Found near the Hill of Kronos and the Treasury Terrace, and inscribed: "The Athenians to Zeus, having taken it from the Medes". It is an "Assyrian" type helmet, paralleled by examples from Urartu and the Caucasus. Therefore while it is uncertain whether it was taken at Marathon or in 480-479 B.C., it certainly recalls Xerxes' far-gathered army.
(b) Corinthian helmet, B 2600. Ht. 18.7 cm. Varying thickness 2.7-7.5 mm. Found at Olympia, and inscribed "Miltiades dedicated (this) to Zeus." There is no mention of his father, his state, or the enemy from whom it was taken. It might therefore be his own helmet dedicated before 493 B.C. when Miltiades was tyrant of the Thracian Chersonese.

68   Copyright (a) Museo Nazionale delle Terme. (b) Alinari 11048a.
(a) The Discobolus of Myron, Castel Porziano torso, restored. In the Museo Nazionale, Rome. Ht. unrestored, including the base, 1.48 m. Date c. 450 B.C.
(b) Harmodius, in the Museo Nazionale, Naples. From the replacement group of Kritias, fairly extensively restored and with the right arm incorrectly placed. The original was a bronze (?) of 477 B.C. See pages 76 and 112.

69   Copyright (a) Alinari 34250. (b) Alinari 24230.
(a) Copy of the Doryphorus of Polyclitus, in the Museo Nazionale, Naples

Plate

(b) Copy of the Diadumenus of Polyclitus, found in Delos, in the National Museum, Athens. See pages 76-77. Date, (a) c. 450 B.C.; (b) c. 420 B.C.

70   Copyright, Hirmer, Munich.
The bronze charioteer found at Delphi, formerly part of a chariot group of which a few other small fragments remain. See also PLATE 72 for the head. It is made up of six separately cast parts. Ht. 1.8 m. A restored inscription seems to indicate that he was the driver of a bronze quadriga dedicated by Polyzalos of Syracuse. Date, 477 B.C. The work, one of the very few great bronzes of the fifth century B.C., has been associated from time to time with the styles of famous sculptors, but without much agreement. Hardly Sicilian.

71   Copyright, Hirmer, Munich.
A relief (generally called The Eleusinian Relief) in the National Museum at Athens. Found at Eleusis. Ht. 2.4 m. Triptolemus crowned by Kore receives the gift of corn from Demeter. Despite the size of the slab the relief is surprisingly shallow. Date c. 450-440 B.C.

72   Copyright (a) and (b) Hirmer, Munich.
(a) Head of the Delphi Charioteer (see also PLATE 70).
(b) Head of the bronze Zeus or Poseidon recovered from the sea off Artemision, North Euboea. In the National Museum, Athens. Ht. 2.09 m. The bearded god strides forward, one arm extended, the other drawn back to hurl some object, more likely to be a trident than a thunderbolt. If so, it was found in a very suitable place since the Greeks honoured Poseidon there for his aid against the Persians. As in the case of the Charioteer many suggestions have been made as to the possible creator of this splendid work, which is somewhat archaic in style. Date, 460-450 B.C.

73   Copyright (a) and (b) Hirmer, Munich.
(a) Sculptured metope from the Temple of Zeus at Olympia, with Athena, Herakles who supports the Sky, and Atlas who brings to him the Apples of the Hesperides. Ht. 1.6 m. In Olympia Museum. Date, c. 465 B.C. The temple was completed by 456 B.C., and may have remained without a cult-statue for twenty years.
(b) The figure of Apollo from the western pediment of the Temple of Zeus at Olympia. Ht. c. 3.3. m. He stands in the centre of the battle of Lapiths and Centaurs at the Wedding of Peirithous. Date, c. 460 B.C. or later.
(c) Late fifth century coin of the Eleans with the head of Zeus. Photographed from an electrotype of a coin in the British Museum.

Plate

74 (a) From a photograph by Tamme. (b) Copyright, Antikensammlungen, Munich (Glypt. 457).
(a) A Roman copy, in the Albertinum, Dresden, of a Phidian work which has been identified as the Athena Lemnia. A. Furtwängler suggested that the head was to be replaced by one in Bologna, see A. W. Lawrence, *Classical Sculpture*, PLATE 50, *a*, and Richter, *The Sculpture and Sculptors of the Greeks*[3], FIG. 614, and page 228. A combined cast (in Budapest) of body and head appears in Richter, *op. cit.* FIG. 616. This combination seems to fit the ancient descriptions.
(b) Bronze head of a boy. Of the highest quality, and influenced by the Polyclitan manner. Date end of the fifth century.

75 Copyright (a) Hirmer, Munich. (b) and (c) British Museum.
(a) The Victory of Paionios. Found at Olympia. Original height of the figure, 2.16 m. It was placed on a high column in front of the Temple of Zeus, and was originally coloured. Date, c. 425-420 B.C.
(b) The so-called Strangford Shield in the British Museum. See page 149.
(c) Iris from the West Pediment of the Periclean Parthenon. See page 146.

76 Copyright, British Museum.
Slabs from the Eastern Frieze of the Periclean Parthenon. See pages 147-148.

77 Copyright, British Museum.
Figures from the Eastern Pediment of the Periclean Parthenon. See pages 144–145.

78 Copyright (a) and (b) British Museum. (c) Hirmer, Munich.
(a) and (b) Youthful cavalrymen from the North Frieze of the Periclean Parthenon.
(c) Armed warrior (*apobates*) in a chariot moving at speed. From the South Frieze of the Periclean Parthenon.

79 Copyright (a) The German Institute of Archaeology at Athens, Olympia Excavations. (b) The American School of Classical Studies at Athens, Agora Excavations. (c) The British Museum.

Plate

(a) A cup of ribbed black glaze pottery, found at Olympia in the workshop of Phidias. That this building, or rather a forerunner on the same site, traditionally so named, was in fact a workshop is clear from the remains of moulds and other debris. The moulds were of two categories, for hammering out metal drapery and for casting glass spangles. The inscription on the cup "I belong to Phidias" must surely refer to the great sculptor. The drapery moulds seem to show a style belonging to the thirties of the fifth century. Consequently it appears that the great Zeus must come after the Athena Parthenos among the works of Phidias.

(b) A potsherd (*ostrakon*) bearing the name of Pericles the son of Xanthippos, and found in the Agora excavations at Athens.

(c) A bust in the British Museum said to be of Pericles wearing a Corinthian helmet. It is a Roman work, and may be a copy of an original of c. 440 B.C. by Kresilas, possibly in the form of a herm.

80   Copyright (a) and (b) Hirmer, Munich.
(a) The Caryatid Porch on the south side of the Erechtheum. See pages 155-157.
(b) The Temple of Athena Nike on the south-west bastion of the Acropolis. The site was long associated with the cult of Athena Nike, but this temple was not completed until after 421 B.C. The balustrade decorated with Victories in clinging drapery (compare the Nike of Paionios and the Iris of the Parthenon) was erected c. 410 B.C.

81   Copyright Hirmer, Munich.
The Doric temple of Athena and Hephaistos, the so-called Theseum at Athens. See page 158 and PLATES 11 and 12 above.

82   Copyright British Museum.
Slabs of the interior sculptured frieze of the temple of Apollo Epikourios ("The Helper"), erected by Iktinos, c. 420 B.C., at Bassai in Arcadia. See PLATE 6 for the site. The frieze, in the British Museum, is of battles between Centaurs and Lapiths, and Greeks and Amazons.

83   Copyright (a) and (b) British Museum.
(a) Attic red-figure hydria or water-jar in the British Museum (E. 224), Signed by Meidias as potter. Abduction of the daughters of Leukippos. Argonauts, Herakles and the Hesperides. Date c. 400 B.C.
(b) Vase in the form of an astragal (knucklebone) in the British Museum (E. 804), from Aegina. Hephaistos and the Clouds. By the Sotades Painter, in the style of Early Classical red-figure painting.

Plate

84 Copyright (a) Museum of Fine Arts, Boston, Mass. (97.371). (b) British Museum.
(a) Attic red–figure *phiale mesomphalos* (libation bowl) (by courtesy of the Museum of Fine Arts, Boston) from near Sounion, Attica. A dancing school, for the education of female entertainers, and its young men patrons. Classical Period. By the Phiale Painter.
(b) An Attic drinking cup with polychrome drawing on a white ground in the British Museum (D 2). From Kamiros, Rhodes. Aphrodite riding on a goose. It bears an inscription "Glaukon is handsome": see note to PLATE 51 (b). By the Pistoxenos Painter. Early Classical Period.

85 Copyright (a) Epigraphical Museum, Athens. (b) Staatl. Museen, Antikenabteilungen, Berlin (East).
(a) Relief (heading a decree of a deme in honor of those who had produced a comedy) with a row of what are taken to be comic masks above. From Aixone, Attica. It is suggested that they form a comic group: father, mother, slave, girl, lover. Date, 340 B.C.
(b) Attic black–figure amphora in Berlin (F 1697), of the sixth century, by the Painter of Berlin 1686. Helmeted men are mounted on men dressed as horses. It is to be dated a century or more before the *Knights* of Aristophanes. There is evidence of other choruses of this type in the Old Comedy, and it has been suggested that the present vase picture shows "an animal masquerade", the forerunner of this aspect of the Old Comedy.

86 Copyright British Museum.
An Attic white–ground funeral lekythos in the British Museum (D 54). By the Achilles Painter. Confrontation of the dead (left) and the living with an offering (right). The stele marks the barrier between them. Second half of the fifth century.

87 Copyright (a) and (b) Hirmer, Munich.
(a) Grave stone in the National Museum, Athens, from the Ilissos (NM 869). Formerly in an architectural frame. Ht. 1.68 m. Youth with his hunting dog and a small child contemplated by an old man. Note the powerful suggestion of the barrier between dead and living. The face of the young man shows the effect of the deepset eyes, a rendering associated with the name of Skopas. Date, c. 340-330 B.C.
(b) The "Mourning Athena" relief in the Acropolis Museum, Athens. Ht. 54 cm. It appears to have been associated with the southern Acropolis wall of Cimon, and to have been buried soon after it was made (some connection with the fall of Cimon?). What it is intended to represent is much disputed: Athena is not certainly mourning and contemplating a funeral stele listing those who have died in some campaign, though this is a possibility; the stele may represent a boundary stone or a decree. Date, c. 460-450 B.C.

Plate

88 Copyright (a) Hirmer, Munich. (b) Staatl. Antikensammlungen, Munich.
(a) Grave stele in the National Museum, Athens, from Salamis (No. 715).
The sculptor seems to have had a connection with the Parthenon frieze.
The animal may be a cat, or a lion surmounting a gravestone. Date, c. 420 B.C.

89 Copyright (a) Museo Nazionale delle Terme. (b) Alinari (6672). (c) Staatl.
Antikensammlungen, Munich.
(a) Aphrodite found at Cyrene in North Africa. It is taken to be an Imperial
Roman copy of a Hellenistic statue, perhaps in bronze, of the third, second
or first century B.C. Opinions have differed widely and violently as to its
quality. It is placed here as illustrating a very different concept of the female
body from (b) which must be felt to be influenced by the athletic tradition
manifest in the rendering of the male body in Greek art.
(b) Copy of the Aphrodite of Praxiteles, the "Aphrodite of Cnidus", in
the Vatican; here reproduced with the tin drapery mentioned in the text,
page 199. Modern illustrations of this work are generally composite reproductions which include the Hellenistic Kaufmann Head in Berlin.
(c) Female head in Munich. Later copy of the head of Aphrodite by Praxiteles.

90 Copyright (a) Hirmer, Munich. (b) Alinari (6510).
(a) Figure of a youth in bronze found in the sea off the island of Anticythera
(Peloponnese), probably forming part of a Roman cargo of works of art
being conveyed from Greece. Now in the National Museum, Athens. Ht.
1.94 m. It may be a copy of the Paris of Euphranor, holding the Apple of
Discord! It is in the Polyclitan tradition, but the stance looks forward to the
Apoxyomenus of Lysippus. Date, c. 340 B.C., but it has been placed considerably earlier. See page 204.
(b) Copy of the Apoxyomenus of Lysippus in the Vatican.

91 Copyright (a) Museo Nazionale delle Terme. (b) Alinari (6505).
(a) Copy of Apollo Sauroktonos ("The Lizard Slayer") of Praxiteles. Both
in the Museo Nazionale delle Terme, Rome. See pages 199-202.
(b) Copy of the Faun of Praxiteles.

92 Copyright Hirmer, Munich. The head of the Hermes "of Praxiteles" in
Olympia Museum, Greece. Ht. of whole figure, 2.15 m. Basically there are
the alternatives (a) that it is a late work of Praxiteles, that is, an original by
the master himself, since the traveller Pausanias associated a Hermes by him

Plate

with the temple of Hera where the statue was found; and (b) that it is a Roman copy of a work by Praxiteles made by a first-class later sculptor. Modern opinion inclines to the latter view, but some excellent judges of Greek sculpture claim it as an original work.

93   Copyright (a) British Museum. (b) Alinari (24287). (c) Alinari (24207).
(a) Winged head of Hypnos ("Sleep") in bronze, in the British Museum. See page 204.
(b) A head from the temple of Athena Alea at Tegea in Arcadia (pediment), in the National Museum, Athens. Date, c. 370-355 B.C.
(c) Relief of a base from Mantinea in Arcadia, in the National Museum, Athens, Date, c. 350 B.C. See pages 201, 202 and 204.

94   Copyright (a) Skulpturensammlung, Albertinum, Dresden. (b) Hirmer, Munich.
(a) Maenad (votary of Dionysus) in ecstasy. Possibly a copy of a work by Skopas. In the Albertinum, Dresden.
(b) Sculptured column-base from the fourth-century temple of Artemis at Ephesus, in the British Museum. Ht. 1.8 m. Date, c. 340 B.C. See page 203.

95   Copyright (a) British Museum.   (b) Hirmer, Munich.
(a) Charioteer from the smaller frieze of the Mausoleum, in the British Museum.
(b) Slabs from the major frieze decorating the same building, in the British Museum. Formerly built into the Castle of Bodrum. It was held in Antiquity that each section of the frieze decorating one side of the building was by a leading artist: Bryaxis (North), Timotheos (South), Skopas (East) and Leochares (West). It is unfortunate that other works possibly by these artists (except in the case of Skopas) exist only in later copies, and there is therefore scant evidence by which to check the attributions of the frieze. (i) from the South frieze, ascribed to Timotheos. Ht. 0.89m. Date, c.350 B.C. and (ii) is a panel from the East frieze, and would therefore belong to Skopas.

96   Copyright British Museum.
Some outstanding coins and important issues of the fifth and fourth centuries B.C.
(a) Ainos in Thrace. Head of Hermes and goat.
(b) Syracuse in Sicily. Four-horse chariot and head of Arethusa surrounded by dolphins.
(c) Athens. Head of Athena and owl and olive twig.
(d) Corinth. Pegasus (and *koppa* beneath) and head of Athena (palmette symbol).

Plate

(e) Syracuse. Ten-drachma piece by the die-engraver Kimon (who signs KI on the headband of Arethusa), issued in connection with the Assinarian Games celebrating the Athenian defeat in Sicily in 413 B.C. (?). Victorious quadriga (below, prize armour), and head of Arethusa with hair net and headband.
(f) Amphipolis in Thrace. Facing head of Apollo and race-torch with inscription around.
(g) Philip II of Macedonia (359-336 B.C.). Head of Zeus and boy jockey on horse, holding a palm of victory.
(h) Philip II. Head of Apollo and two-horse chariot (with trident mintsymbol).
(i) Alexander III (the Great) (336-323 B.C.). Head of Athena and Nike holding wreath and naval standard (with thunderbolt mint-symbol).
All are of silver, except (h) and (i) which are in gold.

97 Copyright (a) British Museum. (b) Alinari (12050).
(a) Head of Alexander in the British Museum, possibly inspired by the Lysippean portraits. See page 225.
(b) The "Alexander Mosaic" in the National Museum, Naples, from Pompeii. See page 225.

98 Copyright National Museum, Istanbul, Turkey.
The "Alexander Sarcophagus" from Sidon, in Istanbul. See page 225. Date between 325 and 300 B.C.

99 Copyright (a) and (b) Hirmer, Munich.
(a) Statue of a dynast from the Mausoleum, Halicarnassus. Ht. 3 m. It is by no means certain that this figure was one of the two (of Mausollus and Artemisia), placed in a chariot, which crowned the summit of the monument. On the other hand it seems generally agreed that it belongs in date to the middle of the fourth century. A recent opinion would identify it as the figure of a later dynast, and place it about 160 B.C.
(b) The Demeter of Cnidus in the British Museum. Ht. 1.53 m. The head is less weathered than the body. It was found in the shrine of Demeter and Kore in Cnidus, and despite what is said in the text (page 203) may be part of a group. It is generally regarded as of fourth century date (350-330 B.C.), but interesting arguments have recently been put forward for placing it in the middle of the second century B.C.

100 Copyright (a) and (b) Hirmer, Munich.
(a) Head of a standing statue of a Hellenistic ruler (?). Ht. of whole figure, 2.37 m. It has been dated to the middle of the first century B.C. by good

Plate

authorities, or, alternatively, to the mid-second and tentatively identified as Demetrius I Soter, King of Syria 162-150 B.C.
(b) Male head in bronze in the National Museum, Athens, from Delos. Ht. 32.5 cm. Eyes inlaid. An excellent example of late naturalism. To be placed somewhere between 150-69 B.C.

101 Copyright (a) and (b) Hirmer, Munich.
(a) The Aphrodite of Melos (Venus de Milo) in the Louvre, Paris. Ht. 2.04 m. Opinions have varied on its date: as early as 300-250 B.C., as late as 150-125 B.C.
(b) The Victory of Samothrace in the Louvre, Paris. Ht. 2.45 m. It has been pointed out that it is wrong to date it by the coin of Demetrius Poliorcetes showing a Victory standing on a prow and blowing a trumpet, since the conception and dynamics of the present figure are different. It is more probably to be dated in the early second century and taken to be a monument for the victory of the Rhodians over Antiochus III (222-187 B.C.).

102 Copyright, Staatl. Museen, Pergamon Museum, Berlin (East).
Part of the major frieze of the Great Altar of Pergamon, with the Battle of the Gods and Giants, in Berlin. Erected by Eumenes II (197-159 B.C.) in the period 180-160 B.C. as a memorial to the victory of his father Attalus I. Ht. c. 2.3 m. The work of many sculptors is apparent, but there must have been one organising artist.

103 Copyright British Museum.
Portrait coins of Hellenistic rulers.
(a) Lysimachus of Thrace (306-281 B.C.). Silver tetradrachm. Head of Alexander with the horn of Ammon.
(b) Eumenes I of Pergamon (263-241 B.C.). Silver tetradrachm. Head of Philetairos, his uncle and founder of the dynasty.
(c) Agathocles of Bactria (second century). Silver tetradrachm. Head of Diodotos of Bactria (king c. 250 B.C.).
(d) Pharnaces I of Pontus (185?-169 B.C.). Uncle of Mithradates VI (the Great). Silver tetradrachm.
(e) Perseus of Macedonia (179-168 B.C.). Silver tetradrachm.
(f) Eucratides of Bactria (c. 180-150 B.C.). Silver tetradrachm.

104 Copyright Hirmer, Munich.
The theatre of Pergamon, erected on the side of the acropolis of this city of Western Asia Minor c. 170 B.C. by Eumenes II. It is reckoned that its 80 rows of seats would give space for more than 10,000 spectators.

LIST OF ILLUSTRATIONS IN THE TEXT

THE GLORY THAT WAS GREECE

INTRODUCTION

αἱ δὲ τεαὶ ξώουσιν ἀηδόνες ᾗσιν ὁ παντων
ἁρπακτὴρ Ἀΐδης οὐκ ἐπὶ χεῖρα βαλεῖ

CALLIMACHUS

Still are thy pleasant voices, thy nightingales, awake,
For Death, he taketh all away, but them he cannot take.

HELLENISM

"Greece" and "Greek" mean different things to different people.
To the man in the street, if he exists, they stand for something proverbially remote and obscure, as dead as Queen Anne, as heavy as the
British Museum. To the average finished product of Public School
Education in England they have long recalled those dog-eared text-
books and grammars which he put away with much relief when he
left school; they waft back to him the strangely close atmosphere of
the classical form-room. The historian, of course, will inform us that
all Western civilisation has Greece for its mother and nurse, and that
unless we know something about her our knowledge of the past must
be built upon sand. That is true: but nobody cares very much what
historians say, for they deal with the past, and the past is dead and
disgusting. To some folk who have read Swinburne (but not Plato)
the notion of the Greeks presents a world of happy pagans, children
of nature, without any tiresome ideas of morality or self-control,
sometimes making pretty poems and statues, but generally basking in
the sun without much on. There are also many earnest students of
the Bible, who remember what St Paul said about those Greeks who
thought the Cross foolishness and those Athenians who were always
wanting to hear something new. Then there are a vast number of
people who do not distinguish between "Greek" and "classical". By
"classics" they understand certain tyrannous conventions and stilted
affectations against which every free-minded soul longs to rebel. They
distinguish the classical element in Milton and Keats as responsible for
all that is dull and far-fetched and unnatural. Classicism repels many
people of excellent taste, and Greek art is apt to fall under the same

I

condemnation.   It is only relatively recently that scholars have been able to distinguish between the true Greek and the false mist of classicism which surrounds him.   Men of Byron's day and before had to look at the Greeks through Roman and Renaissance spectacles, confounding Pallas Athene with Minerva and thinking of Greek art as represented by the Apollo Belvedere and the Laocoon.   We are now able, to some extent but not as much as we would like, through the labours of scholars and archaeologists, to see the Greeks as they were, and not through the eyes of others.   More than this, we can begin to see them against the background of other peoples who were their contemporaries and their forerunners.

Admitting these misconceptions it is my aim here to try and throw some fresh light upon the secret of that people's greatness, and to look at the Greeks not as the defunct producers of antique curios, but, if I can, as Keats with divine intuition looked at them, believing what he said of Beauty:

> It will never
> Pass into nothingness, but still will keep
> A bower quiet for us, and a sleep
> Full of sweet dreams, and health, and quiet breathing.

It cannot be done by studying their history only.   Their history is full of battles, in which they were only moderately great, and petty quarrels, to which they were immoderately prone.   Their literature, which presents the greatest bulk of varied excellence of any literature in the world, must be considered.   But as it can reach us only through the watery medium of translation we must supplement it by studying also their statues and temples, their coins, vases, and pictures.   Even that will not be sufficient for people who are not artists, because the sensible Philistine part of the world knows, as the Greeks knew, that a man may draw and fiddle and be a scoundrel.   Therefore we must look also at their laws and governments, their ceremonies and amusements, their philosophy and manners and religion, to see whether they knew how to live like decent free men. If we can keep our eyes open to all these sides of their activity and watch them in the germ and bud, we ought to get near to understanding their power as a living source of inspiration to artists and thinkers.   Lovers of the classics are very apt to remind us of the Renaissance as testifying to the power of Greek thought to awaken and inspire men's minds.   Historically they are right, for it is a fact which ought to be emphasised. But when they go on to argue that if we forget the classics we ourselves shall need a fresh Renaissance they are making a prophecy which seems to me to be very doubtful. I believe that our art and literature has by this time absorbed and assimilated what Greece had to teach, and that our roots are so entwined with the soil of Greek culture that we can never lose the taste of it as long as books are read and pictures painted. We are in fact, living on the legacy of Greece, and we may, if we please, forget the testatrix.

My claim for the study of Hellenism would not be founded on history. I would urge the need of constant reference to some fixed canon in matters of taste, some standard of the beautiful which shall be beyond question or criticism; all the more because we are living in eager, restless times of constant experiment and veering fashions. Whatever may be the philosophical basis of aesthetics it is undeniable that a large part of our idea of beauty rests upon habit. Hellas provides a thousand objects which seventy-five generations of people have agreed to call beautiful and which no person outside a madhouse has ever thought ugly. The proper use of true classics is not to regard them as fetishes which must be slavishly worshipped, as the French dramatists worshipped the imaginary unities of Aristotle, but to keep them for a compass in the cross-currents of fashion. By them you may know what is permanent and essential from what is showy and exciting.

That the Greek world is peculiarly suited to this purpose is partly due, no doubt, to the winnowing of centuries of time, but partly also to its own intrinsic qualities. For one thing, a great deal of the best Greek work was done not to please private tastes but in a serious spirit of religion to honour the god of the city; that prevents it from being trivial or meretricious. Secondly it is not romantic; and that renders it a very desirable antidote to modern extravagances. Thirdly, it is idealistic; that gives it a force and permanence which things designed for the interest of the moment only must generally lack. With all these high merits it might remain very dull if it had not the charm and grace of youth, which has not lost its first impulse and delight in achievement.

THE LAND AND ITS PEOPLE

It requires more than a glance at the physical map of Greece to understand the sort of country which forms the framework of our story. Certain aspects of it are immediately perceived: its long and complicated coastline; its intricate systems of rugged mountains related to the great backbone of the Pindus north of the Gulf of Corinth and extending into the Peloponnese and out to its capes. Nor do the mountain chains stop there: they continue out to sea, so that they form with their peaks and ridges the multitudinous islands of the Aegean. The Balkan peninsula is one of the three main land masses which stretch out south into the Mediterranean. It is the one which gives the least impression of being a bridge to Africa. On the other hand it seems at first sight less cut off from the land mass to the north than either Spain by the Pyrenees or Italy by the Alps, since the main axis of the Greek mountains appears to lie in the same direction as the peninsula itself, with a north-west south-east trend. This is, however, really a rather fallacious impression. The mountains which lie between modern southern Jugoslavia and Greek Macedonia are less "pervious" than they seem at first sight on the map. Farther south there is the mountainous and broken area between south Macedonia and Thessaly, which includes Mount Olympus and its outliers. There is also the restriction of movement imposed by the mountain backbone of the Pindus laterally; a phenomenon also produced by its continuation in Jugoslavia. Movement east and west is not precluded (at times it has been historically important), but it is not easy, as any one will see who travels from Thessaly via Metsovo to Ioannina in Epirus, or from Lamia in Malis via Karpenision to Agrinion in Aetolia. Nor, indeed, is it an easy passage farther south, from Aetolia eastwards to Delphi and on into Boeotia. What is true of central Greece is equally true of the Peloponnese, as the bus route from Corinth via Argos and Tripolis to Kalamata or Sparta makes clear. It may be argued that the donkey can go where motors cannot, and that the "well-girt" man (as the Greeks called him) can take short cuts, but neither trade nor any other form of intercourse is easily promoted.

On the other hand the sea appears to facilitate communication. There is the outer line of islands, Cythera off the Peloponnese, Crete, Kasos, Karpathos and Rhodes, cosily shutting in the Aegean. It is a commonplace to say that within this line the Aegean islands beckon on the sailor eastwards, and, of course, natives of the east Aegean lands westwards. Between the tip of Attica and Samos the sailor need never be out of sight of land during the day or without a convenient place to put in to at night. The same is true, more or less, southeastwards to

1. The sanctuary at Olympia.

3.   The temple of Athena incorporated in Syracuse Cathedral.

4. Olympia and the Alpheios valley.

5.   The Temple of Apollo at Delphi.

6.   The Temple of Apollo Epikourios at Bassai.

7. Sparta and the Eurotas Valley.

8. The theatre at Epidauros

9. (a) The Acrocorinth and the temple of Apollo.
(b) View from the Acrocorinth looking northwards.

10. The Acropolis of Athens.

11.   Athens from the Hill of the Nymphs.

12. (a) The western side of the Athenian marketplace.
    (b) A plaster model of the same, restored.

13.   (a) Early Neolithic habitation at Cnossus.
        (b) Neolithic pottery from Athens.

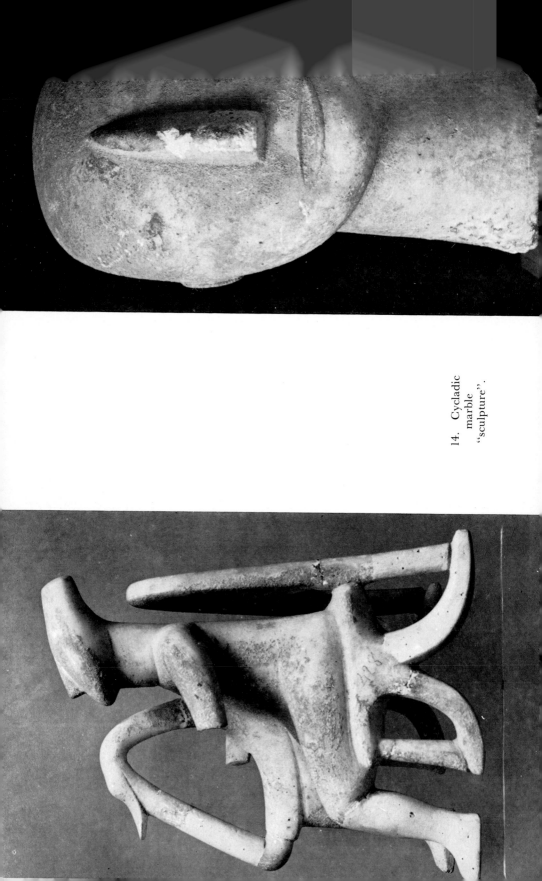

14. Cycladic
marble
"sculpture".

15.   Two views of the citadel of Troy.

16. The Mycenaean "Palace of Nestor" at "Pylos".

Crete. From this protecting arc Rhodes leads on to the south coast of
Asia Minor, Cyprus, Syria and Phoenicia. Directly southward from
Crete the sailor, aided by wind and water, may cross to Africa and
Egypt. The Greek seems positively encouraged to go eastwards.
Movement north and northeast is not perhaps quite so easy. Yet in
this direction, because of the riches of Thrace and of the Black Sea
lands, there came into being one of the great trade routes, via Skyros,
Lemnos and Imbros; at first difficult, it has been suggested, to primitive
sailors (whose adventures give rise to the story of the Argonauts) by
reason of winds and adverse currents, but easier later when ships were
improved. The map, therefore, gives the impression of a land turned
eastwards, for which the sea is its true link with other peoples.

If we believe that Greece is largely cut off from the northern Balkans
we shall probably be right: archaeology appears to support this view.
But not all hasty impressions gained from looking at the map are to
be accepted without condition. There is, for instance, this question of
Greece looking eastwards. It is easy to get the impression that Greece
looks east and Italy looks west, and that the Ionian and Adriatic Seas
were a barrier. This is an impression largely gained by looking at the
upper Adriatic, where, indeed, the mountainous coast of the most
backward region of Greece on the east, and the harbourless coast
(except for Ancona) on the west look rather unpromising. If we look
farther south, the position will be seen to be different. The facts that
the earliest Greek colonisation was in the west, and that the Greeks
exploited and settled on the coasts of present-day Sicily, Italy, France
and Spain, show that Greece looks both ways, not only to the east.
There is a close connexion between the states of South Italy and Sicily
and Olympia in the western Peloponnese (cf. Plate 1 for the line of
"treasuries" which included those of western Greek states). The
importance of western Hellenism is also demonstrated by the temples
(Plates 2, 3) and other material remains of South Italy and Sicily;
Magna Graecia was the name applied, even in days of decline, to
South Italy. Wherever the land promised the Greeks went. Out of
the Corinthian Gulf, up the western coast of Greece via Ithaka (an
early calling-place) and Corfu (Kerkyra) and across to the heel of
Italy, a crossing longer than the island stages of the Aegean, but not
overlong. And so by way of the south coast of Italy to Sicily,
though some Greeks must have been bold and sailed straight across.
As far as the Adriatic was concerned the earlier Greeks found what they

wanted farther south; the later Greeks had no difficulty in penetrating it, both in the late sixth and early fifth centuries when trade with the Etruscans called, and in the fourth century when they were forced to seek supplies of corn in this direction though piracy was rife, which in itself seems to indicate trading activity. If Greece can in any sense be said to turn its back on Italy, it is in that the ancient centres of culture, which so much influenced the Greeks, and the cities of Asia Minor, lie to the east. Furthermore, in the fifth century Athens determined the way Greece looked to a greater degree than Corinth; so did the Persians in the sense that the Delian League was directed against them. Again in the fourth century, despite the continued importance of Syracuse in Greek affairs, the general direction of interest is north and east, culminating in Alexander's invasion of Asia. Finally, however, the rise of Rome forced the Greeks to look west.

There are also other things to be taken into account which are by no means obvious from any map. There is the perpetual problem of differences between ancient and modern times: the altered sea-levels and shore lines, fertile of dispute on ancient naval tactics and navigation. The east-west tilting of Crete since ancient times has brought it about that in the east headlands have become waterless islands, and in the west ancient harbours are high and dry. It is not always easy to restore in the mind's eye, on the map or on the site the land as it was.

The same is true of the soil and its cover. Greece west of the Pindus Mountains with its heavier rainfall is richer in trees and grass (contrast Olympia, Plates 1 and 4 with Delphi, Plate 5, though part of the contrast is artificial); the atmosphere is heavier and moister, hazier and cloudier, and sometimes vaguely depressing. One feels that a Pythian victory at Delphi would be won with less effort than an Olympic victory on the west of the Peloponnese. The east side of the Pindus is drier, or so it seems, from Thessaly southwards. North of Thessaly in Macedonia, locally again, the land often seems better watered. This and the fruit trees make parts of southern Macedonia, little visited by tourists, very pleasant indeed. But here also, as in the rest of eastern Greece (and, indeed, plentifully on the west as one may observe on the sea voyage southward from Corfu), the hills are bare and the land stony and deeply scored by watercourses. Everywhere the drainage is destructive, or has been (Plate 6). So much of Greece is on a slope, how could the soil be retained without the greatest efforts? On level ground also, where the alluvium has gathered from the surrounding hills, there are deep and winding watercourses. They and the rivers of Greece are striking natural features, but not for the regular volume of their waters. Even in western Greece two large rivers, the Achelous and the Alpheius, with wide drainage areas, show, for a great part of the year, a relative trickle amid a sea of stones. The same is true to a great extent of the Peneios in Thessaly and the Haliakmon in southern Macedonia, and, indeed, of the famous Eurotas at Sparta (Plate 8). Only in the north are the rivers moderately impressive, the Vardar (Axios), the Struma (Strymon), the Nestos and the Maritza (Hebros), fed by the snows of the Macedonian and Thracian mountains. Generally speaking the snow water causes less trouble than the sudden precipitation of a rain storm, which is ruinous to the soil and can convert even the streets of Athens into roaring torrents, and used to sweep away children playing in the bed of the Ilissos. So there is a vicious circle from which it is difficult to escape: the loss of the original tree cover means that the soil is swept away by storm water, and reafforestation is thus made much more difficult.

It is common enough to idealise the Greek climate, but in fact there is no such thing as a "Greek" climate, except in very general weather terms. No more in this context than in any other can "Greece" be described as one unit. As often in other connexions, here "Greece" means Attica, the region of the Isthmus of Corinth, and the eastern Peloponnese, the tourist area *par excellence*. Athens enjoys and enjoyed in antiquity "a fair admixture of the seasons"; a long and lovely autumn, a short and sometimes bitter winter, a glowing and dusty summer tempered outside the towns by a sea breeze, and a spring of sudden changes: one day may be dark and overcast with lowering clouds and lasting rain, the next all new-washed blue and green, with a brisk breeze and white caps to the dark blue waves; very different from the times of sirocco when the wind from Africa brings haze and clammy heat and irritated nerves. In our enthusiasm we must not forget that mud and dust were close associates in the Greek poet's mind. For the rest there is, in fact, wide variation. Mainland Greece stretches between the exceedingly mild winters and crushing summer heat of Crete to the grey cold and moderate summers of Thrace. The clear air of Attica, which is a very real phenomenon, is not apparent in Boeotia, which is heavy and rather depressing, or in Thessaly which is dusty and hazy. Both the latter are largely cut off from the sea, which undoubtedly makes a great deal of difference to

Attica, and also a great deal to the islands of the Aegean: they too enjoy the sea breezes, but find less pleasurable the sirocco, the *meltem* and the cold winds from the direction of the Hellespont. In fact, seasons vary, and regional weather varies as the Athenians believed when they expressed the view that their sharp wits owed something to their clear atmosphere, and the dim and stolid Boeotians something to the difference of theirs.

In this point we are already comparing times ancient and modern. What can be said of other things? It may be agreed, at any rate, that the sea is much the same; the Aegean stormy in winter, calm in summer, a mixture of storm and calm in spring. The dangerous rocks and lee shores are the same, but the rest is not, except for the sailor who really sails, without the aid of steam or the petrol-motor to replace or supplement the wind. The true sailor will find things much the same, and the ancient joke concerning the Greek sailors who were found to be using a map of St Paul's voyages as an aid to navigation is less funny on reflection than at first hearing. There are and were the same capes and headlands difficult to round, encouraging the use of harbours on either side and overland portage. The importance of sheltered bays will be the same, and of harbours with several entrances to be used according to the way of the wind. To some extent, also, there will be a concern for suitable landfalls at night. There will always be the same preoccupation with reefs (with which the Aegean is dotted), and sudden storms (to which it is liable). In ancient and modern times alike some regions of Greece produced active and hardy sailors, from necessity for the most part. They were led on from island to island by a sense of adventure and a desire to explore, but they were also forced to take to the sea either to escape poverty on the land, like many island inhabitants of modern Greece, or because it was often their best or only means of transport and communication. They were so much surrounded by the sea that they felt lost without it, like the men of the Anabasis. They also feared and disliked it. Against Aeschylus's "myriad laughing waves" must be set his "Salmydessos, stepmother of ships" and the endless epitaphs lamenting the poor drowned sailor. Odysseus seems to be the very symbol and exemplar of the Greek (Frontispiece); the *Odyssey* is full of sea adventure, but Poseidon was the enemy of Odysseus, and the hero was thankful to be home on dry land; and when he sets out again it is to a place where oars and ships are unknown.

The sea has not much changed. What about the rest? In very general terms it may be argued that the weather was much the same as now. There is, of course, the difficulty of distinguishing between long term and short term variations. That it was not eternal springtime is clear enough from Thucydides and other writers: snow and sleet and frost were all known and to be reckoned with. As noticed above, mud and dust were brothers for the Greeks. In a chorus of the *Antigone* of Sophocles (332) Man the Wonder is hailed for his achievement on the sea:

"the power that crosses the white sea, driven by the stormy south-wind, making a path under surges that threaten to engulf him . . . " (trans. Jebb)

No ideal sea, clearly, challenged the Greeks, and no ideal weather, for the chorus continues:

"And speech, and wind-swift thought, and all the moods that mould a state, hath he taught himself; and how to flee the arrows of the frost, when 'tis hard lodging under the clear sky, and the arrows of the rushing rain . . . (trans. Jebb).

The Greeks (and here we may speak of them in general) knew all about bad weather. Did other conditions of modern Greece prevail also: the loss of tree cover, the shortage of grazing, the denudation of the soil, the intense stoniness (Plate 6), the lack of a capacity to raise large cattle, the extreme fragmentation of cultivation units, the poverty of crops, the lack of wheat-growing land? The emphasis on trees and grass as an amenity of the countryside, the planting of trees as a much stressed benefaction, and the importation of a great deal of timber by Athens, of whose procedures we know most, all suggest that there was no basic difference in Attica then and now. There is no reason to believe that other regions containing a considerable population were much better off. Timber was an essential material both for building (including ships and land vehicles) and for fuel. The use of stone in domestic and private structures, except for foundations, must not be overestimated. Mud-brick was extensively used, as in modern times, but this also required its strengthening timbers; wood was essential for roof-beams and doors, often removed at evacuation in time of war. Charcoal could be made to some extent from scrub, but there were limitations to this, and in the absence of coal charcoal or wood had to be used not only for cooking and heating but for metal-smelting and working, and for pottery and tile-making. It is interesting to note that the Greeks made little use of baked bricks until Roman times. This fuel problem was one which affected different regions of Greece to varying degrees, and was part of the larger timber problem. Woods and forests were not likely to survive very long where they were readily accessible and close to large centres of population; elsewhere the limitations of roads and land vehicles imposed a check, though the charcoal burner with his donkey would eventually make his presence felt even in relatively remote districts. The charcoal burners of Acharnai, who gave their name to the *Acharnians* of Aristophanes, seem to have flourished in the fifth century B.C. when Athens was importing ship timbers, so it is reasonable to suppose that large trees went first, and the smaller followed. The timber problem was in any case part of the still larger transport problem. The many sides of these interrelated economic problems cannot be further examined here, and it is difficult quite to decide when they became fully operative to the detriment of civilised living in the Greek city states. We can be sure, however, that they had started in the classical period of the fourth century, if not before, and in Attica, where we hear of the damage done by storm water as a subject of private litigation, and of the watercourses which resembled roads and the roads which resembled watercourses, which are still a common feature of the Greek country. When cultivation was extended up the mountain sides, as it was in Attica in the sixth and fifth centuries B.C., it became exposed more than ever to ruin through violent rain-storms and neglect of terrace-walling. There at any rate the Greek peasants' life could be a continuous and back-breaking battle against nature. All the more of a blessing therefore were the vine, the gift of Dionysus who received a special welcome in Attica (though the wine of Attica was not highly esteemed), and the olive belonging to Athena the patron goddess. They, or at any rate the olive, helped to bind the soil together; their fruits nourished and cheered the peasant, and they would grow where wheat would not. Nonetheless it was all very precarious. One thing only was in good supply, the stones for walling and terracing.

It will be seen that we know Attica best; so much of Greek literature is Attic literature. For the rest of Greece we are largely reduced to picking up scattered bits of ambiguous information where we can. Expressions of poverty and hardship, which are very common, may be matched by the stereotyped adjectives of fertility and prosperity:

"rich in kin", "horse-rearing", "rich in corn", "deep-tilthed". Significantly enough these epithets appear in the Homeric poems (and are copied from them later), composed in Ionia and, in part at any rate, on an earlier tradition. There is therefore a possibility that they represent the conditions of more fertile Asia Minor and of an earlier age in Greece proper. In any case they are relative as applied to a poor country. So today Messenia around Kalamata, the vale of Sparta (Plate 7), parts of Arcadia, Achaia, Boeotia and Thessaly *look* fertile by contrast, say, with the slopes of Hymettos; so do parts of Attica, such as the plain of Marathon and the Mesogia beyond Hymettos despite Attica's reputation of being light-soiled. Closer inspection shows the poverty of the soil, and the thinness of the green growth. They seem good by comparison with less fortunate areas, where the barley is meagre beneath the olives, or where only the spinifex flourishes amid the jagged limestone. At road cuttings, as for instance in Attica, the traveller perceives how thin is the layer of red soil on the white of the rock beneath. Ancient Greece may have been better in degree, but not fundamentally different, since these characteristics come from the essential structure and nature of the land.

What is true of trees and soil is true also of pasture and the animals which graze on it. In modern Greece grass and fields given up to it, as we in North Western Europe understand them, are largely unknown. Grass is something scant, to be painfully harvested. The fodder which is gathered and transported on the backs of those donkeys which may be encountered on any Greek road carrying their own provender is made up of diverse plants, cut and carried home not grazed on the spot. It is generally used to feed the hard-working donkey, or a few sheep. Horses and large cattle are few and far between, except in fertile Macedonia. In the literature of Ancient Greece we hear of pasture, often along a river bank and wonder what it was like. The word *leimōn*, translated "meadow" is misleading. In the world of the Blessed Dead it is red with roses; in the island of Calypso it bears violets and wild celery. The asphodel meadow in the Underworld of the *Odyssey* is any Greek hillside covered with that unattractive plant. None of these is a place for grazing horses or cattle. In the *Odyssey* (iv 601-608) Telemachos refuses Menelaos' gift of horses, contrasting Ithaka with Lacedaemon:

"But horses I will not take to Ithaka, but leave them here a glory for yourself, for you are lord of a wide plain, wherein is *lotos* in great plenty, and *kypeiron*, and wheat and spelt and white spreading barley. In Ithaka there are no wide ways for galloping, no meadowland at all. It is a pasture land of goats, more pleasant than one that pastures horses. For of the islands that slope down to the sea none is fit for the driving of horses, or rich in meadowland, and least of all Ithaka.''

"Lotos" may be many things from trefoil to fenugreek, cytisus or water lily; "kypeiron" is some form of aromatic reed, which also presents something of a problem in Mycenaean Greek. As pasture for horses they sound unsatisfactory, and in fact it emerges clearly from a closer inspection of Telemachos' words that the real food of horses was almost entirely grains, with some "harvested" greenery as it might be called. True pasture was rare, if it existed at all, and this is a characteristic of Greece to an even greater degree in modern times. So it came about that horses were expensive to rear and feed, the *agalma*, "glory", or as one might say "status symbol" of the great and wealthy. Large cattle also were scarce and difficult to maintain in most parts of central and southern Greece, and consequently a fitting offering on special occasions to the great gods, when man also had his share in the unwonted treat at the feast that followed, while the hides were of the greatest value for the many uses to which they were put. In the west, perhaps, more cattle were kept, and in the case of Macedonia one is struck by the numerous appearances of cattle and horses on the coins of the barbarous tribes of that region; still more by the lions attacking oxen on the coins of Akanthos. These regions may well have possessed large cattle in some quantity, but what, for instance, of the island which stretches more or less north and south off the coast of central Greece, of which the name is *Euboia*, "rich in kine"? What can have been this richness in kine of what now seems to be a mountainous and rather stony island? To be sure, the inhabitants of Chalcis and Eretria, the two chief cities of the island, fought over the Lelantine Plain, which passed as rich. Here we have either the fertility and richness of a bygone day, or else a relative idea, like the reputation of the Eleusinian Plain between Athens and Megara, whence, according to Athenian legend, the gift of corn went forth from Demeter to the world. But in all this we have to be careful to avoid too sure conclusions. As every traveller knows, those rich and wealthy regions especially in the west, in Sicily and Southern Italy, to which the Greeks went forth in early times, do not now look particularly rich in either corn or timber.

Yet we know that they were, and the same is in some degree true of western Anatolia. Perhaps Greece *was* different in ancient times after all. Apart from large cattle, sheep were reared for wool and milk, more perhaps than for meat. The dilemma of Greece was the ubiquitous and omnivorous goat with its sprightly and enterprising character and malignant topaz eyes: eater of the vine (and of everything else) and therefore the proper sacrifice to Dionysus; devourer of trees, but at the same time provider of cheap flesh, cheese and covering.

As far as we can judge, just as cultivation attained no high standard since the soil was thin and only barley and not wheat could be grown in most districts, while the general nature of the land restricted cattle raising, so too the general economic organisation was on a small scale. There may have been large estates, large, that is, in Greek terms, but the cultivation unit would certainly be small, whether tenant farms or free-holdings. This natural tendency was accentuated by the practice of dividing land by inheritance and by the giving of dowries. This tendency to fragmentation has also been a characteristic of modern Greece. The Greeks were always vulnerable, always aware of the power of nature or of the Gods, and always cognisant of the difficulties of making a living from the soil on which they depended, and from which they were never detached throughout their history, even in the largest city communities. Many might live within city walls, but they went out to their country tasks. It was true that in the fifth century B.C. Athens became a great city, and that the Piraeus was the hub of the maritime empire, but Thucydides makes it clear that at the beginning of the Peloponnesian War the Athenians were still close to the soil. The same must have been true of mercantile cities like Corinth and Aegina.

On the other hand every community had its craftsmen and traders. In small communities and at an earlier date it was possible for these to combine craft and trade with cultivation. In the larger cities manufacturing craftsmanship could be highly specialised, as Greek writers commented. As in cultivation the unit was small. There were workshops but no factories. This was of necessity so, because of the severe limitations on equipment and sources of power. The citizen craftsman in his workshop, or working for hire, did piece-work, so that he was in a large measure free of the tyranny of industrial life and free to perform his citizen duties, especially in the democracy of Athens; he was not, of course, free of the tyranny of earning his living. The soulless dealing with men's labour as a commodity, which has been a feature of the modern industrial state, was in effect absent. It was to some extent replaced by slavery; slaves fulfilled those functions which put them at the beck and call of another, which was a position disliked by the free man. Slaves were property and capital, and so could not be too ruthlessly treated or turned off if there was no work. Such manufacturing establishments as there were were manned by slaves. None of them, as far as we know, was at any time large. It has to be concluded, from such knowledge as we possess (which is very defective and relates almost exclusively to Athens), that community needs and export markets were served by a multitude of small establishments. It was all very primitive. The same was true of the distributive process. There existed a multitude of traders and petty huxters, freemen and women, freed slaves (who were relatively rare), and slaves, who often traded for their masters. Trading activity resembled, in fact, the bazaar economy of the modern Near and Middle East, and in some measure our own market system in country towns. There was also in important centres such as Athens and the Piraeus in the fourth century B.C. a class of more important traders, using their own capital or that of others, to trade over a distance, generally by sea. Even this type of trade seems to have been pretty simple compared with that of the Hellenistic period after Alexander and of the Romans. These traders were an extraordinarily diverse body, of scoundrels many would say, drawn from every city of the Mediterranean seaboard, and by no means all Greek. They and the petty trader enjoyed no high reputation, and Plato and Aristotle both animadvert on the moral harm inflicted by trading. It is true that in Hellenistic and Roman times the Greek, like Juvenal's *graeculus esuriens*, gained the reputation of being willing to go anywhere and do anything (which also harmed the repute of later Greeks), but it is an error to suppose, as some have done, that the classical Greek was essentially a trader of sharp wits and dubious morality. It is to be suggested that like the Jew and the Armenian he was driven to this sort of thing. If conditions let him he was naturally a cultivator. The backbone of the Greek *polis*, the heavily armed hoplite soldier, was a yeoman farmer. The partial (it is important to stress "partial") turning of Athens to the sea in the fifth century B.C. under the leadership of Themistocles, with the consequent rise of the "naval mob", was an exception rather than the rule. We cannot speak of the "Greeks" as a sea-going people, without conditioning the statement, nor claim for them all the consequent virtuous and vicious characteristics in thought and action.

One geographical characteristic of Greece was certainly operative for good and ill in antiquity. Nature, it has often been pointed out, has split Greece up into numerous small plains and valleys divided by mountain barriers (*cf.* Plate 7, for the valley in which Sparta lies and Plate 8 for Epidaurus). There are also numerous islands, some of which were the location of active and important city states. The result was a fierce local patriotism, hostile to uniformity, devoted to freedom, and prolific of wasteful quarrels. It is also to be noted that these small and independent units (themselves the product of the union of villages) found for themselves a defensible centre in one of the precipitous hills which dominate the small plains, as at Corinth and Athens (Plates 9, 10 and 11). In the disturbed days of early Greece these were a refuge at some distance from the sea, and therefore safe from pirate marauders; a site for the temple of the protecting deity in some cases (Plate 10), and for the palace of an early ruler. This was true in Bronze Age Greece, and remained so. There is a superficial resemblance to the hill-towns of Etruscan and mediaeval Italy, but peacetime life did not constrict itself within the walls of such an *acropolis*, as the Greeks called it, though the unpretentious and squalid dwellings of a classical Greek town—for such must private as opposed to public buildings have been—huddled around it.

Such acropolis rocks (Plates 9 and 10), some less impressive than others, formed the centre of *polis* life or rather one centre, since there was another, the Agora or Marketplace (Plate 12), and into the *polis* were drawn together a variety of small communities which, in earlier Greece at any rate, had a local loyalty of their own as well as a loyalty to the *polis*, meaning the "city-state". Political union of such small Greek communities was a process of coalescence which went so far and then stopped. Sometimes, as in the case of Athens and Attica, the union was completed as far as the obvious geographical boundaries, or almost so. In other cases, as in Boeotia, separate and independent city states, though of unequal size, survived in some number when the emergence of one unit might have been expected. It is hard to say why. Elsewhere, as in Arcadia and Elis, the passage from village units to a *polis* community was effected only at a relatively late date, while in the regions north of the Gulf of Corinth and west of the Pindus complex the village and tribal life were retained at a barbarous level, and, as Thucydides tells us, men carried arms even in time of peace. This life of scattered communities, which missed the advantages of the *polis*, is present in some parts of Greece today, side by side with the towns. The foreign traveller, journeying by bus, is often puzzled when the vehicle stops in what appears to be the deepest and most deserted countryside. Passengers descend; bicycles, sewing machines, at Eastertime even lambs on spits, are brought down from the roof, and the party then appears to plunge off into nowhere. But high up on the distant mountainside is a small community marked in the day as a patch of white houses, by night, if at all, by a dim light. Our travellers are going to such a village; and such life must have been common also in ancient times.

Of this one thing we can be certain, that the Greeks have been influenced by this geographical characteristic of division. Much else is a matter of opinion, and while giving all due credit to the Greek character and achievement, we must be careful not to romanticize them. Not all of them enjoyed that clarity of thought which has sometimes been ascribed to the clarity of the atmosphere. Moderation and self-knowledge were not always conspicuously present among them. The Greeks admired certain virtues, of *Aidos* or reverence, and *Sophrosyne* or self-restraint. The Delphic Oracle urged Moderation and Self-knowledge, indeed. But the point must be clearly taken. For instance, the Delphic maxim "Know thyself". Stories told of the oracle and of those who enquired of it make clear that Apollo's counsel meant "Understand your motives; do not try to get others to make moral decisions for you, so that you can dodge the blame". The sober student of Greek history and Greek affairs is only too well aware that these principles and these virtues were so much stressed by Apollo because they were so much needed. The Greeks were at least honest in this. Like the rest of us, and like the ancient Romans, they admired those virtues necessary for survival and progress which were often most conspicuous by their absence, more honoured in the breech than in the observance. We must not believe that they were universally practised, any more than we need believe that the virtues praised by implication in the legends of early Rome were present in later Romans to a greater degree than in any one else. They were a useful ideal.

The Greeks were human. They merit our attention because of their achievements. Though most things they did have been done as well or better by others, they are none the less worthy of our attention because of their infinitely puzzling character, especially their strong contrasts; so much about them we fail to understand, and while this in part comes from our sheer ignorance, this is not wholly so. They never seem dull, or respectable or predictable. Thus Aristophanes could be described by a German poet as "a grove of singing nightingales and chattering apes". There was the sinister discipline of Sparta, and the democratic liberality of Athens; the austerity of a Pericles and the exuberance of a Cleon; in art, the remote idealism and the cheerful obscenity. There is their mobility of temperament, as in the modern Greeks, at one time kindly and hospitable, at another savage and violent. They could play many parts: Sophocles, composer of the *Antigone* could also help to put down the insurgent Samians. They appeal to the sympathy and admiration and wonder of us moderns, most of whom, it is to be suspected, would hate to live with them.

AEGEAN CIVILISATION

Vixere fortes ante Agamemnona.

HORACE

A NEW CHAPTER OF HISTORY

I t is the misfortune of historians to be liable to attacks at both extremities. On the one hand Time is continually adding postscripts to their *Finis*, and on the other hand the archaeologist is constantly making them tear up and rewrite their first chapters. In Greek history especially the spade has proved mightier than the pen. We are now only certain that the first page of any Greek history written thirty years ago must be defective; we are not even yet quite sure or agreed what to put in its place. Explorers have succeeded in extending our horizon backwards (as in Neolithic Crete, Plate 13) for some thousands of years; and the evidence is not always easy to interpret as it grows more abundant and more complicated. This is strikingly true of the site of Lerna in the Peloponnese (Plate 30). For many years there lay in the Cretan museum scores of clay tablets inscribed with an unknown writing. Excavation in Greece has added many more. Some of them have found interpreters in recent years to confound, illuminate or confuse us all. In the last century eminent writers like Gladstone and Freeman were still looking to Homer for their ideas of the primitive European and his civilisation. Strange indeed were the results that followed. In politics we were to believe that the earliest Greeks settled their affairs at a public meeting where elders and princes made persuasive speeches, and radicalism, though not unknown, was sternly discouraged. A benevolent monarchy, hereditary in the male line, was supposed by Sir Henry Maine to be the form of government common to primitive Europe and modern England. Literature was believed to have begun with elaborate epic poems written in hexameters of exquisite variety and extreme subtlety. The primitive woman was believed to have been the object of chivalrous and romantic esteem. Strangest of all, religion in this primitive world was held to

18

have included the cheerful bantering of anthropomorphic gods and goddesses. We were to suppose that the European began by laughing at his gods and ended by worshipping them.

Then in the 'seventies of the last century came the redoubtable Dr Schliemann, most erudite of sappers, and dug into the hill at Hissarlik to see if he could find the bones of Hector and the ruins of Troy. Troy he found in abundance, seven Troys at least, one on the top of another. In Schliemann's techniques there was much to be desired; we must honour him for his enterprise and pertinacity rather than for his skill. He called the second city from the bottom the city of Priam. In this he was wrong. It was in effect much earlier and it remained for the American excavator Blegen to show how vastly more complicated the site was, and to distinguish the settlement whose fortunes may have given rise to the epic tale (Plate 15). From Troy Schliemann crossed over with his spades and picks to look for what might be left of Agamemnon at Mycenae. Sure enough, he presently startled the learned world by a telegram to the King of Greece saying that he had found the tomb of Agamemnon. Quite certainly he had found some very important things—things, as we shall soon see, far more interesting and valuable to history than if they had belonged, as Schliemann thought, to the king of all the Greeks. But the point is that for some years to come all the excavators who worked on Greek soil started with the false belief that Homer was the beginning of all things and that their discoveries were illustrating Homer. In a sense they were, for the Homeric poems reflect not only elements of Greece contemporary with the poems but also dim memories of a far earlier and very different day. Yet we now know that the discoveries at Mycenae not only are far older than Homer, but that they themselves are preceded by a long and varied development of civilised life. The excavations of Mycenae have gone on ever since, and astounding discoveries have been made. They have been supplemented by others in Greece, as for instance at Pylos (Plate 16). In Crete, Cyprus, Anatolia, the eastern Mediterranean shores and the central Mediterranean area there is an ever increasing exploration and discovery. We are now in a position to throw the beginnings of European and Asiatic culture in the Mediterranean basin centuries—more, whole millennia—farther back than our fathers' wildest dreams could carry them. The history of European civilisation is no longer a traceable progression from Homer to T. S. Eliot and C. P. Snow, but a long cycle of rising and decaying cultures with periods of seeming darkness intervening. For this revolution in our ideas the responsible weapon is the humble but veracious spade.

CRETE, THE DOORSTEP OF EUROPE

We are to picture the primitive tribes of the world as continually moving under the double pressure of the wolf in their bellies and the enemy at their backs—moving, it might be said in a very generalising way, in the main north and west, as climatic conditions relented before them. Climatic conditions did not always relent: sometimes they grew harsher, as with the desiccation of the land and the formation of desert, when man was once again, like other animals, forced to flee or suffer an ever more straitened life in oases. Later came a movement south and east of a different kind and for different reasons. So long as they were in this nomadic stage little progress could be made in civilisation; tents must form their houses, and their goods could be only such necessary pots and pans as they could carry. Others followed their cattle in constant search for fresh pastures. Some remained nomads, and adapted their culture to a life of movement with no abiding city. They used leather and wood instead of pottery; animal products were their food, and their gods were of the sky and not of the earth. Other moving tribes halted and settled. The attraction was particularly fertile land or an everlasting spring. When they had acquired fruit trees or established irrigation channels, and followed these with more permanent houses and shrines for their deities, they could move no more. Thus it came about that civilisation begins in the oases of the desert, in the river valleys and on the north coasts of Africa, on the western edge of the Iranian plateau and in the great river valleys of Mesopotamia, at Jericho and in southern Anatolia. Settled by force, and to some degree protected by Nature, they could begin to accumulate possessions, and to improve them with art. They could begin to build houses, and, while it is true that poor and nomadic peoples can possess an organised life, rules of society and tenets of belief, it is also certain that settled life is the necessary basis for the full development of what Sophocles called "all the arts that mould the State".

Geography has made it exceedingly probable that Crete would play a momentous part in the earliest history of Europe. That island lies like a doorstep at the threshold of Europe. If civilisation were to rise with the sun in the East, out of the extremely ancient civilisations of Egypt, Mesopotamia, and the rest of what has been called "the Fertile Crescent", certainly this island of Crete would be its stepping-stone to Europe. If one end of it points to Greece and Europe, the other points to Rhodes and southern Anatolia, where again prodigiously early remains of the first stages of settled civilisation have recently been found at Hacilar and Çatal Hüyük. Thus we reason, knowing it to be the truth. But we should never have learned the truth from literature. In Homer, for example, Crete is of ambiguous importance. It was famous for its "ninety cities" and its mixed nationalities, and it was known as the former realm of Minos. It was a place with which adventurers might be associated. There is some suggestion of artistic importance, for there the father of all craftsmen, Daedalus had fashioned a wondrous dancing-place for Ariadne. From Crete important contingents of Greeks followed after Agamemnon to Troy, but their integration into the rest of the body of legend about Crete is clearly awkward. We might almost gather from the pages of Homer that it was a land whose glory had already departed. Outside Homer, Crete, though on the sidelines of history until a late date, takes a much more important place in mythology and legend. Witness the dim memory of the Greeks which is reflected in the story of the Cretan priests whom Apollo settled in his service at Delphi. For religion Crete was the birthplace of Zeus, the king of the gods. In the history of law-making it plays a very important part, for Minos of Crete was said to be the first law-giver, and he was placed as the judge of the dead by later mythology. In religion it produced Epimenides, the early exorcist, and in music Thaletas. Then many ancient historians give us a tradition of early naval empires in Greek waters. Thalasso-cracies they were called, and that of Crete stands at the head of the list. Finally, those fortunate Englishmen whose introduction to Greece has come through the wonderful "heroes" of Charles Kingsley know the story of the Cretan labyrinth and that fearsome beast the Minotaur. They know the story of Theseus: how the Athenians of the earliest times had to send tribute every year of their fairest youths and maidens to King Minos of Crete, until one year the prince Theseus besought old Aegeus, his royal father, to let him go among the number in order to stop this cruel sacrifice; how he went at last, and how the Cretan princess, Ariadne, loved him and gave him a weapon and a clue to the labyrinth, and how he slew the dreadful monster and deserted his princess and returned home; but how he forgot also to hoist the signal of his safety, so that the old king, seeing black sails to his ship, cast himself headlong from the rock in his misery, and gave a name to the Aegean Sea. In old days we read it as a beautiful Greek romance; now we are not so sure. It would be rash to accept the story as it stands and assume that the Athenians in early days did have to pay tribute—

septena quotannis
corpora natorum

to the empire of Minos, but it appears less unlikely than it once did. Sir Arthur Evans, the explorer of Cnossus, at first spoke as if he had discovered the labyrinth, and perhaps even the Minotaur, in his excavations at Cnossus. In any case he discovered a civilisation previously almost unknown to history. As these new discoveries centred in Crete, the excavators naturally took Crete as the fount and origin of it all, and called their new old world "Minoan", just as the followers of Dr Schliemann called their discoveries "Mycenaean". The two cultures are not distinct; Mycenaean objects show the influence, often very strongly, of the later stages of Minoan culture. Earlier than the Mycenaean remains on the mainland of Greece is another culture, or rather an earlier stage of it, called Helladic; the Mycenaean period is sometimes called "Late Helladic" to mark its place in the development. Then on the islands of the Aegean Sea the phases of a culture allied to the Cretan are distinguished as "Cycladic". But we may quite fairly use one name such as "Aegean" for all this world of prehistoric civilisation long before Homer, although it covers an enormous space of time and may be divided into many distinct chapters or phases; because, after all, there is a clear line of ancestry between the earliest of the art forms and the latest in many cases, indicating that the artists followed the same tradition, however many times their cities might be destroyed and their works buried under the soil. We note at times the appearance of novel elements, perhaps indicating the intrusion of new races, but these are absorbed into a distinctive whole covering a wide area of the Eastern Mediterranean. Aegean civilisation seems to have reached its maximum of expansion towards the end of Mycenaean times, when it covered much of the Greek mainland and the Islands, and extended eastwards through Cyprus to Phoenicia, westwards to Sicily. Many Mycenaean objects have been found in

Egypt, testimonies to a flourishing trade. Even the Philistines of Palestine are also to be included in the Aegean circle. But nowhere is that civilisation found in such perfect continuity and splendour as in Crete.

It is the custom among archaeologists to divide early cultures into periods, according to the pottery and certain other materials in use. Accordingly we say that the Aegean periods extend from the Neolithic to the Late Bronze Age, meaning the earliest of these Aegean potsherds are found in conjunction with polished flint or stone weapons and tools, while along with the latest we find a few rare pieces of iron, but mostly bronze of a very high finish and workmanship. Such finds are dated very roughly, and relatively, by the level at which they lie, because it is a curious and certain fact that the level of ground once built over is constantly rising, especially where bricks made of unbaked clay are used, or wattle and daub, through accretions of dust and debris which take the form of layers superimposed one on another. In any case it will be clear to every one that when, as at Troy and Cnossus, we find a series of buildings each resting upon the ruins of another, we can trace the history of such a site by the marks of earthquake fissures and conquerors' burning, for instance, with a fair degree of certainty from early to late. In common or abundant remains, such as pottery, we can detect the development of styles and shapes, and secure a relative date thus. It is not so easy to obtain an absolute date B.C. by a relation with another dated civilisation. Sometimes it is possible to get a date by examining foreign objects found on the same site and in the same layers, such as scarabs bearing the cartouche or sign-royal of Egyptian kings. Only we must bear in mind that such small objects are easily displaced and often preserved for long periods, so that great care must be used in taking them as evidence. More rarely there are larger objects imported into Crete from outside, or an exchange of artistic influences may be detectable. There are also Cretan objects in Egyptian contexts. All these help to date Cretan remains, and a general check, but with wide margins, can be imposed by the use of scientific techniques.

PROGRESS OF AEGEAN CULTURE

I have said that the prehistoric culture revealed by the excavations in Crete and elsewhere forms a continuous and progressive history from the Stone Age to the end of the Bronze Age. Sir Arthur Evans, indeed, divided his discoveries into nine periods, from "Early Minoan I" to "Late Minoan III". Without being quite so precise, let us attempt to sketch a history of "prehistoric" civilisation on Greek soil, taking Crete as the centre of influence. In effect "Greek soil" cannot be very readily separated from adjacent regions: there is Troy, as mentioned already, and southern Anatolia from which the earliest neolithic culture came to Crete, but to consider these would take us too far from our real theme.

Some Neolithic pottery is crude enough: for example the coarse grey and reddish-orange ware from the earliest recorded graves in the marketplace of Athens, which marks the presence there also of a Neolithic culture (Plate 13, b). In Crete "Neolithic man" began to design patterns on the pottery which he produced side by side with his weapons and tools of polished stone. Like Nature abhoring a vacuum, he traced zigzags, triangles, and chevrons upon the plastic clay, scratching or pricking lines and dots with a point of bone or stone, and sometimes filling the holes and scratches with white gypsum to show up the pattern. The body of his vases was generally, though not always, black and shiny. This black pottery is found in the Neolithic repertoire all over Southern Europe.

Of his earliest houses at Cnossus little remains except pits and pot-holes (Plate 13, a), though there is some evidence that the earliest incomers used baked brick, and later changed from this to sun-dried brick. The first dwellings must have been irregularly ordered shanties, but eventually ordered and organised series of rectangular houses appear. In Macedonia traces have been found of very early dwellings, and in Thessaly, where Neolithic culture survived right through the flourishing periods of Crete and Mycenae, there are some examples of stonebuilt houses on a rectangular plan, with three rooms and sockets for wooden pillars. Caves were still used as dwellings, and there is also a round type of hut, derived, no doubt, from the still more primitive tent of skin and wickerwork. Of the religion of the Neolithic stage we can only guess. As primitive cultivators they must have had ideas of fertility powers personified by a female deity of the earth and nature, represented by terracottas mostly with exuberantly bulging breasts and thighs, though it must also be pointed out that Neolithic man could produce figures of the highest artistry in stone (and one of these has been found in Cnossus) and in terracotta: outstanding is the fine statuette from Neolithic Lerna in Greece proper (Plate 17). Their dead they buried with care. This Neolithic period lasted a long time; the deposit on the hill of Cnossus is of great thickness. The end of the accumulation of this mass (which has been affected by the later structures built upon it) must be placed early in the third millenium B.C., and the most recent investigations would set its beginning before 5000 B.C.

Then gradually comes the beginning of the Bronze Age. All civilisation may be regarded as a progress in tools and weapons. Nowhere is the history of Europe traced with a clearer pen than in its armouries. As the guns of Crécy foretold the passing of chivalry, so the discovery of that alloy of copper and tin which produced a metal relatively easy to melt and mould and hard enough to work with meant a step forward for civilisation. At first, indeed, bronze is rare and costly; it is confined to short dagger-blades and spear-points. Along with the earliest bronze we find an advance in the pottery; paint used to trace the patterns, though the designs are still those of dot and line. Experiments are being made with colours and glazes. In experiment is the germ of progress; all cultures show experiment and trial. Some at a later stage lose this tendency to change, and settle into a conventional style; the outstanding example of this is Egypt except under Akhnaten. It is the pre-eminent characteristic of the Minoan artist that he did not lose this quality for many a long day, though at last convention and the stereotyped appeared in Crete also. So, until a late date, in the forms and designs of the pottery we watch a steady upward march, the progress growing faster as the standard of achievement rises. Curves and circles take the place of zigzags and triangles. The potter plays tricks with the colour of his clay, daubs it with red, burns it in patches (Plate 18, b). In the early strata we begin to find imitations of the human form, rude images, or sometimes not so rude, sometimes called "idols". Some are possibly the votive offerings which represent the worshipper (Plate 18, a), or are a substitute for human sacrifice. As noticed above, many of these in the Neolithic period are exaggeratedly curved and bulging; others are conventionalised in a different way into queer fiddle-shaped goggle-eyed figures. All the Cretan artists insisted on the waist to a degree which would seem even to Victorian misses an exaggeration. In Egypt the small waist was regarded, it seems, as a characteristic of the men from the Isles of the Sea. The broad shoulders of the men no doubt are intended to symbolise strength. Along with vases and "idols" are found seals and other objects, especially stone bowls, which suggest the influence of Egypt under the first six Dynasties. This Early Minoan period is in many respects not easy to distinguish from the preceding Neolithic, but it may be said that it covered a long period, most of the third millenium B.C.

Now we take a great upward leap into the "Middle Minoan" periods of Sir Arthur Evans. Here the first indications of signs and signets are followed by a pictographic script, the earliest writing of Europe: and this in turn is followed by two related systems of syllabic signs written on clay tablets (Plate 19). The one, called Linear A, seems to conceal an unknown language; the other, Linear B, has recently been found to write a primitive form of Greek, and to record some of the day-to-day business of an elaborate social and economic order. More will be said of this later. Here it must suffice to say that the earlier of these tablets are associated with structures far more elaborate than anything which went before: namely the earlier palatial structures at Cnossus, Phaistos and Mallia, but especially at Cnossus. There are also the remains of important houses, as at Phaistos to the south of Cnossus (Plate 20). The concentration of life and an increase of wealth produced profound effects on art. Here and elsewhere, as at Petsofà, we find clay figures which are presentments of the costume of the day: and a highly elaborate costume it is (Plate 18, a). Here also we find the Kamares ware, a style of pottery to which we can perhaps for the first time apply honest expressions of admiration: not, indeed, to such monstrous products of misplaced ingenuity as Plate 21, b, but certainly to other examples (Plate 21, a, c), sometimes with walls as thin as eggshell china. There are many varied and graceful shapes: among them the precise form of the modern teacup is common, and beautiful dishes for offerings which resemble the modern épergne. A lustrous black glaze generally forms the background; on it designs are painted in matt colours, white, red, and sometimes yellow. The designs are still chiefly conventional patterns of stripes, curves and spirals, though there are some rare and very stylised human figures. The potter's wheel is by now in common use, as we see from the greater symmetry and accuracy of the lines. It is suggested that this ware in its thinness and its patterns was inspired by metalwork. It must not be forgotten that the archaeologist only finds what the robber and looter has missed or despised. The gold and bronze have been taken and only the humble potsherds left.

In the stage we have been describing the general colour effect of the vase was the artist's first consideration. Presently a new spirit begins to appear, the desire to imitate the forms of Nature. With increasing naturalism the potter reverts to simpler colours, despairing, it would seem, of the attempt to reproduce the colours of his models. Neither greens nor blues could be managed in earthenware. Fortunately, however, a new material was discovered which served the purpose. This was a kind of faience or porcelain. The idea was imported from Egypt, but a native factory was set up in the palace of Cnossus, and we even find the steatite moulds by which the patterns were impressed. Two of the most important examples are illustrated. One is a "priestess" entwined about by snakes (Plate 22), the other is an animal suckling her young, constantly found as a heraldic type on coins and seals (Plate 23, c). Here it is evidently drawn from a direct study of Nature, so living is the pose, so faithful is the expression of the muscles. It is probably a failing of archaeologists to see religion everywhere they go. It may be that the suckling motive was in after times associated with the worship of maternal deities such as Hera. It is certain also that the Bronze Age Cretan did worship powers of fecundity in human and animal form. But we need not transform this she-goat into a goddess. I much prefer to believe that this prehistoric Cretan loved and studied the wild creatures of his native hills and his native blue sea. As well as the production of faience, there was a long tradition of work in stone following on the early stone vases. A superb example is the leopard-axe or mace-head from the palace at Mallia (Plate 24, a); later, but in the same tradition, is the ceremonial vessel in white limestone in the form of the head of a lioness from Cnossus (Plate 24, b), and, most impressive of all, the fantastic vigour and life of the Harvester Vase from the palace of Ayia Triadha (Plate 25), one of a group of relief works in soft steatite, of which the Chieftain Vase (Plate 23, b) is another. Art and Nature are hand in hand now on vases and gems also. We have seal types bearing wolves' heads, owls and shells, scenes from the boxing-ring and the bull-ring. The Middle Minoan period may be assigned to the age between about 2000 B.C. and the middle of the sixteenth century, being roughly contemporary with the Eleventh and Twelfth Dynasties and the Shepherd Kings (the Hyksos) of Egypt.

We pass on to the "Late Minoan" periods, the ages of masterpiece. Crete is extremely liable to earthquakes, which have left their mark on

the palaces and served to delimit cultural periods, for, from each
disaster which befell, art rose again triumphantly above the ruins, to
continue where it had left off before.   In the Late Minoan period
Mycenae enters the story, but the achievement of this related and
mainland Greek civilisation must be treated apart.   Whereas in the
last period the designs on pottery were generally drawn in white upon
a dark ground, they are now drawn in reddish or a darker brown upon
a light ground.   They are naturalistic, and in the best specimens the
artists have achieved the highest triumph of vase-painting, namely to
apply the artistic forms of Nature to serve their purpose of decoration,
subordinating representation to this end but retaining a large measure
of its effectiveness.   It is to be seen how admirably the grass of Plate
26, *a* is at once naturalistic and decorative, how the octopus of Plate

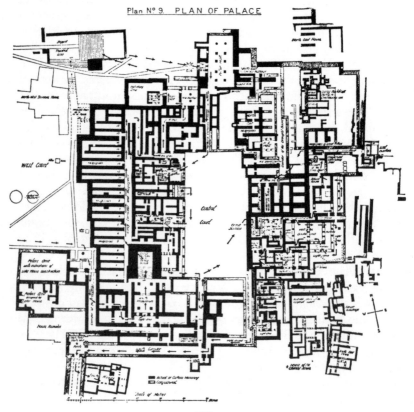

Plan Nº 9.   PLAN OF PALACE

FIG. 1

26, *b* is fitted to the shape of the pot; and how the murex shells (Plate 27, *a*) are used along with conventional patterns and a massing of light and shade. The shapes are now extremely graceful. Those pointed vessels called "filler-vases" were used as we see in the famous frieze of the Cup-bearer (Plate 27, *b*) to serve the wine. We notice how common are marine objects in the natural forms selected. That alone might have given us a hint to look for an island as the centre of this art.

Now comes the great period of Minoan architecture, the final form of the great palaces, with their courts and grand staircases as at Phaistos (Plate 28, *a*). Nor were there only palaces; a whole small town on a hill, with the palace of the local ruler at the summit, has been revealed at Gournia in eastern Crete complete with house-foundations and streets (Plate 29). The final stage of the palace at Cnossus was of vast complexity (Fig. 1), implying extraordinary constructional skill in its making, and a highly elaborate life and administration functioning within it. The cutting and boring of the solid stone as it was cut into the gigantic steatite wine-casks and the building operations as a whole imply, with the relatively primitive tools available, a great deployment of labour and the power to command it. Of the rest of the architectural marvels of these Minoan palaces, their upper stories, their light wells, their great staircases, the magazines and store-rooms, with their Aladdin's jars still standing where King Minos' storekeepers placed them (Plate 28, *b*), of the Queen's Chamber and the Hall of the Distaffs, the Throne Room and its throne with flanking griffins, the Royal Villa and the Little Palace, let the archaeologists relate, and the ground-plan give some idea (Fig. 1). It is believed, indeed, that it was the intricacy of these acres of ruined foundations which provided the later Greeks with their legend of the Labyrinth, the haunt of the bull-man, the Minotaur, to which King Minos made a periodic offering of human victims. The frescoes of palaces and houses are truly marvellous, whether we consider the superb youth called the Cup-bearer (Plate 27, *b*), or the "Prince" proudly striding amid flowers and butterflies, or any of the other frescoes or stucco reliefs which present such an admirable combination of acute observation of nature and masterly formality. Side by side with these are the mainly small objects of a luxurious civilisation, such as the veritable board on which King Minos may have played backgammon according to the Minoan rules of that respectable game. It is of gold and silver, of ivory and crystal and *kyanos*—a board fit for a thalassocrat.

There is something here for every one. The sportsman will observe the methods of pugilism indicated on the steatite Boxer Vase (Plate 23, *a*) and on the clay seal impressions, admiring the muscular development of the Cnossian prize-fighter, though he seems to have neglected his guard. Or we may study the laws of that curious form of bull-baiting which was practised at Cnossus, and which is illustrated in a fresco and in the ivory figure of the Bull-leaper, noting the agility with which toreadors, as we might call them, male and female leap over the animal's head in a form of exercise which was half sport and half religious ceremonial.

The milliner may seek inspiration for new modes from the fashion-plates of the seventeenth century before Christ, and to descend to the apparently ridiculous, the plumber too will find his inspiration in Cnossus. There are toilets, sinks, sewers and man-holes. Professor Burrows, one of the earliest authorities on the Minoan archaeology of Crete, writes thus: "The main drain, which had its sides coated with cement, was over 3 feet high, and nearly 2 feet broad, so that a man could easily move along it; and the smaller stone shafts that discharged into it are still in position. Farther north we have preserved to us some of the terra-cotta pipes that served for connections. Each of them was about $2\frac{1}{2}$ feet long, with a diameter that was about 6 inches at the broad end, and narrowed to less than 4 inches at the mouth, where it fitted into the broad end of the next pipe. Jamming was carefully prevented by a stop-ridge that ran round the outside of each narrow end a few inches from the mouth, while the inside of the butt, or broader end, was provided with a raised collar that enabled it to bear pressure of the next pipe's stop-ridge, and gave an extra hold for the cement that bound the two pipes together". Let no cultivated reader despise these details. There is no truer sign of civilisation and culture than good sanitation. It goes with refined senses and orderly habits. A good drain implies as much as a beautiful statue. And let it be remembered that the world did not reach the Minoan standard of cleanliness again until the great sanitary movement of the late nineteenth century.

THE MAINLAND PALACES

The material culture of mainland Greece has its own special problems. The visible achievements of the ancient people or peoples who preceded the Greeks in their land are the splendid Neolithic figure, goddess or votary, from Lerna in the Argolid (Plate 17), the mysterious "House of Tiles" of the Early Bronze Age (Plate 30), and the superb abraided stone vases and figures of the Cyclades (Plate 14), also of the Early Bronze Age, which were widely exported. Many problems attach to the authors of these, and their origins, and to the time of arrival in Greece of the Greek-speaking people, with their northern heritage. It is quite clear, however, that by the sixteenth century B.C. eastern and southern areas of Greece were being strongly influenced by Crete, and by 1450 B.C. perhaps there were Greeks in Cnossus. Subsequently it was Crete which declined and Mycenaean Greece, so-called from its great centre Mycenae, which replaced it in pride of place in the Aegean. The power and prosperity of Mycenaean Greece is amply testified by the imposing remains. Though there is much to interest the architect in Cnossus and the other palaces of Crete, and though the finest ashlar masonry is to be found there, even more imposing still are the later palaces of Mycenae, Tiryns, Pylos, to name only the most important. They vied in their complexity with Cnossus and Phaistos, though the central element, the great hall with pillars and central hearth (best seen at Pylos in the south-western Peloponnese, Plate 16) is alien to Crete and finds its parallel in Troy and western Anatolia. In Cnossus, as noticed above, there was no fortification— which has been taken as a proof that the Minoan empire rested safe behind wooden walls. Fortifications are not always present on the

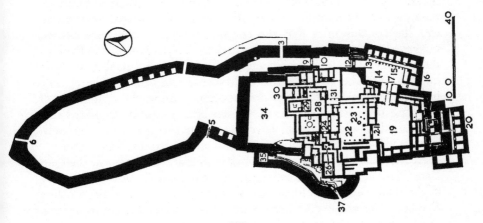

FIG. 2

mainland—there are none at Pylos, for instance, but in Tiryns (associated in legend with Herakles) and Mycenae (the epic stronghold of Agamemnon) we have two magnificent fortresses and citadels, the ponderous walls of which caused the Greeks to believe that they had been piled by the hands of giants. At Tiryns (Fig. 2) the builder has taken the fullest advantage of the natural strength of his position. The top of the hill has been levelled and the summit encircled with a gigantic wall seldom less than fifteen feet thick. In the wall there are galleries opening internally upon a series of magazines (Plate 31). Along it at intervals there are massive watch-towers. One such screens each of the gateways. The main gate on the east side is approached by a long ascending ramp, which is exposed all the way to attack from the wall that towers above. To reach the postern-gate on the west you had also to climb a long flight of steps. The hill, which is more than 900 feet long, consists of a lower plateau to the north, on which no traces of building have been found, possibly because there were only wooden erections there for the soldiers, or possibly because it was left bare as a place of refuge for the cattle and peasants; and a higher plateau to the south, which contains the palace, with its great pillared megaron, or hall. In this there is a circular central hearth. Close behind is a secondary hall, perhaps of another palace, with sleeping chambers at hand, and a strong treasury partly built into the wall. There is an elaborate bathroom, with drain-pipes and water-supply, a little to the west of the megaron. The three inner courts were sumptuously paved with mosaic, and the walls were covered with frescoes. It appears that the buildings on the summit of the hill were all of a palatial description, and the conclusion is that the commons lived in the plain below, governed and protected by their citadel. Tiryns lies on the flank of the plain of Argos, and within a few miles of the sea. As this one plain included also the great fortress of Mycenae and others of lesser note but marked by fortifications or important tombs, the dominions of this king must have been small. It has been plausibly suggested that these citadels, and above all Mycenae, existed to command the highways leading to the Isthmus of Corinth and to exploit transit trade.

At Mycenae the fortification work is similar. The view of the Lion Gate (Plate 32, *a*) will give some idea of the massive Cyclopean masonry of the final stage in the fortification of this great centre of Bronze Age Greece. The great relief itself is clearly a heraldic device; some such grouping of animals is constantly seen upon seals and gems: sometimes there is a female figure between the animals, and sometimes she stands upon a stylised mountain. In view of the cult directed to stones and pillars both in Minoan Crete and later Greek lands, it is not too rash to see in the pillar between the heraldic animals at Mycenae a sacred object forerunner to or substitute for the goddess. But heraldic though it be, this great group, the largest piece of sculpture known from Minoan or Mycenaean times, is far from lifeless conventionality.

If the Lion Gate and the great walls, built for prestige and defence, are the most impressive of the monuments at Mycenae, the tombs are not far behind. Within the great walls, though originally outside them, Schliemann discovered his rich burials which made him believe that he had discovered the very tombs of Agamemnon and his companions, for there was a tradition that they had been buried within the citadel. These tombs, which are called Shaft Graves from their form, were surrounded by a circular enclosure (itself later than the burials) formed by a double series of slabs set into the ground on edge, thus making something like a sacred enclosure. Originally they had been covered by a low mound, with grave stones set upon it. They are now called the First Grave Circle, for in recent years a Second Grave Circle (but with no surrounding slabs) has been found outside the Lion Gate, again with rich contents. Both Circles clearly represent royal burials, the earliest at Mycenae, beginning at the transition from the Middle to the Late Bronze Age. They are followed, over a period of centuries it would appear, by another type of monumental tomb built into the sides of the ridges below the citadel. They are of a circular form like a beehive; they have been found elsewhere in Greece, but nowhere of such splendour. The greatest and perhaps the latest of them is the traditionally-named Treasury of Atreus (Plate 32, *b*). It is a great family tomb, consisting of a circular *tholos* or main chamber, where the bodies were arranged with their funeral gear or disposed beneath the floor; a small side-chamber was probably used as a charnel house, and there was a long *dromos* or inclined approach. The *tholos* is of great interest to architects as providing a forerunner of the dome. But it is not built on the principle of the arch, with wedge-shaped masses and a keystone. This dome is contrived by laying ever-narrowing circles of masonry one upon the other concentrically, the interior being smoothed and richly decorated. The great *tholos* tombs of Mycenae named after the notorious and ill-fated family of Atreus, Clytemnestra and Aegisthus, have stood open and empty since antiquity. We do not quite know how their inmates were disposed, but other and lesser tombs of the same type not very far away in the Argolid, preserved completely or partly with their contents (including a fine set of Mycenaean armour), give some idea of what they were like. Clearly great kings were buried in them.

There are similar tombs elsewhere, notably one with a wonderful carved pattern of rosettes and spirals at Orchomenus in Boeotia. On the slope of the Areopagus Hill at Athens there are also *tholos* tombs, to match the remains of a Mycenaean palace on the Acropolis, the "strong house of Erechtheus" as Homer calls it. From one of the Athenian tombs, perhaps the tomb of a princess, comes a splendid ivory box, carved with deer and griffins from a great tusk (Plate 36, *b*). The palace at Pylos has already been mentioned; there is another currently being excavated in south-eastern Thessaly at Iolkos (Volos), associated with the Argonauts. Indeed all the great centres of Greek saga seem to have strong connexions with the Mycenaean civilisation— except two, for there is no centre in Aetolia to match the Calydonian saga, and none in Laconia to provide a palace for Menelaos and Helen. We are probably to imagine the face of the Greek world in the later second millenium B.C. as dotted with these citadel palaces, and with flourishing villages; some, like Athens and Thebes, were sites famous in after-history; others, like Mycenae and Orchomenus, were not. Contemporary with Bronze Age Greece flourished the settlement of Troy; the Sixth City of the earlier second millenium had its towers and great walls (Plate 15, *b*) shattered by an earthquake; following after it came the meaner settlement (VII a) which may be the Troy of the Siege, in which houses huddle within the walls close under the palatial structures—an index of unsettled times—and show the signs of violent destruction (Plate 15, *a*).

In keeping with its ancient description, "the Golden", Mycenae has yielded many interesting treasures, some certainly Minoan, some imitated after the Minoan style. Schliemann's Shaft Graves contained the gold masks, some of them clearly of individual and powerful personalities, of thin gold laid upon the faces of the dead (Plate 34, *a*). Then there are the wonderful inlaid daggers from the same graves (Plate 33), and the superb ivory group, found near the citadel walls, of two seated women and a child (Plate 34, *b*). Smaller objects such as the gold ring (Plate 35, *b*); from a grave-robbers' hoard reburied in Mycenaean times), like the fresco-fragment (Plate 35, *a*) with processing

demons, show a close connexion with Minoan Crete, as does so much
else about the Mycenaean centres of Greece. We seem to be fairly
certain that at one time there were Greeks at Cnossus, and Greek
legend suggests close links between Greece and Crete. But there is
very much we do not know of the factual background. What, may
it be said as a warning, without detailed information would we make
of the Chinoiserie fashion in England, or of the rooms in Kensington
Palace decorated in the Pompeian style?

Other Mycenaean sites have preserved outstanding objects of
Minoan-Mycenaean work: Athens, Dendra in the Argolid, Pylos and
the region of Messenia with important tholos tombs. Outstanding is
the famous pair of gold cups (undoubtedly Minoan work) found at
Vaphio in Laconia (Plate 36, a). They are of gold repoussé, and their
designs of wild and tame cattle are incomparably living and natural.
Sir Arthur Evans was certainly justified both on grounds of style and
subject in claiming these superb treasures as exports from Crete. The
palm-tree betrays the Cretan origin also.

What came of all this splendour? First, it would seem, Cnossus
suffered a great catastrophe, this time by violence not earthquake,
between 1400 B.C. and perhaps 1350 B.C. For the time being it meant
the end of the Greeks at Cnossus, though exactly what happened is
much disputed, not least as to dates. Minoan civilisation went on
until later Greek penetration, taking place once again, pushed the
remnants of Minoan culture into inaccessible high places; but the glory
and primacy departed in the fourteenth century from Crete to Greece,
where Aegean civilisation continued for something like two centuries
more; indeed, it is at this period, when the supremacy seems to have
passed from Cnossus to Mycenae, that we place the greatest extension
of the Aegean culture, for now Mycenaean products and influences
extend right across to Palestine and Syria in the east, and to the central
Mediterranean, at least, in the west. The fourteenth and thirteenth
centuries B.C. are marked by the great material achievement of the
palaces, walls, great houses, and monumental *tholoi*. There is every
reason to believe that the workshops were active, and that skill of a
high order was lavished on far-fetched materials; there was also a great
volume of production and export in commoner objects, particularly
pottery. But the first freshness and verve was gradually lost in a
progressive stylisation, the effect, no doubt, first of too much prosperity and then of worsening political conditions. The earlier thir-

teenth century was characterised by active building of houses (or so they are identified) at Mycenae, but by the middle of the century they are destroyed, and those outside the citadel are never restored. While on the one hand the great "Treasury of Atreus" may have been completed at this time, we also find that in the latter part of the century the great walls are improved at Mycenae, and there, at Tiryns and at Athens, steps are taken to provide access from the citadel to a fortified spring of water, as if a siege were expected. Somewhere at this time a wall was built across the Isthmus of Corinth. The Linear B tablets from Pylos give evidence of warlike preparations as if in face of an external threat. On a bowl found in a house in the citadel of Mycenae (Plate 37, *b*) the warriors march forth and their womenfolk lament at their departure. In similar fashion, some believe, rather more than half a century before, the Greeks of Mycenaean Greece marched forth against Troy, which perhaps weakened the capacity of the Greeks to resist invaders of their own land. Such attacks had long since been common in Aegean lands as the silver Siege Vase from an earlier Mycenae shows. In the thirteenth century and towards its close they increased in extent and intensity, and the expedition to Troy was one of them or a memory of them. They appear in the Egyptian records as the land and sea raids which also put *finis* to the Hittite Empire. Something of the sort befell Greece about 1200 B.C., for the Mycenaean citadels and palaces, or most of them, were laid waste. Refugees fled to Cyprus, already much influenced by Mycenaean culture as its pottery, some with a quaint animal and figure style (Plate 37, *a*), shows us. The twelfth century was a time of broken-backed existence at Mycenae and elsewhere, with evidence of more disturbance and perhaps invasion at its end. Among the relics of this period are objects which betray the cause or concomitant of the downfall—weapons of iron. Bronze was to yield to iron as stone had yielded to bronze.

THE MAKERS OF AEGEAN ART

It now becomes our duty to sum up this remarkable world, which we know for the most part from archaeology, and to consider its bearings on the character and culture of the Greeks. It will be abundantly clear that many problems arise concerning the identity and origins of the Bronze Age populations of Greece. On certain matters we can be tolerably clear, but in general they present questions rather than supply answers.

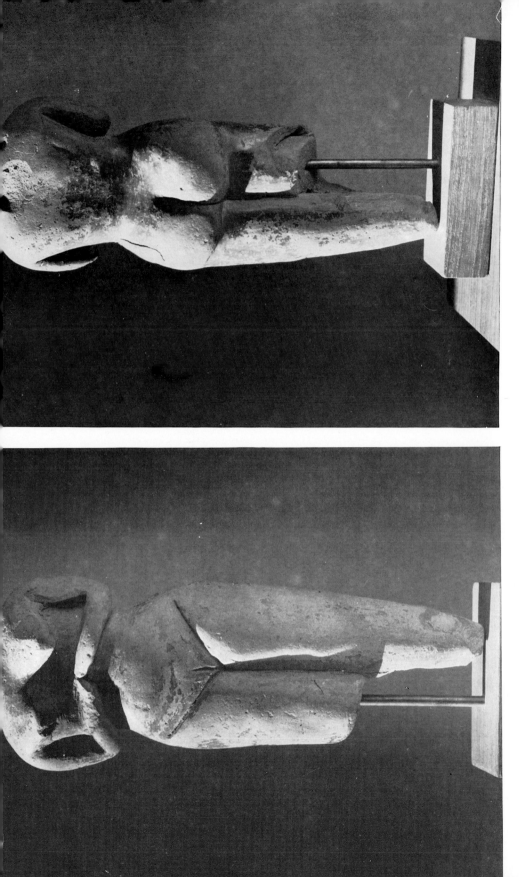

17.   Neolithic clay statuette from Lerna.

18. (a) Votaries in clay from East Crete.
    (b) Vasiliki style pottery.

19 (a) *above* Fragment with Linear A
        inscription.
    (b) *right* Fragment with Linear B
        inscription.
    (c) *below* Tablet with Linear B script.

20 Phaistos. Middle Minoan I houses

(a)

(b)

(c)

21. Vases in the Kamares Style.

22. "Snake Goddess" in coloured faience.

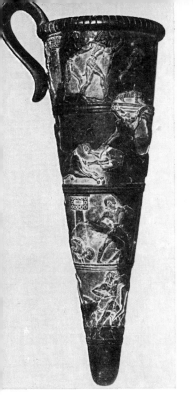

23.   (a) The Boxer Vase.   (b) The "Chieftain Vase".

(c) Faience plaque with a wild goat and two kids.

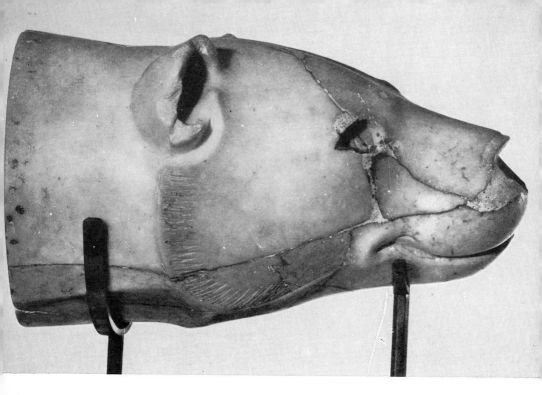

24. (a) Mace-head found at Mallia.
 (b) Ceremonial vessel in the form of the head of a lioness.

(b) Lentoid flask. Late Minoan I.

(a) Beaked jug, Late Minoan I.

26.

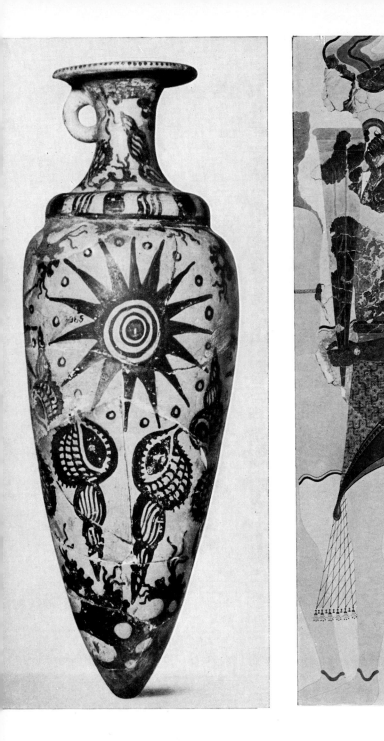

27. (a) *left* Clay rhyton (libation vase), Late Minoan I.
(b) *right* Restored fresco-fragment of the so-called "Cup-bearer".

28. (a) The Western Court at Phaistos.
    (b) The West Magazines of the Minoan Palace at Cnossus.

29. *opposite* The Minoan town of Gournia.

30.
The Early
Bronze Age
"House of
Tiles" at Lerna.

31. *opposite*
The "casemate"
of the
Mycenaean
fortress of
Tiryns.

32. (a) The "Lion Gate" at Mycenae.

(b) The interior of the "Treasury of Atreus" at Mycenae.

It is obvious that Minoan-Mycenaean art has very much which is alien, in certain fundamental principles of observation and rendering, to later Greek art; it is not better but it is very different. A considerable number of separate elements are clearly owed to Egypt, the East Mediterranean and the Middle East, but again it is basically different in approach, if not in purpose, to the art of these regions. Then there is the question of religion, as far as we dare speak of Minoan-Mycenaean religion where we have no written texts to help us understand the material remains. In classical Greece, as everyone knows, there was a prevailing cult of state gods and goddesses, an anthropomorphic Olympian family, Zeus, Hera, Athena, Artemis, Apollo and the rest of them. But recent students of religion have pointed out that side by side with the public worship of these Olympian deities there was a more mysterious but more real devotion to a quite different form of religion, a cult of powers, often female, with mystic or ecstatic rites of which the origins were largely forgotten. To this class belong the Mysteries of Eleusis, to name the most famous example, and the cults of Dionysus. And while it is common to see in "Diana of the Ephesians" and in Aphrodite and Adonis the influence of oriental religions, it might be better to suggest that we have here the re-emergence of the same element, which is a primitive one. It has long been seen that such Greek cults and beliefs have very ancient antecedents. They appear in very odd forms in Arcadia, traditionally the untouched primitive part of Greece. A religion of fertility and the Mother naturally suggests itself, parallel to the other manifold appearances of this in the world. We distantly recall the bulging "Venuses", and the opulent and curvaceous terracotta figures of Neolithic females, and we are forced to admit that in this non-Olympian religion of the Greeks we may well have the emergence of a primitive element, later imperfectly overlaid: the religion not necessarily of pure and primitive cultivators, but rather of peoples following a mixed economy of cultivation and pastoralism for whom fertility was a major preoccupation. The worship of the later Great Mother belongs to such a background, and if the male principle is involved it is as a very junior and youthful consort. The discoveries in Crete have gone far to reaffirm this, and even, perhaps, to throw some light on the nature of fertility worship of later times. It seems that a principal deity of Crete was such a Nature goddess, sometimes associated with snakes (Plate 22). She was worshipped with orgiastic rites, ecstatic dances and the like. Along with this worship, and older, maybe, in origins, as the aniconic precedes the iconic stage of religion, there are many apparent signs of aniconic objects of cult: pillar worship, axe-worship, tree-worship, or something very like it. There are also the monstrous forms of votaries or "demons" which appear on gems, signets and frescoes (Plate 35, *a*). It is not a long step from this to suggesting that the Minoan people who evolved all this were the descendants of an ancient neolithic Anatolian-Cretan ethnic element speaking an alien language perhaps concealed beneath the Linear A signs. But at Cnossus and in Greece we have also indicated in the Linear B tablets the presence of the Olympian Gods, the discovery of whom has been something of a shock to classical scholars. Among them appears, for instance, *A-ta-na po-ti-ni-ja*. Therefore we have a non-Greek element and a Greek element; and even if we do not believe in the decipherment of the Linear B tablets we must assume that the Greeks, as speakers of an Indo-European language, got to Greece somehow from the northern region where that great group of languages was evolved, though it would be too simple to regard them as clearly differentiated sky-god worshipping pastoralists planting themselves on a mother-goddess worshipping agricultural "under-layer". In fact, in terms of ethnic origins and religion we are very much in the dark, as we are on the problem of the social and governmental elements contributed by the Orient. But Greek and non-Greek there were in Greece and Crete. The Greeks arrived sometime at the beginning of the Middle Bronze Age, according to the most generally accepted theory, though some would believe that they came as early as the late Neolithic period or as late as the end of the Middle Bronze. There is a similar divergence of opinion about the region from which they came: either down through the Balkans or across from north-western Asia Minor. By whichever way they came, and whatever the date of their arrival, some of these Greek-speaking peoples pushed on into southern and eastern Greece, while others remained behind in the more northerly and backward regions to evolve a dialect of their own and retain their ancient barbarism. The Greeks who penetrated into the eastern and southern regions imposed themselves on a non-Greek Early Bronze Age stratum, perhaps from Asia Minor, itself imposed on the Neolithic. The account here given is simplified, and perhaps over-simplified, but it seems likely that by the sixteenth century B.C. there was a mixture of peoples in Greece, part Greek-speaking, who

were then influenced by the superior culture of Minoan Crete, to form
the Mycenaean civilisation of which we have spoken, and to take
over in Greece something of the Near Eastern palace order and
economy. In the fifteenth century it may well be that a Greek dynasty
from the mainland established itself by some non-violent means at
Cnossus, until it was overthrown in the fourteenth century possibly
by an attack again from the mainland. It is unlikely that adventurous
dynasty-founders confined their attentions to Crete; it must have
happened elsewhere, including western Asia Minor. There could also
have been a coming and going of dynasts and relations across the
Aegean such as we hear of in the stories of Pelops and Bellerophon.
But from the fall of Cnossus it was mainland Greece that prospered
until the thirteenth century. Then we hear of the movements of
marauding peoples by land and sea, which we have mentioned earlier,
and of assaults on the Hittite Empire and on the Egyptians. The
attack on Troy may, in effect, have been one of these movements.
There was also strife internal to the Mycenaean states; Greek legend
represented one of these struggles as the expulsion of the Children of
Herakles, displaced from their inheritance. In the third generation
they returned, and with them the Dorians and associated peoples, in
effect those who stayed behind in the mountainous regions of northern
and western Greece at the original coming of the Greeks. They, it
may be suggested, were the authors or part authors of the widespread
destruction of the Mycenaean centres. They plunged Greece into a
dark age (or so it seems to us) from which the classical world was to
emerge slowly and painfully.

II

THE HEROIC AGE

ἀνδρῶν ἡρώων θεῖον γένος οἳ καλέονται
ἡμίθεοι.

HESIOD

THE INVADERS

In stepping out of Crete and Mycenae into Homer we are leaving a material world of artists for a literary world of heroes. Incidentally it may be mentioned that we are stepping over some four centuries without any clear history and with relatively scanty archaeological remains. These have been rightly called the Dark Ages, for the analogy between these prehistoric Dark Ages and those of history is singularly close. The greatness of Crete departed very largely about 1400 B.C.; the Mycenaean Empire which stepped into its place survived for two centuries longer; then during the twelfth, eleventh and tenth centuries darkness and confusion seem to cover Greece. Thus the stability and order of life in the Aegean was broken up and the lamp of culture flickered out. Some sparks of it survived, to burn up again with even greater brilliance in the Classical period. Writing seems to have perished and subsequently to have been reimported from the East.* The foreign trinkets and other signs of trade disappear for a time out of the Greek world. These things were closely bound up with a flourishing commerce, and now the sea became unsafe for commerce. The old naturalistic art had gradually become stylised, and though the shapes of pottery in some cases seem to survive right through, yet the designs undergo considerable changes, from debased naturalistic and figure drawings to geometric patterns, so that the period under discussion is called, in its three successive states, Sub-Mycenaean, Protogeometric and Geometric, largely from that imperishable material of the archaeologist, pottery.

The same cause operated here as after the fall of Rome. The world was being remade, new peoples were coming upon the scene; there

*In far-away Cyprus the Minoan syllabic writing, adapted to the use of Greek, survived until a late period.

was a long period of Wandering of the Nations, with no Christian missionaries to mitigate their barbarism—or to chronicle their progress. The Egyptians of about 1200 B.C. observed that there was unrest among the Isles of the Sea. The Hittite empire is overthrown. There are many hints of disturbance provided by archaeology, but they are difficult to interpret, and much stylised and dimly-seen history in the heroic sagas of the Greeks, if we could but disentangle truth from fiction and restore the proper political and temporal perspective.

The invaders are not to be thought of as a single tribe or a single movement. More like our early Danish invaders, they began gradually and continued slowly. Some must have come in as mercenaries, and taken part in internal strife, like the barbarian levies of the Late Roman Empire. In keeping with the story of the Return of the Children of Herakles narrated by the Greeks it has been suggested that a great Mycenaean family helped to bring in the barbarian. It may be there were earlier assaults and destructions in a world weakened by military undertakings such as the expedition against Troy (which some would put in the earlier thirteenth century B.C.), and efforts to improve defences; but the great destruction came at last to Mycenae, Tiryns and Pylos about 1200 B.C. It was followed at Mycenae by a sort of recovery (though there was also migration, to Cyprus for instance), and then there was more destruction; and though the thread of culture was never wholly broken it was a dim and depressed existence with people, native and incomer, building inferior houses among the ruins of the palaces or sheltered themselves like the jackals and owls of Isaiah among the Cyclopean masses. No wonder that legends arose about the magical race of Cyclopes who built so amazingly, and no wonder that the Greeks of later time put their Golden Age into the past instead of the future. The poet Hesiod, writing probably at the end of the eighth century B.C., divided the history of the world into five ages of deterioration. First come the Golden and Silver Ages of Virtue, both, of course, purely ideal. Then comes the Bronze Age, mighty and strong. "Of bronze were their vessels, of bronze their houses, with tools of bronze they worked: dark iron was not yet." At last they passed away, and then came a fourth generation on the procreant earth, "a generation juster and better, the divine race of Heroes, who are called demigods. Cruel war and the stern cry of battle destroyed them, some as they strove for the flocks of Oedipus at Thebes, and some when they had been led on shipboard over the great gulf of the sea to Troy for the sake of Helen with her lovely tresses". Then these too went hence "to dwell in the Isles of the Blessed by the deep-surging Ocean, like happy heroes, and the fertile earth yields them honey-sweet harvest thrice a year". But, alas for the poet, he is doomed to live among the fifth race, the Men of Iron.

This is not all fancy: the Bronze Age is history, as we have seen; so is the Iron Age. What then of the age between, the Age of Heroes? It comes in awkwardly, for it disturbs the poet's picture of degeneration. Also, culturally speaking, there is no "Age" between Bronze and Iron. But it has to be inserted in deference to the beliefs of Hesiod's audience. Hesiod is more or less consciously writing a Bible for the Greeks. The Age of the Heroes, the milieu of Homeric poems and Attic tragedy, has long been supposed to be unhistorical; but the Greeks believed in it, and after long hesitation we are beginning to ask whether they were not right in doing so. The Homeric poems remember vaguely the material civilisation of the Bronze Age, the latter part of which is their Heroic Age; is it improbable that they also retained some tradition of the princely families and of their exploits and achievements? We approach the subject of Greek heroic saga today in a spirit very different from the complete scepticism of past generations.

We have already seen that the earliest penetration of Greek-speaking tribes can be dimly traced back far into the Bronze Age. Then came the Mycenaean Age, which, if it at first showed strong Minoan influences, certainly seemed to be basically Greek to judge from the Linear B tablets, as far as "Greek" means those who used the Greek language; and it is of this, the age of the Achaeans, that Homer some centuries later was to sing. We see it dimly as an age of constant movement, of wars and individual adventure. Homer had heard of one terrible war in which seven princes were banded together to destroy Thebes; later came the greater war in which all the might of the Achaeans went oversea to lay siege to Troy. This is best placed in the earlier thirteenth century, and it seems to have been the last effort of the Achaeans; they came back to find their land in jeopardy from internal strife and external attack, for it was that period of movements of peoples of which we hear in the records of Egypt. These attackers were the Dorians, who put an end to Achaean, i.e. Mycenaean, power and who are generally supposed to have been coming in between 1200 and 1100 B.C.

We cannot with assurance say how important the Dorians were in effecting the destruction which certainly overtook Greece at about 1200 B.C. and left it a depopulated shadow of former greatness. Tradition represented the Dorians as coming into Achaean, that is Mycenaean, Greece under the leadership of the exiled descendants of Herakles returning to claim their rightly inheritance. They are said to have pushed before them those who in part inhabited southern Thessaly and Boeotia in the classical period; and it was even felt that some Dorians had got into the Aegean before the Trojan War. It was also believed that the Dorians proper penetrated the Peloponnese in two streams, and established their rule there: not in Arcadia, but especially in the Argolid and Laconia; and from the Argolid they pushed north through Corinthia and the Megarid to be repulsed from Attica. This series of events, it was also asserted, set in train the movement across the Aegean which established the Greek cities of Asia Minor. Tradition is one thing; reality another. We need not be too sceptical, but we should note that these Dorians were other Greeks: not wholly alien, therefore, or basically different from the Greeks in the country already. The Dorians are elusive, archaeologically speaking, and much of all this story is an explanation of the classical dialect map of Greece, and also of the dispersion of the Greeks to Asia Minor, and of the classical division of Dorian and Ionia, Spartan and Athenian. It cannot all be taken literally, still less as the basis for "racial" arguments in terms of "Northerners" and "people of the Aegean". We can be sure that Greece reverted in large measure to primitive conditions. There was a long period which was dark, certainly dark to us. In it the epic tales of the Age of Heroes were elaborated, and the poetic form; its subject matter was "Golden Mycenae" of the Mycenaean Age.

HOMER AND THE ACHAEANS

There is, it must be reiterated, a temptation to see in the Achaean heroes of the epic and their background the mixture of two concepts: "Aegean" and "Northern", in matters both material and racial. It has to be admitted, indeed, whatever view is taken in detail, that epic largely means "Mycenaean", in its general conception, and that Mycenaean involves the influence of Minoan Crete. But aside from this some have felt an urge to identify "Indo-European" or "Northern" characteristics in material details and in matters of institutions and religion; even in the Linear B tablets. This is the wrong approach.

In what is manifestly an amalgam it is no use stressing certain elements and ignoring others even if we think we can separate them out. Certain things can be identified as characteristic of the Indo-European speaking peoples: horses and sky-gods, maybe, but not necessarily chariots, or iron, or woollen clothing or the pins to fasten it. Above all we must not explain nebulous national characteristics by such supposed origins, or involve ideas of Dorians and Ionians, concepts elaborated much later, with such matters. In effect we have two things which concern us in this consideration of Hesiod's Age of Heroes: the picture in the heroic poetry and the archaeological record, from which we can pick out relevant parallels to co-ordinate with the descriptions of Homer. We shall not find them all in one period. If we reflect that we are dealing with memories which recede into the far past and with a background partly Mycenaean and partly post-Mycenaean, and—most important of all—with a span of four centuries or more, we shall be prepared for contradictions, anachronisms and obscurities. With this in mind, let us look at the epic scene. Although, as I have said, the Achaeans of Homer, had an Olympian hierarchy of gods, a real devotion was also given to heroes—that is, to ancestors of the tribe, whose graves, real or imaginary, were the scene of sacrifices and libations. One such hero was Agamemnon, who was worshipped at Sparta and elsewhere. Another was Achilles, who had the centre of his cult in Phthiotis. Their valorous deeds were doubtless commemorated in ancient lays. But our Homer is not a collection of simple ballads or folk-songs. It is a literary product of such finish and perfection as to postulate centuries of experiment in the literary art and the intervention of individual genius of the very highest order. We are forced to believe in the existence of a real Homer who set himself, as Hesiod did in a different sphere, to collect the praises of the heroes and to fashion them into immortal verse, grouping, the various heroes into one Panhellenic army under the leadership of Agamemnon in a great expedition, almost certainly an echo of real history, against the city of Troy. But it has been thought by many writers that our Iliad and Odyssey are not the untouched composition of a single brain. Not only is the story of the Iliad far too incoherent—warriors killed in one book, are fighting cheerfully in the next, a huge wall and fosse round the Greek camp appearing, and disappearing, unaccountably; not only is the original plot of the Wrath of Achilles forgotten and obscured in later books; not only is the Odyssey in style and diction visibly later than the main part of the Iliad; but it is possible to trace a progressive variation in customs and ideas, with subsequent interpolation and expurgation, throughout. And it must not be forgotten that the ancients applied the term "Homer" to a vast body of epic matter of which our Iliad and Odyssey are only a part. We are asked to conclude that many successive generations of bards had forged the epic style, language and themes. These Homeridae, or "sons of Homer", must have included several men of genius among their number, but they were all trained in a noble school. They were, as has been said, hymning the praises of their patrons' heroic ancestors. They were dealing with a great mass of traditional material, much of which is undoubtedly of great antiquity, and it is curious how successfully they avoided the worst anachronisms and obeyed the epic convention. Thus the Dorians, except for a single oversight, are studiously ignored; writing and coined money (except for one single instance) are avoided. Habits of ancient barbarism like human sacrifice, poisoned arrows, and the ill-treatment of the dead have been carefully expunged, though the sharp eye of modern criticism can detect the traces of expurgation. Although the poet is living in the Iron Age and is well aware that iron weapons are the usual implements of war, he conventionally represents his heroes as "smiting with the bronze". All the named heroes, being somebody's tribal hero and somebody's ancestor, have to receive the title of king, although in the Iliad they are but captains in Agamemnon's army. A patriarchal monarchy is conceived as the normal form of government; yet some parts of the poems seem to betray an acquaintance with oligarchy or aristocracy. The tradition may be true which says that Homer was not edited in our "authorised" version until the tyranny of Pisistratus at Athens in the sixth century.

How far, then, are we justified in using the Homeric poems as material for history? They tell us relatively little of the history of the comparatively late age at which they assumed their final form; but recent research has made it probable that they embody a very large mass of historical matter concerning the Mycenaeans of the Bronze Age. The traditions are so clearly defined in the poet's mind, the genealogies and chronological points so sharply delimited, the material objects can be so exactly paralleled from recent discoveries, that we can only conclude that the greater part of the poems has been religiously handed down from Mycenaean times by generations of bards.

These bards knew that the world they lived in was not the world of their story, and abstained as far as possible from alluding to it; their duty was to preserve the memory of the great days of old—the palaces gleaming with gold; the mighty kings and fair-limbed women who once walked this earth.

But they could not wholly exclude their own present, and if it possessed nothing which was familiar the epic must inevitably have lost its appeal. The mixed background is well illustrated by the tripods which are mentioned again and again in the epic as prizes and symbols of prestige and as objects of use. The clay vessel illustrated on Plate 38, *c* is a cheap funeral substitute to replace the great tripod-cauldrons of bronze, with ring handles, often bearing human or animal figurines, and high legs decorated with circles and tangents. These cauldrons, in their fully developed form, were masterpieces of Iron Age craftsmanship, offered at hero shrines and appearing on vase pictures of epic chariot races at funeral games. When Achilles celebrates the funeral games for Patroclus (Iliad xxiii 259) it is said:

"He brought forth from the ships prizes, cauldrons and tripods and horses and mules, and the mighty heads of oxen, fair women and grey iron."

They are the spoils of the warrior and the plunder of cities. The idea of them is a curious mixture as befits a Bronze Age epic composed in the Iron Age. In the poem cauldron and tripod are separate, and so they were in the Bronze Age, and this was dimly remembered; in another place the cauldrons are called "eared", and this seems to be confirmed in the Linear B tablets. But the men who read or listened to this poem long afterwards, and the artists who decorated some of the later Geometric pottery with epic scenes, were in no doubt what these objects were like: they were the tripod-cauldrons of which the one illustrated is an early model in clay. They also appear in the Odyssey as gifts, and for use when the tired heroes require a warm bath (x 358):

"And a fourth handmaid bare water, and kindled a great fire beneath the mighty cauldron. So the water waxed warm; but when it boiled in the bright brazen vessel, she set me in a bath and bathed me with water from out a great cauldron." The word translated "cauldron" is in fact "tripod", and in this passage once again the ages meet, for the water is poured into a bath, and the word here used is *asaminthos,* one of those non-Greek and perhaps pre-Greek words and names which are so intriguing; and it takes us back to Pylos and its bathroom. Then there is that wondrous shield wrought for Achilles by Hephaestus at the instance of Thetis.

THE SHIELD OF ACHILLES

The description of the Shield in the eighteenth book of the Iliad is of two-fold interest. It is a link with contemporary reality. It gives us a picture of Greek life which must be natural and universal, since neither dramatic nor religious motives interfere to distort it. The writer also is clearly describing a round shield with concentric zones of ornament, such as are found on Phoenician bowls of later date (Plate 42, *b*). The pictures are conceived as inlaid in various metals, gold, tin, silver, and "kyanos", or blue glass; in fact the poet is describing in every detail the technique of the wonderful inlaid daggers from Mycenae (Plate 33), although such weapons had ceased to be made for many hundreds of years. Here is the mixture of periods again. But obviously an idealising poet in describing such objects of art permits his imagination to excel anything that he has ever seen or heard of. Besides, it was wrought by the lame god Hephaestus, and the gods do not make armour such as you can buy at the shop.

First he made a shield great and mighty, decorating it in every part, and round it he threw a bright, threefold, gleaming rim, and a silver baldric therefrom. There were five folds of the shield, and on it he set many designs with skilful craftsmanship.

On it he wrought earth and sky and sea, and an unwearied sun and a waxing moon, and on it were all the signs wherewith heaven is crowned, the Pleiades and the Hyades and the might of Orion, and the Bear, which they surname the Wain, which revolves in the same place and watches Orion, and alone has no part in the baths of Ocean.

And on it he put two cities of mortal men, two fair cities. In one there were marriages and feasts. They were carrying the brides from their chambers through the city with gleaming torches, and loud rose the marriage-songs. The youths were dancing in a ring, and among them the flutes and lyres made their music. The women stood admiring, every one at her porch. But the men were gathered together in the market-place. There a strife had arisen: two suitors were striving about the price of a man slain. One claimed to have paid in full, and he was appealing to the people, but the other refused to take anything. So both had hurried to have trial before an umpire. Crowds of backers stood around each to cheer them on, and there were the heralds, keeping the crowd in order. The old men sat upon polished stones in a holy circle with staves of loud-voiced heralds in their hands. With these they would arise in turn to give their judgments. There in the midst lay two talents of gold to give to the man who should speak the most rightous sentence of them all.

But round the other city two armies of warriors bright in mail were set. And there was a division of counsel among them whether to destroy it utterly or to divide up into two shares all the store that the lovely citadel contained. The besieged would not yet yield, but were arming in secret for an ambush. Their dear wives and innocent children stood upon the wall to guard it, and in their company were the men of age. So the warriors were marching out, and there were their leaders, Ares and Pallas Athene, golden both with golden raiment, both fair and tall, armed like gods, a conspicuous pair, for the hosts about them were smaller. But when they came to a place where they had decided to make the ambush, in a river-bed, where there was a watering-place for every beast, they sat down there wrapped in their shiny bronze. Then some way off two scouts of the army were posted to watch when they might see sheep and oxen with curling horns. And there were beasts moving along, with two herdsmen following that took their pleasure with pan-pipes, for they suspected no guile. But their enemy who had watched them leapt upon them, and swiftly cut off the herds of kine and fair fleeces of white sheep, and they slew the shepherds also. But the besiegers, when they heard the din of battle rising among the kine, from their seats before the tribunes leapt upon high-stepping horses to pursue, and swiftly they approached. Taking rank there by the banks of the river, they fought and smote one another with bronze-tipped spears, and Strife mingled with them, and the din of battle uprose, and ruinous Fate was there taking one man freshly wounded and another without a wound and another already dead and dragging them away by the feet in the noise of battle, and her robe about her shoulders was dappled with the blood of men. They mingled like living men and fought and dragged away the bodies of their dead comrades.

Also he wrought thereon a soft fallow, a fat ploughland, a broad field of three ploughings. Many ploughmen were driving their teams up and down in it. And whenever they came to the baulk of the field at the end of their turn a man came forward with a cup of honey-sweet wine in his hands and proffered it. So they kept wheeling among the ridges, anxious to reach the baulk of the deep fallow, which grew dark behind them, and, gold though it was, looked as if it had been ploughed, so very wondrous was the craft.

There too he put a princely demesne, wherein hired labourers were reaping with sharp sickles in their hands, some swathes were falling thick and fast to earth along the furrow, and the binders were tying others in bands. There stood the three binders close at hand, and behind ran the gleaner-boys carrying the corn in armfuls and busy in attendance. A king with his sceptre stood in silence among them on the furrow rejoicing in his heart. Some way off heralds were laying a feast under an oak-tree. They had sacrificed a great ox and were busy with it, while the women were sprinkling white barley meal in plenty for the harvesters' supper.

On it also he wrought a vineyard heavy-laden with grapes, beautifully wrought in gold. Upon it were the black bunches, and the vineyard was set with silver poles throughout; round it he drove a trench of kyanos and a wall of tin; a single causeway led to it whereby the pickers walked when they gathered in the vintage. Maids and youths were carrying the honey-sweet fruit in woven baskets, and in the midst a boy played a lovely tune on a high-pitched lyre, singing thereto with his dainty voice the Linus-song, while the rest kept time with stamping feet and leaping and song and shrieking.

On it he made a herd of straight-horned oxen. The cows were fashioned of gold and tin; lowing they passed from the midden to the pasture by a plashing river and by a shivering reed-bed. Four cow-herds of gold marched along with the kine, and nine swift-footed dogs followed them. But among the foremost kine two dreadful lions were holding a deep-voiced bull. He was being dragged away bellowing loudly, but the dogs and the hinds were after him. The two lions had torn the hide of the great bull, and were greedily devouring the entrails and the dark blood, while the cowherds followed, vainly spurring on the swift hounds. But they, forsooth, instead of biting the lions, kept turning back; they would run up close to bark at them and then flee away.

On it the far-famed Cripple made a sheepfold in a fair valley, a big fold of white sheep, and steadings and huts and roofed huts and pens.

On it the far-famed Cripple fashioned a dancing-floor like that which Daedalus of old wrought in broad Cnossus for Ariadne of the lovely tresses. Therein youths and maidens costly to woo were dancing, holding one another by the wrist. The maids had fine linen veils, and the youths had well-woven tunics with faint gloss of oil. The maids had fair garlands on their heads, and the men had golden swords hanging from silver baldrics. Sometimes they would trip it lightly with cunning feet, as when a potter sits and tries the wheel that fits between his hands to see whether it will run. But sometimes they advanced in lines towards one another, and a great company stood round the lovely dance delighted, and among them a holy bard sang to his lyre, and among the dancers two tumblers led the measure, twirling in the midst.

And on it he put the great might of the River Ocean along the edge of the rim of the closely wrought shield.

So then when he had fashioned a great and mighty shield he fashioned also a breastplate brighter than the beam of fire, and he fashioned him a strong helmet, fitting the temples, richly dight, and on it put a crest, and he made him greaves of pliant tin.

I trust that the reader may be able to catch some glimpse of the picture even through the bald prose of translation. We are now in Europe for certain. It might be in Dorsetshire or Bavaria or Auvergne or Tuscany that these women come to their doors to watch the weddings go past, these honest ploughmen drain their beakers, and these weary harvesters look forward to the harvest supper. To this day you may see the peasants of Greece dancing in rings and lines, with agile acrobats to lead them, just as they danced on the shield of Achilles. History goes on its pompous way, leaving the peasant un-altered and the ways of country life unchanged.

KINGS AND GODS

The poet even here, not wholly oblivious of the courtly circles to whom he was singing, has, indeed, brought in a "king". But it is a poor sort of Basileus who stands there among the clods rejoicing in his heart. He and his ancestral sceptre cut rather a foolish figure among

> The reapers, reaping early
> In among the bearded barley.

The truth is, of course, that he's a king in buckram. He is only a country squire with a pedigree, dressed up as a Basileus to suit the convention of the epic. Such too are the "kings" of the Odyssey. There the story requires that Odysseus shall be King of Ithaca and that his faithful wife shall be maintaining his throne in his absence. But the poet or poets were so little accustomed to the ways of kings that they constantly forget the political importance of Penelope and speak as if it were only a question of the jointure of a comely widow. Eumaeus the swineherd extols the wealth of Odysseus by saying that no other in Ithaca had so much. They were already in the habit of regarding the market-place as the political focus of the State. So in the town of Scheria "King" Alcinous goes forth daily to the council with the twelve other "renowned kings". Odysseus their visitor prays that this "king" and his "queen" may be so blessed by the gods that they may leave to their children "the substance in their halls, and whatever dues of honour the people have rendered unto him". And the "princess" goes out in a mule-cart with the washing. On the stage of the epic the king is, indeed, a great and mighty ruler. We are often reminded how fearful is the wrath of kings. The king says, according to a quotation of Aristotle, that he has power of life and death. He gives away cities that do not belong to him. He inherits "his sceptre and his dooms" from Zeus and a long line of ancestors. But he cannot live up to these exalted pretensions. He debates policy in the market-place with the other kings (who are often called elders by mistake, though they are young and lusty as an eagle), and matters are settled by the acclamation of the masses. It is the orator who sways the crowds. By occasional slips of the tongue these noble kings are spoken of as a greedy class, just as they are in Hesiod. As for the "dooms" that they receive by inspiration from Zeus, they make no practical use of them. Justice, as we saw on our Shield, is really administered by the elders in the agora. A careless line of the Odyssey tells of "the hour when a man rises from the assembly and goes home to supper, a man who judges the many quarrels of the young men that go to him for judgment". There is no single example of a king acting as judge in Homer, and though the king pretends to give away cities he sometimes humbly accepts the gift of an acre or two from the citizens for services rendered. There is, indeed, one celebrated passage of the Iliad where monarchy is apparently extolled; but the attentive reader will discern that it is in the language not of primitive patriarchal conditions, but of a partisan of aristocracy or tyranny rebuking the presumption of radical demagogy. It is in the second book of the Iliad. Agamemnon had bidden the Greeks prepare for flight from Troy. It was only a ruse to try their temper, but it succeeded all too well, for the people hastily took him at his word. Now Odysseus is bidden by the goddess Athena to hurry down and stop them.

He went to meet Agamemnon, son of Atreus, and took from him his ancestral sceptre, ever indestructible, wherewith he went down to the ships of the brazen-shirted Achaeans. Whensoever he met a king or man of mark, him he would approach and check with soft words. "Sir, it befits not to terrify thee like a coward; nay, sit thee down, and make the rest of the host sit also, for thou knowest not yet the mind of the son of

Atreus. Now he is but trying the sons of the Achaeans; soon he will smite them, and mighty is the wrath of god-nurtured kings. Honour is his from Zeus, the Zeus of counsel loves him."

But when he saw a man of the people shouting, him he would smite with his sceptre and chide with a word. "Sir, sit quiet and hear the speech of others, who are better than thou. Thou are unwarlike and cowardly, thou art of no account in war or in council. We cannot all be kings here, we Achaeans; many-lordship is not good. Let one be lord, one king, to whomsoever the son of Kronos of crooked counsel has given the sceptre and the dooms that he may be king among them."

Thus he went through the host, lording it; and they hurried back to the meeting-place from their ships and tents with a noise as when a wave of the thundering sea crasheth on the mighty shore and the deep resounds.

The others then sat down and took place on the benches, but Thersites alone still brawled with unmeasured words—he who was full of disorderly speech for idle and unseemly striving against kings.

He was the ugliest man that came to Troy. He was bandy-legged and lame, and his two shoulders were humped and cramped upon his breast. Above, his head was peaked, and a scanty stubble sprouted upon it. He was the bitterest foe to Achilles and to Odysseus, and ever he was reviling them. Then too he cried out shrill words of reproach against divine Agamemnon. But the Achaeans were horribly wroth with him, and hated him in their hearts.

Thus he spake reviling Agamemnon, the shepherd of the people. But divine Odysseus quickly stood beside him, and scowling rebuked him with a grievous word. "Thersites, heedless of speech, shrill ranter that thou art, be still and dare not alone to strive with kings, for I say that there is no creature worse than thou, of all that came with the sons of Atreus to Ilium."

Thus he spake, and smote him with his sceptre on the midriff and the shoulders. But he hunched himself up and a big tear fell from him, and a blood-red weal rose up from his back under the golden sceptre. So he sat down and trembled, looked helpless, and wiped away a tear in his pain, and they, for all their anger, laughed sweetly at him. And thus a man would say, looking at his neighbour, "Lo, now! Verily Odysseus hath done a thousand good deeds both in discovering good counsel and in leading the battle, but now this is far his best deed among the Argives, in that he hath checked this word-spattering maker of mischief from his rantings. Never again, I ween, will his ambitious heart stir him up to revile kings with words of reproof"

Thersites is not a product of simple undeveloped monarchy; the

poet who drew this portrait had seen the mob-orator in his native agora. Thersites, it has been said, is the only private in the army. He is the only man who is named without a patronymic. And yet modern research has shown that even Thersites had an ancient cultus as a demigod in Sparta. So true is it that all the figures of the epic stage are figures of tribal ancestor-worship.

That is why the real gods come so badly out of the epics. They are the only immoral people in Homer; they cheat and lie, they smack and squabble. Perhaps we do not expect much decency from Zeus or Aphrodite, but even the stately Hera herself alternates between the crafty courtesan and the scolding fish-wife. And yet Homer is the "Bible of the Greeks"! Herodotus said, and said truly, that it was Hesiod and Homer who assigned to the gods their names, distributed their honours and functions, and settled their appearance and characteristics. In after-times Homer was the universal primer of education. It is extremely probable that Homer and Hesiod selected certain deities out of a vast number for special honour as members of the Olympian family. Why in the world, then, did not Homer honour them? Various explanations have been given. The old explanation was that this is the naive expression of primitive anthropomorphism, which makes gods in the likeness of men, enlarging the human vices as well as the virtues. But no one who really studies Homer can believe in a theory which makes him simple and childlike. Homer's ridicule of the gods is not the unsophisticated laughter of a child or a savage. It is to be noticed that it is only some of the gods who come badly out of the Homeric theology. No figure could be lovelier than that of the sea-goddess, Thetis, or more dignified than Pallas Athena, or more ethereal than Iris, the ambassadress of heaven. Sir W. Ridgeway's belief that Homer was written by a bard of the old Aegean race honouring his Achaean masters might explain the mordant raillery of supposed "Northern" gods as of Zeus by Hera. But then Aphrodite, who is the worst treated of all, would seem to be actually a form of the Nature-goddess of Crete, ever accompanied with doves in Cretan art. It is just the Aegean naturalism which is excluded from Homeric religion. There is nothing to connect even Iris with the rainbow. My own explanation would be that hero-worship is a powerful influence on Homer. So many of his heroes claim descent from Zeus by so many mothers that Zeus cannot be endowed with monogamic morality. The gods can look after themselves; it is the heroes who require the assistance of the bard. I believe, too, in Professor Gilbert Murray's suggestion that in these passages of impiety we have the intervention of the later Ionic spirit of rationalism. As such passages are widely diffused over the Iliad we should have to place their composition in the ninth century B.C. or later.

Once you abandon the absurd belief in Homer's "primitive simplicity" and admit, what is now certain, that the epic poets could consciously archaise their story, omitting all reference to events and customs which seemed to them too modern to fit in with the divine race of heroes, just as Malory does with the Arthurian knights, there is no objection to believing that large parts of Homer were written in the ninth century or even later. Of course, as we have said above, there are much older traditions and older fragments of epic poetry embedded in our Iliad and Odyssey. No real violence is done to ancient tradition by bringing these poems down to the verge of historical times, for Homer and Hesiod were generally regarded as contemporaries in antiquity. In the civilisation depicted by Homer we often observe a conflict between the traditions and conventions handed down from the Mycenaean age and the practices current when the poems as we now have them were composed. Take the armour for another example. Although, as has been said, the heroes generally "smite with bronze" and their shields are sometimes "like a tower" and "reaching to the feet" and "girding the body", as on the monuments of Mycenae and Crete, yet in the ordinary thought of the poets the swords are undoubtedly of iron, since the cut is commoner than the thrust and you do not cut with a sword of bronze, and the shields are "circular", "equal every way", "bossed", and "like the moon". Sometimes, as in the case of the shield of Achilles, or the shield of Agamemnon, they are adorned with a blazon. In fact, the Homeric warrior sometimes is conceived as a Mycenaean of the purest Bronze Age type, and elsewhere is dressed and equipped exactly like the hoplite of Greek history. As regards his methods of fighting, the epic convention naturally requires a series of duels in order to show the individual prowess of the heroes; and; indeed, the various episodes of the Iliad are labelled as "The Prowess of Diomede", "The Prowess of Menelaus", and so forth. But at the back of the poet's mind there constantly appears an ordinary Greek combat between two lines of warriors (Plate 46, c). Agamemnon once divides the host up into companies, tribe with tribe and brotherhood with brotherhood. Finally, by placing Homer late we avoid the absurdity of supposing that a literary form so exquisite and elaborate as the epic should have sprung out of nothing in times of violent unrest, of invasions, migrations, and ceaseless strife. *A priori* any one would say that lyric poetry must precede epic, as it has done in England. Greek tradition places Orpheus, the father of lyric song, before Homer. There would be nothing surprising in placing the early elegiac poetry on the same chronological level as the earliest hexameters. That the ordinary forms of lyric verse already existed in Homeric times we can see, if we read the poems attentively. The boy sings his vintage song of the death of Linus. At the burial of Hector there are bards to sing dirges. There is reference to the Hymenaeus, or wedding-song. There were banquet songs too: in the First Iliad they sing all day long over their cups. Bards like Demodocus sing of the loves of the gods. Thus there is ample evidence that all the common forms of Greek lyric poetry preceded the epic, and that Homer did not spring into existence ready-made out of the void.

ART OF THE EPIC PERIOD

And now the question arises as to what sort of art we are to match with the poetry of Homer. It was the desire to give some literary equivalent for the glorious art of Mycenae and Cnossus which led Schliemann and his school to equate it with Homer; and the remarkable resemblance of some of the objects Homer describes to those discovered at Mycenae has compelled modern scholars to suppose a tradition linking the Homeric poems to the Bronze Age. Doubtless prehistoric Crete had its literature. But that has all perished, unless such tablets as remain undeciphered should chance to yield us something. We must realise that great literature can co-exist with crude art and the reverse. Language being the earliest medium of artistic expression, literature can develop earlier than the graphic or plastic arts. We must therefore be prepared for the shock of finding that Homer belongs to a period characterised by limited activity in the graphic arts. The pages of Homer do not really lead us to expect anything else. Sculpture is scarcely mentioned in Homer. There is only one temple statue, and that is the statue of Athena at Troy, of which we are told that the Trojan women used to lay a richly embroidered robe upon its knees. We are probably, then, to concieve a rude seated figure of wood or stone such as we find at the earnest stages of Greek sculpture; but large scale sculpture in Greece begins far later than the poems of Homer and we have few if any surviving objects to illustrate the Homeric conception of a temple statue, except in small terracottas.

Beyond this there are some obviously imaginary figures in Homer, such as the golden torch-bearers in the fairyland of Phaeacia, but nothing that we can call sculpture. Also there are many "objects of virtue", such as the drinking-cup of Nestor (cf. Plate 40, *a*) and the brooch of Odysseus, some of which are matched by the relics of the Mycenaean tombs; but of course cups and jewels of gold were still preserved from the older civilisation, or their descriptions may have been traditionally preserved, and notably enough such objects are always accounted for: either Hephaestus has wrought them, or they have been handed down as heirlooms, or brought by the Sidonians over the sea. Homer does not take his art for granted. He uses the potter's wheel in similes, but the only art he really describes is that of tapestry-weaving, the domestic art carried on by all his ladies. Thus Helen employs herself at Troy in weaving figures of warriors into her web, and Andromache weaves flowers into hers. What pattern Penelope wove into her everlasting shroud is known only to those who know what song the sirens sang. Appropriate to this prominence of the textile art is the style of ornamentation described, as we have read, upon the shield of Achilles. This reminds us of the long lines of descriptive friezes found in Assyrian palaces at a later date, and for a reconstruction of the shield we might well compare the metal work of Phoenicia (Plate 42, *b*) or Crete of the early Iron Age (Plate 42, *a*).

The typical products of the age when Homer sung are the painted vases of the ninth and eighth centuries, in what is called by modern archaeologists the Geometric style, because the whole body of the vase is divided into bands and panels by strips of regular and repeated geometric ornament. The finest phase of the Geometric style is specially named after the Dipylon Gate at Athens, because huge vases of a certain type were found in great numbers in the ancient cemetery of Athens in that neighbourhood. The subject of these vases is therefore often funeral (Plate 40, *b*). We see the body laid out upon the bier and the mourners indicating their grief by laying their hands upon their heads. The figures are rendered in conventional diagrams. There is no added colour, though in the best Attic products the glaze and clay are good. Nor is there outline drawing: this has to wait until the end of the eighth century. But the use of angular silhouette figures does not produce dullness. It is not all funeral melancholy, either. There are stately chariot races and vigorous sea battles; and scenes of daily life, music and dancing, and the perils of the sea, and ships (Plate 39, *c*). The angular silhouettes fit well with the "geo-metric" decoration. Compared with the following "orientalising" style it looks orderly and precise, and the same impression is obtained when it is compared with the late Mycenaean. It might be tempting to suggest that this Geometric pottery was the product of a new incoming people. Yet there is sufficient evidence to show, from the Kerameikos cemetery at Athens, for instance, that there is a continuous development from the end of the Mycenaean style onwards into the earliest period of the geometric decoration (*cf.* Plate 38), but the reason still eludes us why the later stages of this style, the Geometric proper, show such excellence both in decoration and in the skill of potters who made vases of tremendous size, at a time when Greek art had relatively little else to show, except figures in bronze (such as Plate 39, *b*) or geometrically conceived figures of small size carved in ivory (Plate 39, *a*). It is hard to believe that there was major wood-carving which has perished. There were, of course, the splendid tripods mentioned above (page 46). Like the vast vases, late in the period in Attica, they show great technological skill.

THE HERO'S HOME

In Crete art dwelt in palaces; in classical Greece it haunted the market-place and the temple. For the present art is confined to the house. If we may judge by the charming "interior" pictures which Homer most skilfully introduces as a counterfoil to the everlasting clash of arms in the Iliad, domestic life was at its richest and best in the age of the epics. Everyone has been struck with the dignified and important position accorded to women in Homer, contrasted with their seclusion and neglect in historical Greece. No one but Shakespeare has given us so charming a series of feminine portraits as Andromache, Helen, Penelope, Nausicaa, Thetis, and Calypso. The ingenious Samuel Butler actually attempted to prove that the Odyssey was written by a woman, so sympathetic is the poet's insight into the feminine point of view. But the same is equally true of the Iliad; and, indeed, the respect for women becomes part of the heroic tradition even in Attic tragedy, so that the audience in the theatre of Athens must have seen the heroines on their stage acting with a freedom and treated with a deference which was quite alien to their own homes.

But even at this, its highest point, the domesticity of Greek life falls far short of modern ideas, and the dignity of the heroes' wives is somewhat illusory. Possibly the inconsistencies are due once more to the many voices and successive generations which have had their part in building up the epic. Certainly, for monogamists, the matrimonial ideas of the heroes are far from exclusive. Agamemnon announces his intention of taking Chryseis home, for he likes her better than his dear wife Clytemnestra, and makes no secret of the position she is to occupy. He does actually take Cassandra home to his wife. In the Odyssey, too, we get a hint of arrangements decidedly Oriental in what Penelope says about her son and the fifty handmaidens. Again, there is singular contrast between the tender conjugal devotion of Hector and Andromache, or Odysseus and Penelope, and the extraordinary callousness sometimes indicated with regard to feminine charms. It is often remarked as an instance of Homer's subtlety that he nowhere describes the beauty of Helen, whose face

> launched a thousand ships
> And shook the topless towers of Ilium,

only indicating it by making the old men of Troy look at her as she walks past and say to one another, "No wonder that the Greeks and Trojans should suffer pain so long for such a woman. Her countenance is wondrous like the immortal goddesses". These traditions of the power of love and beauty must belong to the original epic story for the whole plot of the Iliad, so far as it has a plot, turns on the beauty of Helen, as the whole plot of the Odyssey depends on the love of Odysseus for his wife and the constancy of Penelope. Thus both epics have a basis which might be the foundation of modern romantic fiction. Nevertheless, the spirit of romance is as completely absent from Homer as it is from all true Greek art and literature. Though Agamemnon is very angry at losing Chryseis he has no love for her. Odysseus simply gets tired of the lovely nymph Calypso, and parts from the charming Nausicaa without a pang. Such shocks as these are constantly in store for the modern reader, who is fed upon romance in the nursery.

If we look at the houses in which the domestic scenes of Homer are set we shall find that they are of a simplicity in strong contrast with the elaborate palaces of Crete or Mycenaean Greece; and this in spite of the obvious intention of the bard to depict them on a scale of heroic magnificence. They seem to be built mainly of wood. The palace of Paris consists of three parts—*thalamos*, *doma*, and *aule*. The *thalamos* is the private part of the house, and contains the marriage-bed of the royal couple. The *doma*, or *megaron*, is the public hall for meals and receptions. The *aule* is the court with colonnades surrounding it. Priam had a large family: fifty sons slept with their wives in fifty *thalamoi* of polished stone built outside his court, while his daughters slept with their husbands in twelve *roofed* chambers within the court. The palace of Odysseus is more elaborate, and is so intended, for the disguised wanderer says: "Verily, this is the fair house of Odysseus, and easily may it be known and distinguished even among many. For there is building beyond building, and the court of the house is cunningly wrought with a wall and copings, and there are well-fitting double doors". Yet standing outside the front door he can perceive by the smell of roast meat that there is a banquet going on. No great magnificence here. In front of the "well-fitting doors" there is a heap of manure, with an aged hound asleep upon it (a similar dung heap, it may be remarked, graces the court of the palace of Priam in Troy City). Inside the doors there is the *megaron*, where the banquet is going on. Odysseus sits down on the ashen threshold, leaning against a pillar of cypress wood, specially commended for its straightness. Telemachus takes a lump of meat, "as much as his two hands can grasp", and a whole loaf out of the fair basket, and Odysseus (who is disguised as a beggar) devours it on his dirty wallet as he sits on the threshold. This threshold under the portico of the hall is the regular meeting-place of beggars, and it is there that strangers are put to sleep. Somehow related to the hall there is an upper chamber where Penelope sleeps and lives with her maidens. The wooers set up three braziers in the hall to give them light, and heap them with wood and pine-brands; consequently the hall is so full of smoke that the weapons have to be removed to a store-room to keep them useful. Odysseus, sleeping in the "prodomos" of the hall, can hear a remark made by one of the twelve grinding-women who have their hand-mills in the house next door. Under the same echoing colonnade where Odysseus sleeps goats and cattle are tethered by day. The walls of the hall itself are of wood, the ceiling is of wood, and the floor is of stamped earth, for it is cleaned with a spade, and fires are raked out of the braziers on to the floor. As for the bridal chamber, Odysseus had built it himself with stone, and it contained a marvellous bed wrought by the hero out of a living olive-tree. Finally, there was a rather obscure postern-gate set high in the wall of the hall above a stone threshold, and opening on to a gallery or passage. Thus the feature of the house of Odysseus is that it is of two stories; otherwise it consists, as usual, of three parts—hall, court, and chamber.

Our learned archaeologists have been setting their intellects to the task of making these Homeric houses fit in with the palaces and houses of Mycenae and Tiryns, but they have sometimes found it hard work. They have had to admit that the palace of Odysseus is a good deal simpler than the meanest of the Aegean palaces. And yet there can be no doubt that our poet knew traditionally of a long-past time when his heroes dwelt in splendours such as we should find in Mycenae and Tiryns. Such are, in terms of splendid but vaguely conceived materials, the fairytale palaces of Menelaus and Alcinous. When it came to the details of everyday life, then, and only then, his imagination to some extent failed him. What should we think of a novelist who pro-fessed to write about duchesses and described them as sitting in sump-tuous front parlours? Surely we know the explanation. It is hope-less to attempt to synchronise the Homeric Age with the ages of Aegean palaces. Homer lived in an altogether lower civilisation as regards wealth and comfort. Just as we can see that his "kings" are only country squires, so his "palaces" are no more than farmhouses, with all their picturesque squalor and simplicity. Dirt and mag-nificence may go hand in hand, as in our own mediaeval halls, but in the Homeric civilisation the magnificence is only in the memories stored up in the poet's heart.

HESIOD'S WORLD

Hesiod is the Cinderella of Greek poets, in the past somewhat neglected by editors and students. And yet once he stood on a level with Homer. He is in reality the complement of Homer, and no picture of the Greek Middle Ages can be complete without him. The Parian Marble sets Hesiod thirty years earlier than Homer; Herodotus places them both about 850-800 B.C. He was almost certainly later, perhaps of the latest eighth century, or the beginning of the seventh. Hesiod's principal works are two, the "Works and Days" and the "Generations of Gods" or "Theogony". The "Works and Days" is generally supposed to be a treatise on husbandry, but it seems to be in origin a letter of remonstrance to a wicked brother, Perses, who had ousted Hesiod from his property. The letter is embroidered freely with morals, maxims, and examples from mythology. Perses is exhorted to practise industry and good farming, for which some proverbial hints are given. But the main purport of this curious jumble is the reiteration of complaints against the "bribe-devouring kings"—always in the plural—who have given a corrupt judgment against the poet on his brother's lawsuit. No one pretends to see real monarchy or anything but oligarchy in Hesiod, yet his rulers are called βασιλεῖς, just as are Homer's. The "Works and Days" contains also the earliest versions of two most famous legends which together make up the Greek story of creation, the story of how Prometheus stole fire from heaven and the story of Pandora, the Eve of Greek mythology. The chief interest for modern readers lies in a very quaint and curious list of taboos and some personal reminiscences which form, I suppose, the oldest piece of autobiography in existence. He has already described seafaring as a very disagreeable business, to be avoided if possible; he now advises his brother to "wait for a seasonable sailing day, and when it comes, then drag down thy swift ship to the sea, and have a fit cargo stowed away on it, that thou mayest return home with profit; even as my father and thine, most witless Perses, used to make voyages for an honest living. Once he came even to this country, after a long voyage in a black ship from Cyme, in Aeolis, turning not from rich resources and prosperity, but from dire poverty, which Zeus gives to me. And he dwelt near Helicon in this beggarly hamlet of Ascra—Ascra, vile in winter, uncomfortable in summer, and good never at all. But do thou, my Perses, be seasonable in all thy doings, but above all in seafaring praise a small ship, but put thy cargo in a great one. The freight will be greater and the profit greater if the winds keep off their dreadful storms. Whenever thou turnest thy rash heart to trade, wishing to escape debt and joyless famine, I will show thee the limits of the thundering main without being skilled at all in seafaring or in ships, for I have never sailed the broad sea in a ship except when I crossed to Euboea from Aulis, where the Achaeans in times long past were storm-bound when they gathered a mighty host from holy Hellas for Troy of the fair women. There did I take passage for Chalcis to try for the prizes of wise Amphidamas" (i.e. prizes offered at his funeral games), "the many well-prepared prizes which his lordly sons offered. There I boast to have won the prize for the hymn, and brought home a tripod (see page 46 and Plate 38) with handles which I set up to the Muses of Helicon where first they taught me to be a clear-voiced bard. So little trial have I made of well-caulked ships, but still I shall declare the mind of Zeus who bears the aegis, for the Muses have taught me to sing a hymn without bounds."

Quaint old Hesiod! How like the literary man of all ages! He has never been to sea except on the channel ferry, but in virtue of his literary gifts he is competent to instruct other landsmen in navigation. So by help of the Muses he declares the mind of Zeus—"Never put to sea in a storm!"

Well, this is the reverse of Homer's medal: the god-nurtured kings frankly revealed as corrupt nobles, the unrelenting toil on the stony farm, the perilous commercial enterprises in small unseaworthy ships, the emigrant returning home to Boeotia in poverty from his Eldorado in Aeolis, the superstition, and the pessimism.

III

THE AGES OF TRANSITION

οὐ μὴν οὐδ' ὑπαρχόντων τούτων ἁπάντων ἤδη πόλις,
ἀλλ' ἡ τοῦ εὖ ζῆν κοινωνία.

ARISTOTLE

THE COMING OF APOLLO

"He bringeth to men and women cures for their grievous sick-
nesses, he giveth the harp, and he granteth the Muse to whomsoever
he will; he ruleth his oracular shrine, bringing peace and lawful order
into our hearts; he stablished the descendants of Heracles and Aegimius
in Lacedaemon and Argos and most of holy Pylos." Such is the
Theban poet's summary of the attributes of the Dorian god. Healing,
harp-music and lyric poetry, discipline and morality fostered by the
Delphic oracle, and the Dorian government of Sparta, Argos, and
Messenia—these are the gifts of Apollo to Greece. There is nothing
here to connect him with Nature-worship. He is not even connected
with light or sun.

We have already seen something of the earliest strata of religious
beliefs on Greek soil. The Aegean worship clearly incorporated an
element of "aniconic fetishism"—that is, the worship of inanimate,
possibly symbolical, objects, such as stones, pillars, axes, horns, and
trees. Then there were animal deities, possibly totemistic in origin,
such as the snake-goddess and the dove-goddess, powers mainly representing fecundity, and both probably phases of the Great Mother
of all living things. There was probably also ghost-worship; for the
dead in the tholos tombs were later certainly honoured by sacrifices,
as protecting heroes. We are reminded of rain-maker chieftain spirits
in inner Africa, and the cult of dead Pharaohs. There seem to have
been no temples at all in these stages of religion, though small cult-
places have been found; and it will be wise to say more excavation
may force us to change our views. There was certainly a system of
private local cults in great and bewildering variety. But it is probable
that some of the Aegean spirits developed into anthropomorphic
deities before the end. Some of the regular Olympian deities of

63

historical Greece seem to belong partially, and some wholly, to this earlier civilisation. So the linear B tablets of Cnossus seem to indicate. Athena the virgin goddess of Athens, Artemis the mother of wild things, Aphrodite the goddess of love, and Demeter or Mother Earth, can, indeed, be derived from the primitive Mother-goddess idea of the neolithic and Anatolian background, but also certain of the deities associated with the "northern" sky-god background, such as the "Healer", appear in the tablets. From Aegean cultures there may be carried over mysterious forms like the Fates, the Curses, the Harpies, and the Sirens. But there was little exclusiveness about ancient religion; new deities are quite readily accepted into polytheistic systems, though in some cases there was a protracted struggle to keep them out. Hesiod remarks that the deities have many names for a single shape, and often a double name reveals assimilation, such as Phoebus Apollo or Pallas Athena. In most cases, indeed, the great name of an Olympian god covers a host of minor deities with varying and sometimes quite opposite attributes. Thus the national Zeus has swallowed up countless local heroes, as when Laconians worshipped Zeus Agamemnon. Likewise Athena took over many local city-goddesses, and Apollo many local oracles.

All these processes of change are reflected in mythology. It would seem as if mythologists, or, as we should say, expert theologians, set out to reconcile the people to new forms of worship by inventing delightful stories to account for the change. Homer and Hesiod were doing precisely that sort of work. For example, the development of the position of Zeus was explained by means of a curious myth. It was agreed that he had not always been King of Heaven; formerly his old father Cronos, probably a figure taken from Aegean mythology, had ruled, he whose wife was Rhea or Ge. Zeus was born in Crete— that is, he was attached to an ancient Cretan story of a divine nativity in which a she-goat suckled a babe. Here may lurk some relic of animal cult or worship which it is beyond our power to explain. Again, Cronos is said to have tried to crush the usurper in the bud by swallowing his dangerous child, but to have swallowed a stone instead. Who knows what relic of the worship of sacred stones may not lie hidden here, for it was said that the stone was preserved. Still more instructive are the legends of contest between deities for worship at a particular shrine. The ordinary device for the introduction of Zeus was to make him the father of the local hero. "God," says Voltaire, "first made man in His own likeness, and man has been returning the compliment ever since." It is the secret of anthropomorphic religion that the worshipper is worshipping himself, or rather an idealised vision of himself projected upon the public conception of his god. The human heart has an unlimited power of thus adapting its faith to its habits. Anthropologists are continually telling us of the persistence of ancient cults in spite of pretended changes of faith, rituals that belong to Artemis transferred to the Virgin, dirges for Adonis transformed into mourning for Christ. Often when the polite antiquarian Pausanias asked the Greeks of his day about the objects of their worship he got conflicting answers. That is how it becomes easy to make converts if you are content to leave ritual unchanged, and that was how Apollo got himself accepted as the young man's god all over Greece. There was, indeed, a rival young man's god in Hermes, a very ancient deity. Remnants of antique aniconic worship attach themselves to Hermes: his statues even in classical times are three parts pillar to one part god. He is the shepherd-god of Arcadia, and the Arcadians represent a very early, perhaps the earliest, Greek stratum in the country. Hermes is a god of music too, but his instrument is the lyre, which in shape and construction resembles the modern mandoline, for the body was made from the shell of a tortoise, an indigenous Greek creature, with a sounding-board of parchment stretched over it. Apollo properly plays on the cithara, or harp. The popularity of Hermes persisted throughout because he became identified with Luck, and Luck is the one god we all worship. He is also associated with commerce; he it is who drives a sharp bargain; because in his original form a shepherd-god, he was the pillar or pile of stone at the boundary of a field, or along the roads. This attribute the trade-despising warriors turned to his discredit, for poor Hermes in the Homeric Hymn, and generally in literature, becomes a sharper of the worst description. If you ask "Who stole the cows?" the answer is "Hermes". He is the messenger of Zeus, but he is also his spy. Hermes, then, was much too strongly planted to be uprooted by the superior Apollo. In classical Greece there are two Apollos, one the Delian or Cynthian Apollo, the centre of whose cult was the island of Delos; the other was called Pythian Apollo, and worshipped above all at Delphi. To these two shrines mysterious messengers came at intervals bringing offerings from the far north. They were associated, perhaps, with the amber route and the vague ideas of far northern peoples rather than with the "northern" origins of the Indoeuropean-speaking Greeks. The Delian shrine was a centre of the Ionians, and Delos afterwards became the headquarters of the maritime league of Athens and the Ionian States. Delos boasted itself to have been the god's birthplace, and mythology presented an elaborate nativity for this Apollo and his sister Artemis. "Homeric" hymns to both Apollos are preserved, and it is interesting to notice how the Ionian bard who is praising the Apollo of Delos mentions all the centres of his worship in a longish list which tallies closely with the list of Athenian allies in the Delian confederacy. But this Delian Apollo is not the important one; in many respects he is only a pale reflection of the other, and his vogue principally depended on the extreme sanctity of the little island of Delos.

The true Apollo is the god who had his home at Delphi. He and his worship play such a prominent part in the making of classical as distinct from prehistoric and heroic Greece that I put him in the fore-front of this age of transition. Delphi is one of the most impressive sites in Greece, lying high in a narrow glen with precipitous and almost awe-inspiring crags on every side (Plate 5). Several times in Greek history rash invaders failed to penetrate into this mysterious shrine. The god's majesty and the terrors of his abode were sufficient protection. It is clear from the mythological presentation of his com-ing that before Apollo there was already an ancient oracle at Delphi, the source of which was Earth and a snake called Python, symbol of a more primitive chthonic cult. The myth described how Apollo came and conquered this serpent. He built a great temple in this valley under Parnassus, and took the place of Earth, or Themis, as Pythian Apollo, lord of the Delphic oracle.

Apollo is the most characteristically Greek god on Olympus, as he is the representative god also of Dorians. He is the young athlete god. If we trace the history of his type in art we see him as the favourite subject at the very outset of Greek sculpture when, somewhat before 600 B.C., the Greeks learned, perhaps from Egypt, to make great statues in stone. He is always nude in these early statues, and it is not easy to say how many of the so-called early Apollos represent the god, and how many are simply statues of male athletes offered to the god as the fine flower of manhood, or set up over the tomb of a young warrior. It makes little difference in the former case for the god and his worshipper are one. At first there is little expression, and the artist is still struggling with his stubborn material, happy if his chisel can get the semblance of human shape out of marble; yet in the early "Apollos" the resulting effect of simple grandeur is unmistakable (Plate 52, *a*). In the next stage, represented by the "Apollo of Tenea", the sculptor has attained considerable mastery over his tools, and has succeeded in his main object, namely, a moderately faithful expression of the muscles of the male body (Plate 52, *c*). The reader will notice "the archaic grin" on the faces of all gods and goddesses of this period. This is probably not an attempt to indicate the benevolence of the deity; it comes from a technical problem, not yet overcome, found in all the early sculpture of Greece. Apollo was always the god of healing; Asklepios was his son and Hygeia his daughter. By-and-by the artists learnt how to express their ideals less crudely (Plate 52, *b*), and all the time they were learning more anatomy and a fuller mastery over their tools, until in the glorious fifth century a sculptor of Olympia could make a noble figure such as stands calm and powerful, every inch a god, in the midst of battle on the West Pediment of the great temple at Olympia (Plate 73, *b*). Study this god. If you can love him you will have learnt the secret of Hellenic greatness at its best. He is very simple, serious, and severe; he has the asceticism of a good athlete who knows what discipline means for the sake of his club or country. You must judge him as early work, you must allow, when you criticise the stiffness of his hair, for the use of tinting and the crown of gilt bayleaves which once passed through the hollow underneath his hair. You will perceive that there is something wrong with the angle of his eyelids, which meet without overlapping. Sculptors of the next generation learnt to correct that, but they never conceived a grander figure of the sort of god that a gentleman and an aristocrat might fitly worship. Of course this is not a temple image; it is only one detail of a piece of ornament under the gable at the back of a temple, but it is the conception of a great artist. After that they began to think too much about the beauty of Apollo and young athletes in general, worshipping both with extravagant devotion. At last we come to the young exquisite with the elaborate coiffure and the studied theatrical pose, the Apollo Belvedere, who seemed to our great-grandfathers the most perfect of Greek statues, though he was carved to suit a decadent taste in the days when Greece had lost the very memory of manliness. Another conflicting, but, I believe, equally aristocratic type of Apollo represents him in the flowing and almost feminine robes of a musician. This is Apollo the artist, not the athlete, the Apollo who leads the choir of Muses on Mount Helicon.

To return to the god and his oracle: Apollo, already present as Paion in Bronze Age Greece, came truly to the fore after the transition to the Iron Age, that is, after the disappearance of Mycenaean culture which is to be connected somehow with the Dorians. When they had overrun the whole Peloponnesus, except Arcadia and Achaia, occupying the southern islands, including Crete, and overflowing even into the south of Asia Minor, Delphi eventually became their central shrine and oracle and a centre for many others. So cleverly was that oracle managed by the Delphic priests that it became the common centre for advice to all Greece, until it formed a sort of focus of Greek nationality. Even semi-barbarian monarchs like Croesus of Lydia applied to it for advice, and paid for its oracles with lavish dedications. As ambassadors and private individuals kept coming to Delphi from all parts of the Greek world, the priests had good opportunity of collecting information. They were especially strong in geography, and if a city found its population increasing beyond the extent of its land space, or if there were a gang of mischievous young nobles to be got rid of, or if the city sought new commercial openings, it would send an embassy to Delphi to consult Apollo about a suitable site for a new colony. Some, no doubt, asked advice of the priests. The very highly favoured, after due sacrifices and oblations and various mysterious rites to ensure the proper reverential spirit, would be brought to the vestibule of the inmost shrine, where a priestess sat upon a tripod over the identical crack in the ground where the old serpent Python had once made his den. Here was a conical stone representing the omphalos or navel of the earth. Then the inspiration would seize the Pythian priestess, she would fall into a kind of fit or trance, caused, they say, by burning leaves of laurel, and in the course of it she uttered wild and whirling words. Before you left the priests would hand you the substance of her remarks neatly composed in rather weak hexameter verses. Very often the advice would turn out excellently, for the priests knew their business. If it did not they could usually point out that their words bore quite a different interpretation if you had had the sense to understand them, and your own innermost desires. Thus Croesus asked whether he should make war on the growing power of Persia; he was told that if he did he would destroy a mighty empire. After the success of Cyrus, the oracle, of course, explained that Croesus had in fact destroyed a mighty empire—namely, his own.

The supple intelligence of the Greeks devoted a good deal of its ingenuity to inventing smart *double ententes* like this, but I am afraid that the Delphic priests were actually guilty of a good deal of low trickery and corruption, though they would hardly have won the national confidence, as they did, if that sort of answer had been their ordinary practice. In politics they played a very important part until the Persian wars, when their more accurate knowledge, as they believed, of external affairs led them to overrate the power of Darius and Xerxes and to counsel submission, whereby they somewhat injured their credit. They also feared for their treasures. They formed an international bureau for the statesmen of Greece. Two institutions in particular made them a much-frequented shrine; one was the Pythian Games, the second in importance of the four great religious and athletic festivals of Greece, and the other was the Delphic Amphictyony. The latter was an international league for the defence and supervision of the shrine, which looked, at times, as if it were going to develop into a real Panhellenic confederacy. Delphi had crept in here, supplanting a much older religious union of neighbours at Anthela. Even in historical times the Amphictyons or their delegates met alternately at the shrine of Demeter at Anthela and at the temple of Apollo at Delphi. The meeting was mainly for common worship, but some of the proceedings touched international politics, and there was an old Amphictyonic oath resembling the Geneva Conventions, in which the members bound themselves not to cut off running water from any other city of the league. Unfortunately, the inveterate feuds of the Greeks often led to the abuse of this league for political ends, and, instead of enforcing holy peace, we often find it waging sacred wars.

We saw that Pindar placed *eunomia*—good order—among the gifts of Apollo. Like Athena, Apollo was greatly interested in political and constitutional systems. In the course of the eighth and seventh centuries, which is the period when Delphi first began to extend its influence, we find the oracle deliberately claiming the authorship of some of the most celebrated legal and constitutional systems of the day. Sparta became not only the chief Dorian state, with a preponderant influence or hegemony over all Southern Greece, but the possessor of the most elaborate and successful political system in the whole country. We can see the Delphic oracle deliberately inserting itself as the founder of this good order. The historian Herodotus got much of his information from the oracle, and he tells us its version, how a certain Lycurgus had come to Delphi to ask for laws and a constitution, and had received it from the god. But the Spartans themselves had not yet been convinced. They still believed that theirs were the true Dorian institutions—as, in fact, they mostly were—dating back to their original leaders, "the sons of Herakles", and closely resembling or even in part derived from those of Dorian Crete. A generation or two after Herodotus the Delphic claim was admitted, for constitutional writers of all parties were glad to accept the sanction of the god for the constitution as they severally interpreted it. Thus Lycurgus, who had originally been an obscure hero with a half-forgotten cult, came to rank as the Spartan lawgiver and the author of the remarkable system of life and government which we shall presently describe. Delphi did the same for the famous legal systems of the West, claiming to have inspired Zaleucus, the law-giver of Locri, and Charondas of Catana with their codes. There is some indication of similar proceedings with regard to Solon of Athens, but they met with little success among the worshippers of Athena, who was as much a patron of law and order as Apollo himself. Delphi endeavoured to appropriate the wisdom of the Seven Sages, mostly early historical philosophers who belong to these ages of transition. Apollo even claimed the philosophy of Pythagoras, whose name lent itself peculiarly to a supposed Delphic origin. By such means as these the Delphic oracle became the chief sanctuary in Greece, and exerted a very great influence.

ATHLETICS

The same period saw a great impetus given to the cult of athletics in Greece. The boxers and the bull-fighters of Cnossus prove that athletics were already at home on Greek soil before the Dorians came. But the Ionians and Dorians were also devoted to manly sport. With them it seems to have had from the first a religious significance, especially in connection with funerals and ancestor-worship. In the Iliad the funeral of Patroclus is honoured with sports at his tomb. The programme of this early meeting was an elaborate one. It might be described in modern technical style somewhat as follows:

CHARIOT RACE. First Prize: A blameless, accomplished woman and a tripod with handles. Second Prize: A brood mare. Third Prize: A new cauldron. Fourth Prize: Two talents of gold. Fifth Prize: A new two-handled pan.

Antilochus won the toss and took the inner station. In the first lap there was little in it, but on rounding the turn Eumelus' team pushed to the front, with Diomede lying second, close up. Phoebus Apollo knocked the whip out of Diomede's hand, whereupon Pallas Athene responded by breaking the leader's yoke, the driver being seriously injured. Result: Diomede 1, Antilochus 2, Menelaus 3, Meriones 4, Eumelus 0. The fifth prize was awarded to Nestor as the oldest member present. Menelaus' objection to Antilochus on the score of dangerous driving was amicably settled.

BOXING MATCH. Prize: A six-year-old mule. Consolation Prize: A two-handled cup.

Epeius and Euryalus were the only entrants. Epeius was an early winner, finding the Theban champion's jaw in the first round and knocking him out like a fish out of water.

WRESTLING MATCH. Prize: A large tripod, value twelve oxen. Consolation Prize: A clever woman, value four oxen.

Of the two wrestlers Ajax showed superior strength, but Odysseus was more than his match in science. This seems to have been a regular rough-and-tumble, both champions being pinched black and blue; there was nothing to choose between them, and after a ding-dong struggle the match was declared a draw.

FOOT RACE. First Prize: Handsome silver punch-bowl of Sidonian make. Second Prize: Fat ox. Third Prize: Half a talent of gold.

Odysseus, none the worse for his recent encounter, entered in a field of three. Ajax son of Oileus was first off the mark, closely followed by Odysseus. The latter, unable to get on terms with his speedier rival, prayed to Pallas Athene for help. On nearing the prizes Ajax fell, and Odysseus was declared the winner. The objection lodged by Ajax on the ground of celestial interference was dismissed with ridicule.

SHAM DUEL. Prize: the armour of Sarpedon.

Diomede and Telamonian Ajax were so evenly matched that this event also was pronounced a draw.

PUTTING THE WEIGHT. Prize: A lump of natural iron.

Polypoetes won this event, with a record put, amid general enthusiasm.

ARCHERY. First Prize: Ten double axes. Second Prize: Ten single axes.

The mark was a dove tied to a mast. Teucer won the toss and took first shot, missing his bird, but cutting the string by which it was attached. Thereupon Meriones snatched the bow, and, vowing a hecatomb to

Apollo, pierced the dove to the heart, thus proving his title to the first prize.

JAVELIN-THROWING.   First Prize: Ornamental cauldron, value one ox. Second Prize: Javelin.

Agamemnon walked over.

Even in the account of these games it seems very probable that there has been a process of accumulation in which later bards have added events according to their fancy.   Some of the later encounters are described with much less vigour and skill than the earlier.   It is, however, important to notice that from the very first Greek athletics were part of religion.   They were undertaken in a serious, devotional spirit, to honour some god or defunct hero.   It was the same with poetry.   Epic was, of course, devoted to the gods and heroes.   The early choral lyric was also in the main devotional, whatever its subject might be.   We have seen Hesiod carrying his poetic talents to a contest in song arranged to honour the funeral of Amphidamas. Later on (page 164) we shall refer to a theory that Tragedy developed out of funeral choruses.   It appears also that the great games of Delphi —the Pythian Games—developed from a musical contest.   The histories of Herodotus are said to have been declaimed at the Olympic Games, and orators would in later times make them the occasion for Panhellenic orations.   There was no divorce between intellect and muscle among the Greeks.   Each was a necessary part of *areté*, the quality of the perfect man.   Sport-loving people as we are, there is nothing in all literature so hard for us to comprehend as the work of Pindar, the Boeotian poet of the early fifth century.   His professional business was only the writing of the Epinikia, songs and music in celebration of athletic contests at the great games, Pythian, Nemean, Isthmian, and Olympic.   But the spirit in which he approaches his task is that of a man writing about the most solemn and important achievements in the world.   He assumes that success in a boys' wrestling match or a mule-race is an episode in the history of the successful athlete's country, and does not find it inappropriate to speak of the gods and heroes in the same breath.   "Far and wide shineth the glory of the Olympian Games, the glory that is won in the races of Pelops, where swiftness of foot contends, and feats of strength, hardy in labour. All his life long the victor shall bask in the glory of song for his prize. Daily continued blessedness is the supreme good for every man." We cannot understand the devotional spirit of Pindar unless we realise that the Greeks dedicated their bodily strength and grace to the honour and service of heaven. The Hebrew praised Jehovah in dance and song: the Greek honoured Zeus and Apollo with wrestling and races and the beauty of trained bodies.

The Olympic Games (Plate 4) had originally belonged to the service of local heroes, Oenomaus and Pelops, but as they gained in popularity Father Zeus took them under his aegis. Apollo was said to have outrun Hermes in a race there and to have beaten Ares in boxing. The traditional date for the founding of the festival was 776 B.C., and that became the era from which all Greek dates were subsequently settled. But the actual date has no special significance: the great importance of the games begins a good deal later —it coincides, in fact, with the hegemony of Sparta in the Peloponnese. Though the games were not in Spartan territory it was undoubtedly from Spartan support that their importance arose, though the importance of the connexion with the Western Greeks must be stressed.

At first the only contest was a foot-race, but various events were added until at last five days were necessary for the whole meeting. The most important contests were the following: (1) short foot-race; (2) double course; (3) long foot-race; (4) wrestling; (5) pentathlon, consisting of five feats, long jump, foot-race, quoit-throwing, javelin-throwing, wrestling; (6) boxing; (7) four-horse chariot-race; (8) pancration, a mixture of boxing and wrestling—in fact, a combat between two naked unarmed men, with scarcely any rules; (9) horse-race; (10) hoplite-race for soldiers in full armour. Besides these there were six special events for boys and various other contests, such as mule-races and trotting races, which did not become permanent fixtures. There was a regular competition for heralds and trumpeters.

Sacrifice and ritual accompanied every stage of the proceedings. Before the meeting, which took place every four years, ambassadors went from city to city proclaiming a Sacred Truce. All people who could prove Greek nationality were invited. From its situation Olympia naturally attracted support from the flourishing communities of Sicily and South Italy. Whether they sent competitors or not, most of the states would send embassies to the festival, and a great point was made of their lavish equipment. The judges were chosen by lot from the citizens of Elis, who managed the contest; they received a ten month's course of instruction beforehand in the duties of their office. All the competitors had to undergo a strict examination as to their qualifications, and to take an oath on the altar of Zeus that they would compete fairly and that they had been in training for the previous ten months. The only prize was a crown of wild olive, cut from a certain tree of special sanctity, but the victor's name and country were proclaimed to the assembled multitude and the highest honours awaited him on his return. He was welcomed in procession, led in through a breach specially made in the wall of the city, and granted immunities from taxation, or, as at Athens, free meals in the Presidential House for all his life. The chariot-races were especially the object of ambition and the opportunity for display to the wealthy. Tyrants of Syracuse competed in them, but the brilliant Athenian Alcibiades out-stripped all competitors by sending in no fewer than seven teams.

Although the prize was but a spiritual one, we cannot say that the contests were always conducted in what we should call a spirit of pure amateur sport. Perhaps the incentive to trickery was excessively great. Anyhow, there stood at Olympia an ominous row of statues dedicated to Zeus which had been set up as fines by athletes guilty of discreditable practices, generally of the kind we associate with the "pulling" of horses. But when it is considered that the Olympian Games continued in an almost unbroken series for twelve centuries— that is, until the Emperor Theodosius abolished them in A.D. 393— the list of such irregularities is not unduly long.

In the very minute account of Olympia which we owe to the traveller Pausanias there are some curious and interesting anecdotes of the games. For example, he saw the statue of the boy Pisidorus, who was brought to the Olympic Games by his mother disguised as a trainer, because no women were allowed to be present. "They say that Diagoras came with his sons Acusilaus and Damagetus to Olympia, and when the young men had won their prizes they carried their father through the assembly, while the people pelted him with flowers and called him happy in his children." Then there is Timanthes, the strong man, who won the pancration. "He had ceased practising as an athlete, but still he continued to test his strength by bending a mighty bow every day. Well, he went away from home, and while he was away his practice with the bow was discontinued. But when he came back and could no longer bend his bow he lit a fire and flung himself on the flames." There is the plough-boy Glaucus, whose father noticed him one day fitting the ploughshare into his plough with his fist instead of a hammer. His father thereupon took him to Olympia to box, but as he had no skill in boxing he was badly punished and almost beaten. Suddenly his father called out, "Give him the plough-hammer, my boy!" Whereupon he knocked his adversary out, won the prize, and became the famous pugilist. "The mare of the Corinthian Phidolas was named Aura; at the start she happened to throw her rider, but continuing, nevertheless, to race in due form, she rounded the turningpost, and on hearing the trumpet, quickened her pace, reached the umpires first, knew that she had won, and stopped."

The formal athletic exercises can be reconstructed in some detail from the description left by ancient writers and from vase-paintings. On the less formal sports and games of Greece we are naturally less well-informed, but mention may be made of some sculptured bases found by chance in 1922 during the demolition of an ancient wall at Athens. One of them depicts a scene which at once recalls a modern game of football; there are also representations of athletic exercises (Plate 59, b). Another shows a "bully-off" at hockey (Plate 59, b); the game seems to have been single-handed, not between teams, and the players at the sides are awaiting their turn to play. These reliefs belong to the late sixth century, just about the time when the Delphic oracle induced the Spartans to expel Hippias the tyrant, son of Pisistratus, from Athens.

That there was a good deal of extravagance in the cult of athletes was not likely to escape the critical eye of a people who so detested extravagance in any form. The outspoken Euripides had a violent tirade against athletes in his satiric drama *Autolycus*. "It is folly," he says, "for the Greeks to make a great gathering to see useless creatures like these, whose god is in their belly. What good does a man do to his city by winning a prize for wrestling or speed or quoit-heaving or jaw-smiting? Will they fight the enemy with quoits? Will they drive the enemy out of their country without spears by kicking? No one plays antics like these when he stands near the steel. Garlands of leaves should be for the wise and good, for the just and sober states-man who guides his city best, for the man who with his words averts evil deeds, keeping battle and civil strife away. Those are the real boons for every city and all the Greeks." Twenty-three centuries stand between this and "The flannelled fool at the wicket, the muddied oaf at the goal". I fear that Euripides got no more attention than did Mr. Kipling.

As with us, professionalism grew upon them in later days. The old ideals of bodily grace and all-round excellence were deserted. In their place the boxing and pancration encouraged a coarse type of heavy-weight bruiser. The training and meals of the athletes became a by-word in vegetarian Greece, and romantic sporting reporters enlarged upon the gastronomic feats of the famous athletes.

Athleticism, however, gave one thing to the Greeks that we lack. It was from the models in the palaestra and the stadium that the sculptors of Greece drew their inspiration. It was of course an immense benefit to that art to be able to see the stripped body at exercise in the sunlight, and that, coupled with the natural Greek sense of form, is the secret of the unchallenged supremacy in this category of Greek sculpture. Perfect anatomy of the body was achieved even before the face could be properly rendered. The nude male figure was the favourite theme of fifth-century art, and extraordinary perfection was reached by Myron and Polyclitus. Myron's "Discobolus" is, of course, one of the best known of ancient statues. Myron, an Athenian artist, is an elder contemporary of Phidias, and therefore belongs to the earlier stages of the great period. But he had already begun to feel the artist's sense of mastery over his material, and he delighted in rather strained poses, therein starting a tendency for sculpture which would surely have led to a premature decadence if it had not been for the extraordinary genius of the inspired Phidias. The original statue has disappeared, but several Roman copies are preserved (Plate 68, a). But they are leagues removed from the original bronze. The "Discobolus" is an instantaneous photograph of an athlete just poising the heavy disk and preparing to throw. In another moment he will turn right-about on the pivot of his right foot. There are few statues of the fifth century which thus select an instant out of a series of movements. For athlete statues two types stand pre-eminent. One is the athlete (Plate 69, b) just fastening the diadem upon his victorious brow ("Diadumenus"), a type due to Polyclitus, whose examples of figure-drawing were taken even by the Greeks as "classics"—that is, as models of perfection in the direction attempted. His "Doryphorus" or "Spear-bearer" (Plate 69, a) was known as "the Canon", as being a model of proportion, on which subject Polycleitus wrote a treatise. Unfortunately, we are compelled here again to rely upon inferior marble copies of an original in bronze, copies which probably do injustice to their model in exaggerating its heaviness and muscularity. Another fine athletic type, of later date, is that of the "Apoxyomenus", the athlete engaged with the strigil in scraping off the oil with which all athletes, and especially wrestlers, were anointed (Plate 90, b). Of all statues dealing with the Games one of the most impressive is the bronze charioteer discovered by the French at Delphi (Plate 70 and Plate 72, a). There is a wonderful calm and dignity about the robed figure. The long folds of his charioteer's dress, like those of the garment of Athena on the metope from the temple of Zeus at Olympia (Plate 73, a) seem to match the columns of a Doric temple.

To be naked and unashamed was one of the glories of the cultivated Greek. It astonished (and still shocks) the barbarian. When Agesilaus, the Spartan king, was fighting on Persian soil he caused his Oriental captives to be exhibited naked to his men, in order that they might have no more terror of the great king's myriads. Alone among civilised peoples of the earth the ancient Greek dared to strip his body to the sun, and this too, as Thucydides witnesses, came from the manly city. "The Lacedaemonians," he says, "were the first to use simple raiment of the present style, and in other respects were the first to adopt a similar scale of living for rich and poor. They were the first to strip and undress in public, for anointing with oil after exercise. Originally the athletes used to wear loin-cloths about their middles even at the Olympic Games, and that practice has not long been discontinued" (actually in 720 B.C.). "Even now some of the barbarians, especially the Asiatics, continue to wear clothes at contests of boxing and wrestling. One might point to several other analogies between the customs of ancient Greece and modern barbarism." With female nudity the case is different. Although the girls of Sparta used to strip for their gymnastic exercises, that was a notorious Spartan idiosyncrasy. It is only in the later periods that feminine nudity is exhibited in Greek art. Hear Plato on the subject: Socrates has been led by the logic of his argument into the assertion that the women of the Ideal Republic ought to be educated just like the men, to go through the semi-military training of the wrestling school and the gymnasium along with them. The only objection he can see to such a course is that the public exercises of women would appear *ridiculous* to the Athenians of his day. That objection he dismisses as follows:

"Well, then," says Socrates, "as we have begun the argument we must take the rough with the smooth, and we must beg the wits to leave their usual trade and be serious. They must remember that it is not very long since it seemed to the Greeks ugly and ridiculous that men should appear naked, as it does now to most of the barbarians. And when the Cretans first, and after them the Lacedaemonians, began their stripped exercises the wits of the day had occasion to make fun of such things. Don't you suppose they did?"

"I do indeed."

"But when experience showed that it was better to strip than to cover the body, what the eye thought ridiculous was overwhelmed by what logic declared to be best, and it became apparent that it is only a fool who thinks anything ridiculous, except what is evil."

SPARTA

We turn naturally from Apollo and the Dorians to Sparta which was, in ancient times, the symbol and leader of the Dorian element in Greece, as Athens was of the Ionian. Yet it should be remembered that a city as different as Corinth was also Dorian, and that Argos the inveterate foe of Sparta was too. As the most important part of Greek history consists of the long duel between Sparta and Athens, and all our literature comes from Athens, posterity naturally tends to take sides against Sparta. And yet all those writers, from Herodotus to Aristotle, had a very real admiration for Sparta. Liberals, on the other hand, dislike Sparta, as representing oligarchy against democracy and as having sold the liberty of Greece to the Persians. And yet the Spartans practised a sort of equality, which the Athenians praised, as no people on earth have ever practised it, and in selling Greece to Persia they were only bidding against Athens with the freedom of others as the coin. Other people despise Sparta as the one Greek people which contributed hardly anything to literature and art. Yet until the later sixth century there is a recognisable if derivative and inferior Laconian art (though this is certainly the work of non-Spartiates), and the Spartans appear to have appreciated the uses of elegy and choral lyric, but mostly the work of alien poets. The fact is that Sparta is a paradox. One of the chief interests of Greek history is the extraordinary psychological contrast between the two chief actors. Sparta is the antithesis of Athens, and yet, if any one would know Greece, he must realise that both are essentially and characteristically Greek. Each is the complement of the other. Without Sparta

Greece would lack its most remarkable figure in the realm of politics, as well as its chief bulwark in land warfare. These are the two sides of Sparta on which we ought to fix our attention—the political system which gave her the best, or at any rate the most stable, government in Greek history, and the military education and discipline which gave her the finest army in the period of citizen armies.

Politically, all the Greek states, whether democracies or oligarchies, rest upon a double structure of council and assembly. In democracies the assembly is based on a very wide franchise, and possesses the actual control of the state, the council being limited to subordinate functions, executive and deliberative. At Athens, as we shall see, the council is more like a committee to prepare business for the assembly. In oligarchies, on the other hand, the assembly consists of a compara-tively small and select body of richer or nobler citizens, while the actual government is in the hands of the council. Sparta contained both these elements: an assembly of all the warriors, or Spartiates, with full rights, though these were comparatively a small proportion of the population of Laconia, and a *Gerousia*, or Senate, of thirty elders. But Sparta, though ranked as an oligarchy by the general opinion of Greece, was not, as Aristotle saw, a true or typical oligarchy. In the first place, the ruling council of regular oligarchies generally consisted of a close corporation co-opting its members, while the Spartan *gerontes* were elected by the whole body of the full citizens. In the second place, Sparta had developed an executive magistracy, which had a far more real share in the direction of the state than either the Senate or the Assembly. This perhaps was the secret of their efficient and stable government, for most Greek states had such a dread of personal ascendancy that they sacrificed unity and efficiency of admini-stration by placing their executive magistracies in a position wholly subordinate. It was not so at Sparta. There they had retained a recognisable kingship from the early times of the Dorian invasion right through their history, as no other really Greek state was able to do. They had two kings descending in parallel dynasties from pre-historic times, or, as they put it, from two Heraclid families. The origin of this double kingship is really lost in antiquity, though there are many theories about it, both ancient and modern. The most probable is that of two separate bands of Dorian invaders, each under its own king, uniting to conquer the valley of the Eurotas, and com-bining to form the state. In reviewing the kingship of Greek history

Aristotle places this Spartan system in a class by itself, calling it a "permanent hereditary generalship". By this time the office had lost, indeed, much of its political significance, and was notoriously subordinate to the Ephorate. The military leadership was by far the most conspicuous duty attached to the office. This is curious, for political experience commonly shows the opposite case; one of the first duties to be taken from a hereditary office is the military leadership, because of the peculiar need for personal capacity in that department. But Sparta was a singularly conservative and religious, not to say superstitious, city, devoted to ritual, and firmly believing in the general's luck. Such a people does not feel confidence under the leadership of mere talent; it much prefers to fight under the orders of a descendant of Herakles. And as Spartan warfare was always a very simple business, requiring no strategic skill in its direction, the Spartans were not likely to find out the weakness of a hereditary system in generalship. Beyond the leading of armies, the Spartan kings had few rights or duties. They had ex-officio titles to two of the thirty seats in the *Gerousia*, they had legal jurisdiction in some unimportant cases connected with religion, and they represented the state in certain festivals and sacrifices.

But the political executive in the fifth and fourth centuries was in the hands of the five Ephors, who controlled and sometimes even oppressed the kings. The origin of this peculiar and distinctive office is also lost in antiquity. Spartan tradition certainly believed in a time when the Ephorate was not; and on the whole the most probable theory is that the Ephorate was originally created by the kings as a subordinate office to act in their absence. Judging from actual history, it is too much to say that the Ephors were always supreme over the kings in practice; nearly all the great men of Spartan history—Leonidas, Cleomenes, Agesilaus, Agis, Cleombrotus—are its kings, and we know the names of relatively few Ephors. It was, in fact, a long fight between kings and Ephors for pre-eminence. As a general rule the board of Ephors no doubt directed the state's policy, but kings like Agesilaus seem to have had far more than a mere executive duty. What struck all observers was that Ephors sometimes summoned kings before them for trial, sometimes condemned them to death, and in ceremonial remained seated in the presence of the kings. The fact is that at Sparta sovereignty was felt to belong in a very real sense to the warrior body, and the Ephors expressed that sovereignty, as being directly elected by it. Especially in judicial matters they were supreme, and in a state which moved by clockwork under the control of a rigid discipline and fixed customs, though all the laws were unwritten, the heads of the judicial system naturally held the reins of government. The fact that the Ephors held their position by popular election is held to constitute a democratic element in the constitution. This gives rise to the theory, evolved by the successors of Aristotle in political philosophy, that the stability of the Spartan constitution depended on its adjustment of the three elements of policy—monarchy, aristocracy, and democracy. Sparta was thus considered to be the type of a Mixed Constitution. From Sparta the Greek historian Polybius applied the same theory to the government of Rome. Thence it was transferred by Montesquieu to the British Constitution, and thus has played an important part in the history of political science. So far as Sparta is concerned, the theory rests upon a false basis. Aristotle was undoubtedly right in terming Sparta an aristocracy, for the Spartiate body itself was a minority and a jealously guarded close corporation. Both the democratic and the monarchical elements in the state were largely an illusion. Moreover, Aristotle did not admit the propriety of applying the term "democracy" to a state which merely had some choice in the persons by whom it should be governed. "To govern and be governed in turn" was the essence of democracy to Aristotle, and he would certainly have called both the other examples of the Mixed Constitution, ancient Rome and modern England, aristocracies. To him, however, aristocracy was the best kind of rule. Did it not mean etymologically "government by the best"? Besides, there was the practical proof of excellence that Sparta alone was free from the ever endemic Greek disease of "stasis" or civil strife, and that Sparta alone of Greek states had never witnessed a successful revolution.

In the common meaning of the term also Sparta was an aristocracy. Her citizen body—the Spartiates, as they called themselves—were always a minority of nobles, living armed and watchful amid a great subject population of serfs. These helots were of the same blood as the neighbouring peoples of Messenia and Arcadia—that is to say, they were the old stratum of the Greek-speaking population—and if they had a chance would no doubt prove as intelligent and artistic as their ancestors. But no chance was given them; they were ruthlessly oppressed, cruelly exploited, and there was an organised secret service to remove any men of mark that might arise from their ranks. On the battlefield of Plataea every Spartan soldier was followed by seven Helots. Thus every Spartan is to be ranked with the mediaeval knight, though he fought on foot. Between these two classes of knights and serfs there was also an intermediate element—the Neighbours, or Perioikoi. They must represent a Dorian wave of conquest which in its turn had to yield, but which, being not alien, was treated on a superior footing. Though they had no political or social standing, the Perioikoi were not oppressed. They lived mostly in the country and on the sea-coast. They provided the sailors, the farmers, the craftsmen, and, so far as Laconia had any trade, the traders. They seem to have been generally contented with their lot, but we know singularly little about them.

The city of Sparta itself—the only unwalled city in Greece, planted on the banks of the Eurotas, under Mount Taygetus (Plate 7)—consisted, then, of a circle of knights and their slaves. The Spartiates formed a very exclusive and haughty clique of military men, extremely narrow and oppressive to those about and beneath them, ever vigilant against rebellion, and conscious that their spears and shields had to take the place of a wall for Lacedaemon. Among themselves they lived an absolutely equal communistic life. Their meals were provided at common mess-tables, each a little club with power to elect and reject its members. As this institution also prevailed among the Dorians of Crete, it is to be regarded as something very ancient and characteristically Dorian—unless, as some traditions say, Sparta in this point was copying Crete. It meant, of course, the complete absence of home and family life. It was by such habits that the Spartans remained a conquering race, victorious first over their Messenian neighbours in two long wars, the details of which are legendary, and then gradually extending their influence over the whole Peloponnesus, including their Dorian kinsmen of Argos and Epidaurus.

It is possible that the remarkable discipline and asceticism of Sparta which is proverbially linked with her name had gradually increased. British excavations have shown that seventh-century Sparta was not destitute of art, just as Dorian Crete was not. From the lyric poets of the seventh century, as noted above, we get glimpses of a Sparta not entirely ascetic or contemptuous of culture. On the contrary, she is a patroness of foreign poets like Tyrtaeus if, indeed, Tyrtaeus was foreign. But already she appreciates most the martial song and dance.

It must be remembered that in Greece poetry, music, and the dance were far more closely allied than with us. Not only did Greek dramatists originally train their own choruses in the dance and compose their own music, but even Hesiod in that Euboean competition had to chant his verses aloud. So at Sparta Terpander and Alcman were first musicians and secondly lyric poets, and Tyrtaeus, the elegist, whom some called an Athenian, was there to conduct martial dances and to train the boys of Sparta in their musical drill. Thus there was no contradiction in early times between strict military discipline and a love of choral lyric poetry. Afterwards, when music grew softer and poetry less martial, the Spartans banished all musicians and poets from their midst, though they retained the old marching tunes of antiquity. One of these poets, Alcman, seems to have come to Sparta as a captive from luxurious Lydia, and he does sing of unmartial things, but the small fragments of Tyrtaeus are all military themes:

> Come, ye sons of dauntless Sparta,
> Warrior sons of Spartan citizens,
> With the left advance the buckler,
> Stoutly brandish spears in right hands,
> Sparing not your lives for Sparta
> Such is not the Spartan custom.

Terpander (who came, it should be noted, from Lesbos, and was much admired at Sparta) praises Sparta for three things, the courage of her youths, her love of music, and her justice. A Spartan proverb, apparently ancient, runs: "Sparta will fall by love of wealth, naught else". They were, and always remained, a covetous people; but for that very reason when coined money began to be used in Greece about the end of the seventh century Sparta forbade its introduction lest commerce should taint the warrior spirit of her citizens, so that Sparta had no coinage until the third century, but continued to use, where money was necessary, the ancient clumsy ingots of iron. Change for five pounds at Sparta needed a cart to bring it home. But money is not the only form of wealth, and it is probably an Athenian lampoon which represents the Spartan as living on nothing but the celebrated black soup. As every Spartan had his land (the equality and inalienability of the lots is probably a later fiction), with a number of Helots to till it, while the young men spent their leisure in the chase, there was plenty to supply the Spartan larder, and to provide wine and sweetmeats for Lydian poets as well.

It was in education that the discipline is most characteristically "Spartan". From birth to death the Spartan was in the grip of an iron system. Indeed, it began before birth, for the Spartans are the only people in history who have dared to carry out the principles of modern eugenics. They trained the bodies of their girls with running and wrestling and throwing of quoits and javelins, that when the time came they might bear stalwart sons, and bear them bravely. "The Law-giver," says Plutarch, "put away all coquettishness and hysteria and effeminacy by making the girls strip for processions, dances, and choruses at the temples, with the youths present as spectators. This stripping of the maidens involved no shame, for modesty was there and lewdness was absent, but it produced unaffected manners, and a desire for physical fitness, and it gave the female sex some taste of a not ignoble pride, in that they too had their share of manly worth and ambition to excel. Whence came to them that thought which is expressed in the traditional repartee of Leonidas' wife Gorgo. A foreign woman remarking to her, 'You Laconians are the only women who rule the men', 'Yes', she said, 'we are the only women who are the mothers of *men*'."

The strongest moral suasion compelled Spartan men to marry. The marriage customs of Sparta were peculiar and carry us back to the remotest antiquity. The bridegroom carried off his bride by a pretence of violence, and the bride cut her hair short and dressed like a man. There was no marriage feast; the young husband dined at his mess-table, visited his young wife by stealth, and returned to barracks. Sometimes a wife bore children to a man whose face she had never seen. The child was not considered to belong to his father, but to the city. "The Law-giver thought it absurd to take trouble about the breed of horses and dogs, and then let the imbecile, the elderly, and the diseased bear and beget children." There was another celebrated Spartan repartee about adultery:

"We have no adulterers in Sparta."

"Suppose you had, what is the penalty?"

"The fine is a big bull that jumps over Taygetus and drinks up the Eurotas."

"My dear sir, how could there be such a monstrous animal?"

"My dear sir, how could there be adultery at Sparta?"

33. Inlaid daggers from Shaft Grave Circle A at Mycenae.

34. (a) *left* Gold death-mask from Shaft Grave Circle A.
    (b) *above* Ivory group of two women and a child. Found on the citadel of Mycenae.

35. (a) Fresco fragment from Mycenae.
     (b) Beazle of a gold ring from Mycenae.

36. (a) *right*
Gold cup found in the Vaphio *tholos* tomb in Laconia.

(b) *left*
Ivory pyxis from the grave of a Mycenaean "princess" on the side of the Areopagus Hill at Athens.

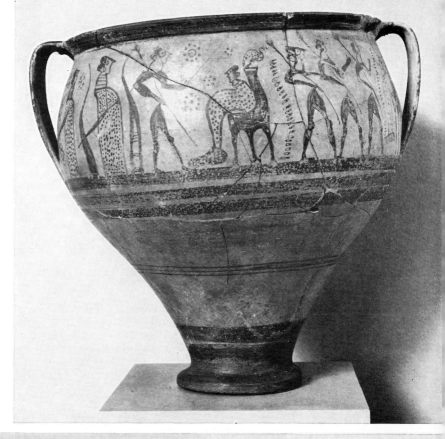

right
Mycenaean
riote mixing bowl.

below
Mycenaean
ng bowl from the
use of the Warrior
e" at Mycenae.

(a)

38. Pottery from the Potters' Quarter (Kerameikos) of Athens, showing the transition
from Late Mycenaean to Protogeometric.

(b)

(c)

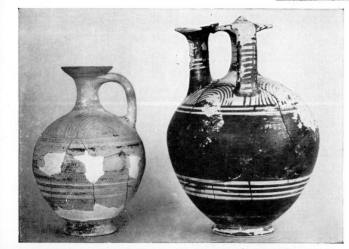

39. (a) *left*   Geometric style ivory "goddess".

    (b) *above* Bronze stag group in the Geometric Style.

    (c) *below* Corinthian Geometric mixing bowl.

40. (a) Cup found in the Austrian excavations on Ischia (Pithekoussai).
    (b) A scene of "lying-in-state" from an Attic standed mixing-bowl.

1. (a) *above* Bronze bowl from the Kerameikos Cemetery, Athens.

(b) *right* A bronze libation bowl from a great tomb at Gordion.

(c) *below* Athenian Geometric jug from the Dipylon Cemetery.

42. (a) *above* Bronze gong from the Idaean Cave.

(b) *top right* "Phoenician" silver-gilt bowl from an Etruscan tomb at Palestrina, Italy.

(c) *right* Alphabet incised on an ivory writing-tablet from Marsigliana.

43. (a) *far left* Bronze relief plaque found at Olympia.

(b) *centre* Ivory figure, "The Lion Tamer", found at Delphi.

(c) *right* Ivory sphinx from Perachora.

(d) *Below* Ivory plaque from the archaic temple of Artemis at Ephesus.

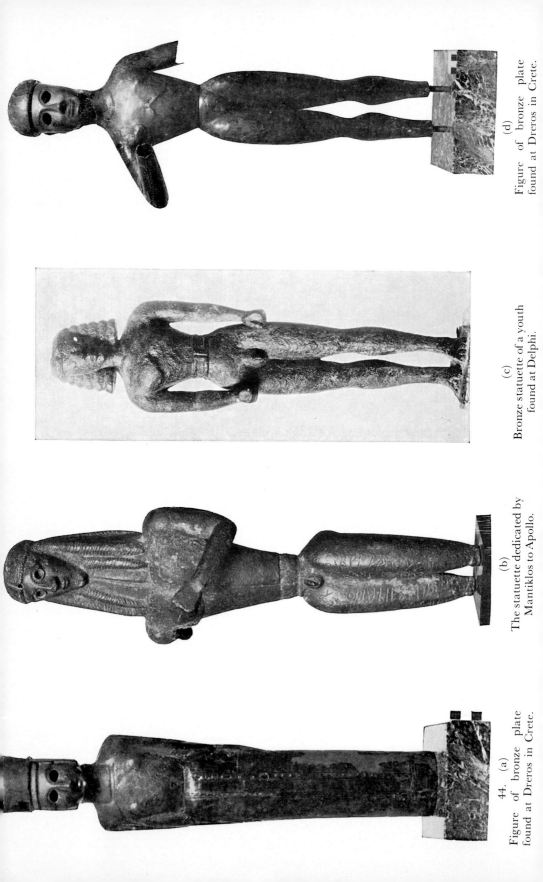

44. (a)

Figure of bronze plate found at Dreros in Crete.

(b)

The statuette dedicated by Mantiklos to Apollo.

(c)

Bronze statuette of a youth found at Delphi.

(d)

Figure of bronze plate found at Dreros in Crete.

(a) *right* The Auxerre Statuette.

(b) *above* Ivory figure of a priestess from the archaic temple of Artemis at Ephesus.

46. (a) *above* The Macmillan aryballos.
    (b) *left* Corinthian jug (olpe).

(c) A portion of the Chigi Jug (olpe) from Formello.

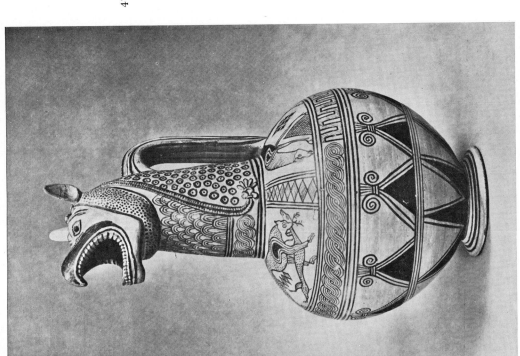

47. (a) *left*
Jug from one of
the Cyclades islands.

(b) *right*
An "Island" style
amphora (so-called
"Melian").

48.
The site of Olympia,
the Altis enclosure
and the temple of
Hera.

At birth the babe was taken away from its parent to a hall where the elders of the tribe sat to examine it. If it was plump and strong they said, "Rear it". If not it was exposed to die in a cleft of the mountain. "For they thought better, both for it and the city, that it should die than that it should live if it was not naturally healthy and strong. That was why the women washed it with wine instead of water as a test of its strength." They had scientific methods of rearing babies, no swaddling-clothes, no fear of the dark or solitude. Foreigners used to hire Laconian women for their nurses.

As soon as they were seven years old the children were drafted off into "herds". The most "sensible and combative" of each herd was made prefect, whose orders the others had to obey implicitly and suffer his punishments without wincing. The older men watched them at their play, and set them to fight one another. They learnt letters, but nothing else except music and drill. They walked without sandals, and generally played naked.

At the age of twelve they were allowed one mantle a year but no tunic. "They had no experience of baths and unguents; only for a few days each year they were allowed such luxuries." They slept in their "herds" on rushes, which they had to gather from the river-banks. "In winter they used to mix thistle with their bedding, from the idea that there was some warmth in them." At this age they began to associate with older youths on those curious terms of male love peculiar to the Greeks. Their elders would take a fatherly interest in the achievements of their beloved, chastise and encourage them.

Also, there was a public tutor appointed from among the grown-up nobles for each "herd", as well as prefects from the wisest and most warlike of the youths of twenty. The latter had his "fags" entirely under his orders. Stealing of food was encouraged as a martial virtue likely to lead to sharpening the wits for warlike purposes. In a state which practised communism there was, of course, no dishonesty involved. If they were caught they were thrashed for their bad stealing. To encourage theft, their public rations were kept short. They were also thrashed for the good of their souls, to encourage endurance. "We have seen many of the youths die under the blows at the altar of Artemis the Upright," says Plutarch, or rather the authority he is quoting. But modern students consider that this flagellation at the altar was probably a religious ritual, of which there are many other examples. If the beater spared his victim the goddess manifested her displeasure.

After mess, at which he was waited on by his "fags", the prefect would address himself to their intellectual education. Some had to sing, to others he would put questions in ethical casuistry. "Who is the best of men?" "What do you think of this or that action?" The answer had to be brief and pointed—"Laconic", in fact. The boy had to give reasons for his answer. A bad answer was punished by a bite on the back of the hand, but if older men were present the prefect had to justify his punishments. If a boy cried out ignobly in fighting, his lover was punished also. But the real source of their education was in music, marching songs, and hymns in praise of the heroes of Spartan history. One such song is preserved:

> *Old Men.* We were warriors of old.
> *Men.*   As we are. Who doubts? Behold.
> *Boys.*   Some day we shall be more bold.

Laconic, but Spartan!

The Spartan youths did not neglect their personal appearance, especially in the matter of fine armour. They prided themselves on their long and well-groomed hair. In the pass of Thermopylae the Persian monarch was astonished to see the three hundred Spartans, who ought to have been trembling and saying their prayers, carefully combing their long hair. In war-time discipline was relaxed. When the line of battle was drawn up in the face of the enemy, first the king sacrificed a goat, and the warriors crowned themselves with garlands of flowers, while the flute-players played the song of Castor. Then they stepped forward gravely to the sound of the marching paean, all in step, without disorder or confusion, but "led gently and cheerfully by the music into danger". There was no fear, for the hymn "made them feel that the god was with them". When they had routed their enemy they only pursued so far as to assure defeat, "considering it neither gentlemanly nor Hellenic to cut and slay those who yielded and retired". This was the spirit of all their warfare; they never destroyed a beaten city, though they might dismember it.

As soon as they were of military age the army and the secret police, which kept watch on the Helots, took most of their time and thought. Arts, crafts, and business they considered the work of slaves. Dancing, singing, modest banquets, and hunting were their relaxations. It was not until the age of thirty that a Spartan could go into the agora and enjoy his rights as a citizen. Even then lounging in the market-place was not encouraged; most of the day was spent in the gymnasiums and clubs. There was no private family life whatever. King Agis, coming back victorious from a campaign, asked permission to dine with his wife. It was refused by the Ephors, whose power, no doubt, was derived from their position as overseers of this singular disciplinary system. The old men were highly honoured, and the supreme object of an old Spartan's ambition was a seat on the Senate.

And what type of character did this strange system produce? Well, it produced the three hundred warriors who died to a man round their king Leonidas at the pass of Thermopylae. It produced the Spartan king who refused the request of his allies to destroy Athens. It produced the women who mourned after the great defeat of Mantinea because no sons or husbands of *theirs* had died for Sparta. It produced the only good infantry of Greece, and the only stable form of government. It produced good men like Brasidas and Gylippus. Sparta was the state that swept tyranny out of Greece, and bore the brunt of the landfighting against the Persians. But, on the other hand, the system encouraged that stupid and bigoted conservatism which ruined Sparta, partly through refusing to learn anything new in the art of warfare, and partly through declining to supplement the dwindling warrior caste by extending the franchise to the other inhabitants of Sparta. No doubt, also, the strict discipline of life in the city led to the moral breakdown of her victorious generals Pausanias and Lysander when they came in contact with the fascinations of Eastern luxury. It made the Spartans oppressive and unjust when they had to govern an empire. The typical Spartan is narrow-minded, superstitious and covetous, but he is always brave, patriotic, and often chivalrous. Sparta has left us no art or literature after her early days, but she has left us an extraordinary experiment (for a warning) of aristocratic communism combined with unfettered militarism.

PALLAS ATHENA

Sparta and Athens are the counterparts and complements of one another: Sparta drilled, orderly, efficient, and dull; Athens free, noisy, fickle, and brilliant. Sparta's watchword in history is Eunomia (order); the motto of Athens is Eleutheria (liberty) and Parrhesia (free speech and free thought). But Sparta was orderly and powerful over the Peloponnese long before Athens was free or cultured.

Both Apollo and Athena were deities specially concerned with cities and good government. If Apollo was the god of prophecy music, poetry, and athletics, Athena's arts were those of the craftsman, the potter, and the weaver. Athena, though a fair, grey-eyed goddess, was nevertheless an enemy to love, wise in counsel and fond of battle. So strictly maidenly was she that they gave her a virgin birth. No female had a hand in her making, for she sprang fully armed from the head of Zeus at a blow from the axe of Hephaestus. That was the scene depicted on the front gable of the Parthenon. The worship of Athena seems singularly pure and civilised; it is almost entirely free from magic and mystery, for Athena is emphatically a civic goddess, having hardly any obvious connexion with the powers of Nature. She is pure intellect. True, she has a pugnacious aspect, she is armed with spear and shield, and with a breastplate, or aegis, bearing the Gorgon's head and snaky coils of hair. It has been ingeniously suggested that the aegis had been evolved by art from the skin of a beast worn over the shoulders, with the fierce head hanging over the breast of the wearer, and the legend of Medusa the Gorgon invented to explain it. Or it was the magic goat-skin (aegis) combined with the rude grimace which averts evil. Anyhow, Athena is a hoplite goddess. Whatever connexion she may have with water elsewhere, at Athens she is armed for land warfare.

All these signs might suggest to us that the Athena worshipped on the Acropolis of Athens is not a primitive goddess. But most scholars are now agreed that her origin is to be sought in the remote past. Her name does not seem to be Greek, and Athena, the virgin goddess living proudly alone, is only a refined version of the Aegean Great Mother, dominating all created beings and owing allegiance to no man. She was the Lady of Athens, and from the city she took her name. Yet Athena has not only won her way into the circle of Olympian deities, but in that circle she holds a place of high honour. Already in Homer she is second only to Zeus, the most powerful champion of the Greeks at Troy. She is far more thoroughly Hellenised than other aspects of the Great Mother: than Artemis for instance, round whom something of the Aegean flavour of wild life always clings, or Aphrodite, who in Homer receives scant respect. Probably she was the first form of the Mother to be encountered by the Greeks. The Athenians boasted themselves to be an aboriginal people of the old stock, whatever that might mean (though they distinguished themselves from the mysterious Pelasgians), but at the coming of the earlier Greek speakers, most probably at the beginning of the Middle Bronze Age in the twentieth century B.C. Attica received its quota like other regions. Thucydides tells us that in the periods of disturbance invaders passed by the stony promontory of Attica as beneath their notice, and hence the Athenian boast that they were of unmixed blood, but this statement of Thucydides only refers to the latest invaders, the Dorians. Other Greek tribes, whose Greek we know from the Linear B tablets, and whom we may call Old Achaeans, were in Greece so early that practically all tradition of their coming was lost; among these, in the combined ethnic and dialect pattern evolved later by the Greeks, were the Ionians, and the dialect of Athens is akin to Ionian. Once it was believed that a celebrated mythological event, represented on the western pediment of the Periclean Parthenon, had some ethnical significance, a struggle of two peoples variously identified. This was the contest of Athena and Poseidon for the land of Attica; when, some said, Poseidon smote the rock of the Acropolis and produced the horse, or at any rate a salt spring and was outdone by Athena with her more useful gift of the olive. The most obvious identification, for those who hold to a division of "Aegean" and "Northern" peoples, is of Athena (as suggested above) with the old fertility goddess of the primitive layer of Aegean cultivators, and of Poseidon with the "northern" incoming pastoral nomads. After all Poseidon was god of horses and protector of aristocrats, brother of Zeus the Sky God. But it is not quite so easy. The same difficulties arise in these ethnic appropriations of gods as with Apollo and Athena. Poseidon was god of earthquakes, and brother also of Hades god of the underworld, and bulls are his offerings. Sometimes, even in Attica, we find Poseidon associated closely in cult with Athena, as Poseidon Hippios, god of horses, but with Athena Hippia. Some of his characteristics, such as bulls and earthquakes, seem to fit well into a Minoan context; and even if he is an in-comer, he is not a late in-comer, for he appears as a recipient of offerings in Old Achaean Greek Cnossus, and at Pylos, where Nestor in the Odyssey is also found offering him a splendid bull. It is a complex and confused situation, in fact, and for the moment we should be content in our ignorance.

In all the elaborate rebuilding of Periclean days the rock of Acropolis was pretty thoroughly scoured of ancient remains. But we still see the remains of prehistoric masonry, as at Tiryns and Mycenae, forming what the Athenians called "the Pelasgic Wall". In fact quite a fair amount of Mycenaean Athens survives, even traces of the palace which stood on the Acropolis, and Mycenaean tombs (cf. Plate 36, *b*) on the slope of Areopagus. To that period we might ascribe such traditional royalties as Cecrops, Erechtheus, and Pandion, possibly real names of prehistoric kings who ruled over the rock and part of the plain below, but by no means over the whole of Attica. In artistic representation these ancient worthies are rather apt to develop serpents' tails in place of their lower limbs; if some of them are just culture ancestors or faded gods, others of them may be really half-forgotten Aegean princes. It is not likely that Athens was ever a citadel of equal importance with Mycenae or Cnossus. Its inhabitants lived mainly by agriculture and the soil of Attica was proverbially thin and poor. There was an Athenian contingent in the Achaean host before Troy, but together with its king Menestheus it plays rather a humble part. Yet Attica has yielded a fair number of relics of the Bronze Age.

The great legendary King of Athens was Theseus, a figure much embroidered by later mythologists because he had been made the patron hero of the Athenian democracy and the synoecist of Athens—that is, the man who made Attica into a city-state instead of a congeries of village communities. That is certainly not history. Prehistoric Attica, which may variously be defined as Achaean or Late Bronze Age or Mycenaean Attica, was certainly not united in the manner of the classical land, even if it was dominated by the king who ruled from the rock of the Acropolis. There is clear evidence of other centres, of which dim memories survived in legend. After the dissolution of the Bronze Age civilisation of Greece, in what we call (for want of a better term) the Dark Age, Attica must have suffered the same fragmentation as other regions, and had to be united or reunited. It seems to have been a long process. In fact it was not physically completed until the seventh century, or spiritually until the late sixth. Theseus was a symbol of this union or synoecism, and a curious figure in himself in some details of his career. Some legends seem to represent him as an alien, others as a son of Poseidon; his adventures resemble those of another mixed Mycenaean ruler and culture-hero, Heracles.

Theseus' Cretan adventure with the Minotaur in the Labyrinth links Athens and Cnossus in some obscure way. Legend also credited him with a carrying-away of Helen in her earlier youth before she received the attentions of Paris; she was recovered by her brothers Castor and Pollux and Theseus was expelled to be replaced by Menestheus, who led the Athenian forces to Troy. Theseus died in exile at Scyros, and his sons served at Troy under an alien banner; but then they replace Menestheus as rulers of Attica. There were thus narrated confusion and changes of rulers, as before in the earlier saga, which told of Pandion and his sons, and later, when Melanthus came from Messenia displaced by the Dorians, took the place of an unworthy descendant of Theseus, saved Athens, and founded a Neleid dynasty. He was followed by Codrus who preserved Athens, so it was said, from the Dorians at the cost of his own life. Both Codrus and Theseus show elements of folktale, and Theseus was a useful symbol of union, as mentioned above. When, after the Persian Wars, the bones of a giant were found in Scyros they were at once recognised as those of Theseus, and brought with great ceremony to be reinterred at Athens.

In terms of heroic saga Athens and Attica appear as the scene of much strife. Later, however, when the Dorians came to Greece, it was believed that Athens escaped conquest thanks to Codrus, in whose honour the kingship was abolished. We need not believe that events went quite like that. Under the story must lurk the truth that Athenian kingship dissolved into an aristocracy, and in any case may well have exercised dominion over part of Attica only, which had yet to be united. Then there follows a long period of obscurity, in which we are hard put to it to find anything to say about Attica at a time when other states were sending out colonies and suffering internal strife.

Archaeologically speaking the picture is also difficult to interpret. Attica was held to be the recipient of refugees in the disturbed times after the Dorian invasion, and a spring-board for emigration to Ionia. This process of colonisation appears, from excavations in Asia Minor to have commenced some two hundred years after the great disaster which overtook late Bronze Age Greece. What happened before that is obscure. Western Attica may well have suffered in the inroads of the Dorians, while Eastern Attica largely escaped. In any case the record of burials and excavation in the Potters' Quarter of Athens (the Kerameikos) is not easy to explain. But it seems clear that a pottery tradition of continuous development (see above, page 40 and

Plate 38) existed and continued in Attica, and that Athens may well have been a centre of diffusion of the earliest style of Geometric decoration which characterised this post-Mycenaean period, just as later Athens is the chief exponent of the developed Geometric style, shown in the splendid great vases displaying in silhouette scenes of funerals, sea-battles, chariot-processions and the like (Plate 40, *b*), which may be epic scenes or else scenes of contemporary daily life. If they are the latter then the wealth of some Athenians must have been high to match the remarkable potters' and painters' technique it encouraged. In the later eighth century objects of oriental material (Plate 39, *a*) appear, and objects of oriental style and manufacture (Plate 41, *a*). In common, therefore, with other centres such as Crete (Plate 42, *a*), Corinth (Plates 46, *a*, 43, *c*), Delphi (Plate 43, *b*), Olympia (Plate 43, *a*) Athens shows renewed contact with the Eastern Mediterranean. The effects are abundantly apparent as these new influences break up the Geometric style of decoration and replace it (as elsewhere) with the exuberant turmoil of what is called the Orientalising style. This, by the first half of the sixth century, is sobered into the splendid earliest stages of the monumental black-figure and its derivatives (Plate 50, *a* and *b*).

Athens as a state did not engage in colonisation; earlier she may have possessed a fleet and engaged in sea battles, but this maritime activity had disappeared by the seventh century. Athens must also have developed a hoplite army, but we know nothing of any stresses set up in this way. She must certainly have had a wealthy aristocracy, who somehow in the late seventh century became a clique of oppressive landowners whose farms were largely worked for them on the *métayer* system, by which the tenant pays a certain proportion of the produce to the proprietor. There is much obscurity in all this, but in this connexion we hear of the first Athenian statesman who emerges as a clear personality, namely Solon, and of the first major appearance of Athens in Greek history. The events of Solon's times and after seem to show that Attica had not yet attained the unity it subsequently had, and this may account for the obscurity of her earlier history.

The troubles which Solon had to face were agrarian troubles connected with boundary-stones. He reckons income in bushels of corn and oil. His enactments, or the ancient laws which pass under his name, are largely concerned with dogs and wolves and olive-culture. The only export permitted is that of olive oil. Even after Solon the local parties that divide the state are not divisions of city-dwellers, but of country folk—the shepherds of the hills, the farmers of the plain, and possibly the fishermen of the coast—or so the story goes. These facts emerge in spite of subsequent Athenian historians, who, to please the *amour propre* of a democratic city, tried to make out that democracy had existed long before the tyranny of Pisistratus—in fact, as far back as Theseus, and certainly Solon. But it is fairly clear to any one discounting this tendency and reading their early traditions impartially that until the time of the tyrants Attica was by no means a true city-state, much less a democracy. Until city life was developed democracy was impossible.

Strange relics of this agricultural life survive in the religious customs of Athens—as, for example, in the sacrifice called Diipolia or Ox-murder. "They choose," says Porphyry, "some girls as water-carriers, and they bring water for sharpening the axe and the knife. When the axe has been sharpened one person hands it and another hits the ox, another slaughters him, others flay him, and they all partake of him. After this they sew up the hide of the ox and stuff it with hay and set it up, just like life, and yoke it to the plough as if it were going to draw it. A trial is held about the murder, and each passes on the blame for the deed to another. The water-carriers accuse those who sharpened the knife, the sharpeners blame the man who handed it, he passes the guilt on to the man who struck, the striker to the slaughterer, the slaughterer blames the knife itself; and the knife, as it cannot speak, is found guilty and thrown into the sea." All these offices are held in certain families by hereditary right. The whole ceremony clearly points back to days when the ploughing ox was held sacred. The older worship of Attica is all agricultural. The Eleusinian mysteries are in honour of Demeter (the Earth-Mother), Kore, her daughter, also called Persephone, and Triptolemus, who brought corn from Egypt (Plate 71). There are the Athenian mysteries called Thesmophoria, in which the women cast mysterious objects, really pieces of decayed pig and dough in the shape of snakes and men, into clefts in the earth. They were intended to produce fertility in fields and women. There was the Hersephoria or Arrhe-phoria also, in which maidens carried baskets containing objects whose nature they must not know to the precinct of the goddess of child-birth. Tradition said that two girls did peep in, and saw a child and a snake, and cast themselves off the Acropolis in terror. The Skirophoria was similar; it included a rite of daubing the image of Pallas with the white clay which was used as a dressing for olive-trees. There was another ceremony in which young girls dressed as bears danced in honour of Artemis of Brauron. There were the three sacred ploughings of Attic soil every year. Besides snake-heroes and snake-kings, there was the wolf-god who became identified with Apollo, and the goat-god Pan. It is possible that Athena's owl is a relic of those days of Nature-worship in far-off Bronze Age times. Most of these cults may be Attic rather than Athenian, and are specially localised in the country demes. They visibly belong to the same religious area as the snaky figures of Cnossus; and, indeed, Crete figures largely in the mythology of this period. Anthropomorphic religious representation probably began at Athens with a rude female *xoanon*, or wooden pillar-like or plank-like statue, which received in due course the name of the warrior maiden Pallas Athena.

Athens thus comes rather late into Greek history. Only two facts stand out with any clearness from the period before the sixth-century tyrannies: the attempted tyranny of Cylon and the early law-giving. Both these facts were recalled by events of subsequent history. The attempt of Cylon involved a curse upon one of the greatest of Athenian families, the Alcmeonids, to which were related celebrated names like Megacles, Cleisthenes, Xanthippus, and Pericles. The Law-givers of Athens are indeed historical personages, which is more than we can say with any confidence for the Spartan Law-giver Lycurgus, but they have served as pegs for much legend and a good deal of deliberate falsification. Athens undoubtedly possessed ancient wooden tablets of laws (though it is rather a question whether they could have survived the two burnings of Athens by the Persians), and some of these laws probably bore the names of Dracon and Solon; but it is very certain that later orators lent weight to any old law they wished to quote with approval, by giving it one of these respectable names. On the other hand, we know that when Athenian writers began to take an interest in constitutional history, which was not until two hundred years later, they used Dracon and Solon to father their own theories, because it was possible to form the most conflicting views of what those legislators had really done. One great point was to make out that the democracy was as old as the hills, and in this sense Solon was made the inventor of the Assembly, the Council, and even the popular jury courts. Some ascribed to him the invention of the old Council of the Areopagus. Others maintained that Solon was not a democrat, but the author of a limited franchise on a property basis—in fact, of just the system that Theramenes and his party were proposing in 411 B.C. Others, again, went one better, and attributed a sort of democratic system to Dracon, a still earlier Law-giver, in spite of the fact that Solon had abolished all his laws except those about murder and blood-guiltiness. Thucydides, however, being a scientifically minded historian with an impartial love of truth, passes over this early period with the remark that people will accept without testing any sort of traditions even when they concern their own country. And that is the right attitude for us. There were no historians until the fifth century, no contemporary records whatever, except a very few ancient inscriptions, and the work of the lyric poets who flourished in the eighth, seventh, and sixth centuries. We have, indeed, a considerable bulk of poetry which passes under the name of Solon. Some of it is not above suspicion, for it includes a so-called prelude to a versified edition of his laws, and other lines written in a tone very unsuitable to a philosopher. But from the undoubtedly genuine portion we gather that Solon, so far from being an impartial mediator, collected a partisan following, vehemently attacked the rich, and then "gave to the people so much power as sufficeth, neither diminishing nor increasing their honour". His principal work was to codify the laws which had hitherto existed only in the bosoms of the nobles. He did a great deal to fix the existing social classes in Athens by arranging the people in four ranks according to their incomes, reckoned, of course, on the basis of land-holding. And he removed agrarian grievances by forbidding loans on the security of the person, a custom which had led to the actual enslaving of the poor by the rich land-owners. In these ways he did an immense service to the future liberty of his country. Even a cautious estimate of his work makes him a very great man. But he was not the inventor of democracy.

His personality is hopelessly involved in legend. He is one of the Seven Sages, doubtless real personalities whose names have served as a peg for the inventive faculties of the Greeks. Some of them were natural philosophers, like Thales of Miletus, whose knowledge of astronomy was so exact that he predicted the eclipse of 585 B.C. He is said to have learnt his scientific knowledge, as Solon is said to have learnt his legislative skill, in Egypt, where he measured the height of the pyramids by their shadows. There is very likely a substratum of truth in the stories which make the birth, or rather the revival, of learning in Greece come from Egypt and Babylon. Thales knew that the light of the moon came from the sun. He was the first of those natural philosophers of Greece whose main object was to find the "principle" of the universe. Thales held that all things originated from water. Another of the Seven was Bias of Priene, whose activities were mainly political, and who invented maxims like "He is unfortunate who cannot bear misfortune", and "If thou hast done a good deed ascribe it to the gods". At least two of the other four were tyrants. Solon is also associated with a curious figure who went about expounding religion and conducting purificatory rites, Epimenides the Cretan, who was supposed to have lived for fifty years in a cave on nothing but asphodels and water, the father of all hermits. Whatever constitutional enactments Solon did make were not fully effective. They were intended to avert a tyranny; but in fact the tyranny of Pisistratus and his sons followed after a period of party strife.

To return to the goddess: only two passages of Homer refer to Athens, and both may have been interpolated at the editing of Homer in the days of Pisistratus or later. Both allude to the connection between Athena and Erechtheus. The goddess is described in one place as visiting "the goodly house of Erechtheus", which probably means the old Mycenaean palace on the Acropolis; in the other she has received Erechtheus, the son of Earth, into "her own rich shrine". The early shrine of Athena upon the Acropolis has been discovered on the north side of the Parthenon and south of the so-called Erechtheum. It would seem to have been a building of the sixth century or earlier, and to have been surrounded with a peristyle of columns by a later hand—whose we shall presently see. This is the "old temple" later overshadowed by the Parthenon. Our "Erechtheum", so well known for its Caryatid porch, was built right up against this old temple, so that the Caryatid porch juts out over the stylobate of it. In the old temple was the old cult image of the goddess afterwards supplemented by the splendid creation of Pheidias. It was an archaic image, of olive-wood, in a sitting posture, its rude shape doubtless concealed with offered drapery. Later another statue may have been set up on the Acropolis, armed with spear, shield, aegis, and helmet, and standing in act to strike. As the illustration (Plate 50, *a*) shows, this became a favourite motive in the portraiture of the goddess; she stands there as the champion and protectress of the city. Phidias idealised this type in his Athena Promachos. But it does not seem to be very ancient. Certainly in Athens, as at Troy, the earlier Pallas was seated, upon whose knees the women laid their embroidered "peplos". It may not have been until Athens became a real city-state, that the great cult of the Warrior Goddess began on the Acropolis.

TYRANNY AND CULTURE

All this time art has been slowly reviving. Lyric poetry and music had found a patroness among others in the advancing city of Sparta. The Heroic and Olympian cults which were fostered by the epic poets and by the influence of the Delphic oracle undoubtedly gave an impetus to art, partly by requiring temples and temple statues, and partly by fixing certain artistic types for the principal deities.

It is also true to say that an increase in trade and wealth had something to do with it. The vase-painter, as noted above in the case of Athens, was influenced by objects imported from the eastern Mediterranean (Plates 41, a; 42, a and b; 43), and by imitations of these in Crete, Asia Minor, and Greece, to get away from the rigidity and convention of the Geometric style, and broaden his repertoire to include curvilinear and floral motives, sometimes in a rich carpet-like manner, with outline drawing and added colour. This happened alike in Greece, as for example in Athens, Corinth (Plate 46), in Crete, and in Asia Minor and the Aegean Islands (Plate 47). In some cases it must be agreed that oriental craftsmen, such as metal workers, came to Greece, and Greek craftsmen went to the East Mediterranean and saw Assyrian palaces and the like, or brought back carpets and Phoenician bric-à-brac, including those bowls decorated with concentric bands of figures (Plate 42, b) which combined with memories of Minoan-Mycenaean inlay to inspire the description of Achilles' shield (above, page 47). In the repertoire of the East were not only floral patterns but also figure scenes and animals, real and imaginary—and the Greeks imagined still more. There was also much major sculpture, late Hittite, for instance, and Egyptian; there were also great buildings to amaze the Greek visitor. The latter, in the limited circumstances of the earlier Iron Age had been accustomed to art mostly on a minor scale, though there had been fine tripods of bronze, also imitated in clay (Plate 38, c). But the angular geometric models of humans and animals were small, whether in ivory (Plate 39, a), terracotta, or bronze (Plate 39, b), though there could be larger terracotta cult statuettes and bronze figures built up of plates on a wooden core, not unlike the later examples (Plate 44, *a* and *d*) from Dreros in Crete. This is still true in the seventh century (Plate 44, *b* and *c*), and some works of art show a pronounced oriental character (Plate 43, *b*). But some larger works were also produced (like the Auxerre statuette, Plate 45, *a*), which might be brightly coloured; and architectural sculpture, used for the decoration of buildings, is also known from this period. Thus the foundations were laid for the development outlined earlier (above, pages 76-77).

The vase-painter now introduces a figure style proper and identifies his pictures by inscriptions. He was enabled to do this by the introduction of alphabetic writing. Those who went to the east Mediterranean encountered there the Phoenician alphabet and adapted it to Greek uses. It appears to have been in common use by the Greeks in the eighth century, as the clay cup from Ischia shows with its scratched reference to the Cup of Nestor (Plate 40, *a*). It appears in Athens in mid-eighth century on a jug, perhaps a prize for dancing (Plate 41, *c*), and at Corinth. Alphabetic writing was not confined to the Greeks. It appears in Phrygia at Gordion scratched in beeswax on a libation bowl (Plate 41, *b*), and on a writing-tablet from Etruria (Plate 42, *c*). It represented a great step forward, and made possible the writing down of epic poetry, and other verse as well, the recording of laws and the inscription of dedications (such as the Apollo dedicated by Mantiklos, Plate 44, *b*), and the drawing up of lists such as names of yearly magistrates. For the vase-painter an anonymous figure scene could become an illustration of an epic incident.

The opening up of Egypt showed the Greeks what might be done in sculpture and architecture, and the accumulation of wealth was facilitated by the development of trade and the invention of coined money following on the use of unstamped ingots (Plate 49, *a*). There was a consensus of opinion in Greek antiquity that coinage was an invention made in Asia Minor, and we may suggest that the inventors were either the cities of the western coast or the rulers of Lydia inland, and the purpose either trade or the payment of mercenaries. From Asia Minor where coins were struck of a natural mixture of gold and silver called electrum, with rude stamps (Plate 49, *b*, *c* and *e*), in the second half of the seventh century, the invention passed to Greece, to Aegina (Plate 49, *d*) and to other Greek states (Plate 49, *h-j*) including Corinth and Athens. From the electrum coinage of Lydia

(Plate 49, *f*) were evolved a bimetallic coinage of silver and gold by Croesus (Plate 49, *g*) and the famous Persian gold daric (Plate 49, *k*) and silver siglos. So began the period when money not birth made the man, and the period of the evolution of Greek art when artists begin at length to depict the heroic mythology, and to evolve types which can be imitated and improved. Of this something has been said already. This fixing of types or motives was essential to the progress of ancient art. The Greek sculptor does not carve a statue, as novel and original as possible, to send to an exhibition of art. He is commissioned to make, we will say, an Athena; in that case he has to express the armour, the aegis, the owl, perhaps the snake. He tries, indeed, to make the goddess as lovely and strong and benignant as he can. Perhaps he is allowed to choose between the Promachos type or the seated statue, but in any case the type is fixed for him. Or he may be asked to make an athlete statue; in that case he will have to carve a nude male figure as physically perfect as possible, in an athletic attitude. He will not be asked, yet, to portray accidental facts, such as the lineaments of the particular man the statue is to honour. That is how, by concentrating on a limited number of motives, Greek art succeeded in a few generations in approaching so near to perfection.

This development did not depend purely on artistic competence, though this played a great part. The small and poverty-stricken potentates and cities of the "Dark Age" could do little, by reason of their low standard of life. For the most part their cult statues were primitive and their temples of mud-brick and thatch; their "palaces" were very modest places compared with the Mycenaean (see above, page 59). Certain developments had to take place in ideas, in politics, in trade, and the concentration of wealth; the great religious centres of Delphi and Olympia also had to grow up. We must look to changes particularly in the polis to explain this artistic development.

The little states of old, with their natural citadels, provided a splendid opportunity for any ambitious and unscrupulous person who wished to make himself tyrant. All you had to do was to stand forth as champion of the oppressed "demos" against the oppressive aristocracy, declare that your life was in danger, acquire a bodyguard of a few score stout knaves armed with spears, or even cudgels, then seize the citadel, and, if you had not forgotten provisions, you were an established tyrant. It was a simple trick that was often tried in Greek history, and it nearly always succeeded. They had to have followers, and these were not always the socially and economically most depressed class in the state. It is interesting to note that there is a connexion with the *hoplite* army, the army of sturdy foot soldiers, modest farmers who had an opportunity of asserting themselves against a steadily narrowing aristocracy when arms and armour became more plentiful (Plate 46, *c*). For example, at Corinth there was a singularly offensive aristocracy called Bacchiads. One of them had a deformed daughter who was permitted to marry beneath her. Her son, Cypselus, was not received in Bacchiad circles; he felt aggrieved, and he adopted the programme I have indicated. He founded a little dynasty which lasted more than seventy years, until it was put down by the Spartans in the first half of the sixth century. The same thing had happened a little earlier at Sicyon; it was repeated at Megara a little later, and at Epidaurus. At Athens the first attempt by Cylon, about 630, failed; at Miletus a similar attempt succeeded. In the sixth century tyranny broke out everywhere in Sicily. In 560 Athens followed suit with the tyranny of Pisistratus. Polycrates of Samos comes about thirty years later. Thus many states in Greece went through the tyrannical phase about this time.

Although the Greeks, to their eternal honour, ever afterwards detested the name of tyrant, and although they tried to expunge the benefits they owed to them from the tablets of their history, yet we can see that tyranny was a valuable, almost a necessary, stage in the progress of the Greek state. Anything is better than aristocracy of Bacchiad type; even a tyrant has the merit of possessing a single throat. As a matter of fact, most of the Greek tyrants, with the exception of Phalaris of Acragas, who had a habit of roasting his subjects in a brazen bull, were intelligent and not oppressive rulers. They were able to form a consistent foreign policy, which is always the strong point of autocracies, to found colonies, acquire empires, form alliances, and marry their neighbours' daughters. We hear of tyrants having relations with Egypt and Lydia, and importing copper from Spain. At home they policed their cities and made them appreciate the benefits of order. Above all, no doubt from sordid motives, they encouraged commerce. The flourishing commerce of Minoan days had ceased with the end of the thalassocracy. Piracy had become rife on the Aegean, as we see in Homer, where no visitor thinks it impolite to be asked whether he is or is not a pirate. For art and literature, here at last were the patrons. It is under the tyrants of the late seventh and sixth centuries that the art revival begins.

Corinth, with her mighty natural fortress (Plate 9, *a*) more than a mile in circuit and 1800 feet high, her two seas and her command over a narrow isthmus (Plate 9, *b*), was admirably situated for commerce. She was one of the earliest states to develop a tyranny, to found an overseas dominion, and to revive the arts. Her colonies were mostly towards the west, and in Corcyra she had a valuable stepping-stone for Sicily and Italy. It is at Corinth that the new type of "orientalising" vase-painting reaches its maximum of development in the second half of the seventh century.

Through the seventh century at Corinth as elsewhere the Geometric style (Plate 39, *c*) was disintegrated by influences from the Near East. Floral patterns from Assyrian palaces, late Hittite and Assyrian lions, monstrous animals and everyday ones make their contribution to a style which eventually, in its close texture, resembles an embroidered or woven textile or carpet. And such from the East may in part have inspired it. Eventually, however, its neat precision (Plate 46, *b*) and fantastic miniature quality (Plate 46, *a*) could not stand mass production; nor could the best of its vases decorated in a figure style such as that of the Chigi Jug (Plate 46, *c*). Decline was inevitable, though Corinthian pottery left its mark on other fabrics including that of Attica. Later in the seventh century and in the early sixth Corinthian potters depicted Greek legends on their vases, but in this they could not compete with Athens who overshadowed and displaced them. The coin types of Corinth in the sixth century are already beautiful designs (Plate 49, *i*). It was Cypselus, tyrant of Corinth, who dedicated at Olympia a famous chest covered with mythological scenes in parallel bands, of which Pausanias has left a long description. A celebrated gold bowl in Boston Museum is also a dedication of the same family. Periander, his son, was originally one of the Seven Sages, though Plato wanted to cast him out for a tyrant. The name of the third, Psammetichus, proves the close intercourse of Corinth with Egypt. The appearance of the name Cypselus at Athens seems to show the same for Corinth and Athens. It was Corinth under her tyrants that evolved a new poetical form, the dithyramb; and in Corinth still stands part of a Doric temple, one of the earliest that remain in Greece proper (Plate 9, *a*), where, however, excavation has laid bare the foundations of more primitive structures; there are older temples also in the Greek colonies overseas. The grave and splendid Doric style of architecture took its rise from very humble beginnings in the Dark Ages; the tradition of the *megaron* of a Mycenaean palace may be preserved in it, for the home of the prince was a fit model for the house of a god. Egyptian influence may have played a part in determining that it should be built of stone, for the earliest Greek temples seem to have been of wood and sun-baked brick with thatched roofs. Such originally was the temple of Hera at Olympia, but as the wooden columns fell down one by one they were replaced with stone (Plate 48). In many features of Doric architecture it is possible to trace development from wooden technique. The whole roofing system is one of joists and beams, even when the roof is of stone. The triglyphs are the ends of the beams, translated into stone. The metopes were originally left open, then filled with painted terra-cotta slabs, and finally with slabs of stone carved in high relief. In the earliest Doric temples the columns are very thick and heavy and the intercolumnar spaces very narrow. These things indicate that the architecture had not yet fully realised the superior strength of stone. An ignorant or hasty glance might suggest that there was no progress in Greek architecture, but the close observer sees how the succeeding generations of architects continued to make subtle improvements rendering the shafts more graceful, the mouldings more refined in their curves, correcting most cunningly the optical illusions of a straight row of tall columns, improving the lighting arrangements, improving the masonry, substituting stone for wood and precious marble for stone, adding ornament where it was appropriate, as on the frieze inside the peristyle, rejecting it where it was unsuitable, as on the architrave, which, being a main beam, *ought* to look heavy and strong;—reaching forward, in fact to the *telos*, the ultimate end of the type which his predecessors had set him. That is the Greek way. The Parthenon is the goal at which this old temple of Corinth had been aiming.

Seven columns of the temple at Corinth (Plate 9, *a*) have stood through the Roman destruction of Corinth and all the subsequent batterings of history. Their antiquity is shown by their clumsy strength. The height of the columns is only about four and one third times the diameter of the base. Each column is a monolith of rough limestone which was originally covered with stucco and painted, in height 23½ feet, in diameter tapering rather sharply from the base

(5 feet 8 inches) to the top (4 feet 3 inches). The temple was peripteral—i.e. it had a colonnade all round the interior structure or cella, six columns at each end, fifteen on each side. Already there is an attempt to correct the optical illusion which makes horizontal lines seem to sink in the middle and vertical lines seem to bend inwards, the stylobate, or floor from which the columns rise, being slightly curved, so that the centre columns stand about 2 centimetres higher than those on the wing. The interior building consists of two oblong chambers back to back, without communication between them. The side walls are prolonged at each end under the colonnade. From the existence of the two separate chambers we conclude either that the temple united two distinct cults, or that one of the chambers was a treasury, for temples in Greece were always used as banks. I have gone into some detail in describing this building, because it is the oldest standing Doric temple of the full classical type in Greece; its date is about 550 B.C. Roof-tiles, which made a sloping roof possible, were said to be an actual Corinthian invention.

It was under these Cypselid tyrants that Corinth began to acquire her historical character of a luxurious, sensual, and cosmopolitan city particularly linked with the East. Aphrodite, as she was worshipped at Corinth, was none other than "Ashtoreth, the abomination of the Sidonians", and was imported along with the Tyrian purple from Phoenicia. She had a famous temple on the citadel of Corinth, which was thronged by her sacred slaves, the courtesans. Their numbers grew to more than a thouand, and they were a notorious snare to the commercial travellers of antiquity. You had to be a rich man to visit Corinth, as the proverb said:

οὐ παντὸς ἀνδρὸς ἐς Κόρινθον ἔσθ' ὁ πλοῦς.
non cuivis homini contingit adire Corinthum.

That this immoral state of affairs began under the tyrants we can be sure, though Periander is said to have collected all the procuresses he could find and drowned them in the sea. Pindar delicately sings of "the hospitable damsels, ministers of persuasion in wealthy Corinth". And we are told that when the Persians invaded Greece the courtesans flocked to the temple of Aphrodite to pray for the deliverance of the land. In gratitude for their patriotism bronze statues of them were erected, with an epigram by Simonides. Lais, the most celebrated of all these erring females, belongs to the time of the Peloponnesian

War, though there would appear to have been others who adopted her famous name. The other Greeks were apt to speak of Corinth in much the same tone as a modern Englishman or German speaks of Paris. The wealth of Cypselus is proved by his dedication of a colossal gold (or gilt) statue of Zeus at Olympia. Periander cut a canal through the promontory of Leucas, and projected another through the isthmus of Corinth.

One of the tyrants of Sicyon won the chariot race at Olympia, and dedicated two large model shrines of Spanish bronze. But Cleisthenes was the most celebrated for his luxurious court, for his hostility to Argos, which made him forbid the recital of Homer at Sicyon because it honoured the Argives, and for the wooing of his daughter Agariste, a famous event of the earlier sixth century which marked his greatness as much as his championship of Delphi in the First Sacred War. Cleisthenes had issued a general invitation to any one who wished to marry her to come to his court, offering them hospitality for a year. All the rich young gentlemen of Greece assembled. For a whole year Cleisthenes tested their accomplishments. By that time two Athenians were the favourites, Megacles, of the famous Alcmeonid family, and Hippocleides, who had the most charming social graces in the world. At last came the final day of decision. Hippocleides braced himself for a great effort. There had been a banquet, and perhaps Hippocleides had poured too many libations to Dionysus. After dinner the flute-players struck up, and Hippocleides began to dance. Let Herodotus continue the story: "And he danced, probably, for the pleasure of dancing; but Cleisthenes, looking on, began to have suspicion about it all. Then Hippocleides, after a short rest, ordered a slave to bring in a table: when it came, he began to dance on it, first Laconian figures and then Attic ones; finally he stood on his head on the table" (and this was perhaps an old ritual dance) "and gesticulated with his legs. But Cleisthenes, when he danced the first and second time, revolted from the idea of Hippocleides as a son-in-law on account of his indecorous dancing, yet he restrained himself, not wishing to make a scene. But when he saw him gesticulating with his legs he could not restrain himself any longer. 'O son of Tisander,' he cried, 'you have danced away your marriage.' But Hippocleides answered: 'Hippocleides doesn't care!' Hence this answer became a proverb." So Megacles married the lady, and lived happily ever afterwards, becoming the ancestor of Pericles, while

Hippocleides probably took to drink and went to the bad altogether. But this Herodotus does not inform us.

The tyranny at Megara was a brief one, but we know that Theagenes built an aqueduct for his city. More than this; Cylon of Athens was his son-in-law, and Theagenes aided him in his attempt at tyranny, and thus engaged Athens and Megara in a long struggle over Salamis which brought fame to Solon and Pisistratus.

At Athens this man Pisistratus stood forth, it is generally believed, as champion of the poor shepherds of the Hill against the wealthier parties of the Coast and the Plain. He succeeded where Cylon had failed in gaining command of the Acropolis with his bodyguard. Twice the Athenians managed to expel him, but each time he got back, the first time by dressing up a tall and handsome woman as the goddess Athena and driving into the city with her, and the second time by hiring support from elsewhere, with money which he had obtained by prudent operations in the goldfields of Thrace. From first to last he and his sons were in power from about 560 to 510. It is difficult to estimate his services to Athens, for later generations did their utmost to deny and conceal them, giving some of his achievements to Solon and some to Theseus, and some even to Erechtheus. He founded an early Athenian overseas empire. He recovered the island of Salamis from Megara, and until she possessed Salamis Athens had no open road to the sea. Later Athenians ascribed this feat to Solon. He regained Sigeum, on the Troad, after a war with Mitylene. He established the elder Miltiades as tyrant of the Thracian Chersonese. In these movements his policy was obviously to exploit trade with the Black Sea, the trading region of Ionia and the future granary of Greece. He extended olive-culture in Attica. He probably developed the silver-mines at Laurium, which were thenceforth an important source of Athenian revenue. He made the poverty-stricken tillers of the soil into peasant proprietors by confiscating the estates of his noble opponents. He was allied with Sparta and Argos, Thebes and Thessaly and Naxos. He introduced a police armed with bows into the city of Athens.

He probably did much of what Theseus is supposed to have done in synoecising Athens—that is, transforming Attica from a number of villages with a capital into a city-state with surrounding territory. We know that he sent judges on circuit round the country districts. The other indications are that Pisistratus constructed a proper water-supply, and that he fostered the worship of the Olympian or State deities. At the same time he fostered agriculture, and tried to get the poor of Athens back to the land. As he had owed his return to Athena, he signalised his gratitude by surrounding the old temple of Athena Polias with a marble peristyle and sculptures. Some of the sculptures of this period and earlier are preserved on the Acropolis of Athens. They were generally carved of the softer *poros* or rough limestone, and freely adorned with colour. But the decorations of Pisistratus' temple are of Parian marble. In the sixth century Athens became possessed of an outstanding school of sculptors in marble, not uninfluenced as time passed by the artists of the Aegean islands and of Ionia; while the dedications on the Acropolis, including the young women carved in marble, called *korai*, sometimes with painted patterns on their garments, show works obviously by foreign artists, including Ionians (Plate 56, *a*). These latter in their delicacy and grace (withdrawn and sweetly-smiling), the very embodiment in stone of Sappho's maidens, like some works found in Asia Minor (Plate 54, *b*) contrast strongly with the sturdy and powerful Attic works, such as the early Berlin Standing "Goddess" (Plate 53, *b*) which was perhaps a grave monument, the so-called Peplos Kore (so named because of the garment she wears), Plate 56, *b*, and, among male figures and much earlier, the Calf-Bearer dedicated by Rhombos (Plate 55, *a*). On the other hand, an Attic artist also produced the curled and elegant "Rampin Horseman" put together by the late Humfry Payne from a head in the Louvre and body and horse fragments from the Acropolis (Plate 55, *b*). In fact the sack of Athens by the Persians in 480 B.C. and the subsequent clearance and burial of the debris by the returning Athenians have preserved for us a great deal which would otherwise have been lost. On the plain below the Acropolis Pisistratus began a temple to Olympian Zeus on so huge a scale that republican Athens was unable to complete it until the Emperor Hadrian brought his immense resources into play.

But Pisistratus did more than building for religion. He may fairly be called the founder of the state cults of Athens. He reorganised the Greater Panathenaea as the symbol of union for Attica. This was a most solemn procession, held every four years, of all the people, to carry up a new embroidered robe as a gift to the Virgin Goddess on the Acropolis. That is the scene depicted on the frieze of the Parthenon which is now the chief glory of the British Museum

(Plate 76, *a*). Later Athenians, of course, ascribed the Panathenaea to Theseus or Erechtheus. Along with the procession there were athletic games and sacrifices. And the prizes in the games were those fine big oil-jars, the Panathenaic amphorae, of which we have a long series preserved (Plate 50, *b*). From the first half of the sixth century Athenian pottery rose (not without the aid of Corinthians and other foreigners, often slaves) to be the finest and most admired pottery of Greece, of unsurpassed excellence, parallel to the sculpture and showing at a certain point the same Ionian influence. The beautifully proportioned vases with their painted scenes from Greek life and legends which are the pride of our museums today were exported even to far-off Etruria and the region of the Black Sea; in fact everywhere where Greeks penetrated and beyond, as, for example, into Gaul. At first the figures were painted in black silhouette on a leather-coloured clay ground, with inner details incised through the black glaze paint into the clay, and with added red and white enhancement. Later the clay ground was improved to a rich red by treatment with ruddle. After a stage where the influence of Corinth is strong, two styles in effect emerge, a miniature style best illustrated around the middle of the sixth century by the cup with the Introduction of Herakles to Olympia (Plate 51, *a*), and superlatively by the François Vase with its many friezes (Plate 50, *a*), and a larger style (a continuation of the fine late Protoattic painting of the seventh century and its immediate successors), associated with the names of such painters as Exekias. Some of these painters, it should be noted, were foreigners, and probably even slaves, like Lydos, "the Lydian". The subjects of this vase painting were heroic stories, such as the duel of Achilles and Penthesilea (Plate 51, *b*), or everyday life, like the olive-gatherers (Plate 51, *c*). This black-figure style was highly decorative, sometimes splendidly monumental, but it had its limitations. It is not surprising that about the beginning of the last quarter of the sixth century the pattern was reversed to red figures reserved against a black ground, which allowed much more delicate interior detail. Some vases were decorated in both techniques. (A rare alternative took the form of black or polychrome figures on a white ground, cf. the much later Plate 84, *b*.) It is at this stage that influences from Asia Minor manifest themselves, as in sculpture, with an elegant style (Plate 58, *a*) which is in fact just one part of the cultural development under the tyrants Hippias and Hipparchus. It may be noted here that it is an illustration of that drain of talent which took place when the Persians conquered Asia Minor, and which went on and was intensified when the Ionian Greeks rose against the Persians. The emigration which took place to Greece and the West did these regions a great deal of good, but, as the drawing on a fragment of sculpture from Persepolis shows (Plate 58, *b*), some Greek artists must also have gone East, willingly or unwillingly. This early red-figure vase-painting had a close connection in detail of anatomical rendering and postures with contemporary sculpture, especially relief sculpture such as the Acropolis Base (Plate 59, *b*). Early Attic red-figure vases are among the most beautiful products of Greek art, cf. Plate 58, *c*, a plate by Epiktetos, and the charming cup from the Agora of Athens, Plate 59, *a*.

Pisistratus greatly encouraged the idea of Athens as the leader of the Ionian states of Greece. Up to this time great Ionian cities like Miletus and Ephesus had been ahead of Athens in wealth and civilisation. Solon had called Attica "the oldest Ionian land", and on the same conviction, not altogether unbiased, rested the tradition of Messenian Neleid dynasties in Athens in the latest Bronze Age (see page 91 above) and in Ionia as a result of a migration from Attica across the Aegean. It is hard to say how Pisistratus persuaded them that Athens was in some sort their mother city unless such was the fact. He inaugurated the solemn purification of Delos, by removing the dead from the island. Henceforth the Apollo of Delos was to share with the Poseidon of Mycale the patronage of Ionia. Both at the Panionic festival of Delos and the Panathenaic festival at Athens the solemn recitation of Homer formed an important part of the proceedings. It was Pisistratus, according to ancient tradition, who caused an authorised version of Homer to be prepared at Athens. Certain portions were selected and edited. Thus at length, it was believed, Homer became a fixed canon, though some have doubted this.

Another festival instituted by Pisistratus led to important literary results. This was the Great Dionysia. Dionysus, as a name, does appear in the Linear B tablets at Pylos just once, but apparently not as a god, and the ancient conviction was that he came as a late-comer to the Olympian assembly, probably from Thrace. As the god of wine and ecstasy, his coming had to face some opposition from the temperance party, and those who feared possession, but like a god he triumphed, and those such as Pentheus, who opposed him, did so at their peril. It was at the Dionysia that, as we shall see, the Athenian drama took its rise as a service of worship to the god.

Literature found a whole-hearted patron in the great tyrant's younger son Hipparchus, associated in the tyranny with Hippias. At his court were, among others, Simonides, Anacreon, and Onomacritus. Simonides of Ceos is specially associated with the dithyramb, the chorus in honour of Dionysus, which played a great part in the development of the chorus of tragedy. He was also a composer of odes of victory for successful athletes, though here his fame was eclipsed by his young rival Pindar. But it is chiefly as a writer of elegies and epitaphs and epigrams that his fame survives. It is not quite certain whether he actually wrote the epitaph that everyone knows on Leonidas and his Three Hundred Spartans at Thermopylae:

> Go tell at Sparta, thou that passest by,
> That here, obedient to her word, we lie.

But a fine ode by him on the same subject is still in part extant Anacreon is known even to the "general reader", through Byron:

> Fill high the bowl with Samian wine!
> We will not think of themes like these!
> It made Anacreon's song divine,
> He served—but served Polycrates
> A tyrant; but our masters then
> Were still, at least, our countrymen.

Anacreon's main business was, as our poet suggests, the writing of banquet songs on love and wine. It is rather melancholy to reflect that his anacreontics were composed—according to his own prescription—on ten parts of water to five of wine; but all the ancients watered their liquor. How closely tyranny is to be associated with the revival of culture is proved by the careers of these two poets. Anacreon passed from the court of Polycrates, tyrant of Samos, to Hipparchus, one of the tyrants of Athens, following as mentioned above, in the steps of vase-painters and other artists. When he fell Anacreon went to the still more brilliant court of Hiero, tyrant of Syracuse. Simonides went with him, and there they were joined by Bacchylides, Pindar, and Aeschylus.

Onomacritus was a strange person. It seems that Hipparchus had a hobby of collecting oracles, and had commissioned Onomacritus to edit a famous collection of poetical prophecies by Musaeus, a half-mythical bard. Onomacritus was detected inserting some of his own compositions, and very properly expelled for a forger. If all the historical forgers of this and later periods had been detected the modern historian's lot would be a happier one.

One monument to be dated about 510 B.C. is of especial interest, the *stele* or gravestone of Aristion (Plate 60, *b*). It is a bas-relief, once adorned with colour, of a warrior in armour with a long spear in his hand. It is not likely that any attempt was made at a portrait of the deceased. As the *stele* was found near Pisistratus' birthplace it has been suggested that this may be that very Aristion who proposed the decree which gave the tyrant his bodyguard. In reality it is to be dated too late for such an identification but some connection with the family of Pisistratus' supporter is not impossible. The "stele of Aristion" is the best known example of a whole series of tombstones and fragments (including the sphinx which topped the stone), so often in memory of young men, which like the kouroi, or some of them, and the Berlin Standing Goddess, stood in the sixth-century cemeteries of the great Athenian families, not only in the Keramcikos at Athens but also in the country. They illustrate at once the pride and wealth of these families, and the quality of Attic sculpture. Among the finest is the stone illustrated in Plate 60, *a*, in New York and Berlin, of a youth and his little sister, to be dated around the middle of the sixth century. The fragmentary epitaph does not clearly reveal to what great family they belonged, but it was clearly one of the foremost.

It was the custom after dinner at Athens to pass round the harp, and for each guest as it came to him either to improvise a verse or to cap his neighbour's impromptu or to sing a stave of some famous song. The most popular of all these "skolia" was "The Myrtle Bough". One version of it runs:

> I will wear my sword in a myrtle bough,
> Like Harmodius and Aristogeiton
> When they killed the tyrant
> And made Athens free.
>
> Dearest Harmodius, thou art not yet dead.
> They say thou art in the Isles of the Blessed,
> Where dwells Achilles swift of foot
> And Diomede, Tydeus' son.

I will wear my sword in a myrtle bough,
Like Harmodius and Aristogeiton
When at the sacrifice of Athena
They killed Hipparchus the tyrant lord.

Everlasting shall be your glory upon earth,
Dearest Harmodius and Aristogeiton,
For that ye killed the tyrant
And set Athens free.

Right down in the days of Demosthenes, nearly two hundred years later, these two men were still mentioned in most of the public decrees, because immunities had been granted to their descendants for ever. They are the only private individuals for more than a hundred years who had statues erected to them. All this extraordinary honour was theirs because they had killed a tyrant.

Although we can see the blessings that the tyrants of Greece had brought to their cities, it is to the credit of the Greeks that they could not. They much preferred to govern themselves badly than to be governed ever so efficiently by someone else. A tyrant might give them wealth, peace, culture, and happiness, but no Greek ever lost sight of the tyrant's *telos*, or goal. The tyrant governed, as Aristotle says, "for his own advantage, not that of his subjects". Hence their execration of tyranny and the extraordinary honour they paid to tyrannicides. Such a sentiment has had an enormous influence in history. The Greeks taught it in their schools, their orators embroidered the theme, the Roman schoolboys learnt declamations against tyrants from their Greek teachers of rhetoric, until finally this old legend of Harmodius and Aristogeiton whetted the daggers of Brutus and Cassius against Caesar.

It was a legend, I am afraid. The Athenian tyranny was put down by a Spartan army persuaded by a bribed oracle at the bidding of the Alcmeonids. All that Harmodius and Aristogeiton had done was to kill Hipparchus, the younger brother of Hippias, by surprise, as he was marshalling the Panathenaic procession. Apparently, too, the motive was merely a love affair of a kind that we consider disreputable; but that only added the necessary touch of romance to the story. No ancient historian supports the belief expressed in this ancient assertion, that Harmodius and Aristogeiton had set Athens free.

This story provided the subject of one of the most famous of archaic statues, the "Harmodius and Aristogeiton" of Antenor. It was carried off by Xerxes to Persia when he sacked Athens in 480, but returned eventually by Antiochus the Great. Meanwhile two other sculptors had been set to reproduce Antenor's group. It is probably this reproduction from which our many copies have been made. We have them on coins, on vases, on a marble throne, and above all in two separate statues in the Naples Museum, where unfortunately Aristogeiton, who should have been the bearded elder, has been degraded by the addition of one of the pretty curly-haired heads of the fourth or third century. But the Harmodius is a fine type of archaic work, even though it has been freely restored and is of course only a copy (Plate 68, *b*).

From Aristophanes it would appear that it was the mark of a jingo democrat at Athens to sing "the Harmodius" on every possible occasion.

Hippias, then, was expelled by the machinations of the Alcmeonids and the strong arm of Sparta in 510 B.C. It was the Alcmeonid Cleisthenes who was called upon to draw up a new constitution. After emerging from the tyrannical stage all the Greek states developed a republic, either oligarchical or democratic. In the oligarchic type the citizenship was confined to a few hundreds of the richer citizens and the actual government was carried on by a small council of ten or fifteen members. This was the normal type of Greek government. The democracy of Athens was the rarity. All Greek states had inherited from the earliest times the public meeting in the market-place as one of the rights of citizenship. At Athens eventually all administrative decrees were made at this Assembly, or Ecclesia, and all adult male citizens could attend and speak if they chose. It amounted to government by mass meeting. It was, of course, an ignorant, fickle, excitable body, especially in conducting a war or a piece of foreign policy. But it was a wonderful instrument of education, and it gave the Athenian citizen that sense of direct participation in the affairs of his state which alone could satisfy the political aspirations of a Greek. Who shall call it a failure because it bungled a war and an empire, if it made Athens the eye of the world for ever and ever? Cleisthenes set up a Council of five hundred members, fifty elected from each of his new ten tribes, which was a committee to prepare business for the Assembly. One tenth of it, the members of one tribe in a recognised order, acted as an executive for one tenth of the year. Also there still remained the old patrician council of notables, now chiefly consisting of ex-magistrates, who met upon the Areian Hill and were called the Council of the Areopagus. These had the guardianship of the laws, amounting probably to a veto upon the Assembly's proceedings, and a general censorship over morals. They were also the highest criminal court for cases of blood-guilt—a solemn and awful tribunal. Consisting of ex-officials, they naturally had great influence over the merely annual magistrates, or *archons*; and, indeed, later it was claimed that they managed most things in Athens until after the Persian Wars. This was something the rivals of Themistocles wished to believe. The chief executive magistrates were still the nine annual *archons*, chosen as before by popular election. With the new ten tribes of Cleisthenes were later instituted ten *strategoi*, or generals, to lead them under command of the War Archon. The ten tribes were so grouped as to prevent any recurrence of the local factions which had enabled Pisistratus to rise. And Cleisthenes may have devised the ingenious system called ostracism, by which any unpopular statesmen who had six thousand votes or more cast against him was sent into polite and honourable banishment (Plate 79, *b*). It was generally the leader of the Opposition who suffered this fate, and such was the intention. Though Greek democracy inevitably developed a party system, it was never recognised. Opposition was considered treachery to the state, as, indeed, it generally was.

Such in general was the constitution under which Athens rose to glory. It was modified, as we shall see, in a democratic direction by Pericles. As yet it can hardly, with its powerful Areopagus and elective magistrates, be called a democracy. But it tends that way, and the course before it is plain. Cleisthenes has lost much of the credit due to him in the process which has assigned superhuman wisdom to Solon. He, with Pericles, is the father of the Athenian democracy.

IONIA

At this time, when the mainland cities of Greece were thus actively developing their culture, their kinsmen across the sea, particularly the Ionians, were their equals, and, indeed, probably in advance of them in civilisation. They were primarily the descendants of the Greek inhabitants, who had been forced across the Aegean on to the coast of Asia Minor as a result of the disturbances caused by the

Dorian invasion. They went to Aeolis and Lesbos in the north, to Ionia and the islands of Chios and Samos in the centre, and to Caria and the adjacent islands in the south. The most promising land was in Ionia. We know relatively little of the peoples who were there before, but it is clear that sometimes the immigrants had to build forts, so that they may have encountered resistance (or were the forts built against other Greeks?). Eventually they dominated the local inhabitants and exploited them, which may explain their subsequent prosperity. They must have emigrated from Thessaly, Boeotia, Attica, and the Peloponnese in small and mixed bodies, and established many settlements which afterwards were reduced by coalescence or elimination to form the group of cities which worshipped Poseidon at Mount Mycale. The excavations at Old Smyrna seem to show that the settlements go back to about 1000 B.C. In some cases, such as Miletus, they follow on Mycenaean centres. They were lucky in the earlier stages of their settlement when they were small and weak since inner Asia Minor was in an inchoate state for centuries, until the development of a flourishing Phrygian kingdom in the region of the Sangarios river, and of the kingdom of Urartu about Lake Van to the east. The Phrygians certainly had contact with eastern Anatolia, with Urartu (famous for its metalwork, Plate 43, *a*) and the Assyrians, and probably got their system of writing independently from the East (Plate 41, *b*). The Ionians, or all the Greeks, were the Iawana of the Assyrian records. It is difficult to decide to what degree the Ionian Greeks made contact with the East through Anatolia, or with the Phrygians. They certainly did make contact, as finds from Ephesus at the temple of Artemis, in Samos at the temple of Hera, and in Rhodes show. There was also contact with the nomads, perhaps, to judge from objects found at Ephesus (Plate 43, *d*). The link with the eastern Mediterranean was most likely by sea, to northern Syria, though this was an area where the Aegean islands appear to have had early associations.

Undoubtedly the existence of a rich hinterland could benefit the Ionians; it also exposed them to attack from the East. Thus in the seventh century B.C. they suffered from the attacks of the nomad Cimmerians (who destroyed Phrygia), and were the victims of aggression by the Kings of Lydia who eventually reduced them, with the exception of Miletus. This gave them needed peace, though they fought among themselves also, and encouraged them to colonisation as an outlet. If they did in fact dominate a local population it gave them leisure to develop their culture. So we find them passing for a soft people, plump (cf. Plate 62, c) and luxurious, cultivating their minds and expressing their feelings with uninhibited passion: very different from our picture of the Spartans, who, none the less, admired some of their poets. But perhaps we do them wrong: they were also mercenary soldiers, merchant adventurers to Egypt, and colonisers of the far Euxine.

In the late seventh, and early sixth centuries cities like Miletus, Ephesus, and Mitylene on Lesbos were among the greatest cities of the Greek world, in size, riches, and culture. They in their turn were sending colonies into the Black Sea, to tap its rich sources of corn, timber, and other natural products. We have seen something of the wisdom of Thales, and we must allow our imaginations to suggest what a vast amount of preliminary knowledge and culture is required before a man can calculate an eclipse. This learning must have come in the merchant ships from Egypt when that country was opened up through Naucratis, and it must also have been passed along the caravan routes from Babylonia to arrive on the coast of northern Syria, and to be conveyed from there, by visitors, to Ionia. It was in Ionia, too that the mass of Achaean traditions which forms the subject-matter of the Homeric epic seem to have been preserved, by those who emigrated from Greece; and here lived the great Homer himself. It is here too that lyric poetry both choral and personal reaches its apotheosis. We have agreed, I hope, that the epic did not come into being out of the void, but that there must have been songs before there were long poems. Hence we need not make the extravagant assumption that Sappho and Alcaeus were beginners at their trade. The same consideration would apply to the two elegiac poets who, as Ionians, represent the very antithesis the one of the other: Callinus of Ephesus who sought to stir up his countrymen from sloth to martial deeds, and Mimnermus of Colophon, writer of poetic myth and of laments for the passing of the joys of life and the onset of old age.

The great lyric period of the seventh and sixth centuries belongs politically to an era of aristocracies and tyrannies. The aristocracies here must have lived mainly from their landed estates like those of Athens and Sparta. There may have been "merchant princes", as is sometimes suggested, though it is to be wondered whether at this early date there was a sharp division between landowner and merchant.

These aristocratic landowners may well have been served by a subordinated population of cultivators, a circumstance which allowed them to develop their personalities and the arts: in the case of poetry, in particular, by personal participation, not merely by the exercise of patronage; for some of the great poets seem to have been members of the aristocracy.

Sappho is a remarkable figure in the history of literature, the only woman who has ever reached the front rank among poets. Her poems were for long represented almost entirely in extracts preserved by the diligence of grammarians for other than poetic reasons. Of relatively recent years its volume has been greatly increased from the papyri found in Egypt, but it is still pitifully fragmentary. Yet even from these ruined remnants we can feel across the ages the vital throb of her passion, speaking in music of altogether unequal beauty. It is impossible to describe the emotion which scholars and poets of all ages have felt when they first stumbled upon

> Immortal Aphrodite of the starry throne,
> Daughter of God, weaver of guile, I beseech thee
> Neither to disgust nor to distress subdue,
> Lady, my heart . . .

Or the broken marriage chorus:

> MAIDENS
> Like the sweet apple blushing on the topmost twig,
> Top of the topmost, which the gatherers forgot.
> Forgot? Nay, but they could not reach to it.
> YOUTHS
> Like the hyacinth on the hills which the shepherd swains
> Tread underfoot, and down to the earth the bright flower . . .

But translation inevitably spoils the fragrance, as even Rossetti and Swinburne found. It is of Sappho that Swinburne writes in her own metre:

> Ah the singing, ah the delight, the passion!
> All the Loves wept, listening; sick with anguish
> Stood the crowned nine Muses about Apollo;
>   Fear was upon them,
> While the tenth sang wonderful things they knew not.
> Ah the tenth, the Lesbian! the nine were silent,

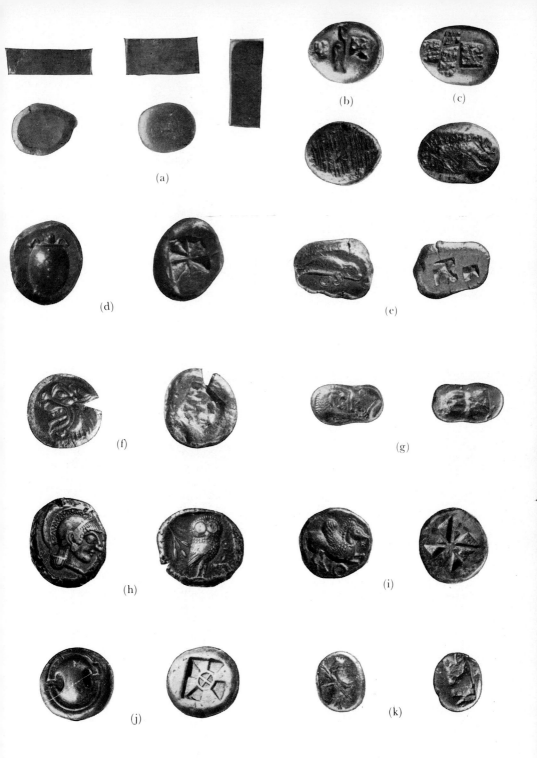

49. Dumps and coins showing the early development of Greek coinage.

(b) The Burgon Panathenaic amphora.

50. (a) The François Vase.

51. (a) *above* A black-figured lip-cup signed by Phrynos as potter.
    (b) *below left* Black-figured amphora, signed by Exekias as potter.
    (c) *right* Black-figured amphora by the Antimenes Painter. Olive-gathering.

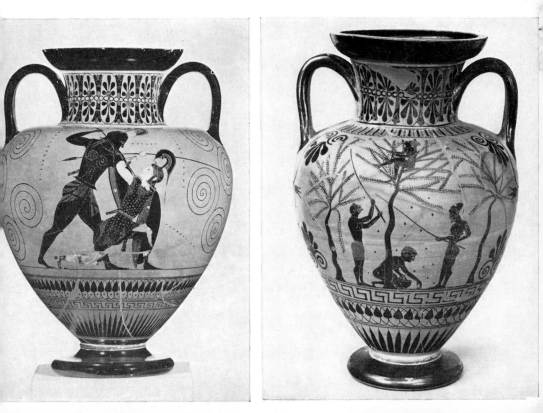

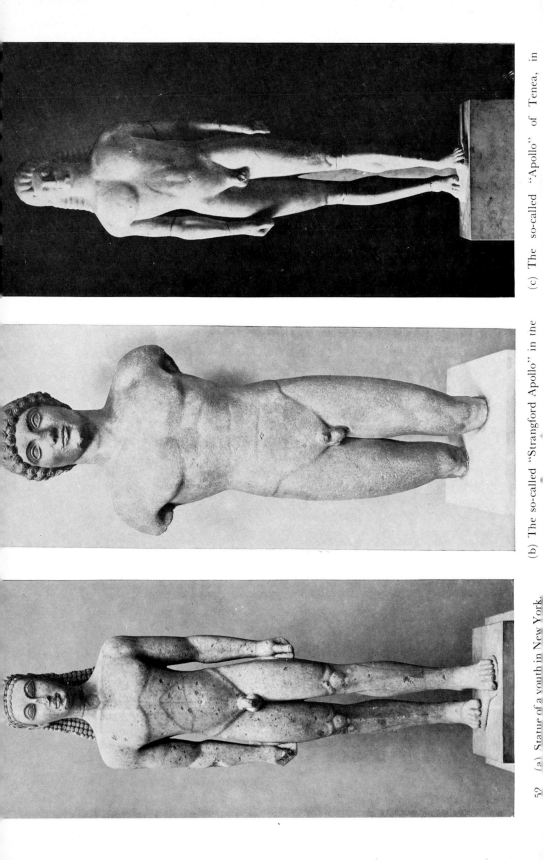

52 (a) Statue of a youth in New York. (b) The so-called "Strangford Apollo" in the (c) The so-called "Apollo" of Tenea, in

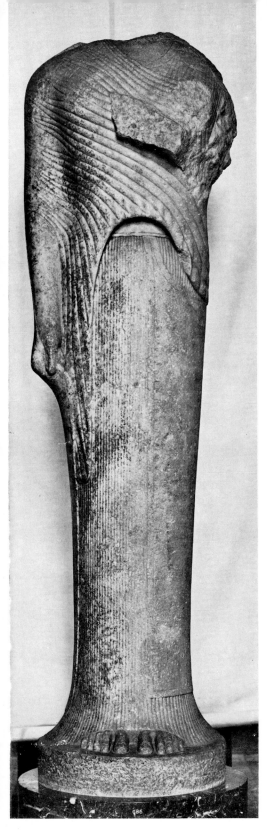 

53. (a) Standing female figure in the Louvre, dedicated to Hera at Samos by one Cheramyes.

(b) The so-called Berlin Standing "Goddess".

54.   (a) Fragment of a female head in the British Museum.

55.
(a) *left*
The so-called
"Calf-bearer",
in the Acropolis
Museum,
Athens.

(b) *right*
The head of a
horseman, the
"Rampin Head"
in the Louvre,
Paris.

56

(a) *above* Statuette of a young woman from Chios.

(b) *right* Statue of a young woman (*kore*), the so-called "Peplos Kore".

57.   Slabs from the sculptured frieze of the Treasury of Siphnos at Delphi.

58. (a) *left* From an amphora from Vulci (Etruria). An elegant young man acts as judge at a wrestling contest.
(b) *right* Fragment from a relief at Persepolis. (c) *below* From a red-figured plate. Signed by Epiktetos as painter.

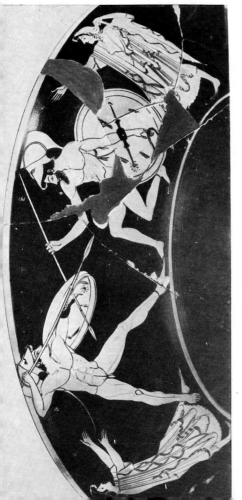

59.
(a) *left* Exterior of a fragmentary red-figured drinking cup found in the Agora excavations at Athens, signed by the potter Gorgos.

(b) *below* Base of a statue found in Athens.

60.

(a) *left*

Funeral monument of a youth and girl fr[om]
Attica, in New York and Berlin.

(b) *above*

The funeral slab (*stele*) of Aristion, in Athens

61. A view at Delphi down the Sacred Way.

62. (a) *above* Female head from the archaic
temple of Artemis at Ephesus.

(b) *below* One of the reliefs from the so-called
"Harpy Tomb" at Xanthus.

(c) *right* Seated figure from the oracular shrine
of Apollo at Didyma south of Miletos.

63. (a) *left* Seated goddess in Berlin.

(b) *below* Metope from the temple of Hera at Selinunte.

64.   Metope from Temple C at Selinunte.

Nine endured the sound of her song for weeping;
> Laurel by Laurel
Faded all their crowns; but about her forehead,
Round her woven tresses and ashen temples,
White as dead snow, paler than grass in summer,
> Ravaged with kisses,
Shone a light of fire as a crown for ever.
Yea, almost the implacable Aphrodite
Paused, and almost wept; such a song was that song . . .

From her own works, we can gather some interesting details. She belonged to the governing aristocracy of Lesbos, and, for a time at least, went into exile with it. The women of Lesbos seem to have formed rival *salons* of literary culture, and Sappho herself was the head of one. There was a good deal of jealousy between them. Strangely, the most ardent of her verse is addressed to one of her own sex, and since it cannot be true that she is only writing the amatory language of male poets, we must conclude that the women of Lesbos imitated the men in that strange passion which ignored sex. To contradict the celebrated fable of her dramatic suicide from a cliff in consequence of an unrequited love, we have a fragment of her message to her daughter from a calm death-bed:

> . . . For it is not right that in a house that Muses haunt
> Mourning should dwell: such things befit us not.

We are naturally unwilling to dismiss as mere gossip the story of tender feeling, or at any rate tender expressions, between Sappho and Alcaeus. They were contemporary poets of the same city. Sappho sometimes used the alcaic measure, and Alcaeus the sapphic. Besides, we have it on the authority of Aristotle. One line of Alcaeus to Sappho is preserved:

> Sappho, pure sweet-smiling weaver of violets.

Alcaeus too was a member of the Lesbian aristocracy. He alludes with bitterness to a tyranny which was ended by the appointment of a constitutional tyrant or dictator, Pittacus, who enjoyed a noble reputation except among his political opponents, of whom Alcaeus was one. In the course of these disturbances Alcaeus went into exile—among other places, we should note, to Egypt—while his brother took service under the King of Babylon. Such were the cosmopolitan relations of this period. The poet also fought for his country against the Athenians in the struggle for Sigeum, and humorously records the fact that he lost his shield in the rout. Such a loss was the regular mark of defeat, and generally regarded as a brand of ignominy to a soldier. But the Ionians may have taken love, drink, and politics seriously, but not, it appears, the honour of a soldier. It seems also to have been *de rigeur* that lyric poets should lose their shields in battle—Archilochus, Alcaeus, and Anacreon—while the Roman Horace was too careful an imitator of the Greek lyric tradition to neglect their example in this respect, rather than follow that of Callinus and Tyrtaeus. The poetry of Alcaeus falls into two classes—banquet-songs in praise of love and wine, and political songs attacking his enemies. He too chiefly survives in fragments like

> Wine is the mirror to mortals . . .
> Wine, dear child, and Truth . . .

Though there is not the fire of Sappho in his work, it is singularly artistic, polished, and rich in the language of pure poetry. For the rest we must be content to admit his great reputation in antiquity and to enjoy him through the medium of Horace's Latin.

These two great poets, who both flourished about 600 B.C., their predecessors Archilochus, Arion, Callinus, and Terpander, and their successors of the next generation Anacreon and Simonides, are the best representatives of the early culture of Ionia in the broader sense. To complete the picture we must remember her philosophers. Besides Thales and Bias, the two Sages (Bias, by the way, is credited with having proposed that the Ionians should leave their homes *en masse* and found a united state in the west), there were students of natural philosophy like Anaximander, who made the first map and the first sun-dial and explained the evolution of life from the Infinite by the interaction of heat and cold and other opposites, Heraclitus of Ephesus, "the weeping philosopher", or Hecataeus of Miletus, the grandfather of history and geography. Hecataeus first explained away the gods as only deified mortals of past ages, a doctrine afterwards called Euhemerism. This was the Ionian attitude of scepticism which in some degree is to be discerned in Homer's attitude to the gods. Even Sappho, the worshipper of Aphrodite, says in one fragmentary line:

> I know not what the gods are: two notions have I . . .

In matters of the graphic arts the same factors promoted their development among the Asia Minor Greeks as among the Greeks of Greece proper; namely peace and the increase of wealth. It has been seen (above, page 114) that they had little peace in the seventh century B.C. until the ascendancy of Lydia and its benevolent domination of the Greek coastal communities. It has also been pointed out that their connection with the Orient was not in advance of that of the other Greeks, though their great temple centres were obviously concentrating points of imported objects (brought by sea) and of artistic development. As colonists of the Black Sea region they were not earlier in this field than the rest of the Greeks in theirs. In fact they were later.

In one thing they were in advance of the other Greeks. The invention of coinage took place in Asia Minor, perhaps for the payment of mercenaries rather than for trade. Tiny lumps and bars of precious metal must have been used first (cf. Plate 49, *a*, though these are from Crete), and then the dumps with striated face and punch-marks on the reverse (Plate 49, *b*). These striations were replaced by types, some of which may have belonged to individuals who used coins for their own mercantile or other purposes (Plate 49, *c*). In course of time the Ionian cities issued coins (some with "canting" or punning types, such as the seal, *phoke*, of Phocaea, and the initial *phi*, Plate 49, *e*), and so also did the kings of Lydia (Plate 49, *f*). All these were of electrum, and like the seals and gems of the time they possess little artistic quality.

Temples and shrines were small until late in the seventh century, with the exception of Samos where the development of the temple and sanctuary of Hera appears to have been in advance of other centres of Greece. Pottery, especially the Geometric, lacked the quality of that of the mainland. When the "orientalising" style came in it was attractive with its gay ibex friezes and liking, subsequently, for colours, but again it was inferior to the products of the islands and mainland of Greece. Ivory carving on the other hand appears to have been a highly developed pursuit, as finds at Samos show, and also objects found in Greece (Plate 43, *b*) which may be from Greek Asia Minor. But it is frequently difficult to decide where exactly such things were made. Some small bronzes of a later date show a plump and podgy "Ionian" habit of body, the contrast of which to the taut and lean "Doric" type (Plate 44, *c*) is a temptation to a racial antithesis. The same plump type is apparent in the sixth century in the celebrated small ivory figures from Ephesus, the moon-faced priestess (Plate 45, c) and her companion the eunuch priest. The increase of Ionian wealth in the sixth century meant the development of Ionic architecture in the enormous temples of Ephesus and Samos, the latter under the patronage of Polycrates, and the former aided by King Croesus of Lydia, who was said to have helped with the columns and bases of the temple decorated with high reliefs now in the British Museum (Plate 62, a). These are something of a landmark in the development of Ionian art because of the suggested connection with Croesus. This famous monarch was in power from 560 to 546 B.C., with strong Hellenic sympathies and in close relation to the Delphic oracle; his growing power was overcoming and absorbing the independent cities of Ionia, who made no very violent resistance. But he himself had to face a still greater power then swallowing up the ancient kingdoms of the East—Cyrus of the Medes and Persians. Croesus lost a great battle, and died, some said, as ostentatiously as he had lived, on a splendid funeral pyre. The Greeks loved to invent stories about this plutocratic potentate, all illustrating one of their favourite maxims against pride, "Call no man happy until he is dead". In defiance of chronology edifying interviews were composed between him and Solon. It is clear that the Greeks were tremendously impressed by his magnificent life and dramatic end. The fall of the Lydian power brought the Greeks face to face with Persia, and gave them their great struggle for freedom, and their greatest inspiration through their victory.

There is a good deal else, some of it earlier, which shows the development of sculpture in Asia Minor; much of it in the same plump and obese tradition, like the seated figure of about 570 B.C. (Plate 62, c), one of a number in the British Museum, from the avenue leading to the oracular shrine of Didyma near Miletus.

Sedet, aeternumque sedebit!

There is also a standing figure, equally plump and well wrapped, from Samos. The fine detail of linen garments, which seem characteristic of Ionia, combines with a stylised cylindrical rendering of the body in the "Hera" dedicated by Cheramyes, in the Louvre (Plate 53, a) of about 560 B.C. Each reader must define for himself the similarities and contrasts between this and the rather earlier Attic on the same page. A series of fragments show the development of the head: such as Plate 54, *a*, in the British Museum, of about the same date. The grossness of the male figure is counterbalanced by the female figures with their more suitably rounded contours, delicacy of detail in drapery, and archaic charm, quietly smiling in the archaic fashion like the young lady of the relief from Didyma, Plate 54, *b*.

In fact there is a great variety of artistic rendering in which the islands such as Samos, Chios, and Naxos form a bridge to Greece proper. Collections of sculpture, like that of the *korai* from the Acropolis of Athens, show varied styles and sources, and unitary works of decorative sculpture like the frieze of the Siphnian Treasury at Delphi (Plate 57) show diverse hands. We have, in fact, Greek art becoming an inter-state affair, a foretaste of what was to happen in the fifth century.

Greek influences penetrated also to the Hellenised areas of Caria and Lycia, where a peculiar type of pillar tomb was decorated with relief work such as that of the Harpy Tomb at Xanthos now in the British Museum (Plate 62, *b*), to be dated between 510 and 500 B.C. It is of interest not only for its style, showing a sturdy rendering of both male and female figures, but also for the "heroic" scene, and the winged spirits, not unlike the Harpies of Greek fable, which carry off the souls of the dead.

A contemplation of the Ionians and their art tends to involve us in one of those dangerous "cultural" and "racial" arguments which are only too common. It seems at first sight wholly right that these plump and inactive men, so much all things to all men, should be reduced by the Persians, rise in revolt at the beginning of the fifth century—a revolt which was a failure because of unwillingness to bear hardship and avoid treachery, and follow the Persians tamely to Salamis, waiting on the turn of events. We need to be reassured by the example of the Athenians that high culture and resolute spirits can go together. Yet it has to be remembered that the Ionian mind was keen and active; and if in the late sixth and fifth centuries the Asia Minor Greeks apparently declined, losing their poets and artists to the rest of Greece and to the barbarian, their contribution to Greek culture was the greater for it.

THE WEST

Wheresoever the patron is there will the poets be gathered together. When tyrants like Polycrates and Pisistratus ceased to exist in the

East, and when the Ionian cities had fallen under the Lydian and Persian despotisms, the courtly poets migrated with their lyres and other luggage to Sicily and South Italy, where there were aristocracies as elegant and tyrants as bountiful. The centres of commerce in this period before Athens rose into prominence were Miletus, Corinth, Aegina, and Sybaris, but above all the first and the last. The ancient Greek West was then one of the greatest granaries of the world. Sicily in particular, with its fertile volcanic soil and its equable climate, was regarded as the original home of wheat. Milesian wool and eastern wares found a ready market among the Etruscans, a wealthy aristocratic nation of Italy, whose language and origin are a mystery. This trade could pass either through the straits between Italy and Sicily or, because of natural and political hazards, overland to the Tyrrhenian Sea across the "toe" of Italy. Among those who took part in this carrying trade to the West were the Ionians. Most of this traffic passed through the hands of Sybaris. As a result, Sybaris, on her soft, warm gulf, became proverbial for wealth and effeminacy. In the early sixth century Sybaris seems to have been held to be larger and richer than any other state of the time. Her walls had a circumference of over eight miles, her population was 100,000, she kept a standing force of 5000 horsemen, and in her last great battle is said to have put 300,000 men into the field. We need not accept these figures literally, but we must take serious note of the belief in the greatness of Sybaris which is their basis. The Sybarites passed for the inventors of many of the refinements of civilisation—including the chamber pot—and about them clustered tales of extreme luxury and indolence. Of these luxurious people the most luxurious was the Sybarite who came to the Wooing of Agariste. But in the midst of her opulence and luxury she fell—and was destroyed for ever, so that not a vestige was left to mark her site. It was her neighbour and rival Croton that destroyed her. Croton was not nearly so wealthy, but she was better organised for war. She prided herself on the number of prizes her athletes won at Delphi and Olympia, and she was led by the famous strong man Milo, he who

> Could rend an oak
> And peg thee in its knotty entrails.

It is said that in the great battle on the river Traeis in 510 the cavalry of Sybaris were so much better accustomed to musical drill than to fighting that at the sound of the enemy's fifes the Sybarite horses began to dance! The asceticism which led to Croton's efficiency was a result of the teaching of Pythagoras of Samos, the great philosopher, a refugee from the tyrant Polycrates. A strange person was Pythagoras; his philosophy largely consisted of sound mathematics run mad on metaphysics. He attached mystical meanings to odd and even numbers; harmony was the principle of the universe. The abiding doctrine of his philosophy was that of metempsychosis, or the transmigration of souls:

Clown. What is the opinion of Pythagoras concerning wild fowl?
Malvolio. That the soul of our grandam might haply inhabit a bird.

These doctrines of the immortality of the soul may have come from the East, for Pythagoras is reported to have sojourned in Egypt and visited Babylon. He founded a great semi-religious society, which lived on monastic (and of course vegetarian) principles. He had considerable influence on the mind of Plato. His followers, banded together by mystical rites of initiation, took to playing an important part in the politics of their country, and fell into disrepute in consequence.

When Sybaris was destroyed some of the survivors took refuge at Posidonia, her colony. Here, at the modern Pesto, are some of the most splendid remains of Doric architecture—three well-preserved temples; the largest, the "temple of Poseidon" as it is normally called. belongs to the middle of the fifth century.

Zenophanes of Colophon was another Ionian philosopher of the sixth century who came to instruct the West. He was the founder at Elea, near Posidonia, of the important Eleatic school of philosophy, teaching that God was one, and was one with Nature. Like others of his kind, he devoted a great deal of attention to Nature-study, especially geology. He thought little of two staples of Greek culture, myths and athletics. In him, as in Pythagoras and others, we have the Ionian who flees his country to his country's loss, but to the advantage of greater Greece. These regions also boasted two of the most celebrated law-givers of antiquity, Zaleucus of Western Locri, said to have been the first to put laws into writing, and Charondas of Catana. We have seen reason to believe that the Law-givers of Greece represent rather a conception of Greek history than a fact.

Doubtless these two sages are as historical as Solon, but there is even less doubt that they have both been made the peg for elaborate forgeries of some late Pythagorean philosopher, who succeeded in foisting off a whole series of excellent moral doctrines upon their shoulders, to the great confusion of later writers, such as Cicero and Diodorus, who believed them to be genuine.

Lyric poets too arose in Sicily as in Asia Minor. Stesichorus of Himera, who was stricken blind because he spoke ill of beautiful Helen of Troy, and Ibycus of Rhegium, who sings with almost Sapphic fire of roses and nightingales and Eros,

> Who shooteth his melting glance from under his shadowy eyelids.

But most remarkable for its volume of talent is the galaxy of poets gathered at Syracuse round the great tyrant Hiero. His wealth is indicated by his frequent victories in the chariot-races of Greece. To these athletic triumphs we owe not only the incomparable coin-types of Syracuse, but some of the immortal victory-songs of Pindar also. The eagle flights of Pindar I have already described as indescribable. We cannot, I think, put ourselves into the attitude of the Greeks with regard to horse-races. Heavily as we may bet about them, we do not associate them with history and religion. Until we do so Pindar must remain largely a stranger to us. He is like some fairy juggler throwing up strings of jewels which vanish when we try to grasp them. Bacchylides is a lesser, more facile Pindar; his works, long lost, were recovered in 1897 as the result of a chance find of a manuscript in Egypt. I have mentioned that his uncle Simonides and Anacreon also migrated to this court. Presently they were joined by a greater than them all—the tragedian Aeschylus. But this was later.

As the East had powerful barbarian kingdoms to withstand, so the West had a terrible enemy always at the gates—the Semites. These Phoenician traders were far more powerful and aggressive in their colony of Carthage than in the mother cities, Tyre and Sidon. Admirably organised as a state, with able generals and highly trained mercenary troops, they coveted the rich island of Sicily. They seem to have effected a lodgment on the west end of the island about the time when the Greeks came to colonise the east and south. Thanks to the great resources of the tyrants of Syracuse, the Greeks here were more successful in resisting the barbarians than were the Ionians of the East. The great conflict came in the battle of Himera, fought, according to tradition, on the same days as Salamis, and won by Gelo, who preceded his brother Hiero on the throne of Syracuse. This victory thrust the Phoenicians back into their corner for nearly a century.

It is to be observed that Himera and Plataea meant far more than physical victories. Neither Persians nor Phoenicians were in our sense barbarians; indeed, so far as political organisation and material comfort are concerned they were far ahead of the Greeks. It was a question which of two civilisations, which of two spiritual and moral standpoints, would prevail.

The town nearest to the Carthaginians in Sicily was Selinus. The wealth and piety (or local pride!) of this city are indicated by the remains of eight Doric temples, seven of which belong to the sixth and early fifth centuries. Several of them were richly adorned with sculpture. Among the earliest is the well-known metope (Plate 64) which shows Perseus cutting off the head of the Gorgon, who is clinging to a small Pegasus, while Athena stands behind to encourage the hero. The heads are full-face, while the legs are in profile. The Gorgon is the happiest effort (she looks the happiest of the three), because this was a recognised art type of ugliness and terror. It is a clumsy, old-fashioned work, of between 550 and 540 B.C. The other metope (Plate 63, *b*) here illustrated is of about 470 B.C. a little before the Olympia metopes. It represents with great dignity and beauty the appearance of Hera to Zeus when she came in all her finery, as related in Homer, to beguile his heart. It is in fact a Hieros Gamos, or Sacred Marriage. Observe how admirably the scene is designed to fill the space of the panel without overcrowding.

Another work of art from the West is the beautiful seated goddess (Plate 63, *a*), perhaps Demeter, which is said to have been found at Locri and which found its way to Berlin in the middle of the First World War. The statue is probably contemporary with the battle of Salamis, about 480 B.C. Much of the rich painted decoration may still be traced, though the paint has faded.

From Sicily, perhaps, comes one of the most enigmatic works of art, found in Rome in the grounds of the Palazzo Ludovisi and preserved in the National Museum of the Terme, the so-called Ludovisi Throne (Plate 65), perhaps to be dated between 480 and 470 B.C. Does it represent the Birth of Aphrodite or a ritual baptism? Do the two female figures on the sides, one youthful and nude, and the other older and draped like a matron, represent Profane and Sacred Love? What purpose did the object serve, since it was assuredly not a "throne", and how was it related to the other puzzling work of art in the Boston Museum, which is of much the same form and seems to represent something like a Weighing of Souls? Is the Boston Throne a forgery, do they belong together, and did they come from the temple of Aphrodite of Mount Eryx in Sicily? To discuss such problems would take a whole volume and get us no further. So let it suffice to point out the naive yet mysterious charm of the Ludovisi relief, and its freshness, a quality which seems to have lived longer in the West than in Greece as so many coins show.

Acragas, too, the home of the tyrant Theron, has left us ruins of many temples (Plate 2), superbly arranged on a long ridge, among them the largest in existence. Its columns are so huge that a man can stand inside the fluting of them. The most remarkable feature is the row of Telamones, or pillars carved to represent men, bearing up the heavy entablature, as the Caryatids of the Erechtheum carried their portico upon their heads (Plate 80, a). But the motive at Acragas was to indicate the strength of the bearers and the weight of the burden. The refined Athenian put maidens in their place, with a very light roof to carry. It was not an idea that found much acceptance among the Greeks, though it is rather popular with the modern architect—witness the Hermitage Palace at Leningrad.

Of all the splendours of ancient Syracuse the most impressive memorials are the lofty Doric columns built into the walls of the Christian cathedral (Plate 3). Yet perhaps the greatest distinction of Syracuse is her coinage. It bore on one face the racing chariot and horses, and on the other the head of Arethusa surrounded by dolphins even as her spring on the citadel island of Syracuse, Ortygia, is surrounded by the sea. Within the compass of these types the coin-engravers, many of whom proudly signed their work, displayed their virtuosity. Among these splendid coins is the Damareteion, the ten drachma piece which Gelo caused to be struck from the gift the Carthaginians gave his wife Damarete for securing them better terms, or so it was said. Of the following series Plate 96, b, is one of the most charming. Then at the end of the fifth century come two other great series of ten drachma pieces by the die-engravers Kimon and Euainetos (Plate 96, e by Kimon), but it is a melancholy thought that this time they may commemorate not the victory of Greek over barbarian but of Greek over Greek, for the Assinarian Games when these may have been issued, celebrated the crushing defeat of the Athenian expedition against Syracuse in the Peloponnesian War.

Fig. 3

IV

THE GRAND CENTURY

ὅθι παῖδες ᾿Αθαναίων ἐβάλοντο φαεννὰν κρηπῖδ᾿ ἐλευθερίας.
PINDAR

THE RISE OF ATHENS

Rarely in all the world's history was there such a leap of civilisation as in Greece of the fifth century. In one town of relatively small size during the lifetime of a man and his father these things occurred: a world-conquering Power was defied and defeated, a naval empire was built up, the drama was developed to full stature, sculpture grew from crude infancy, so to speak, to a height it has never yet surpassed, painting became a fine art, architecture rose from clumsiness to the limit of its possibilities in one direction, history was consummated as a scientific art, one of the most influential of all philosophies was begotten. And all this under no fostering despot, but in the extreme human limit of liberty, equality, and fraternity. One Athenian family might have known Miltiades, Themistocles, Aeschylus, Sophocles, Euripides, Socrates, Phidias, Pericles, Anaxagoras, Aristophanes, Herodotus, Thucydides, Polygnotus, and Ictinus.

No historical cause will account for genius, no historian can predict its coming. Some say that great literature is produced by outbursts of national emotion, as Shakespeare was "produced" by the defeat of the Spanish Armada (though he was twenty-four when it happened) and Milton by the Puritan rebellion (though he wrote "Comus" in 1634). Others maintain that art is the blossom of decay. It is vain to look to politics for the real cause of the uprising of genius. But when a whole state rises simultaneously to an intellectual heat, at which masterpieces are thrown off almost daily, in almost every department of human activity, we may, and must, look for some historical and political explanation.

Pisistratus, as I have argued, had laid the foundations of Athenian civilisation, partly by making Athens into a real city-state, partly by direct encouragement of art and literature, partly by promoting commerce, and thus opening the way to foreign influences. Then in 507 Cleisthenes and, oddly enough, in one sense the Spartans had given Athens a free republic, with distinctly democratic tendencies. Thus the cold domination of the conservative, old-established aristocracy, which had mainly been occupied in agricultural pursuits, had lost ground, although, no doubt, the Areopagus, which still "directed most things", maintained its influence to a considerable extent. What now grew into the most powerful element in the state was the seafaring commercial population, which lived mainly on the sea-coast. These were the restless, eager brains which were beginning to think things out, and to find their bearings in the big world outside Attica. They would be in constant business relations with their Ionian kinsmen across the sea, and thus catch a tincture of their cosmopolitan culture. Accordingly, when at the close of the sixth century the Ionians rose in revolt against their Persian masters, Athens, with Eretria, another city with Ionian connections, alone responded to their cry for help. It was only a raid, but it singed the Great King's beard by burning one of his capitals, Sardis. For this revenge was promised. The Great King of those days was no effeminate, luxurious Oriental. The Medes and Persians were then invincible conquerors, who had just devoured all the great empires and ancient civilisations of the East. It seemed as if they were out to conquer the world, and now nothing but a narrow sea lay between them and the presumptuous Greeks. Accordingly, ambassadors were sent in the usual fashion to Greece, to demand earth and water in token of submission. The Athenians are said to have thrown their envoys into the barathron where the bodies of felons were flung for burial, there to collect what earth they could. The Spartans, with whom originality was never a strong point, threw *theirs* into a well, indicating thereby that the answer was in the negative. So Darius collected a very great host from all his vassals, and sent it round by land, with the ships coasting alongside. It may have been planned to conquer Greece, or it may only have been intended to prepare the way in Thrace and Macedonia. In either case, fortunately for the Greeks, the fleet met with fearful shipwreck off the dangerous Chalcidian promontory of Mount Athos. In 490 Darius tried again. This time it was a much smaller force, designed not to conquer Greece, but merely to punish Athens and Eretria. It was a naval expedition only, but room was provided in the ships to bring back the Athenians in chains for summary judgment. Datis and Artaphernes were the leaders, but the ex-tyrant Hippias was there to show them the way to Athens, where he felt he still could reckon on friends and supporters. But Athens also had an ex-tyrant among her generals, one who knew the Persian method of fighting and had the strongest motives for resisting them. That tyrant was Miltiades, an Athenian noble who had family possessions in Gallipoli, where he had been tyrant, and from which he had been expelled by the Persians. He had experience of warfare (cf. Plate 67, b), and knew the enemy. Hippias' plan was to cross over the strait from Euboea, where the Persians had succeeded in enslaving Eretria, land on the north coast of Attica with a large force, and while the land army of Athens was engaged there, slip round with the fleet to Piraeus and catch Athens undefended. His plans miscarried, for the Athenian line swept down the hill at Marathon upon the Persian archers before they were fully deployed, and with their lightning charge hurled them back into the sea with great slaughter, then marched back at full speed to the city, in time, it may be, to prevent Hippias' partisans from opening the gates.

This was the triumph of the Athenian hoplite—his only really great feat in history—led by aristocrats in a limited democracy. The hoplite himself was a comfortable burgess who could afford a full suit of armour. It was not a victory for full democracy, and the clamorous proletariat of the Piraeus had little, if any, share in it. But it was a purely Athenian triumph and a Persian helmet dedicated at Olympia may commemorate it (Plate 67, a). Alone—with the help of her little Boeotian friend Plataea—alone she had done it. The great Dorian city had been urgently entreated by the runner Philippides to send aid. But Sparta was busy with a festival and had to wait until the moon came right for marching. Athens now, by virtue of this supreme achievement, stepped up into the second rank of Greek Powers.

A few years later some slaves working in the Athenian silver-mines at Laurium chanced to strike a rich vein of metal. All Athenian citizens were shareholders in all the state's property, and naturally expected to divide the profits. Then stood up a certain Themistocles—an aristocrat, but an unusual one, and a persuasive speaker with the supplest brain that Zeus had ever created since Hermes stole the cows—and proposed to spend the whole bonus on ships. This is the turning-point of Athenian history. The stout hoplites who had won the day at Marathon stood aghast, we may believe, at the proposal. They would point out that the strength of Pallas lay in her spear, that to create a navy would be to encourage those turbulent radicals at the Piraeus. Besides, what was it for? The Persians had gone home again. Themistocles, in reply, drew attention to the war then on hand with Aegina, an island obviously not to be conquered by hoplites only. Doubtless a Greek neighbour was the more persuasive bogey, but Themistocles must have known that Persia was the enemy. Athens did not require a hundred new ships to fight Aegina, which had many less than this number for use in battle. No doubt Themistocles had the support of the "nautical rabble", for he gained a majority for his proposal, and soon afterwards got rid of his chief opponent, Aristides, by ostracism. Thus Athens acquired a fleet beyond all comparison the most powerful in Greek waters. It was needed.

Persia had spent the interval in suppressing Egypt; Darius was dead, and Xerxes reigned in his stead. But still the slave stood behind the royal chair to whisper every day at dinner, "Master, remember the Athenians". Soon he had time to remember them. This time there were to be no miscalculations; no mere raid this time, but the hugest armament in history. No shipwrecks this time: where the army had to cross the sea at the Dardanelles a bridge was constructed; where the fleet had to round the promontory a canal was dug.

The host was on the same scale. Herodotus and Aeschylus alike delight to parade the outlandish names of the Oriental leaders, to display the numbers of that mighty host of all the nations of the earth, how they drank the rivers dry as they marched, to dwell on the strange equipment of the remote barbarians of Thrace, India, and the Sudan, the wealth and magnificence of the Great King, how he lashed the sea when it broke his bridge, how he questioned the exiled Spartan king Demaratus, unable to believe that these little people would dare to stand up against him. Even more than the life and death of Croesus, this immortal story of the Persian monarch's great Armada and its fall, with the tragic contrast between his glorious setting out and miserable return, stirred the imagination of the Greeks for ever afterwards. Did it not illustrate their favourite philosophy of "No excess" and "Know thyself"? All their art, if not their behaviour, was based on this motive: "Know thyself; practise Reverence, because Wealth and Prosperity lead to Insolence, and that arouses Envy in gods and men. Wrath (Nemesis) follows on the heels of Insolence, beguiling with false Hope, and finally leading into Ruin." That is the doctrine of all Greek tragedy; both Herodotus and Thucydides illustrated it in history, the former taking Persia and the latter Athens for its examples and victims. But it governed their art also; it is the secret of the self-restraint that characterises all the best of their work. That virtue of *Aidos* was present in their spirits. That is why it is so absurd to think of the Greeks as happy pagans. They walked in the fear of the Lord, in the shadow of tragedy.

The news of that marshalling of the host found Greece in a state of disunion if not terror. Some states submitted at the first summons. All sent for advice to the Delphic oracle. Apollo, I regret to say, was panic-stricken or politic. He told the Cretans not to interfere, he told the Argives to guard their own head; to Athens in particular he sent the most terrible menaces: "O wretched men, why sit ye here? Fly to the ends of the earth, leaving your houses and the high citadel of your wheel-shaped city . . . For fire and swift Ares, driving the Syrian chariot, destroyeth it. And he will destroy many other castles, and not yours alone; and he will deliver many temples of the immortals to devouring fire, which now stand dripping with sweat and shaken with terror; black blood trickles from the topmost roofs, foretelling inevitable ruin. Go from the sanctuary, and steel your hearts to meet misfortunes." Conceive the effect of such an oracle at such a time, and conceive the courage of Athens in preparing to resist! Thessaly submitted; Gelo of Syracuse, the most powerful Greek ally they could have, had declined to help, being himself fully occupied with the Carthaginian invasion of Sicily; Corcyra was sitting on the fence. Thebes was supposed to be traitorous, but there is little doubt that history has been unfair to Thebes. Nevertheless, the Persian was invited to do his worst. The Spartan plan was to draw strong lines across the Isthmus of Corinth and to fight there in defence of the Peloponnese, which was all the Greece that Sparta cared about. Besides she had Argos and the Helots as her worry. This meant the desertion of all the northern parts. Eventually she was persuaded to try resistance at the northern passes, but she did so half-heartedly. Tempe was found to be indefensible, for the invaders were pouring over another pass to the west of it. The first resistance was therefore made at Thermopylae, where the mountains left only a narrow track along the shore.

The battle of Thermopylae and the death of Leonidas with his three hundred Spartans are often represented as a forlorn hope and a gallant suicide. It was a reasonable plan of defence, which failed because the Greeks had not fully made up their minds whether the positions were to be held as a line of serious resistance or merely as outposts. Six thousand Greek hoplites marched with Leonidas, and they should have been sufficient to hold that narrow pass, and the mountain track, which alone could turn it, against a great force. Of course, the Persians were coming by land and sea, but Themistocles, with the Greek fleet, was to hold their fleet in check at a parallel point. But the Phocians, who were guarding the mountain track, instead of standing their ground fell back towards their own territory, leaving the flank of the main position exposed. The Peloponnesian allies who were then sent back by Leonidas were not being dismissed because the case was hopeless, but despatched to defend the point where the mountain track debouches into the main pass. This they failed to do. The Persians were expected to take a longer road round the mountain, whereas they came straight over the crest; and thus Leonidas was caught between two fires, and perished valiantly with all his men. It was not the less glorious because it was reasonable. Meanwhile a great storm had inflicted loss on the Persian fleet.

Now the strategy of defending the isthmus seemed the only hope, and that, of course, meant the abandonment of Athens. Sadly the Athenians saw the necessity. Indeed, under Themistocles' leadership they may have seen it earlier, before Thermopylae. They removed their wives and children to the Peloponnese and put all their fighting men on board their fleet, which amounted to nearly two hundred vessels. It has been suggested that the defence of the Acropolis was a serious attempt, probably a scheme to occupy the Persians before Athens until winter set in, rather than a fanatical misinterpretation of that second oracle which bade Athens trust to wooden walls. The Persians swept on irresistibly, wrecked and ruined Attica, and burnt the city of Athens and her citadel—not, however, so completely as to destroy all the old sculptures there.

The great sea-fight of Salamis needs no describing here. It was Themistocles' victory. He had cajoled, threatened, and finally deceived the Spartan admiral into remaining there instead of retiring to the Isthmus. He craftily persuaded the Persian monarch to attack the Greeks in narrow waters where numbers were only an obstacle; the fleet which won the day was his creation. The battle has gained its deathless glamour from the picture of Xerxes sitting on the hill above, enthroned on marble, to watch the engagement taking place at his feet. In that narrow strait between Salamis and the mainland, and in that lucid atmosphere, every detail of the fight must have been visible to the monarch, and his courtiers, his eunuchs, and his concubines. There was no smoke or dust; the manoeuvre was simply "full speed ahead and ram", steering, if you could, so that the metal prow of your ship struck the enemy obliquely, and sheared off the whole row of protruding oars on one side. Then, unlesss the enemy sank under the impact, it was a case of hand-to-hand fighting with spear and shield against arrows and scimitars.

Thus there was no need of the lines at the Isthmus. Athens had conquered at sea as she had conquered on land at Marathon. The Persian determination to subdue Greece was unaltered, but with winter coming on and the control of the sea lost, a change of plan was necessary. Part of the army, with Xerxes himself, fell back to protect the long line of communications against a possible Greek naval counterthrust; but a great force under Mardonius, a force of picked Persian cavalry and infantry, was left behind to hold what had been won in Northern Greece. In the following spring this army resumed the offensive and perpetrated a second sack of Athens. At last it came to the great campaign of Plataea (479). Here the Spartan infantry got its opportunity and proved worthy of it, though the Athenian hoplites slew their thousands also. So at length the Persian peril rolled away and Greece was able to breathe again.

This whole episode was the great achievement of the Greeks in the field of action. It passed into the realm of heroic history. It is almost the only historical episode which the drama, usually devoted to heroic and epic subjects, was permitted to use. No public oration was complete without a reference to it. Vase-painters, influenced by the drama, also depicted the story of Darius and Xerxes as they did that of Hector and Priam. It remained on the border-line of the permissible, however, for when temple sculptors wished to allude to it they generally did so under cover of Homeric contests between Greeks and Trojans or mythical battles between gods and giants or Lapithae and Centaurs. The memory of this united action had some influence in counteracting the local separatism of the Greeks.

The side of this great contest which chiefly concerns us is its effect in promoting Athenian civilisation. Salamis and Plataea had pushed Athens forward into the front rank of Greece, to a position almost on a level with Sparta herself. It is true that she still had to ask Sparta's permission, or to trick her into acquiescence, before she could build the walls she desired. But above all it was a triumphant vindication of the policy of Themistocles. Even Aristides, who had come home to help his country in her hour of trial, had to admit that. In this crisis he seems to be working with Themistocles on the "democratic" side. For Salamis had outshone even Marathon. The "nautical rabble" had justified itself. The party of cautious hoplites, who feared full and radical democracy, could no longer control the policy of the state. They gradually lost ground, and from their farms grumbled at the "demagogues", and issued forth to support conservative politicians like Cimon and Nicias. Their great champion in literature is Aristophanes, who loves to depict the old Marathon men as the real bulwark of the state. When Athens was rebuilt Themistocles saw to it that the Piraeus should henceforth be part of the city, eventually connected with it by Long Walls. The Piraeus stood for naval interests and naval empire, for commerce (though not for peace), and for democracy. It was not so far off but that the voters could flock up to Athens when an Assembly was to be held. It contained a large population of resident foreigners.

This was how Athens became a democratic city-state. Democracy advanced in various stages: the poorest were made eligible for the magistracies, except for the generalship, which always remained, as an elective office, an "aristocratic" element in an increasingly democratic state; the supervisory power of the Areopagus was reduced; the magistrates (archons) and the Councillors were no longer leaders elected for merit or reputation, but ordinary burgesses chosen by lot; the Assembly became actually sovereign over administration within the terms of the constitution. At an early date after the repulse of Persia, Themistocles himself was ostracised, being far too great and clever to be a comfortable companion in a democratic city-state. Curiously enough, time has spared some of the "ostraka", or potsherds, bearing his name by which he was condemned to banishment see Fig. 3. Then an empire fell into the Athenians' lap. It began, as most ancient empires did begin, with an alliance gradually transformed into a tyranny. Some Ionian cities had already won their freedom on the defeat of the Persian navy, but some had still to be liberated, and all needed protection for the future. The year after Plataea was spent by the Greek fleets in cruising about the Aegean, doing the work of liberation. At first Spartan admirals were in command, but the Ionians disliked Dorian discipline, and Pausanias, the victor of Plataea, was puffed up with pride and power. So they turned to Athens, whose commanders were Cimon the rich and generous son of Miltiades, Aristides the Just, and Xanthippus the father of Pericles, all men of the aristocracy, but loyal servants of Athens and capable seamen. Thus they formed the Confederacy of Delos, a league of maritime states, with a kernel of Ionians who worshipped the Delian Apollo. On his sacred island was to be the treasury of the league, and there the common synods were to meet. This league Athens eventually transformed into an empire. From the first some of its members were too poor to supply the normal unit of subscription, the trireme galley. These, then, contributed money on the assessment of Aristides. Athens built the ships for them in her own dockyards and sent her collectors round for the money. Sooner or later all the states except Chios, Samos, and Lesbos, found their naval contribution converted into a money payment. Some states were coerced into joining the league, garrisons and magistrates were sent from Athens to hold them in subjection. Often colonies of Athenian citizens were planted on their territory. When the Persian danger seemed finally removed by the destruction of the Phoenician fleet at the river Eurymedon some allies began to contemplate withdrawal. They were very soon taught that membership was not a voluntary privilege. Now the empire of Athens was a naked despotism, only mitigated by the fact that many of the states were permitted to manage their own internal affairs and benefited from the order maintained in the Aegean. The treasury of the league was removed from Delos to Athens, and the money was spent at her discretion. Meanwhile the ambitions of Athens had extended with success. She was no longer content with a naval empire. She began to cherish plans to extend her influence in the West; she seized the opportunity of taking over her shrunken neighbour, Megara, in order to have an outlet to the Corinthian Gulf; she took Naupactus on those waters as a base, and built up diplomatic connections in Sicily and planned a great Panhellenic colony at Thurii,

in South Italy. Moreover, she mixed in the affairs of great foreign
powers like Egypt. She attacked Cyprus and overran Boeotia. But
these adventures ended in disaster and after a defeat at Coronea in
Boeotia (447 B.C.) Athens was compelled, at any rate for the moment,
to abandon her claim to land empire and to content herself with
supremacy at sea.

In all this imperial policy from about mid-century onwards the
leader of the democracy, who by his personal ascendancy was almost
as powerful as a monarch at Athens, was Pericles (Plate 79, c). He
was one of those aristocrats who succeed in securing the allegiance
of the masses, like Tiberius Gracchus, or Pitt, or Salisbury, by their
very aloofness though not everyone loved him as some ostraka show
(Plate 79, b). His single aim was to make Athens free, powerful, and
glorious. In Greece imperialism was allied, as it is not with us, with
radicalism. At home the last vestiges of power had been taken from
the Areopagus; Pericles had introduced payment of jurymen, payment
of soldiers and sailors, payment to enable the poor to attend the
theatre. He was, in short, what we should now call a Socialist.
Abroad, he was the advocate of imperial expansion by land as well
as by sea. He was for keeping a tight hold over the "allies", and he
justified the appropriation of their subscriptions to the private purposes
of Athens. He had apparently come into power over Cimon's
shoulders as the advocate of Athenian supremacy. The Peloponnesian
War, it might seem, was of his making. There is much in this sketch
of his policy which displeases us. But there was something in the
personality of Pericles which made even men like Thucydides
venerate his name, while they execrated the men who carried on
precisely the same line of policy after his death. This was his idealistic
patriotism, free from all sordid and selfish motives. He believed in
Athenian liberty, and he was prepared to extend it by force if
necessary. This illogical and paradoxical state of mind is common
to idealists; we ourselves have our pugnacious "pacifists", our well-
doers prepared to extend their views by force.

Conflict with Sparta was inevitable. Athens was constantly treading
on her toes in various parts of Greece. She was an upstart rival
aspiring openly to the foremost place in Hellas. That being so, we
have no need to inquire closely into the occasion of the great war
which filled the latter quarter of the century from 431 to 405, and
ended in the humiliating defeat of Athens. In any case the causes of

it must be sought much earlier in the century, since Athens and Sparta had long been subsisting on terms of truce only.

The main features of the Peloponnesian War, which forms the theme of the great history of Thucydides, may be briefly stated. It was a duel between land- and sea-power, for Athens had already lost her land empire, nor could she ever turn out a hoplite line fit to stand against the Spartan charge. The strategy of Pericles, dictated by necessity, was to retire within the walls of the city, relying upon the fleet to keep communications open and effect reprisals on the enemy. The weakness of this strategy lay in the fact that no fleet could touch Sparta, and that it put a very serious strain on the rural population of Attica, who had to desert their homes and see their crops ravaged in yearly forays from Sparta. That state of affairs led to a disastrous plague at Athens, and to a feeling of bitterness against Pericles which darkened his closing years. He died two years after the war began, and his place was taken by Cleon, who walked in his footsteps as democrat and imperialist, but, lacking his lofty personality and high birth, has come very badly out of the hands of history and literature. Aristophanes' perpetual appellation of "tanner" directed against him probably has its point in the fact that he openly represented commercial interests. He was responsible for the shocking decree which condemned all the male inhabitants of Mitylene to death in punishment of their revolt, a decree which was repented of and repealed at the eleventh hour, and he was a frequent obstacle to peace. But there is no ground for charging him with selfishness or dishonesty, and he was certainly not devoid of talent. He should be credited with the most brilliant achievement of the Athenian campaign, the taking of Sphacteria and its Spartan garrison.

It would seem that the war might have gone on for ever, but for the insane ambition of the Athenian democracy, which led her to despatch a huge fleet in 415 to Sicily for the subjugation of that island. It was the hare-brained scheme of that good-looking rascal Alcibiades. No one except Socrates could refuse him anything, much less the mass meetings on the Athenian Pnyx. So Athens squandered two great armadas on an enterprise undertaken in ignorance and entrusted to ill-matched commanders. Terrible as was the loss in men and ships, still more fatal was the realisation by her enemies that even the dreaded Athenian warships were not invincible. They resumed the fight with greater confidence, and Persia, not unwilling to pay off old scores against Athens, lent them money with which to build ships. Using her last reserves, Athens just managed to fit out a new fleet and with this she fought on for eight desperate years, even gaining a few more sea-fights, but the end could not be delayed for ever. Nor were the lessons of defeat learned. At last an Athenian admiral was caught napping at Aegospotami. There were no more ships, no more money in the treasury. After a brief siege Athens capitulated to Lysander in 404.

Such in briefest outline is the historical content of the Great Century, and such is the story of the first of European empires. What bearing has it upon our original inquiry as to the causes of the artistic and intellectual brilliance of the fifth century? We have, to start with, a people singularly endowed by Nature with quick intelligence and a marvellous sense of form. The Persian wars and the rise of Athens had added to these natural advantages a passion of pride in their city and an almost fanatical belief in her mission. Thus even her lowly citizens were eager to do their utmost to increase the beauty and honour of the violet-crowned city and her virgin goddess. A city-state makes a much more direct appeal to the emotion of patriotism than the large modern territorial state. Lastly, there was freedom in Athens such as no state in history has ever enjoyed, freedom in thought as well as in politics. This has been denied, but the attacks made upon Phidias and Pericles, and upon the philosophers Anaxagoras and Socrates, may all be explained on political grounds. We have only to look at the plays of Aristophanes to see what amazing liberty of speech prevailed at Athens. More-over, it was a privileged and educated equality. We must never forget the thousands of slaves whose cruel toil in mine and factory rendered this brilliant society possible at such an early stage in history nor that it was aided by the revenues of an Empire. It must not be forgotten that Greek liberty and communism was that of an aristocracy, however democratic might be the relations between its members. Thus you have at Athens a citizen body living a very full social life in the open air, with everything to stimulate intellectual interests— the daily speeches and debates in law-court and Assembly, the continual festivals and dramatic exhibitions, the endless conversations in the agora, the palaestra, and the various colonnades, the daily coming and going of ships from all quarters, constant embassies from the cities of the League, visits from all the talent of Greece, just sufficient intercourse with Egypt and the East—everything to stimulate the intelligence and make the "common man" a sharer in cultural pre-eminence.

PHIDIAS

In the great oration over the bodies of the dead Athenian soldiers which Thucydides ascribes to Pericles the statesman is made to express his ideal of Athens. She was "the instructress of Greece". She alone, he said, followed "culture without extravagance, and philosophy without softness". She alone combined daring with reflection. She alone welcomed strangers, and, while reverencing the gods and the laws, permitted freedom of speech and conscience to all men. He congratulated her upon the happiness of life in the city, the public displays and sacrificial banquets which afforded daily delight to her inhabitants. He did not lay much stress upon the outward magnificence of the city, for that, in a large measure, was his own work. But it is that aspect of his policy which we can all appreciate, whether we are democrats or imperialists or neither or both.

Pericles himself set the example which Athens followed of encouraging talent from all quarters to devote its abilities to the service of Athens. It was a rare opportunity for the artists. Here was an imperial city to be rebuilt, and plenty of money to build with. The directors of the work were Phidias the sculptor and Ictinus the architect. Phidias had learnt his craft under Ageladas of Argos and stands at the very summit of the period of fine art. Technical mastery over stone and bronze was by no means complete in his youth at the beginning of the century. The "archaic smile" still hovered over the lips of contemporary sculptures, the eyes were too prominent, the eyelids were still cut to meet at the corners instead of overlapping, hair was still conventionally rendered by parallel grooves, or spirals, or roughly blocked out for colouration.

The body, however, thanks to athletic models, was already much more successfully delineated than the head. Among examples of fifth-century sculpture before Phidias come first the pedimental figures from Aegina. These figures from the temple of Athena-Aphaia were discovered on the island by the English architect Cockerell in 1811; they were acquired by the King of Bavaria, restored by Thorwaldsen, and are now in Munich. Plate 66 shows the style in all its archaic vigour despite the restorations. All but the face is highly successful; the naked muscular forms of the warriors follow the poses of athletics, and the leadership of the vase-painters (Plate 59, *a*). It taxed the ingenuity of artists to compose scenes which would fit the triangular space of the temple pediment. Here, it should be noticed, the problem was well on the way to its solution. The ordinary rule is that the east pediments should depict a scene of divine peace and grandeur, that being the end at which the worshippers entered the temple. The west pediments, on the contrary, generally display a struggle. In this early Aeginetan temple both ends are filled with scenes of warfare from the epic glories of Aegina, one of Ajax, and one of his father, Telamon. These Aeginetan sculptures are assigned to the period between Marathon (490) and the years immediately following Salamis (480). The Harmodius group of which I have already spoken belongs clearly to the same phase (Compare Plate 68, *b*).

Later in time, midway between Aegina and the Parthenon, come the sculptures of the temple of Zeus at Olympia, which were brought to light during the German excavations of 1875-1881, and which are now in the Museum at Olympia. Here the rule of variety between east and west is strictly observed; at the east end, the subject is the preparations for the chariot race between Pelops and Oenomaus; not the race itself, but the moment before; the principal figures stand quietly in idleness, and the only movement is supplied by the grooms who tend to the harness. In contrast, the western pediment is filled with a mass of struggling, contorted figures; the myth represented is that of the marriage feast of Peirithous, when the Centaurs invaded the house and strove to carry away the womenfolk. Over the wild struggle stand Apollo in surpassing grandeur (Plate 73, *b*), Reason against Savagery. The metopes, which are earlier, decorated the eastern and western ends of the temple with the Labours of Hercules. The superb bodies, monumental drapery and noble heads are (Plate 73, *a*) equal achievements with the great bronze Zeus or Poseidon from Artemision (Plate 72, *b*); the columnar folds are in the Doric tradition and remind us of the Charioteer of Delphi (Plate 70). In style as in time these sculptures from Olympia occupy the middle place of the three sculptural units of the century; they have freed themselves from the archaic stiffness of Aegina, but have not yet attained the perfect freedom of the Parthenon pediments and frieze; there are still little crudities and errors which offended an earlier generation of critics, and it is only in comparatively recent times that full justice has been done to their overwhelming excellence.

If we turn from these to the Parthenon sculptures, we shall see the amazing swiftness of the maturing of Greek sculpture, apparent in one building and from a comparison of metopes and frieze. With Phidias, and largely no doubt owing to his genius, the plastic art has conquered its stubborn material, but it has not yet attained that fatal fluency which induces carelessness or conscious elaboration and extravagant striving for effect. This is the stage at which the arts and crafts produce their masterpieces, even in architectural sculpture where the volume of the work to be executed requires the piecework of the craftsman carrying out the plans of the superintending artist. Of such craftsmen we know something from the building accounts of fifth-century Athens, but it must be confessed that we have not a single work which we can ascribe with certainty to the hand of the master himself. His great masterpieces, the Zeus of Olympia and the Parthenos of the Parthenon, were of ivory and gold. Of course they have perished utterly. We have to content ourselves with descriptions and casual attempts at copying on coins or statuettes. The coins of Elis do indeed give us a Zeus of considerable dignity (cf. Plate 73, c) which may impart some faint notion of the glorious original, but of the Athena Parthenos we have not even this relic. I decline to follow the text-books on Greek architecture by presenting the woolly-headed Zeus of Otricoli or the well-groomed but fatuous old senator known as the Dresden Zeus for the works of Phidias. Nor will I insult him by depicting the Parthenos by means of the stumpy Varvakeion or the inchoate Lenormant statuettes. Such caricatures only disturb our judgment. For these statues we had better trust our imaginations, working upon what Pliny tells us: "The beauty of the Olympian Zeus seems to have added something to the received religion, so thoroughly does the majesty of the work suit the deity."

But can you, after all, imagine the splendour of these two statues made by the greatest sculptor who has ever lived? The flesh parts were of ivory, the clothing of solid gold on a core of wood or stone. Zeus was of colossal size, forty feet high. On his head was a green garland of branched olive; in his right hand he bore a Victory of ivory and gold, in his left a sceptre inlaid with every kind of metal. On the golden robe figures and lilies were chased. The throne was adorned with gold and precious stones and ebony and ivory, with figures painted and sculptured upon it. Even the legs and bars of the throne were adorned with reliefs. Round it were low screens, plain dark-blue in front and painted in panels by the sculptor's brother, Panainos, at the back and sides. The stool on which the god's feet were resting was adorned with figures in gold; the base, on which the throne rested, likewise. We must not picture ancient Greek art as cold and colourless like the marble statues by which it is represented in our museums. The Greeks loved colour, and used it everywhere. We have grown so accustomed to plain white statues that some of us are offended by the idea of colour in statuary and architecture. In this matter we may safely trust the good taste of the artists who could design and carve so wonderfully. The two favourite Greek marbles, the Parian and the Pentelic, are both of themselves very beautiful fabrics, far more lovely, with their glistening coarse grain and the intermixture of iron which gives them a warm yellowish glow, than the favourite modern marble of Carrara, which is so coldly white and so fine of texture as to dazzle and fatigue the eye and to blur all the delicate outlines. But the Greeks of that day looked upon even their lovely marbles as we do upon brick, good enough for building temples, but not worthy of the high gods. Ivory and gold for the gods, if the worshippers could afford it, otherwise bronze.

Regretfully, therefore, we must seek the genius of Phidias in works which were probably constructed according to his designs, minor works, mere decorative reliefs applied to architecture, much defaced by accident and time, but still bearing the stamp of grandeur and dignity. The sculptures of the Parthenon seem to have been about fourteen years in the making; the metopes were being worked between 447 and 442 B.C.; the frieze then occupied some four years, and last came the pediments, which were not finished before 433. Phidias left Athens, a victim to political intrigue and attack directed against Pericles, perhaps about 437 B.C. The recent discoveries at Olympia, in the so-called Workship of Phidias (which include a cup inscribed with his name (Plate 79, a), a small goldsmith's hammer which might have been his, and moulds for glass spangles and hammered golden drapery), seem to show that the great Zeus was later than the Athena. The work of many men can be recognised on the marbles of the Parthenon, as the accounts would confirm. But the general design is homogeneous, and we may well believe that the whole mass of sculpture had been designed by the master. In any case they are originals of the great period, and thus far better guides than any copies, however skilfully executed. Plutarch tells us that as the buildings of Periclean Athens rose "majestic in size and inimitable in symmetry and grace, the workmen rivalled one another in the artistic beauty of their workmanship. Especially wonderful was their speed. Phidias was the overseer". The surviving relics of the Parthenon sculptures fall into three groups, according to their place on the temple—the pediments, the metopes, and the frieze.

Of these the pediments are the most important for their size and prominence in the building. For example, they are the only external sculptures noticed by the traveller Pausanias. Moreover, each figure is a separate statue carved in the round, and perfectly finished back and front alike, though by no possibility could they be visible except from the front. Ruskin would inform us that this is evidence of the moral excellence of the artist. But the Greeks were a practical people who disliked waste in any form, and Professor Ernest Gardner is probably right in suggesting that the sculptor finished his statues in order that he might be sure they were rightly made. Such fidelity to his religious duty is evidence, after all, of moral excellence. Time has wrought cruel havoc with the sculptures. The central group of the east pediment had gone even before Carrey made his drawings for the Marquis de Nointel in 1674. In 1687 a great explosion occurred, when a Venetian gunner dropped a bomb into the Turkish powder magazine stored in the temple, and wrought further havoc. Then the victorious General Morosini tried to remove some of the figures from the west pediment, and broke them in the effort. In 1801 Lord Elgin, armed with a *firman* authorising him to remove a few blocks of stone, carried off the greater part of the surviving sculptures. From him they were purchased by the British Government for the British Museum. Whatever the morality of this capture, it was a blessing in effect, for the Parthenon suffered further damage during the War of Liberation, and those stones which remain *in situ* have deteriorated far more than those which were removed. Forlorn as they stand in the Museum, battered and bruised as they are, all headless but one, and he much defaced, they still convey an impression of unsurpassed beauty and perfection of art.

The subject of the front or eastern pediment (Plate 77) was the birth of Athena from the head of Zeus. The central scene was in all probability destroyed as early as the fifth century A.D. to make room for an apse when the temple was converted into a Christian church. Perhaps the armed figure of the goddess standing in front of the enthroned Zeus filled the apex with a flying Victory between them. n attendance, to judge from a Roman altar in Madrid, were the Three Fates (concerned with all births), and Hephaestus, who set Athena free with a blow of his axe; possibly also Hermes, the messenger of the gods, balanced on the other side by the swiftly moving woman with the wind-swept draperies who is still preserved (Plate 77, c) and who is universally recognised as Hebe, not Iris, for she lacks wings. The angle-groups still remain and are mostly among the Elgin marbles. In one corner the Sun is just rising in his chariot from the sea; the horses' heads dash up from the soft ripples of the water. At the other corner the Moon in her chariot is sinking below the horizon. That depicts the time of the great event. The identification of the other figures is uncertain, but most authorities incline to regard them as deities; some however prefer to see in them impersonations of scenery. Thus the glorious youth, commonly known as "Theseus", facing Helios with his back to the centre scene (Plate 77, a), may be either Dionysus, or perhaps a mountain, its side lit up by the early rays of the morning sun; would not Phidias have meant him for the Athenian Mount Hymettus or Olympus, setting the scene for the great event? Next come two seated goddesses who are generally thought to be Demeter and Persephone, mother and daughter (Plate 77, c).

At the other side of the gap artists have sighed over the perfection of those three seated female figures (Plate 77, b), headless alas! but wonderful in the perfection of craft which renders the elaborate folds of the soft Ionic draperies without impairing the massive grandeur of the bodies beneath. We used to call them "The Three Fates" but these have disappeared. It is probable that they are not a group of three; one reclines in the lap of her sister, the third sits alone. If the geographical interpretation is to hold good, we cannot improve Walston's suggestion that the sisterly pair is Thalassa (Sea) in the lap of Gaia (Earth). Or are they Aphrodite and Dione? That, however, leaves us without a clue to the third. Some say Hestia. But would not the moon set beyond land and sea over the island of Salamis?

The back or west pediment denotes a contest always, but here, as befits Athena, a contest moral rather than physical, the strife between Athena and Poseidon for the tutelage of Athens. The high angle in the centre would be filled with the olive-tree, and the two contestant deities may be seen in Carrey's drawing. Poseidon is starting back in amaze at the sight of Athena's gift, and she is advancing triumphantly; a winged Victory would be at hand to place the crown upon her head. The central group was flanked by the chariots of the two deities, and in the angles are again either deities or geographical personifications. Though in a sadly broken condition, many figures from this gable are known. The most considerable relic is a nude male reclining figure from one of the corners, the "Ilissus", now in the British Museum, superb in its mastery of anatomy, and the splendid torso of a winged and lightly-clad Iris (Plate 75, c).

Not only the execution of the figures, but the composition of the two scenes, with their subtle correspondences and distinctions, their intricate rhythm (notice in detail the arrangement of the drapery folds on "The Three Fates"), and yet their simple, broad dignity, is typical of what the fifth century was striving for. We might at first glance take the almost severe simplicity of fifth-century art, as we see it, for example, in the dramas of Sophocles or the history of Thucydides or the lines of Doric architecture, for the result of immaturity. But the more we study these things the more we find to study. The apparent simplicity has been produced with infinite labour and loving care.

The metopes of the Parthenon, originally ninety-two in number, consist of separate panels, almost square, adorned with figures in the highest possible relief, often quite free from the back wall. Each one represents a single combat, Gods against Giants, Lapiths against Centaurs, Greeks against Amazons, Greeks against Trojans, on the various sides. These subjects, with the contests of Theseus and the Labours of Heracles, are the regular themes of sculpture on Greek temples. They all represented to the Greek mind the everlasting contest between Hellenism and Barbarism, or between culture and savagery. Heracles destroying monsters like the Hydra snake, Theseus slaying robbers and oppressors of mankind, are symbolical of the conflict between the two sides. They also, no doubt, bear historical reference to the Persian wars. Because of the requirements of architectural construction, they were the first of the sculptures to be executed and in some we recognise the work of old sculptors trained in the school of archaic sculpture; many of these metopes recall the sculptures of Olympia. Others approximate more closely to the free style of the pediments and frieze. All are remarkable for the ingenuity of the composition. It was no easy matter to fill ninety-two square panels with struggling figures without monotony or iteration.

Lastly, we come to the frieze. To judge it rightly, the spectator must remember its position on the temple, for its character is entirely changed when it is seen at the level of the eyes on the walls of our museum. It ran round the top of the cella wall, 39 feet above the floor, inside the colonnade of the Parthenon. It could be examined by mounting the stylobate and craning your neck uncomfortably, but in an ordinary case you would merely catch glimpses of it between the columns as you passed along outside. Moreover, it was in the shadow of the roof, lighted from below by reflection from the white marble pavement. This the artist has foreseen and provided for by making the relief of the upper part deeper than below, so that the heads lean forward from the panels. Where deep shadows are required below they are often secured by cutting into the background. Here is another proof of the advantage art gains when her ministers are practical craftsmen rather than luxurious gentlemen who spend their time between the studio and the drawing-room. The designer of this *frieze*—and surely the designer was no less than the master himself—had a free hand here, with no laws of tradition to bind him, for such a frieze is without previous example. He had to cover an uninterrupted space of 524 feet with ornament. He chose for his subject the great procession representing the glory of Athens which went up every four years at the Panathenaic festival to offer a new saffron robe to the goddess. Observe how he has conceived it. Over the eastern front (Plate 76) he placed the immortal gods and goddesses, not in the awful majesty of Olympus, but down on earth in their beloved city of Athens. He depicted them at ease; only their added dignity of countenance and their greater stature (their heads reach the cornice, though they are seated) indicates their divinity. They are not overladen with attributive emblems. They are at home in Athens. They sit, they almost lounge, in comfortable attitudes. Dionysus leans on the shoulder of young Hermes. Ares, the dreadful Thracian warrior, has left his armour at home; he rests pleasantly with his right knee clasped in his hands. Hera unveils her head, turning to say a word to her royal husband, who sits a little apart in his simple dignity. Athena, the heroine of the hour, is marked by no pomp; she is conversing in friendly fashion with Hephaestus. Apollo turns his beautiful head to say a word to the grave Poseidon. Artemis sits before him (Plate 76, *b*). Eros is a naked human boy leaning at the knee of Aphrodite; she is fully draped, and even veiled, as becomes the deity of Heavenly Love. It is a warm, peaceful day; the gods have flung back their tunics from their shoulders, the goddesses are clad in soft Ionic robes. The sculptor has not chosen to represent the ceremony at its crisis. The procession is on its way, the music can be heard in the streets below. Close by Athena, separated by no extra space, a priest is handing a folded garment, the old *peplos*, no doubt, to a lad (Plate 76, *a*). It cannot be the offering of the new one, for Athena has her back to the scene. Groups of grave elders converse together, leaning on their staves. Attendant maidens stand near with baskets on their heads. This eastern end shows us the peace and happiness of an earth at its best.

Turning the corners, we have on each side the approaching procession, advancing towards the front at a slow pace. As the passing visitor glances up between the columns the procession actually moves. First on north and south come the young men leading the sacrificial beasts, oxen and sheep, with attendants bearing the trays and water-jars. The flute-players and harpers follow at the head of the warriors, the war-chariots with their dismounting warriors (Plate 78, *c*), men with branches of victory, and the hoplites with shield and spear. And then, most brilliant of all, the young knights, scions of the best families of Athens, sitting their fiery horses barebacked with charming ease and grace (Plate 78*a* and *b*), some wearing the broad hat and short chlamys, some in chitons, some with mantles flying in the wind, some in armour. Here and there you see the marshals ordering the procession. Farther back it is just forming; the young knights are mounting their horses and attendants are holding them ready. We must supply to the frieze a dark red background and bronze fittings such as spears and bridles.

But why in the world has he left out the sacred robe itself? Well, he might have chosen to put Athena on her throne in full panoply, and to have made the whole scene far more devotional and impressive to the religious sense. Instead, he has slackened the tension everywhere. The soldiers might have marched in disciplined ranks of Doric precision. The animals might have walked in two by two, as well-behaved beasts going to sacrifice should. The whole thing might have been formal and grand. Phidias preferred to make it charm by its simplicity and grace. His procession glows with youth and beauty, modest but unembarrassed. The young knight lacing up his military boot is quite unconscious that you and I are looking at him. It would not have done for the solemn pediments, it would have been out of place on the violent metopes, but here, just to glance at between the pillars, as a piece of light, supererogatory ornament, the artist felt at liberty to express the joy of living.

If you needed to look upon divinity in its awful grandeur, you had only to enter the shrine and worship before the temple statue. This was the chryselephantine Athena Parthenos, 39 feet high, with a great fortune of refined gold as her raiment, with her triple-crested helmet, her shield and Victory, her aegis and her serpent. Like the Olympian Zeus, she was to be as splendid as art could make her; there was colour and ornament everywhere. I do not suppose that even here she was very terribly militant. Loose tresses of her hair escaped to mitigate the ferocity of the helmet, with its fierce sphinx and monsters. Her pet owl was perched somewhere on her helmet. The Strangford Shield in the British Museum (Plate 75, *b*) is of great interest, because it seems to copy the design of the original shield with some fidelity, and it belongs to an interesting anecdote told about the sculptor. About 437, when Pericles was being attacked through his friends, they charged Phidias with embezzling some of the gold entrusted to him for this statue, and with blasphemous impropriety in putting his own portrait, together with the portrait of Pericles, on the goddess's shield. The first charge he could answer, because Pericles had warned him to make all the gold detachable so that it could be weighed. The latter bears a family resemblance to the whole class of sacristan's tales which attach to every artistic monument in Europe. There was, and there is, on the shield an old man's head which looks so realistic that it might be a portrait. Near him there is a warrior with his arm across his face, and that is said to have been the artist's device for concealing from common view a speaking likeness of Pericles. Nevertheless Phidias was condemned by the angry people, as Aristophanes, his younger contemporary, tells us:

Phidias began the mischief, he was first to come to grief.

Few other details of the sculptor's life are worth repeating. Many are given, but their contradictions involve us in hopeless difficulties. Neither portraits nor biographies belong to the fifth century, so wholly was the individual merged in the community. Later centuries had to provide them, and invent them.

The number of works credibly assigned to Phidias amounts to twenty-four. He was specially famed for his divine statues. He was able to practise for his chryselephantine work on what is termed an acrolithic image—that is, of gilt wood and marble—for little Plataea. He worked also in bronze. At Olympia he made a statue of the boy victor Pantarkes, whom he loved. For the Athenian Acropolis he made two other statues of Athena, one the colossal bronze figure which faced the visitor as he passed through the Propylaea on to the sacred citadel. Her spear was visible above the roofs to the sailors at sea, and it is so represented on the coins of the city. It was a work of his early years, executed for Cimon. It was removed to Constantinople, and the historian Nicetas tells us of its destruction by a drunken mob in A.D. 1203. There was also the Lemnian Athena (Plate 74, *a*), dedicated by the colonists of that island about 450 B.C. Here she was represented in a peaceful aspect without her helmet, "with a blush upon her cheek instead of a helmet to veil her beauty". The statue which Furtwängler compiled by setting a head from Bologna upon a body at Dresden has been claimed as a reproduction of this statue. Of course it is only a copy. If it be true that Phidias made dedicatory offerings for the Athenians at Delphi immediately after the Persian wars he must have had an artistic career of fifty years. In that time he had brought the art of sculpture from its childhood to the prime of manhood.

ICTINUS AND THE TEMPLE-BUILDERS

One of the characteristics of Greek art is the subordination of the artist to his work, as of the art itself to its purpose. This is but a part of the general subordination of the individual to society in Greek life. Hence it follows that we seldom have to think of isolated genius, and never of the genius of Greek artists as of some fitful and inexplicable freak of nature. For this reason it is not as incredible that there might have been several different Homers *all* men of genius as that two Vergils should have arisen at Rome, or two Shakespeares in England. Sappho is one among a group of superlative lyric poets.

Sophocles is one of four. Demosthenes is the greatest of a group of great orators. This remains a remarkable fact, in view of the natural tendency of time to sharpen the outline of peaks in the ranges of culture, and the national tendency of the Greeks, to personify all processes and movements.

Great as Phidias is, he is nevertheless surrounded by a circle of sculptors and architects, engravers and painters, who are all great. In execution they may be ranked in grades of ability, and their individualities are clearly discernible, but they are all inspired by the same nobility of artistic character, so that the spirit of fifth-century art is a thing that the eye can easily perceive. Reserve and dignity are its most prominent characteristics. It shares with all the best Greek art the qualities of grace and erectness, by which we mean a vivid and logical intelligence which knows its aim and pursues it unswervingly, manifesting itself alike in the major arts of sculpture and architecture, and in the minor arts of vase-painting (Plates 58, 59, 84) and coin-die engraving (Plates 49 and 96).

Phidias had Myron for a fellow-student. Of Myron's athletic work I have already spoken. He was as original as it was possible to be in the fifth century. As he was chiefly engaged in works of a private and occasional nature, he has naturally caught the attention of the epigrammatists. We hear much of the animal statues he carved and of their extraordinary realism, for that was the thing that appealed to the ancient art critic. Myron seems to have been a master of bronze technique and a skilful goldsmith. The marble copy of his Marsyas in the Lateran shows the satyr advancing to pick up the flute which Athena has just discarded, while Athena herself, identified not many years ago in a statue at Frankfurt, forbids him contemptuously. As in the Discobolus (Plate 68, a), we see the love of distorted poses which enabled Myron to exhibit his fine draughtsmanship and anatomy. Herein, indeed, he is *peu cinquième siècle*; but we must remember that this figure is one of a dramatic group. I have spoken of Polyclitus too as an athletic sculptor. It is rather remarkable that this youthful art should already in the fifth century be producing its "Canon" and its technical treatises. Though the Doryphorus (Plate 69, a) is the most famous of his works, yet the Diadumenus (Plate 69, b) was probably more popular in antiquity, to judge from the number of copies which have come down to us. Other names are mentioned by ancient writers as being worthy to be classed with

Phidias; Calamis, for example; but they are mere names to us, and the ingenious attempts of modern archaeology to fit them with appropriate works on the score of qualities attributed to them by ancient critics are hazardous, and for the most part unsatisfactory, as, for instance, in the case of the Delphic Charioteer (Plate 70; 72, *a*). Considering the few facts so recorded and the multitude of difficulties they raise, we cannot put much faith in the ancient art critic. Alcamenes and Paeonius, for example, were said to have been the sculptors of the two pediments at Olympia, and yet Alcamenes is described as a pupil of Phidias, which to anyone comparing the Apollo of the west pediment with the pedimental sculptures of the Parthenon is absurd. The other name is also doubtful, for Paeonius was the author of the famous Victory at Olympia (Plate 75, *a*), with its superb study of flying drapery. The inscription testifies that it was set up by the Messenians and Naupactians from the spoil of the enemy—presumably their Spartan adversaries of the Peloponnesian War sometime before 421 B.C. The statement of Pausanias therefore remains an unsolved puzzle, and most modern critics incline to suppose that he was misinformed.

So much for the named sculptors of the period. We have several other works which obviously belong to the same date. The fine portrait bust of Pericles (Plate 79 *c*) is, no doubt, a copy from the statue of Cresilas. I have said above that portraiture is rare in the fifth century. The extraordinary significance of Pericles in the art of the period is one reason for this exception. Moreover, it is, after all, scarcely a portrait in the Cromwellian sense, but rather an idealised type of the soldier statesman: so far from breaking, it notably illustrates the rule of idealism in the fifth century. It was said that all the portraits of Pericles represented him in a helmet to *conceal* his inordinately long head, which is a frequent subject of wit to the comic dramatists. Typical of the period too are the Eleusinian relief (Plate 71) and the Mourning Athena (Plate 87, *b*). The glorious bronze head of a Boy Victor (Plate 74, *b*) is one of the rare original bronzes of the great period. It is part of a full-length statue, formerly restored as a bust, and it is of great importance to students of ancient bronze workmanship. The eyeballs, when the statue was first found at Naples in 1730, were inlaid with silver and the pupils with granite. The lips are gilded, and there was silver and gold on the diadem.

From sculpture we pass to the sister art of architecture. Here we can safely affirm that Periclean Athens reached perfection within the limits it had set for itself—namely, the Doric style. For temple architecture the religious feeling of the day had prescribed a definite programme which it would have been almost blasphemy to outstep. That is to say, the outline of the temple was bound to correspond to the norm of Doric architecture, laid down more than a century before. The artist's originality was therefore confined to the task of improving its details in a manner which would pass unnoticed by the general public, who would but vaguely feel a heightened sense of rhythm and harmony. Here we find proof that Greek simplicity is the outcome of extreme subtlety. Until Penrose everyone had imagined the lines of the Parthenon to be straight. On the contrary, the apparently flat stylobate or floor rises 1 in 450 towards the centre over a length of 228 and a breadth of 101 feet. The columns do not only taper, as they seem to do, but they swell in the middle (*entasis*) in order to counteract the diminishing effect of light behind them, although in pure Greek work the diameter of the shaft is never greater than that of the base. The axis of the outside columns slopes inwards 1 in 106; the inner columns have a slightly smaller inclination, 1 in 150. Even the fluting is studied; the fine shadow effect is produced by diminishing the width but not the depth of the grooves as they approach the echinus. Nor are the columns all exactly the same thickness, for the corner pillars are made a little higher and thicker than their neighbours, because a fiercer light beats on them. Like the stylobate, the entablature also curves upward in the centre, but still more slightly—2 inches in 100 feet. The planes of the moulding are sometimes inclined forwards to prevent foreshortening. Thus to secure the effect of straightness Ictinus cut every stone of this great building on a slant measured to a hair's breadth. To the lay mind these facts throw a revealing light upon the nature of Greek art and the true meaning of Greek simplicity. Judge of the self-restraint shown by Ictinus (and of course *entasis* is not confined to the Parthenon) in expending this infinite trouble in a matter which would escape the eye of nine out of ten spectators. Nine out of ten? Yes, but the tenth might be a brother architect—or it might be Pallas Athena. Now that the measuring-tape has proved how subtle is Greek simplicity in one art, we must be prepared for it in other arts where we cannot measure so accurately—in literature, for example, when Euripides seems commonplace or Socrates illogical.

While the white marble columns and the white marble roof presented this appearance of simple strength and purity, the decorative mouldings between were enriched not only with the sculpture we have described, but with brilliant colour. The background behind the sculpture of the pediment was red, the ground of the metopes probably red, and that of the frieze probably red. The simple echinus and abacus mouldings of the capitals were enriched with leaf patterns in red, blue, and gold. The architraves had holes which once held bronze pegs for a row of gilt shields and wreaths. The grooves of the triglyphs were painted blue. A bright key-pattern ran along the upper edge of the triglyph. The *guttae*, or "drops", were probably gilt. On each corner of the roof-angle and at the apex of each gable rose an open-work acroterion carved and coloured.

Inside the colonnade is the cella, 194 feet long, with six columns of its own within the peristyle at each end. The interior was divided into two main parts—the Hekatompedos, exactly 100 Attic feet in length, where the great gold and ivory statue stood in solitary grandeur, and the Opisthodomos, to the west of it, strictly called the Parthenon, which was a sort of museum or bank for all kinds of offerings. The interior seems to have been lighted only from the doors. Ionic columns were used to carry the ceiling of the Parthenon proper. The wooden ceiling itself was adorned with sunken panels brightly painted. Battered and decayed as this marble building is today after its centuries of use as a temple, as a church, as a mosque, and as a powder magazine, it is still most wonderful in its majesty (Plate 10). We can hardly imagine the impression it produced when it glowed with life and colour on the day of the Panathenaic festival in 438 B.C., when it was opened to the public after nine years of building, with the sculpture probably still unfinished.

Let us glance at the principal buildings beside the Parthenon which crowned the flat-topped citadel hill. I suspect that most modern spectators feel a secret sense of discontent when they see a reconstruction of the Acropolis (Plate 10). The unregenerate Goth in our bosoms cries out for spires and pinnacles upon such a splendid site, for domes and towers and battlements to fret the sky above it. Indeed, it must be conceded that a Byzantine church often fits better into the landscape of Greece than the classical Greek temple.

When the Long Walls of Athens were completed there was no longer any need of fortifications to the Acropolis, though the archi-

tectural conception of the whole mass remained that of a shrine and
citadel combined. The Mycenaean rulers who dwelt on the Acropolis
levelled the top, probably fortified it at the west end, where alone it
was readily accessible, and surrounded it with a wall. The whole
plateau rises to a height of 200 feet. Approaching it from the agora
to the north-west, the pilgrim passed up a flight of low steps, with a
ramp in the centre, to the porch or Propylaea. This was begun in
437 by Mnesicles on the site of an older and much humbler gateway
perhaps of the sixth century. Modern investigators have shown
that it was planned on a far more extensive scale than the actual
execution, and that room was left for subsequent completion. It
may have been that religious scruples combined with a threat of war
with Sparta to restrict and curtail the execution. Even so it was
celebrated in antiquity, and is far the most impressive building erected
by the Greeks for secular purposes (Plate 10). It consists of a gateway
formed by a wall with five openings and fronted by a Doric colonnade,
with gable roof and pediment, flanked on each side in the original
plan by two colonnaded halls, a smaller one in front and a larger
behind. The entrance might well be a development of the gateways
of prehistoric citadels like Tiryns and Mycenae. Indeed, once a
Mycenaean gateway must have stood here too. One of the wing
chambers was used as a picture gallery, the walls being frescoed by
Polygnotus and other celebrated painters. This hall is still in excellent
preservation, due to its use by the Franks as a council chamber and
by the Turks as the palace of their Pashas. Some of the stone beams
are as long as 20 feet.

The front chamber of each wing rested on an artificial stone bastion,
but that on the south was never completed for the reason that it would
have encroached upon the precinct of a goddess, that of Athena Nike.
Here about 450 a little temple had been begun, which however was
not completed for many years, until about 420 or later. The delay
may have been due to a hope on the part of the party of Pericles that
they might be allowed to remove the temple and thus obtain
space in which to complete the Propylaea according to the original
plan. This temple, though its stones were totally scattered and
built into a Turkish bastion, was reconstructed in 1835 by European
architects and again since, with such success that it is one of the most
charming things in Athens (Plate 80, b). It has four columns of the
Ionic order at each end, surmounted with a sculptured frieze, of

which four panels are in the Elgin collection. The whole shrine, which is only 18 feet by 27 feet, was surrounded by a railing supported on a marble balustrade carved with Victories in low relief. Though they are mostly headless, these figures show wonderful delicacy of marble carving; the rendering of the soft transparent draperies clinging to the limbs dates them to the very end of the fifth century. From the platform in front of the shrine there was a lovely view over the Attic plain towards Eleusis. Beyond it, over Salamis and the blue Saronic gulf, you can see the citadel of Corinth and the distant mountains of the Argolid and the Peloponnese. It was here that old Aegeus stood watching for the sails of his dear son from Crete.

Pass through the wide portals of the Propylaea. On your right was the marble terrace where the little girls of Athens dressed up as bears to dance in honour of Brauronian Artemis. Here was Myron's group of Athena and Marsyas, and here Praxiteles was to make his statue of Brauronian Artemis. Beyond the Brauronian precinct was one of Athena the Craftswoman. At this point the colossal bronze Athena "Promachos" of Phidias towered above you, thirty-six feet high. We have visited the Parthenon already; to the left of it, just behind the foundations of the old temple of Athena Polias and the site of the Mycenaean palace, is the wonderful Erechtheum. This building, on a time-honoured site, was probably begun just before the outbreak of the Peloponnesian War, which delayed its completion; from an inscription in the British Museum, it is known to have been unfinished in 409, but was completed soon after. Here the task set to the architects was a peculiar one. It was a temple not only of Athena, but also of Poseidon-Erechtheus, a combination of god and ancestor-king of Athens. Also it had to include a number of immovable sacred objects, such as the salt spring which gushed up when Poseidon struck the rock with his trident, and the sacred olive-tree with which Athena defeated him. This patriotic tree had sprung up into new life after the Persians destroyed it, and had to be treated kindly. The architect overcame these problems with an unconventional building of extraordinary grace and charm. The main building has a colonnade of six Ionic columns in front, and a north porch of six Ionic columns projecting from one side; at the west end a precinct of Pandrosus (daughter of Cecrops), enclosing the sacred olive-tree, adjoined it and on the south side the portico of the Maidens on which tastes will differ (Plate 80, a). This is its most celebrated feature, from the

figures of the six statuesque girls who carry the graceful Ionic entablature. One of the Caryatids (a name derived from the town of
Caryae, in Laconia) was taken to London by Lord Elgin, and has
been replaced by a terra-cotta copy. The capitals on their heads are
designed like baskets. I have already spoken of this use of sculpture
for columns in connexion with the Telamones of Acragas. There
are also more archaic but neater and more charming maidens who
serve as supporting columns to be seen in the museum at Delphi
from the Cnidian and Siphnian Treasuries.

Besides the objects already mentioned, the Erechtheum contained
a number of very ancient relics. There you were shown the marks of
Poseidon's trident on the rock; there were spoils taken from the
Persians; an old wooden Hermes dedicated by Cecrops, a chariot by
Daedalus, a lamp by Callimachus kept perpetually burning, and above
all the ancient wooden image of Athena Polias.

I have only mentioned some of the wonderful objects on the sacred
rock. When Pausanias saw it, it was crowded from end to end with
works of art, sacred or commemorative and no profane person
inhabited it.

It was to the Acropolis that the attention of Pericles and his artists
was first directed when the time came to beautify Athens. In the city
below you would be struck by the ruin of the Persian sack of 480 B.C.,
with the plainness of the private houses, presenting no decorative
aspect whatever to the narrow and tortuous streets. They were of
one or two stories, with flat roofs, the larger ones built round open
courtyards; the women's apartments were often upstairs. The existing
area of the Plaka on the northern slopes of the Acropolis with its
narrow lanes and cobbles, its in-turned houses and courts must give
some fair idea of ancient Athens, just as the small open workshops of
Hephaistos Street must reproduce the industrial area which lay in
that region. The Agora (or market-place) was the centre of commercial, social and political life. Its excavation (or rather the excavation
of part of it, since the region beyond the Piraeus railway to the north
could not be dealt with) (Plates 11 and 12) is a triumph for American
archaeology, and revealed the core of Athenian history from the
earliest times to the last days of the ancient city in the sixth century
A.D. Along the western side of the Agora were such public buildings
as the Council Chamber of the Five Hundred and the Record office,
and hard by, the Law Courts (Plate 12, *a* and *b*). Close by were some

famous porticoes or cloisters, shady and cool to lounge in. In the Royal Portico the "king archon" sat to do his business, mostly connected with religion. Here the Council of the Areopagus met in later days. Here Socrates conversed, and here he was tried for impiety. Ancient laws were inscribed upon the walls of it. The Portico of the Liberator contained statues and celebrated frescoes painted by Euphranor in the fourth century. The Decorated Portico (Stoa Poikilé) in the Agora was even more famous for its historical and mythological pictures, including one of the battle of Marathon by Panainos or Micon, and one by the master Polygnotus of the taking of Troy. It was in this Stoa that Zeno developed in later times his Stoic philosophy. All these pictures have perished utterly, but we can still see reflections of them in the vase-painting of the day.

Above upon a low hill stands a Doric temple (Plates 12, *a* and 81) of the fifth century in almost perfect preservation. This is commonly called the Theseum, but it is certainly the temple of Hephaestus mentioned by Pausanias, and contained cult statues of Hephaestus and Athena (as patrons of arts and crafts) which may have been cast in pits recently found nearby. The temple is of Pentelic marble, surrounded on all sides by columns, with six at each end. It is roughly contemporary with the Parthenon, a date confirmed by finds of pottery and other objects in its foundations. It was not a very important building in ancient Athens; in fact, it is scarcely mentioned in antiquity; but as the best preserved building in all Greece it is of great architectural interest to us. It appears to be the earliest work of the same architect who was responsible for the temples of Sounion and Rhamnous, and for the temple of Ares in the Agora, moved to its present site in the Roman period. Fragments of the pedimental sculptures of the temple of Hephaestus have been found, and also the remains of the garden area which flanked the temple, with flowerpots for the plants. The metopes were not all carved; some were probably painted. There is also a sculptured frieze, at either end, carried across to the peristyle. The subject of the metopes was the Labours of Hercules and Theseus. They are rather badly weathered, and in their present condition not very attractive. Not far away is the Dipylon Gate, with its ancient burial-ground, excavated by the German School of Archaeology at Athens, of which we shall see more in a later section. At the opposite end of the city the visitor in the fifth century B.C. would have been struck by the immense columns of the temple of Olympian Zeus begun by Pisistratus, but never finished. Close under the Acropolis rock was the Theatre of Dionysus, in its present state belonging to a late period, where the tragedies and comedies were performed after this activity was removed (following on an accident) from a temporary structure in the Agora; and a music hall, or Odeion, erected by Pericles. There was a Cave of Pan on the precipitous slope of the rock. The public meetings of the Athenian Assembly were held on the hill of Pnyx, to the west of the Acropolis. Here there was a sort of open-air theatre in which the audience faced north and the speakers south towards the sea until the end of the fifth century, after which the positions were reversed, for practical reasons, perhaps, more than spiritual and political.

So entirely does Athens focus upon herself the culture of the fifth century, that we are apt to forget Athens was not Greece. The Temple of Zeus at Olympia (Plate 4), was the most celebrated temple in all Greece, because of its great Zeus from the hand of Phidias, while the shrine as a whole was famed as the centre of the Olympic Games and for the wealth of the dedications there and the number of athletic statues. Delphi too was enriched with countless artistic offerings sent, in spite of the Pythian's faint-hearted counsels, from the spoil of the Persian and other wars. There was a famous tripod with a stand of twisted serpents, on whose coils were inscribed the names of those cities which had taken part in the battle of Plataea. A forlorn remnant of it still exists at Constantinople on the site of the Hippodrome. Both Olympia and Delphi have been excavated, the former by the Germans and the latter by the French. They have both (Plates 5, 61 and 48) been veritable mines of material for the illumination of the history and art of early and classical Greece (cf. Plates 43 a and b; 44 c). The greatest finds at Olympia were the Hermes, an original or, more likely, a copy of a work by Praxiteles (Plate 92), which belongs to the next epoch, and the temple pediments, which I have already mentioned. At Delphi the long-robed charioteer, one of the noblest fifth-century bronzes (Plate 70), was the most conspicuous treasure. Traces were found of a great number of small shrines which acted as the treasuries of the various states and were grouped round the great temple of Apollo, and some of these, notably the Siphnian (Plate 57), and Athenian (Plate 61) treasuries, have yielded important relics of sculpture. The holy precinct was crowded with treasuries, shrines, votive groups, colonnades and theatre. The

Altis at Olympia was similarly filled with treasuries (Plates 4 and 48); round it just outside were the stadium (of which recent excavations have produced multitudes of fine bronzes including historically important dedications: cf. Plate 67), the hippodrome, the palaestra, and the gymnasium.

Hidden away in a remote mountain glen of Arcadia there is a lovely ruin amid the most solitary and romantic scenery (Plate 6). This is the temple of Phigalia, the modern Bassae. It was dedicated by the Phigalians to Apollo the Helper in consequence of an epidemic. The story, which is doubted by modern writers, runs that they sent for the most famous architect in Greece soon after the completion of the Parthenon. Ictinus used, since his clients were poor mountaineers, the local limestone for the building, but the roof and sculptures were of imported marble. He had also to modify the normal Doric plan in accordance with local religious conventions of sun-worship. In the cella of the temple the interior Ionic columns are joined to the wall by short stone partitions, thus forming a row of five chapels on each side: in the centre stood a free Corinthian column, the earliest example of that order. A door was made in the east side to shed the light of the rising sun full on the statue of the sun-god; for the main building is unique among Greek temples in running north and south. The narrow frieze which ran round the interior of the cella represented, as usual, contests of Greeks and Amazons, Centaurs and Lapiths. It is now in the British Museum. It is of the very finest workmanship, and here we see a system of design hardly less subtle than that of the Parthenon frieze applied to scenes of vigour and violence (Plate 82). The frieze was removed bodily by Baron von Stackelberg and bought at auction by the British Government for £15,000.

We find another example of the versatile genius of Ictinus at Eleusis. Eleusis was the most important town of Attica except Athens, and had long been independent. It formed an agricultural centre for the plain around it. Its famous mysteries were of agricultural significance to start with, and were chiefly concerned with the worship of Demeter and Persephone (Plate 71) in their characters as grain-givers. The cult went back to ancient beginnings, at the latest Mycenaean, and was developed by the tyrant Pisistratus in the sixth century. It was no doubt a later development when the Greeks began to graft the deepest religious and metaphysical doctrines relating to immortality upon them. We can easily see how rustic rites celebrating the death and rebirth of the cornfields should come to bear this exalted meaning for reflective people. Every year on the fifth night of the Greater Eleusinian festival in spring the Athenian people trooped out along the Sacred Way in a torchlight procession. Only the initiated, the Mystae, were allowed to witness the secret ceremony, which seems to have consisted of a ritual marriage and some form of revelation.

The Great Hall of the Mysteries was begun, but not completed, by Ictinus, either because of the death of Pericles or because the plan of Ictinus was too grandiose and difficult of execution. In either case the work was continued under other architects, and many problems attend the interpretation of the fifth century and later remains. There may have been other difficulties, for the Peloponnesian War put a stop to the Eleusinian worshippers from Athens—not the least of their deprivations. But the Mysteries were resumed when Alcibiades came home, and continued until Alaric the Goth destroyed the shrine. The peculiarity of this building is that it cuts into the living rock. The interior somewhat resembled a theatre, with eight stone tiers all round it. It is not likely to have had a second story supported on the columns of the hall, but perhaps an upper series of columns, or a balcony, or even some sort of frieze. The building itself was square, with a portico in front only, added in the late fourth century. The upper levels of the site were reached by a rock-terrace cut out of the hill-side at the back. The whole complex, with outbuildings, was enclosed by a wall. The visitor to Eleusis, already repelled by the presence of modern industry, will be dismayed by the complexity of the site, but he should persevere to understand it both for the importance of the cult in Antiquity and as an exercise in archaeological interpretation.

Summing up the architectural character of the period, we should say that it was severely limited by the conservatism of religion to the austerest outlines and the simplest plans. Such laws it loyally obeyed, and yet found scope for exquisite workmanship and subtle varieties within them. Ictinus and Mnesicles were quite capable of adapting themselves to any local peculiarities, but the strict Doric style still reigned supreme. Finally we note that fine architecture is almost entirely confined to the service of religion and patriotism, while private and secular buildings are still on the most unpretentious scale. The only architectural work of a strictly utilitarian character that we can mention is the planning of the Piraeus, which was as orderly, as regular and as dull as "town-planned" towns generally are, for Hippodamos of Miletus the planner was a philosopher, and there is nothing worse than the architect-townplanner with philosophical theories.

TRAGEDY AND COMEDY

It was clearly the policy of Pericles, when he trusted his fellow-citizens with so much power, to attempt to train them to be fit to wield it. Fond as the Athenian was of political and social equality within his own circle of citizenship, his tone and temper were, I think, like those of all the other Greeks, inherently aristocratic. The Greeks were a chosen people. They stood aloof, with slaves and helots beneath them, and with barbarians all round them. Few Greeks would have disputed the doctrine by which Aristotle justified slavery: the Greek is by nature superior; set him down in a barbarian city, and in a short time the Greek would be king. They would have laughed sweetly at Lafayette's "Rights of Man". Man only gets his rights as a member of a partnership, a corporate community—to wit, a city. This community he entered, when he was acknowledged as a citizen, not without a strict scrutiny into his claims, as formally as we enter a club. Having once joined partnership with such a state as Athens, his rights become precise and important. Among other rights, a democracy offered him that of taking his turn in the government if the lot or the votes of his fellow-citizens designated him for office. Political philosophy maintained as an axiom that the better people ought to rule over the worse, condemning all democracy, and Athens in particular, because there the many ruled over the few, and therefore necessarily the worse over the better. Pericles would not have denied the doctrine, but only its applicability to Athens. He would have claimed that the whole Athenian citizen body possessed "virtue" in the political philosopher's sense of the word; they were all *aristoi*, for he had seen to it that the Athenian citizens should all receive a training, which, though utterly different from the Spartan in its aims and methods, was even more capable of turning the masses into an aristocracy of manners and intelligence.

It was a liberal education even to walk in the streets of that wonderful city, to worship in her splendid shrines, to sail the Mediterranean in her fleets, to lounge in her colonnades and listen to the wisdom of the wise. The temple services, the festivals, and the banquets were

intended with solemn symbolism to uplift the minds of the worshippers. There was actual practice in public business for everyone,
whether in the Assembly or the Council Hall or the large Jury Courts.
Thus it was hoped that any man whom the lot might appoint to be
archon or president would be fit for his duties.

But of all instruments of public education perhaps the most important
was the Drama. This word, which we in our day (or most of us)
associate predominantly with entertainment, and at best cultural
entertainment, meant to the Greeks a religious solemnity destined
to the praise of gods and the edification of men. During the fifth
century at Athens the stage was far the most powerful form of literary
and artistic expression—so much so that, as Greek literature in this
period is almost entirely absorbed by Athens, all the other voices of
poetry are for a time reduced to silence. The amazingly rapid development of this form of expression was largely due to the concentration
with which the literary genius of Greece pursued it. Athenian drama,
Tragic, Comic, and Satyric, was produced at the festivals of Dionysus,
and it has generally been supposed (though there are many different
opinions, nearly as many as there are experts) to have taken its rise
from rude choruses in honour of the wine-god, developed by Arion
and others into the Dithyramb. This is an ancient and respectable
theory. The Satyric Drama is obviously connected with wine and the
wine-god's goatish followers, the Satyrs. Comedy was derived
either from *kömos*, a revel, or from *kömë*, a village, being originally the
rustic form of the same species of mimetic worship. As for Tragedy, that
was traced etymologically to the Greek for a goat, and of course the
goat has a family relationship with Dionysus. Another theory has
been based on the fact that ancient Tragedy has, as was often remarked
by the ancients themselves, nothing to do with wine or Dionysus, and
is scarcely of the festive character that we should associate with that
cheerful deity. The late Sir William Ridgeway accordingly suggested
that the drama took its rise in quite a different manner—namely,
from the cult ceremonies held at the tomb of a dead hero. He cited
the frequent appearance of tombs in the scenery of Tragedy, and
adduced evidence to prove that the Greeks did include mimetic
representations of the dead hero and his deeds among the ceremonies
performed in his honour. This would account not only for the
character of Tragedy, with its sombre musings upon Death and Fate,

but also for the milieu in which its scenes invariably moved—namely, the Epic circle of heroes.

What is certain and most important for the understanding of Tragedy is that the Drama was evolved from the song and dance of the Chorus. First one and then two members of the *corps de ballet* were brought out from the ranks to perform solo impersonations, to narrate an episode in descriptive verse, or to exchange information by rapid questions and answer. Important stages in this evolutionary process were attributed in antiquity to Thespis, the so-called "inventor" of Tragedy, and to Phrynichus and Aeschylus, all Athenians of the late sixth and early fifth centuries. Then the part played by the "Answerers" (*hypokritai*), as the actors were called, gradually gained in magnitude and importance. In Aeschylus the choric passages are still the main feature of the play, but he introduced the second actor. In Sophocles they form a kind of lyric commentary on the action of the drama, in which the interest now begins to centre. In the later work of Euripides the Chorus is largely a superfluous concession to dramatic conventions. Already by the end of Sophocles' career there were as many as four actors, and since each performed several impersonations, the range of character was considerable. Grand as Athenian drama is, even regarded as a vehicle of literary composition, the mere writing of the "book" was a subordinate part of the work of producing a play. In fact Greek tragedy is far more closely akin to the modern oratorio than to the modern stage-play. The task of providing, equipping, and training a chorus was one of the "liturgies" or public duties laid by the Athenian state upon her richer citizens. It lay in the archon's discretion to "grant a chorus" to a poet.

The stage (compare the later great theatre at Epidaurus (Plate 8)) consisted originally of a circular dancing-floor (*orchestra*) with an altar in the middle. Here the fifteen members of the chorus marched in, headed by a single flute-player, chanting in unison. As soon as they had arrived in position they formed a line three deep, the coryphaeus in the middle of the front row, with the leader of each semichorus on his right and left. While they sang they performed simple rhythmic movements of a solemn character. At first the individual actors simply stepped out from the ranks to deliver their lines, but in later times (when, precisely, is a matter of burning controversy) they appeared behind the orchestra on a raised stage. The performance was, of course, always given in the open air. In the fifth century there

65. "Back" panel of the so-called Ludovisi "Throne" in the Museo Nazionale delle Terme, Rome.

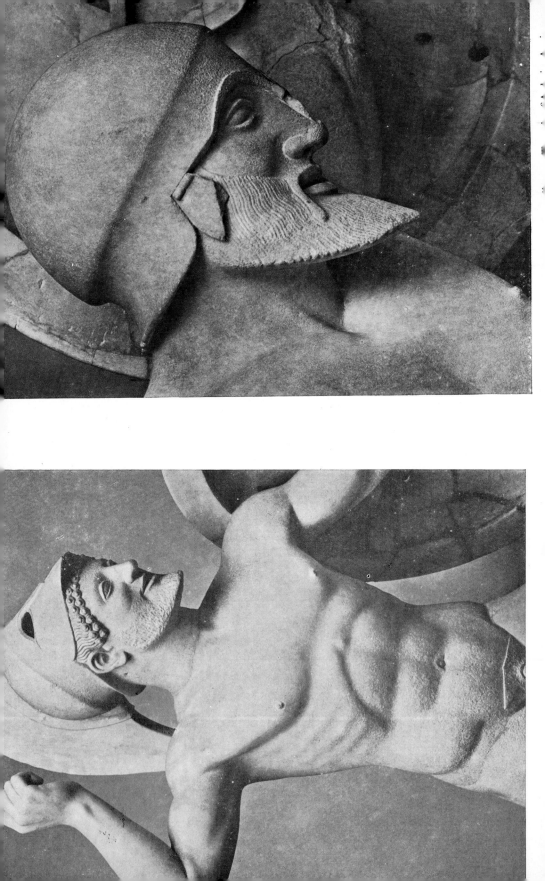

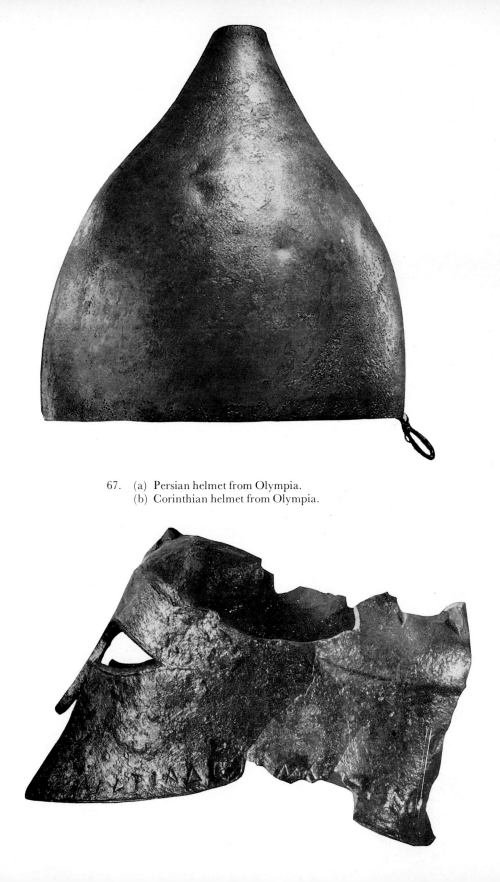

67. (a) Persian helmet from Olympia.
    (b) Corinthian helmet from Olympia.

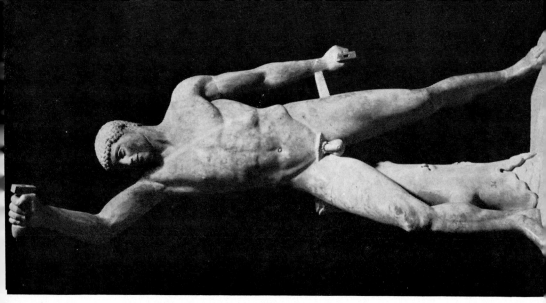

68. (a) *left*
The Discobolus of Myron, Castel Porziano torso, restored. In the Museo Nazionale, Rome.

(b) *right*
Harmodius, in the Museo Nazionale, Naples.

69. (a) *opposite, left*
Copy of the Doryphorus of Polyclitus, in the Museo Nazionale, Naples.

(b) *opposite, right*
Copy of the Diadumenus of Polyclitus, found in Delos, in the National Museum, Athens.

70. *left*
The bronze chariote
found at Delphi.

71. *opposite*
The Eleusinian Relief
the National Museu
at Athens.

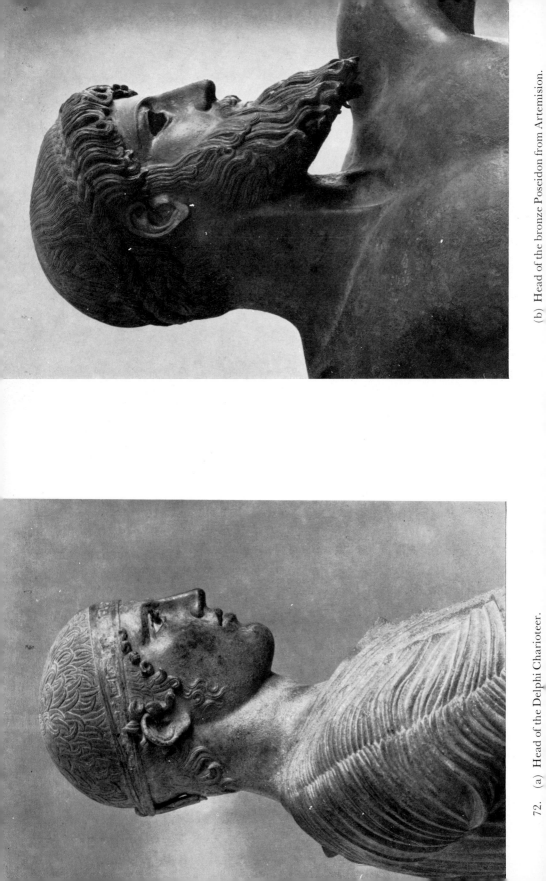

72. (a) Head of the Delphi Charioteer.

(b) Head of the bronze Poseidon from Artemision.

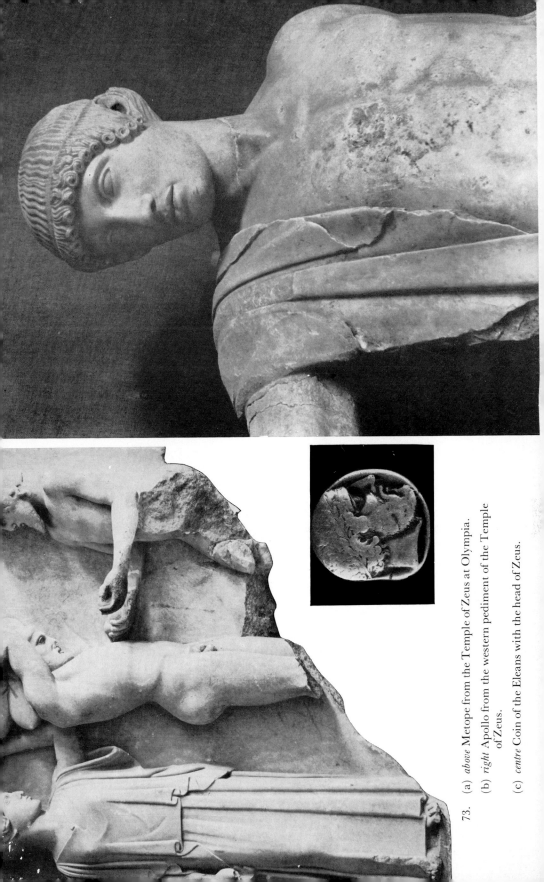

73. (a) *above* Metope from the Temple of Zeus at Olympia.
(b) *right* Apollo from the western pediment of the Temple of Zeus.
(c) *centre* Coin of the Eleans with the head of Zeus.

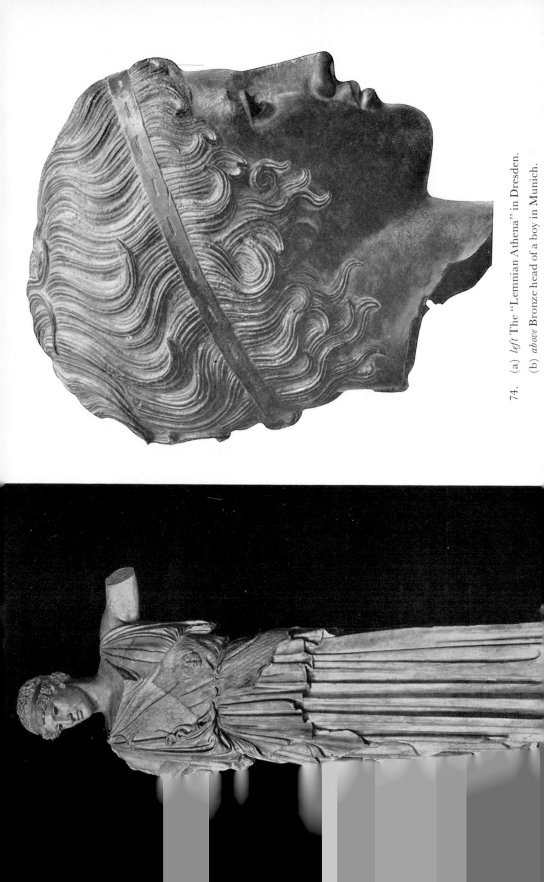

74. (a) *left* The "Lemnian Athena" in Dresden.
    (b) *above* Bronze head of a boy in Munich.

75. (a) *above*
    The Victory of Paeonius.

(b) *right*
    The Strangford Shield.

(c) *top right*
    Iris from the West Pediment of
    the Parthenon.

76. *above and below* Slabs from the Eastern Frieze of the Parthenon.

77. *opposite* Figures from the Eastern Pediment of the Parthenon.

78. (a) *left and* (b) *above*
Youthful cavalrymen from the Nor
Frieze of the Parthenon.

(c) *below*
Armed warrior in a chariot. From the Sou
Frieze of the Parthenon.

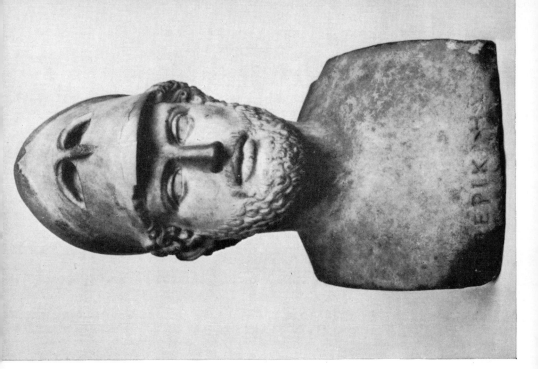

79. (a) *above* A cup found at Olympia in the workshop of Phidias.

   (b) *left* A potsherd bearing the name of Pericles.

   (c) *right* A bust in the British Museum said to be Pericles.

was only a primitive "theatre", at first in the Marketplace, with
wooden staging for seats. After an unfortunate accident there, the
slope under the south-eastern end of the Acropolis was adapted, still
in a primitive manner, near a temple of Dionysus. It was not until
late in the fourth century that the great Theatre of Dionysus, with its
tiers of stone seats resting on the living rock, was constructed in the
same place. It has been remarked that the Greek stage was not, as
ours normally is, pictorial, but rather plastic, giving the effect of
figures in relief against a background. This, the size of the theatre,
the distance from the spectators, and the open air were the reasons
why the actors wore high boots which gave them super-human
stature, and padded garments and trailing skirts, The masks they
wore were part of the traditional convention of Greek drama
(Plate 85, a). The mask would, of course, preclude any facial expression
whatsoever. The Greek actor showed his skill in the grace of his
movements, the expressiveness of his gestures, and the clearness and
force of his articulation. Dramatic declamation was his main business.
Under these circumstances it is clear that we must not expect subtle
nuances of meaning to be conveyed by the actors in Greek tragedy,
though modern interpreters are always on the look-out for them.
It is obvious that the whole character of the representation was thus
transformed. The female parts, too, were, as on our own Elizabethan
stage, invariably taken by men or boys. The scenery was relatively
simple and unsophisticated. There could, indeed, be exotic effects or
rich and splendid costumes (both of these were characteristic of
Aeschylus) but the costume was one conventional to the tragic stage;
there was only the slightest attempt to dress the parts. The plays thus
had the simplicity and breadth of treatment which we have seen in
the statuary and architecture of the period. The art of Phidias
is the most illuminating commentary upon that of Sophocles. As
we saw in Cresilas' portrait of Pericles, idealistic treatment is maintained
so faithfully as a principle that realistic and individual characterisation
is only admitted so far as it does not conflict with the ideal. In both
arts the heroes and heroines must have, as an essential basis, the profile
and contours of physical and moral perfection. It is only within these
limits that Deianira can be soft and womanly, Antigone stern and
faithful unto death, Ajax bluff and bold, Neoptolemus young and
generous. There are broader strokes of character-drawing in the
minor characters. Messengers, slaves, and sentinels are sometimes

permitted the homely sententiousness of Juliet's Nurse. But there is nothing that can truly be called relief from the stern shadows that encompass the world of Greek tragedy.

It must not be forgotten that the themes upon which Tragedy drew were, almost exclusively, the heroic or epic legends. One or two exceptions there are; the "Persae" of Aeschylus is one such, for reasons which I have already explained. Phrynichus also wrote a tragedy founded on contemporary history, "The Sack of Miletus", an episode of the Ionian revolt. But such a theme came too near home, touched too closely on politics, and the poet was punished with a fine. Otherwise the dramatist had little scope for originality or for the element of the unexpected in the choice of his plot. It is as if our dramatists were restricted to the Bible for their choice of subjects instead of being largely debarred from it. The audience knew the main outline of the story as soon as the play began. Thus the audience was often in the secret while the characters on the stage were not, and this fact gave scope for dramatic irony, which is especially connected with the name of Sophocles.

Sophocles is for literature the supreme embodiment of the Athenian spirit at this its purest and highest period. The tragedies of Aeschylus have the grandeur and incompleteness of archaic art. He wrestles with the most awful problems of human destiny and divine purpose. His style matches his themes; it is a whirlpool of foaming imagery in which great masses of poetry in phrase and metaphor appear and disappear without end. He continually baffles the transcriber and the modern interpreter, and it is only the most reverential spirit that can refrain from occasional sensations of ludicrous bathos. Euripides, on the other hand, is so fluent and easy in his craftsmanship that he often seems by contrast commonplace. He is probably the cleverest of all dramatists, and he often dealt with his religious themes in the spirit of an unabashed sceptic. Like Plato, he saw that the gods of anthropomorphic creation were very far from ideal; and he used all the craft and subtlety of the rationalist to exhibit them at their weakest. Aeschylus is the poet of the religious men of Marathon; Euripides, "the human", is the prophet of the New Age of the fourth century, liberal, cosmopolitan, restless and fearless in inquiry. He is also the forerunner of the Romantic drama, and the New Comedy of Menander. Sophocles is the true exponent of Periclean Athens in the realm of literature.

With his inflexible idealism, the poetry of Sophocles is sublimated almost beyond human ken. Moderns sometimes find him too perfect, too statuesque to be interesting. It is both their misfortune and their fault. The appreciation of Sophocles is a test of refined scholarship and an ear sensitive to the inner voices of poetry. This makes translation almost impossible, but Mr. Whitelaw, of Rugby, has come so near to achieving that impossible that I would venture, through his medium, to present a specimen of this poet's exquisite art. This is the famous choric ode on Love from the "Antigone".

STROPHE

O Love, our conqueror, matchless in might,
Thou prevailest, O Love, thou dividest the prey:
In damask cheeks of a maiden
Thy watch through the night is set.
Thou roamest over the sea;
On the hills, in the shepherds' huts, thou art;
Nor of deathless gods, nor of shortlived men,
From thy madness any escapeth.

ANTISTROPHE

Unjust, through thee, are the thoughts of the just;
Thou dost bend them, O Love, to thy will, to thy spite.
Unkindly strife thou has kindled,
This wrangling of son with sire.
For great laws, throned in the heart,
To the sway of a rival power give place,
To the love-light flashed from a fair bride's eyes:
In her triumph laughs Aphrodite.

Me, even now, me also,
Seeing these things, a sudden pity
Beyond all governance transports:
The fountains of my tears
I can refrain no more,
Seeing Antigone here to the bridal chamber
Come, to the all-receiving chamber of Death.

In this ode we have the Greek tragic view of the passion of Love, as the destroyer and distractor of man's peace and sanity. Love is one of the means whereby tragic fate fulfills its purposes of vengeance. The circumstances of this particular case are these: Of Antigone's two brothers one had marched against his native city, and the other had taken arms in its defence. Both had fallen on the field of battle. Creon, the city's tyrant, forbade anyone, under pain of death, to give burial to the slain enemy. In this, of course, he was violating one of the most sacred laws of Greek religion. Now Antigone was betrothed to Creon's own son, Haemon; nevertheless her duty was to brave the tyrant's decree and give the honours of formal burial to her dead brother. She did so. Creon thereupon pronounced her doom, and Haemon in his despair slew himself upon the tomb in which she was immured. The whole story is but an episode in the doom of the house of Oedipus, father of Antigone. The Greek view of Love, then, is the antithesis of the romantic view of it. Where Love conflicts with duty it must be rigorously suppressed, as a source of folly, weakness, and wickedness. So much is this the case that Sophocles puts into the mouth of Antigone words which he had probably borrowed from Herodotus, and which give a view of the Great Passion so painfully unromantic that the modern commentator, who for all his prosiness is a thoroughly romantic person, is tempted to use the shears by which he commonly cuts his knots and call it an interpolation. "My duty," says Antigone, "is to my brother first. You speak of my duty to my future husband, and my future children. I reply that a brother is more than husband or children; *they can be replaced, a brother cannot.*"

An even more disconcerting display of common sense in a presumably romantic situation is seen in that amazing play, the "Alcestis" of Euripides. Everyone knows the tale, how Admetus was allowed as a boon from Apollo to get someone else as a substitute in his place when Death came to fetch him. His faithful wife, Alcestis, took his place, being consoled by Admetus with the promise of a handsome funeral. Then the king's old father appears upon the scene to offer his condolences to the widower, but is immediately assailed with the most vehement reproaches for not having himself, as an old man with one foot in the grave, shown sufficient pluck to volunteer death. He not unnaturally retorts that if it is a question of daring to die, Admetus himself had not been remarkable for courage. The point is one that pleases Euripides; it is a nice point of casuistry; he lets the speakers dispute it at some length. I think these two passages are significant of much. When we think of the Greeks as a race of poetic and artistic genius we must not forget that practical, unsentimental common sense is among their most prominent characteristics. They habitually exposed weakly infants to death. Their comedy is singularly merciless to disease and deformity. Plato's treatment of the sex problem in his ideal republic is strikingly cold-blooded, but hardly more so than the actual treatment of the same problem in the real republic of Sparta. Before we leave this question of the romantic in the Greek character two things should be observed. The romantic element unquestionably grows stronger as Greek civilisation approaches its decline: there is a good deal of it in Menander and Theocritus, still more in Heliodorus; Alexander the Great is romantic to the finger-tips. Secondly, although there is so little of it in Tragedy, or generally in the relations between the two sexes, it is found in a degree of almost modern intensity in the relations between Herakles and Hylas, between Theseus and Peirithous, between Harmodius and Aristogeiton. It was not foolishness to the Greeks for a man to face death for the youth he loved. Indeed, upon that theory Epaminondas the Theban organised that Sacred Band which for a time revolutionised Greek history.

Another characteristic excellence of Greek drama, and especially of Sophocles, is its extraordinary power of narrative. With its severe scenic limitations, the Attic stage wisely refrained from attempting to reproduce realistically exciting spectacular incidents. The actual "tragedies" seldom occur in the sight of the audience. Far more often the hero or heroine leaves the stage in despair, the chorus intervenes with a mournful ode, and then a messenger arrives with a narrative of the fatal occurrence. Shakespeare, with scarcely less severe limitations, faced the impossible, and courted ridicule by representing battles in full detail on the stage by means of a handful of overworked "supers". What they could not represent the Greeks narrated; and Horace, indeed, exalts it into a principle of dramatic art that "Medea must not butcher her babes in public". That the Greek dramatists so refrained was probably due to dramatic tradition as well as to the practical necessities of the case. When there was only one speaking actor in addition to the chorus his part must have been chiefly what our composers of oratorios call "recitative". For these two reasons, and perhaps also in obedience to the Greek spirit of self-restraint, narrative declamation by "messengers" is a striking feature of all Greek tragedy.

We have seen already the religious theory upon which tragedy is generally based, the logical sequence of Success, Pride, Vengeance, and Ruin. The tragedians deal largely with stories of the doom which had pursued certain of the heroic houses like that of Labdacus or Atreus. In such cases a prophetic curse rests upon the entire dynasty: Atreus slays his brother's children and bequeaths doom to Agamemnon. Agamemnon is slain by his guilty wife Clytemnestra, whereby a duty of vengeance devolves upon their son Orestes, who *must* slay his mother, and therefore *must* incur the celestial doom of matricide, unless Apollo himself can intervene to release him from the vengeance of the Furies. Such stories were pursued by all three great tragedians, often in sequences of three tragedies called trilogies. They have no "moral", except that sin breeds suffering to the third and fourth generation, but the sin is often an involuntary one and "learning comes through suffering". The purpose of the tragedian is to show the struggles of man against fate. According to Aristotle's oft quoted theory, the purpose of Tragedy is to act as a "purgative of the emotions by means of pity and terror". As the surgeon lets blood in order to reduce fever, so the drama enables the spectator to acquire peace of soul through the vicarious sorrows of its heroes and heroines. Aristotle declares every tragedy to consist of two parts, the tying of the knot and the loosing of it. The "loosing" commonly involves a *peripeteia*, or sudden reversal of fortune, as when Agamemnon's triumphant return is changed to death and mourning; often it is brought about by an *anagnōrisis*, or recognition, as when the stranger in the palace is found to be Orestes come home for revenge. The so-called Aristotelian "unities", which have loomed so bulkily in the history of dramatic criticism, and under the fear of which the classical dramatists of France were imprisoned, are not to be found in Aristotle. He does, indeed, advocate unity of subject, but unity of time and place are nowhere demanded. The natural limitations and the consequent simplicity of the Greek stage generally imposed these unities as a practical necessity.

Greek simplicity is often, as we have seen, a studiously contrived impression and the result of elaborate concealment of art. That it is not entirely so in the case of the drama is proved by the astonishing fertility of the principal dramatists. Aeschylus wrote more than 70 plays, Sophocles 113, Euripides 92, and another tragic poet whose work has not survived 240. They were written and produced in competition. In 468 B.C. or thereabouts Sophocles began his public career by competing against Aeschylus for the prize of Tragedy. As the judgment seemed equally divided, we are told, the presiding archon left the decision to the ten generals who had just come back victorious from their warfare in Thrace. The prize was awarded to Sophocles, who, it is significant to notice, had been specially trained under a famous musician. But not every one believes the story. Euripides won the prize five times only in a poetical career of fifty years. A prize was likewise awarded to the choregus who produced and trained the best chorus. It was the custom for the successful choregus, who was always, of course, a rich man, to dedicate his prize—a tripod—in a certain street in Athens. One such monument of the fourth century by a certain Lysicrates is still standing in fair preservation. It is a pretty example of the luxurious Corinthian order of architecture and is said to have served as a study for Lord Byron. This particular award was for another type of chorus.

Tragedies were performed in Athens twice a year, at the festivals of the City Dionysia at the end of March, and of the Lenaea at the end of January. There was also the country festival of the Rural Dionysia which fell in December. The poet had an audience of thirteen thousand including (in the great city Dionysia) strangers from all parts of Greece. At first, it would seem, admission was free, but so great was the crush that a small entrance fee was charged. It was one of the really popular measures of the fifth century to start a fund for enabling the poorer citizens to enter free, since this was a public and religious duty from which no one should be debarred. Besides, as noticed above, there was the cultural and educational aspect of the Drama. After all, why should the privileges of free education be lost by the citizen merely because he is an adult? Why should we have to pay to enter the theatre, when the doors of the National Gallery are opened to us for nothing?

Some find it much more difficult to speak of the Attic Comedy with unqualified approval. It is to be suspected that many feel it was unworthy of the great days of Athens. It is also true that ideas of humour differ. Scholars of unblemished reputation and unimpeachable sense of humour do unquestionably find the plays of Aristophanes, even when produced by English schoolboys on speech-day, excessively diverting. There is, it is true, in Aristophanes a good deal of simple honest fun of the type represented by Mr. Punch or Mr. Pickwick and his spectacles in the wheelbarrow. When the wrong man gets a thwacking or when an ignorant amateur, told to sit to the oar, proceeds to sit *on* it, it is, I suppose, no less funny in the twentieth century *anno Domini* than it was in the fifth century before Christ. But there I must leave the humour of Aristophanes to those who can appreciate it and still laugh even when they have laboriously picked out the point of the joke from the notes at the end of their text-book. Some of the humour is of this type. It was written to burlesque the well-known figures of the day, and no doubt served its purpose extremely well. Ancient historians have been known to find it important. Indeed, there is no more certain proof of the liberty of speech which prevailed in Athens than the fact that Aristophanes was permitted to represent Cleon the Leader of the Radicals in successive plays in the most ludicrous and offensive situations. There are elements in the Old Comedy of Athens which rest largely upon a basis of venomous personal slander and libel without self-restraint, without even common decency. It is a phenomenon which must be accepted, one aspect of the many-sided character of the Athenians, based on that lively and cynical interest every man took in his fellow. There are also strong elements of obscenity which would have been much more apparent in the stage production. It would be both foolish and ignorant to condemn it, for this obscenity belonged to the very origins of Comedy and its connections with fecundity. Tradition retained it, for a time, to disconcert the squeamish in modern times. This element and the ruthless abuse are a useful corrective to too idealising a picture of the Athenians in the days of their political and social vigour. A later, more sophisticated and more decadent age would have understood these objections. It is not only thus with literature; the comic vase-paintings of Athens and the comic frescoes of Pompeii present the same problem.

The same Aristophanes was a poet of the highest order, and every now and then in a parabasis he turns to talk to his audience, so to speak, in his own person, dropping for the moment into serious vein. In such passages he is often superb.

In the following dialogue from "The Frogs" we have an interesting and characteristic piece of literary criticism. Aristophanes is clearly a Tory (though the Toryism does not extend to imperialism) with conservative tastes in poetry and in his admiration of the manners of a byegone age. Here Aeschylus as the poet of the old order is at issue with Euripides, and Dionysus himself is there to umpire, disguised as an irreverent Philistine. The spirited and very free translation is by Hookham Frere. Euripides has already expounded his principles, and Aeschylus now takes his turn.

AESCHYLUS

Observe then, and mark, what our citizens were,
When first from my care they were trusted to you;
Not scoundrel informers, or paltry buffoons,
Evading the services due to the State;
But with hearts all on fire, for adventure and war,
Distinguished for hardiness, stature, and strength,
Breathing forth nothing but lances and darts,
Arms, and equipment, and battle array,
Bucklers, and shields, and habergeons, and hauberks,
Helmets, and plumes, and heroic attire.

EURIPIDES

But how did you manage to make 'em so manly?
What was the method, the means that you took?

DIONYSUS

Speak, Aeschylus, speak, and behave yourself better,
And don't, in your rage, stand so silent and stern.

AESCHYLUS

A drama, brimful with heroical spirit.

EURIPIDES

What did you call it?

AESCHYLUS

"The Chiefs against Thebes"
That inspired each spectator with martial ambition,
Courage, and ardour, and prowess, and pride.

DIONYSUS

But you did very wrong to encourage the Thebans.
Indeed you deserve to be punished, you do,
For the Thebans are grown to be capital soldiers.
You've done us a mischief by that very thing.

AESCHYLUS

The fault was your own, if you took other courses;
The lesson I taught was directed to you;
Then I gave you the glorious theme of "The Persians",
Replete with sublime patriotical strains,
The record and example of noble achievement,
The delight of the city, the pride of the stage.

DIONYSUS

I rejoiced, I confess, when the tidings were carried
To old King Darius, so long dead and buried,
And the chorus in concert kept wringing their hands,
Weeping and wailing, and crying, Alas!

AESCHYLUS

Such is the duty, the task of a poet,
Fulfilling in honour his office and trust.
Look to traditional history, look
To antiquity, primitive, early, remote:
See there what a blessing illustrious poets
Conferr'd on mankind, in the centuries past.
Orpheus instructed mankind in religion,
Reclaimed them from bloodshed and barbarous rites;
Musaeus delivered the doctrine of medicine,
And warnings prophetic for ages to come.
Next came old Hesiod, teaching us husbandry,
Ploughing, and sowing, and rural affairs,
Rural economy, rural astronomy,
Homely morality, labour and thrift:
Homer himself, our adorable Homer,
What was his title to praise and renown?
What but the worth of the lessons he taught us,
Discipline, arms, and endurance of war?

All Greek literature and art is judged by critics of all sorts from a standard almost exclusively moral. "Did he teach well?" "Did his art make people better?" Such are the questions constantly applied. The doctrine of Art for Art's sake would have seemed to the Greeks ridiculous or wicked. The actual charges made against Euripides in these scenes are (1) that he was an innovator; (2) that he was a realist, introducing lame people and beggars in rags on the idealist tragic stage; (3) that he was fond of casuistry, and thereby cultivated dishonesty; (4) that he chose immoral subjects dealing with such revolting topics as women in love! Sophocles is evidently regarded by our irrepressible bard as a personage too sacred to be brought upon his stage. That lofty spirit would have no part in such a strife either here or in the underworld.

I look upon Greek Comedy as a Saturnalian product. The Old Comedy also clearly retained a great deal that was archaic, including the choruses which had some curious forerunners as the black-figured vase Plate 85, *b* shows. A people apparently accustomed to a strict, self-imposed discipline in the rest of its art and morals deliberately throws off its restraints and lets itself go on occasions, like a Scotsman at Hogmanay. The Greeks were not in the least shocked by occasional and seasonable ebullitions of high spirits. If you had an enemy or an opponent in politics, the production of a comedy was the time when you might reasonably assert that his deceased mother had been a greengrocer, or that his wife had eloped with a Thracian footman, or that his face was ugly and his person offensive to the senses. You were expected to include some references to Melanthius, a tragic poet, who was notoriously and most laughably afflicted with leprosy, or Opuntius, who provoked great mirth by having only one eye, or Cleonymus, who lost his shield on the field of battle, or Patroclides who suffered a celebrated accident in the theatre. Any reference to leather was sure of a hearty laugh, for Cleon was interested in the leather-market. Anything about crabs tickled the audience, because they all knew Carcinus, the tragic poet. Impudent personalities are generally amusing for the moment, and they were the mainstay of old comedy. And it may be pointed out that when the Old Comedy declined the back-biting, the slander and the personalities appeared all the more strongly and deleteriously, perhaps, in the Law Courts, the Council Chamber and the Assembly. Who shall say the Old Comedy was not a safety valve?

AIDOS

It is a very remarkable phenomenon that a people of such a sort nonetheless had a subconscious yearning for restraint, or some of them did; they admired it as a standard even if they did not always follow it as a rule. There was nothing in the Greek temperament to account for it: on the contrary, they were excitable and hot-blooded people of the South. There was nothing at all in their religion to preach asceticism. It was not a product of reaction, a result of surfeit from extravagance, because it belongs to the earlier phases of culture only. I think it was due in a large measure to the force of historical circumstances. The same influences of external barbarism which forced them to fence their states behind a ring-wall on a rocky citadel also led them to enclose their souls within a wall of reserve. The West was not yet awake; it was against the East that they had to fight, spiritually as well as bodily. Eastern "barbarism", which was really civilisation, ancient and splendid, visibly exhibited all the lusts of the flesh, all the pomps and vanities of this wicked world. Notably, the Ionian Philosophers, who saw the East close at hand, were the first to preach "Know thyself" and "Nothing too much!" And the Athenians, who had personally inflicted the Nemesis that attends pride, were the first to understand this.

But they seem to have had some congenital craving for perfection. Some have attributed it (dubiously) to perfect physical health. Aristophanes, as we have just seen, laughs scornfully at disease and deformity. Euripides is arraigned for getting dramatic pathos out of rags and tatters. When Pericles delivers his oration over the dead soldiers he never once alludes to an individual's prowess or fate. When Phidias designs his long frieze, though there is infinite variety in the poses of his people, though every fold of drapery, every limb of man and beast is separately arranged with an eye to its own value in the design, the faces are allowed to express almost nothing in the way of transient or personal emotion. A monster, such as a Centaur, or a Giant, or a Barbarian, may be allowed a wrinkled forehead to express age, or a twisted mouth to express pain or emotion, but a Greek must be perfect and serene.

This principle may be studied in detail upon the tombstones of Athens. You may often get much illumination about the character of people from their attitude in the presence of death. The Turk plants cypresses in his cemeteries, carves a turban on a shaft over his graves, and then leaves the dead to keep their own graveyards tidy. The Frenchman adorns his tombs with conventional wreaths of tin flowers. The Englishman advertises the virtues of the wealthy deceased and the emotions of the survivors in Biblical texts or rather insincere epitaphs. The Italian, when he can afford it, erects florid monuments in Carrara marble with photographs of the deceased. The nomad barbarian burns his dead, the jungle savage leaves the corpse in a tree for sepulture by the birds of heaven. The Egyptian preserves the body in balms and spices in the service of immortality. The Roman generally used the pyre and stored the ashes in tombs and catacombs.

The practices of disposal were many and various. Some seem to incorporate ideas about the passage of the soul, and the afterlife. Such is the Harpy Tomb at Xanthus, and the sculptures upon it indicate the religious beliefs which accompany that form of burial—

the winged spirits which carry the soul away after death, whether called Fates or Harpies (Plate 62, *b*). Then the soul itself is often represented as a tiny winged figure (cf. Plate 86), sometimes issuing from the mouth of the dead. It was thus that the Greek word Psyche came to mean both "soul" and "butterfly" and we are reminded of the butterflies in Minoan-Mycenaean art. Tombs of an architectural character look as if they were intended as houses for the dead, and, indeed, their design often follows the character of the houses occupied by the living. In accordance with the same idea, or with that of a journey or another life, objects dear to the living are buried with the dead, such as the weapons and accoutrements of a warrior, the jewels and personal belongings of a woman, the toys of a child. Sometimes economical motives lead to a mere conventional copying of the real object, and many of the axes and swords found in the old tombs are far too weak ever to have been made for practical use. Blood and libations were sometimes poured into the graves, and vessels containing oil, or even food and drink, were often placed in the tomb, and when money came into use a token sum of that too. That too was conventionalised into the penny due to Charon, who ferried souls across the Styx.

But what looks at first sight a different conception of the fate of the dead is revealed by the practice of those, such as the Achaeans of Homer, who burned their dead upon the funeral pyre, collecting their ashes in jars and urns, and in the case of a great man raising a barrow over the spot. But the Homeric practices are at variance, oddly enough, with those of the Mycenaean Bronze Age. It is difficult to decide what beliefs lay behind them both, and it would be unwise to be too sure that they believed that the soul of the happy warrior departed to a Valhalla or Paradise in the Isles of the Blessed, where he lived thenceforth as he had lived on earth at his best, in continual feasting and athletic exercise. At a later stage in Greek belief this was often true, but only Menelaus among the heroes was destined for the Isles of the Blessed or the Elysian Fields, and that as the husband of the divine or semi-divine Helen. The rest flit as unhappy shades, seemingly dwindling in strength. The diversity of burial practice, inhumation, or cremation, is difficult to interpret, like the attitude to the Dead, buried in pomp and riches for a time, and then swept unceremoniously aside to make way for others. Was there some idea of a journey completed or of a spirit which faded away and at length became too feeble to do harm? Later some certainly believed that the soul attained a place of rest, but that it could not do so until it had received the rites of burial, and to deny burial was an awful crime against Greek morality. In keeping with the same background of ideas, to be a poor drowned and unburied sailor was the worst of fates. After a battle one side generally had to acknowledge its defeat by asking for a truce in order that it might bury its dead.

Historical Athens practised both burial and cremation, after a period of lying in state. We have seen that Pythagoras taught the immortality of the soul; but then, as now, it was not philosophy which created the popular ideas about death. The belief in immortality, by no means universal in Greece, seems to have been connected rather with the oldest religion of agricultural days. Such, it has been guessed, was the mystical hope given to the initiated in the secret nocturnal rites of Eleusis. It was intimately connected with the agricultural deities (Plate 71), Demeter the Earth Mother, Persephone the Maiden her daughter, Triptolemus, the boy-god, and Eubouleus, the divine swineherd. The beautiful mythological representation of the doctrine in the story of Persephone, who was carried off by Hades to be his bride in the underworld while she was gathering flowers, and then at her mother's powerful intercession was granted as a compromise the liberty to return to earth for half the year, is visibly a parable of summer and winter. It seems that somehow Greek belief, so far as it related to Death, was founded on observation of the revival of the seasons and the rebirth of the crops. This idea was strongest across the water in Asia Minor, in its connection with the worship of Adonis and its Eastern background.

The epitaphs of the classical period in Greece, unlike our own, halt at the tomb or else look back to life. There is appeal or warning to the passer-by, lament at untimely death or comment on the virtues of the deceased, but little mention of an after-life. Even when it was present, belief in immortality was not in Greece, any more than it is with us, strong enough to assuage the sting of Death or to enable the Greeks to dispense with the formalities of funerals. The Athenians practised the usual rites of mourning with professional musicians and dirge-singers, black clothes, women tearing their hair and beating their breasts. All this was and is inevitable, but the public sense of Greece continually demanded a certain decency and reserve in the presence of Death. Solon's old laws attempt to limit funeral displays.

The Spartan system was very rigorous on the point, and there the women were held in such discipline that the death of a warrior on the field of battle was sometimes actually received with patriotic rejoicing by the women of his family.

Our archaeological museums are much indebted to the practice of burying with the deceased the objects of his use in life both in Greece itself and in other Mediterranean lands such as Etruria. Indeed so many objects of Greek manufacture, and especially vases, were found in the Etruscan chamber tombs that Attic vases were once called "Etruscan urns". An athlete would have the strigil, with which he scraped off the dust and oil of the exercise-ground, buried in his tomb; a lady would have her mirror, and her "pyxis" or jewel-box (Plate 84, *a*). Most of the little terracotta figures in our museums come from the tombs. Some of them were children's toys: often the figures seem to have been deliberately broken before interment. Among the most beautiful of such contents of the tomb are the funeral oil-flasks, or lecythi, of the fifth and early fourth centuries (Plate 86). They were specially painted for the purpose, as we can perceive by their choice of funereal subjects, and they are of a distinct type of pottery. The usual vase technique of the best period has the background painted with a fine black glaze and figures reserved in rich red. But these funeral lecythi have the body of the vase covered with a slip of white or cream colour, and upon it the figures and scenes are painted in polychrome and black glaze lines. It is a technique also used on other vase-shapes (Plate 84, *b*). In this way we have surviving very rare and beautiful effects of colour-drawing in this noblest period of Greek art. The work of the great artists such as Polygnotus and Zeuxis has, of course, perished utterly, and we must rely on these little oil-flasks, probably the work of quite obscure craftsmen, for our nearest representation of it, or at any rate of its polychrome effect, for as far as the drawing is concerned the red-figure vase painters were also influenced by it. On the white-ground lecythi, as they are called, we are amazed at the effect produced by simple means. Even where the colours have faded we trace a delicacy and precision of line in the drawing which is simply astonishing. No artists have ever done so much with a single stroke of the brush. It implies a wonderful confidence and mastery of technique to match the restrained and austere pathos of these scenes of farewell.

Our museums also contain a great number of the marble slabs, decorated in high relief, which in varying quality formed the tomb-stones of the Athenians buried in the cemetery of the Kerameikos, outside the Dipylon Gate at Athens. A few of them are still *in situ*, and present a remarkable picture as they stand. One of the most famous is the tomb of Hegeso, in the Athenian National Museum. But there are a great many more, less known but equally beautiful, both there and elsewhere. None of them is, so far as we know, the work of named artists. The great works constructed under Pericles and Phidias on the Acropolis must have collected many competent minor craftsmen in Athens, and given them a noble training in their craft. Some show the round contours and delicate drapery of the Phidian style, some the heavy muscularity of Polyclitus, and some show the small, finely poised heads of the school of Lysippus.

The subjects represented on the lecythi are generally either a scene at the tomb with mourner and mourned confronted, or the bearing away of the dead by Sleep and Death, or else Hermes escorting the soul to Charon and his boat. The sepulchral slabs generally exhibit a scene or rather an atmosphere of departure, which is always treated with extraordinary dignity and reserve. Not a lamentation is uttered, not a tear falls. Perhaps the gaze of our athlete's father (Plate 87, *a*) is more searching and intense than if it were a mere earthly separation from his stalwart son. There is, I think, no portraiture even here. If it is a woman who has gone to her long home, she is sometimes shown putting away her jewels for the journey or taking leave of her maid (Plate 88, *b*). On one archaic relief now at Rome, a mother, with a smile upon her face, is placing her child on the knees of Persephone. A very beautiful one, also at Rome, bears the mytho-logical scene of the parting between those types of married love and constancy, Orpheus and Eurydice. The head of Orpheus is bent a little, but Eurydice is smiling farewell, and the hand of Hermes, the Escort of Souls, is very light upon her wrist. Most typical of all, perhaps, is the Mourning Athena, (Plate 87, *b*), which was probably a public memorial of soldiers fallen in the wars, since it was found built into a wall on the Acropolis. It is strangely simple and restrained. The goddess, clad in her helmet, leans upon her spear, with head bent down, to read the names once painted on a short pillar which is part of the relief. The severe lines of her drapery indicate the austerity of the unknown artist's treatment of his patriotic theme. This is the speech of Pericles in stone, more impressive in

81.
The Doric
temple of
Athena and
Hephaistos, the
so-called
"Theseum," at
Athens.

82.   Slabs of the frieze of the temple of Apollo at Bassai in Arcadia.

83. (a)
Attic red-figure hydria. Abduction of the daughters of Leukippos, Argonauts, Herakles and the Hesperides.

(b) Vase in the form of an astragal. Hephaistos and the Clouds.

84. (a) *above* Attic red-figure *phiale mesomphalos*. A dancing school.

(b) *below* An Attic drinking cup. Aphrodite riding on a goose.

5. (a) *right*
Relief with comic masks.

(b) *below*
Attic black-figure amphora.
Helmeted men mounted on
men dressed as horses.

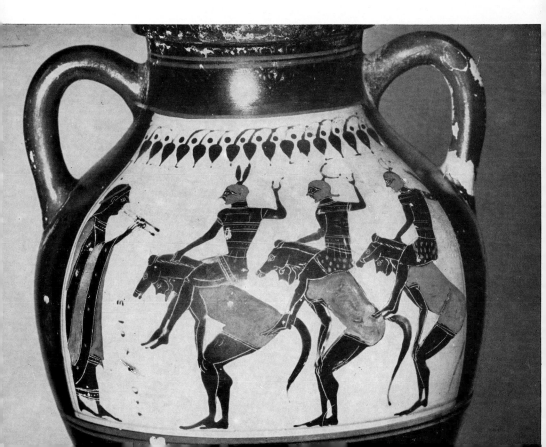

86.   An Attic white-ground funeral lekythos. The Dead and the Living at the tomb.

87. (a) *left*
Grave stone in Athens,
from the Ilissos.

(b) *right*
The "Mourning Athena"
relief in Athens.

(b) The grave stele of Mnesarete in Munich.

88.   (a) Grave stele from Salamis in Athens.

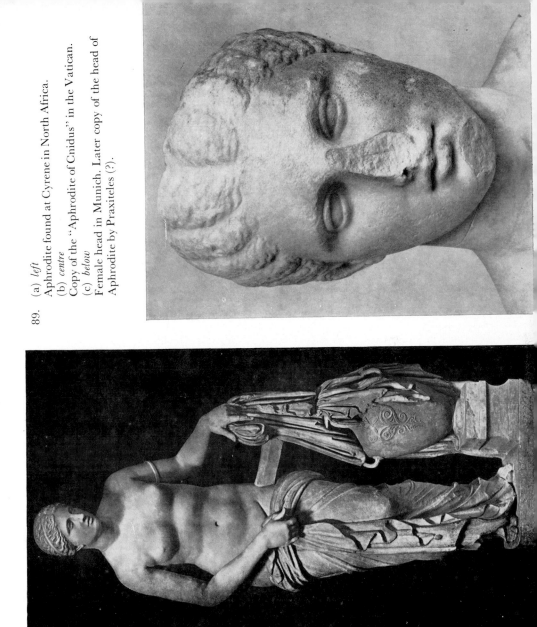

89. (a) *left*
Aphrodite found at Cyrene in North Africa.
(b) *centre*
Copy of the "Aphrodite of Cnidus" in the Vatican.
(c) *below*
Female head in Munich. Later copy of the head of
Aphrodite by Praxiteles (?).

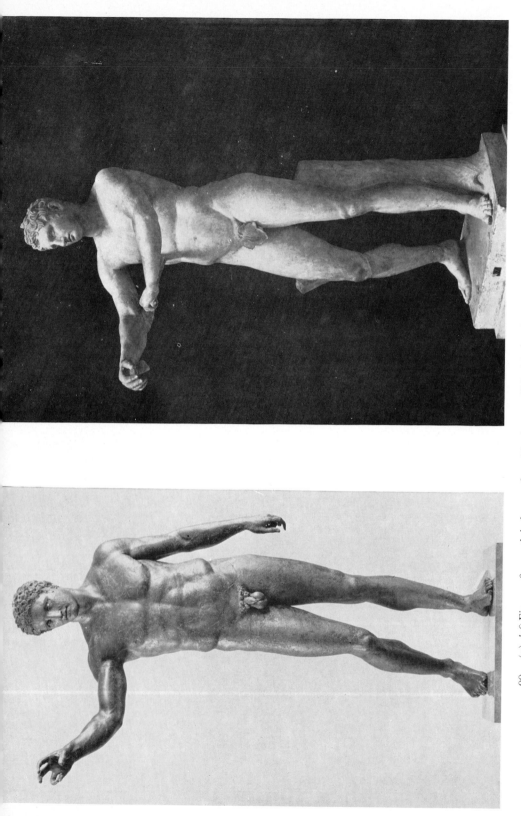

90. (a) *left* Figure of a youth in bronze found in the sea off the island of Anticythera.
     (b) *right* Copy of the Apoxyomenus of Lysippus in the Vatican.

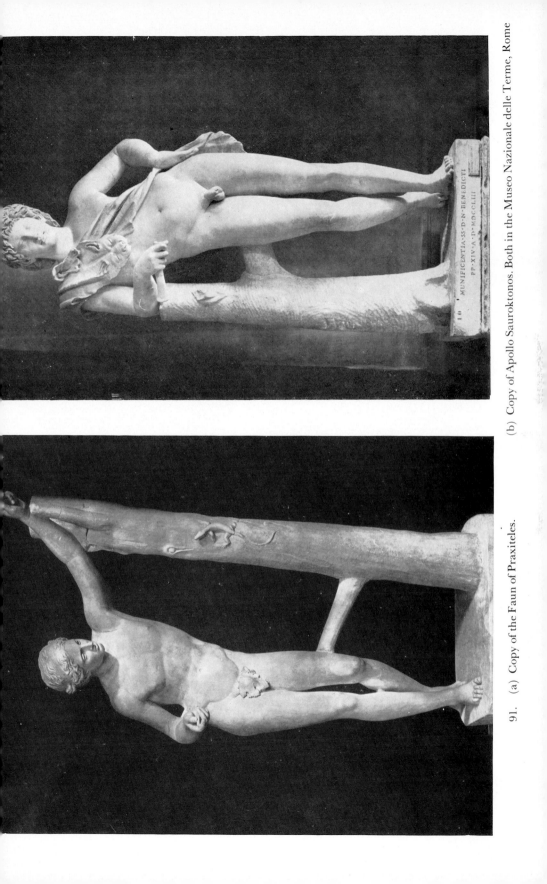

91.   (a) Copy of the Faun of Praxiteles.

(b) Copy of Apollo Sauroktonos. Both in the Museo Nazionale delle Terme, Rome

92.   The head of the Hermes "of Praxiteles".

3. (a) *above* Winged head of Hypnos in the British Museum.
   (b) *right* A head from the temple of Athena Alea at Tegea, in Athens.
   (c) *below* Relief of a base from Mantinea, in Athens.

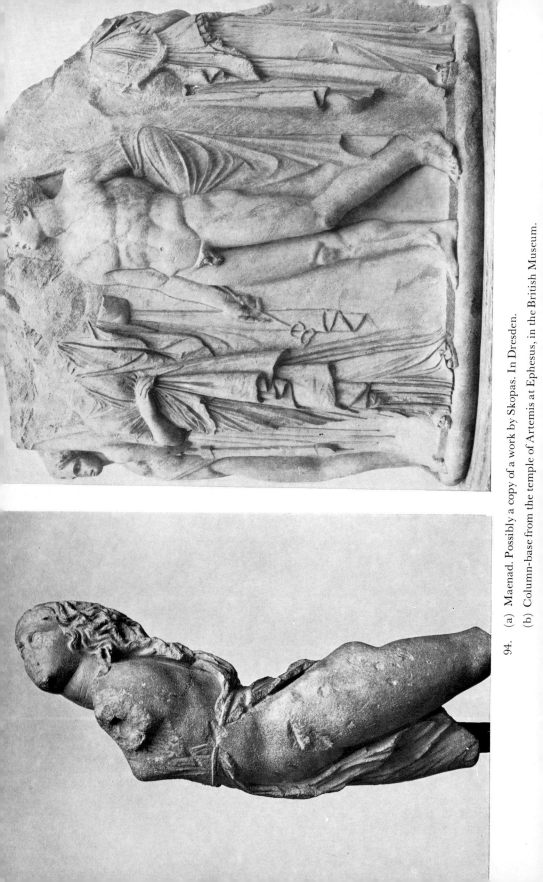

94. (a) Maenad. Possibly a copy of a work by Skopas. In Dresden.

(b) Column-base from the temple of Artemis at Ephesus, in the British Museum.

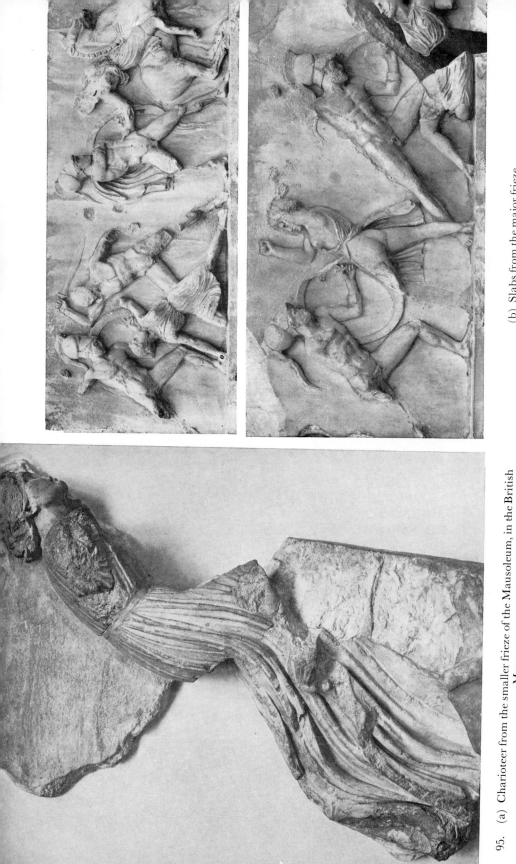

95. (a) Charioteer from the smaller frieze of the Mausoleum, in the British
Museum.

(b) Slabs from the major frieze.

96.   Some outstanding coins and important issues of the 5th and 6th
centuries B.C.

its simple fashion than representations of heroic battle and victory such as also figures on public grave memorials. I have chosen also two less-known monuments from the Athenian National Museum to show the Athenian view of death more clearly. The dead hero does not mourn, but his humbler friends, like the Giants and Barbarians of the friezes, may express their emotion visibly and naturally. Young men nearly always have their hounds to accompany them upon their tombstones. They are big animals, perhaps of the famed Molossian breed, akin to our pointers. Their descendants may be seen (and felt, unless the traveller knows the local artifice of sitting down and pretending not to be afraid) on any upland farm in Greece today. Girls are often accompanied by small pet dogs, curly and excitable. The big hounds clearly show dejection in every line (Plate 87, *a*). There are other subtle gestures of farewell, as of the young man letting his doves go free for the last time (Plate 88, *a*), and as you see, the little slave-boys may look sorry when their masters go. They are not Greeks it might be said; they may express human emotions.

THE FOURTH CENTURY

But Greece and her foundations are
Built below the tide of war,
Throned on the crystalline sea
Of thought and its eternity.

SHELLEY

ATHENS

THE pre-eminence of Thucydides among Greek historians has, I venture to think, somewhat distorted the true perspective of Greek history. The absorbing interest with which we follow his account of the Peloponnesian War to a crisis in Athenian affairs leads us to regard all the rest of Greek history with that slackening of interest with which we commonly regard a sequel and especially (in this case) one narrated by a man like Xenophon. The truth is that Athens rose from her knees after an interval, much chastened, considerably exhausted, certainly poorer, but with as much intellectual vigour and power of artistic creation as before. The Athens that we know intimately is the Athens of the Restoration. Really we know almost nothing of fifth-century Athens but her external politics and the remains of her monuments. The restored Athens is the city of Plato, of Demosthenes, and of Praxiteles. She has still to be the mother of philosophy, ethics, oratory, political science, comedy of manners, logic, grammar, and the essay and the dialogue as forms of literature. This is the only Athens which we know at all intimately from within.

The Long Walls were to be pulled down in order that Athens might be separated from her harbours and become in fact an inland city like Sparta herself. Down they came to the music of flutes, and Athens consented to become the "ally" (euphemism for "humble servant") of Sparta. The moral of it all for imperial cities would seem to be: (1) the precarious nature of sea-power unless backed very strongly by purse-power; (2) the danger of having unwilling allies or dependents; and (3) the impossibility of conducting war by means of public debate in a democratic assembly. On two occasions near the end of the war and the century the Athenians had tried experiments in constitutional revolution. For, indeed, during the closing stages of the war even the citizens of Athens could see what was painfully obvious to the rest of the world, that she was not well governed for the purposes of external politics. Popular institutions exist for the sake of popular liberties. There are better ways of maintaining order, if that is your prime object, and much better ways of securing "efficiency". Democracy may "reign", it cannot "govern"—not, at any rate, without the help of a trained bureaucracy. Above all, in the conduct of a war a meeting of citizens in the market place is the clumsiest deliberative body that can be conceived. We have seen how ignorant they were when they embarked on the Sicilian expedition without knowing anything more than interested parties chose to tell them of the resources of their allies and the disposition of the other Sicilian Greeks. Besides ignorance, they had shown hasty passion in condemning the whole male population of Mitylene to death; they had been ferociously unjust in sentencing their admirals to death for not stopping to pick up the shipwrecked survivors after the victory of Arginusae. They had made childish blunders in strategy, as when they chose three ill-assorted generals to conduct the Sicilian expedition, and in statecraft when they refused peace and drove their cleverest citizen, Alcibiades, into exile. But the most effective argument of the oligarchic party was based on finance. With the cessation of the tribute from the allies it became simply impossible to maintain the structure of government which democracy developed and demanded. Further, democracy was, as we have seen, identified with anti-Spartan policy; Sparta would make no terms with democracy. And, lastly, when the brilliant Alcibiades had been banished by the democracy, he professed to have the Persian satrap, the universal paymaster, in his pocket, and he demanded a revolution as the price of his return. Such were the arguments insinuated by the oligarchs. This party was working incessantly in clubs and secret societies. In 411—that is, two years after the failure of the Sicilian expedition—these intriguers had their way, and Athens consented to try the experiment of oligarchy "until the end of the war". Government henceforth was to be in the hands of a council of 400, for government by council is the prevailing feature of oligarchy. But, like most Greek oligarchies, Athens was also to have a sort of select Assembly, consisting of five thousand of the well-to-do citizens. Thus Athens was imitating Sparta in limiting citizen rights to her upper classes, and in excluding the "naval mob" who were her real strength in war. As usual in oligarchies, even this purged Assembly seems to have been for show rather than for use. The government was, in fact, what it is generally called, a Government of the Four Hundred. Fortunately for human liberty the experiment was not a success. It only lasted for three months. The Four Hundred had, it is true, come rather late upon the stage if they were to bring the war to a successful conclusion. But they failed to do anything useful, and their accession to power was marked by a failure at sea and the loss of Euboea. Assassination, a pleasantly rare weapon in Greek politics, removed the leader of the oligarchs, and Athens reverted to democracy.

Once more, however, at the very end of the war, when the city surrendered, Athens had perforce, at the bidding of Lysander, her conqueror, to revise her constitution in an oligarchic direction. Once more the sacred laws were thrown into the melting-pot, and there were elaborate programmes, and discussions as to the precise form of oligarchy which should be adopted. But while the preliminaries were going on the administration fell into the hands of a board of so-called commissioners charged, like Oliver Cromwell, with the revision of the constitution. Like Oliver these men soon found themselves in a position of power too good to be lost. They were called the Thirty Tyrants, and they deserved the name. They ruled with a strong hand, banished their enemies, disarmed the citizen army, and began a system of private plunder, with the spears of the Spartan garrison to enforce their commands. Athens never forgot and never forgave this nightmare of the Thirty. Most of them were men of talent, some of them were philosophers and literary men who had sat at the feet of Socrates. Critias, the Robespierre of the party, quarrelled with Theramenes, its philosophical Danton, an advocate of the "moderate Constitution", and sent him to execution. Before very long, one is glad to know, honest men (by which term one means, in this instance, democrats) were gathering on the borders of Attica, and under the leadership of Thrasybulus won their way home and crushed the "gentle Critias" and his gang for ever.

The year 403 is the year of restored democracy. It is called the archonship of Eucleides. We hear no more at this time of oligarchy at Athens. Henceforth she is a democracy, as before and more so. Where Athenians had formerly received a fee of threepence for public duties they now got fourpence-halfpenny. Formerly members of the Council had been paid, but not those who performed their citizen duty of attendance at meetings of the Assembly; now the latter too were added to the payroll. According to Aristotle more than twenty thousand persons were in receipt of state payment. However little business the company might transact, the share holders were determined upon one thing—to pay dividends to one another, with a bonus in exceptional years. It is hard to say where the dividends came from. No doubt there was a good deal of commerce and banking business at the Piraeus, mostly in the hands of half-naturalised foreigners. The rich were bled, they felt, unmercifully, so that they tended to emigrate or conceal their wealth. And yet in the fourth century Athens was steadily rising in the political scale. A glad day came when her admiral Conon, with Persian help, was able to rebuild her Long Walls. She started a new maritime league, under better safeguards, this time, for the allies. She even recovered something of an empire. She could not afford statues in ivory and gold, but she eventually built her theatre with stone, laid out a stadium, and produced many charming works of art. In short, though her ambitions were curtailed, life was very free and full, and, I believe, very pleasant, in fourth-century Athens. Her statesmen had to be content with smaller schemes; they were a good deal concerned with finance: indeed, it was hard work to make both ends meet. Generals complained that they got no pay; and now that hired troops were in vogue warfare was an expensive pastime. The Athenians were rather more hysterical than before, even more apt to make Byngs of their unsuccessful admirals. They talked more than ever, and did rather less. But on the whole they were well governed, and they played a not unimportant part in the warfare and diplomacy of Greece. The restored democracy was a success.

While Athens is recuperating her strength, we may turn aside for a moment to watch two other states make their successive attempts to hold the overlordship of Hellas; remembering all the time that the northern horizon is already dark with the storm that is going to sweep the whole of ancient Greece into political insignificance.

SPARTA AND THEBES

The first episode of Greek international history in the fourth century is a Spartan domination, lasting less than thirty years, but generally considered as one of the imperial experiments of Greece.

In addition to her own permanent hegemony over the greater part of Southern and Central Greece, Sparta had now stepped into the uncomfortable shoes of Athens, and found herself the mistress of more than a hundred island or seaport "cities". Now Sparta, as she was frequently reminded, had gone into the Peloponnesian War as champion of the liberty of Hellas against a tyrant city. She had gained the day partly through the virtue of that charming phrase, but I doubt whether anybody seriously expected her to set the Ionian cities and islands at liberty. They were not used to liberty, and would not have known what to do with it. They had utterly lost the habit of fighting or doing anything but pay for their own safety. They were too lazy and broad-minded to care very much where their tribute went. None of them had been enthusiastic about its previous destination. We hear of no bitter lamentations when they discovered that Sparta was selling them wholesale back to the Persians. Under Persia they were at any rate assured of their trade with the hinterland; probably they were heartily sick of being bandied about between Athens and Sparta. Pharnabazus and Tissaphernes, the western satraps of the Great King, seem to have been easy-going gentlemen of normal Eastern calm and duplicity. They were not of the stamp of conquerors or despots, but they had heaps of money and were adepts at making and breaking treaties. Sparta both by geography and by habit was an inland power. She never produced more than one competent admiral, and that was the man now at the zenith of his power, Lysander. As Sparta had now inherited a maritime empire, and as she was unable and unwilling to embark definitely upon a naval career, it became necessary to organise a system of garrisons and governors in every city under her sway. This work of organisation fell to Lysander—the nearest equivalent to a Caesar that Greece ever produced. The Spartan empire, such as it was, was Lysander's handiwork. Of course every state that came into Spartan hands was forcibly converted to oligarchy. This has often been represented as another example of Sparta's tyranny. But a survey of Greece will soon convince us that oligarchy, and not democracy, is the normal condition of the Greek *polis*; and, in fact, with a few rare exceptions, it is only Athens and the states directly under her influence which are democracies. But Lysander was corrupt in the exercise of power, and he entrusted the government in each town to a group of local aristocrats who had won or purchased his interest. Thus the states of the Spartan empire were generally governed by a Council of Ten, working hand in glove with a Spartan captain and a Spartan garrison. Athens, as we have seen, was also accustomed to send garrisons where she conquered. But all that we know of the Spartan temper assures us that the little finger of Sparta was thicker than the loins of Athens.

Like Pausanias before him, Admiral Lysander became intoxicated with success. A very little liberty and luxury was enough to bring giddiness to the ascetic heads of Sparta. Lysander began to think revolutionary thoughts of a Sparta where men could be rich and free like the rest of the world. And the infection spread. Sparta was now earning a thousand talents a year from her empire, and though money was still forbidden at home, and though Sparta had as yet absolutely no coinage of her own, private Spartans were unquestionably getting rich quickly. A rich Spartan was a horrid anomaly: there was nothing that money could buy in Laconia except land. Hence family estates began to change hands faster, and the class of landless, therefore voteless, men of Spartan blood rapidly multiplied. It was Sparta's boast that she alone in all Greece had never suffered a revolution. She never came so near it as on the present occasion, when Lysander with his riches was trying to subvert the Lycurgan constitution by bribing the Delphic oracle, and the discontented Inferiors at home were planning a secret rebellion. Both failed: the conspiracy of Cinadon was detected by the vigilant Ephors and ruthlessly crushed, while Lysander in playing the part of king-maker unwittingly made a king who was his equal in ability. Very soon the conqueror of Athens found himself unnecessary to Sparta, and had to submit to the indignity of being tried and pardoned.

The new king was Agesilaus, whose long and important career was the subject of many biographies. He it was who pointed the path of glory to Alexander by revealing the utter incapacity of the Persians to guard their treasures. For Sparta had quickly fallen out with the satraps, and Agesilaus marched about the Phrygian and Lydian coasts gathering plunder with very little difficulty. One of the biographers of Agesilaus was his friend and admirer Xenophon, who was concerned in a great adventure which likewise served to betray the weakness of the Persian empire.

The British schoolboy, fleshing his young teeth upon the "Anabasis" of Xenophon, struggling in a wilderness of parasangs and paradigms and puzzling out what Cheirisophus said and where they pitched camp that night, seldom realises the romantic nature of the enterprise. There was a dynastic struggle in Persia. Cyrus, a bold and able prince, was disputing the succession to the throne with the rightful successor, Artaxerxes. Knowing the weakness of his native troops, Cyrus conceived the idea of stiffening them with ten thousand hired Greeks, for by now the use of mercenaries was growing more frequnte in the Greek world. These troops were mostly Spartans, their leader was Clearchus, a Spartan, and Xenophon of Athens was a volunteer under his command. They were recruited without knowing the full nature of the enterprise, and it was only when they found themselves in the heart of Asia that they learnt to their horror that the objective was the far-distant capital. At length they reached Cunaxa, near Babylon, where a mighty host opposed their advance. In the battle Cyrus was killed and the native portion of his troops fled or surrendered or were slain. But the Greeks had fought so valiantly that the victorious army of Artaxerxes did not care to attempt their capture, though the crafty Tissaphernes succeeded in assassinating their leaders and leading the army astray into the wilderness. Thus the Ten Thousand found themselves stranded in a hostile country, without generals and without guides, nearly two thousand miles from home. But being Greeks, with a proper contempt for the barbarian, they scorned to lose heart, though the chance of a safe return must have seemed hopeless. The strong political instinct of the city-state was their salvation. They resolved themselves into a wandering *polis*, held assemblies, made speeches, elected generals, with Xenophon among them, and preserved perfect self-control and discipline. So began the Catabasis, an immense and dangerous march north-westward, through the passes of the Taurus and the uplands of Armenia, fighting the wild Kurds of the hills, struggling with cold and hunger, utterly ignorant of geography except for the belief that if they went on long enough in the same direction they would some day reach the sea. Their glad cry of "Thalassa! Thalassa!" when at last they saw the shining water of the Euxine is a cry that has echoed through the ages. Henceforth they were passing through the series of Greek colonies that fringed the south coast of the Black Sea. Though many more adventures awaited them and they were seldom very welcome visitors, yet no fewer than six thousand came safely back to Greece. Not so much the fighting as the courage of the march and the sense of discipline make this one of the finest exploits in Greek history.

As for Xenophon, he retired to spend his leisure and his money close to his beloved Sparta. Purchasing an estate near Olympia, he devoted his veteran days to literature and sport. His life in Triphylia is a picture of the retired sporting colonel of religious and aristocratic tendencies. He regards his estate as a stewardship for the goddess Artemis. He builds her a shrine, an altar with a statue of cypress-wood modelled on the temple and golden statue of Ephesus. Hard by was a river full of fish, and an orchard, with pasturelands and upland game preserves, abounding in wild boars, gazelles, and deer. Every year he gave a sacrifice to the goddess, and invited his neighbours to the feast. There would be barley porridge, wheaten loaves, and sweetmeats. Game had previously been supplied by a day's hunting on a large scale, in which Xenophon's sons conducted the operations and all the neighbours took part if they liked.

Xenophon is one of the most accomplished and versatile of minor writers. He wrote, besides his "Anabasis", a treatise on hunting, with valuable information on the breeding of horses and hounds; he wrote memoirs of his beloved but little comprehended master in philosophy, Socrates, who had been put to death at Athens while Xenophon was on his expedition; he wrote also perhaps the earliest European work of prose fiction, in which he sketched the proper training of a prince and a gentleman, under the title of "The Education of Cyrus"; he wrote a history of Greece beginning where Thucydides left off and ending with the downfall of Sparta; among his minor works are treatises on the duties of a captain of horse, and a glowing panegyric on the Spartan constitution. An equally warm indictment of the Athenian democracy, in fact written before his time, is falsely ascribed to his pen. A pamphlet on finance, in fact on the ways of making ends meet (the great preoccupation of fourth-century Greece), is dubiously his. He was an aristocrat and philo-Laconian by sympathy, and the democracy of Athens had earned his displeasure by slaying Socrates and by banishing himself. That was only natural, seeing that he had taken Spartan service in the field against her, and she seems very generously to have allowed him to return home before the end of his life. In his versatile intelligence, his cosmopolitan habits as a soldier of fortune, in his youthful enthusiasm for philosophy, and in the journalistic spirit which prompted him to write pamphlets on any topic which interested him, no less than in his dislike of democracy, Xenophon is perhaps the most characteristic figure of the fourth century, though he is too military and too conservative to be a typical Athenian of any age.

Greece did not, of course, enjoy peace during the thirty years of Spartan predominance. It could never be said at any point of Greek history that "the land had rest forty years". There was fighting in Asia Minor against the Persians, and fighting in Greece round the Isthmus, a tiresome and lengthy struggle with discontented allies, generally called the Corinthian War. We cannot get a clear conception of the life of a Greek state unless we realise that peace was an abnormal condition in both foreign and internal affairs.

During the period of which we are speaking there had been some important developments in the art of war. As the soldier is the most conservative of men with the exception of the priest, so next to religion warfare is the most conservative of human activities. Field tactics had altered little since the Persian wars. A Greek battle still depended on the shock of two lines of hoplites, largely a question of weight in impact. If you could once cut your opponent's line the victory was yours, because then you found his right or shieldless side open to your spear. A Greek soldier with his heavy shield on his left arm could only defend his front and left. For this purpose the men stood shoulder to shoulder in a line made as deep as possible, for the sake of weight in the scrimmage, and, I fear, to prevent the Greek disorder of running away.

It was the secret of Spartan pre-eminence in war that a Spartan hoplite never thought of running away. But now in this fourth century we enter upon a scientific age when men are beginning to apply their reason logically to all the activities of life instead of trusting to habit. Soldiering, as in the case of the Ten Thousand, is passing over from amateur patriots to mercenary professionals. It is clear that if new ideas are to revolutionise the art of war, the supremacy of Sparta is doomed. Strong arms and thick skulls flourished in the vale of Eurotas. Sparta had a rude shock when an Athenian condottiere named Iphicrates cut up a Spartan company of hoplites with a new-fangled battalion of his own training, a body of drilled light infantry. And now in the fullness of time Boeotia was to produce its man of genius—Epaminondas the Theban.

In 387 Sparta had sold the Ionian cities back to the Great King, who sent down from Susa a beautiful treaty saying, "King Artaxerxes thinks it just that Asia Minor and the Ionian islands shall belong to him, and that the rest of the cities of Greece, both great and small, shall be independent". That was really the end of Sparta's dream of an oversea empire. She had found it too fatiguing for a land power. Armed with this treaty, she began to run amuck among her neighbours. She assailed the Arcadian city of Mantinea and tore it up into villages. She adopted the same policy in North Greece, and one of her captains seized and garrisoned the citadel of Thebes on his way north. Boeotia had been deeply divided and no unshaken friend of Sparta. It now came about that Thebes and Boeotia were held by pro-Spartans and Spartan garrisons. One of these garrison commanders made a dash for the Piraeus, but came to grief. The result is easy to understand. There was a delightfully romantic conspiracy organised from Athens, and a body of Theban patriots liberated their city. Among the patriots was Pelopidas, a brave and skilful soldier, and his friend was Epaminondas, one of the most striking heroes of Greek history.

Two qualities, in addition to the ordinary human virtues of courage and wisdom, seem to distinguish Epaminondas: he showed originality even in the art of war, and he had the broad mental vision which we demand from statesmen but seldom find in Greeks. I do not see any proof that he possessed the full spirit of Panhellenism; he was emphatically a Theban first, whatever he might be afterwards. But he had, it seems, an eye for an international situation. It is the measure at once of his success and of his failure that the rise and fall of Thebes is exactly conterminous with the rise and death of Epaminondas.

Thebes and Athens had both suffered from the wanton aggression of Sparta. They now made common cause to avenge it, and at the battle of Leuctra (371) Sparta suffered defeat in a pitched land battle on a great scale for the first time in her history. The victory of Thebes was wholly due to the new tactics of Epaminondas. He had formed a Theban *corps d'élite*, composed, in a fashion strikingly characteristic of the Greek mind, of 150 pairs of lovers sworn to conquer or die together. Thus he pressed into his service the only romantic feeling which the Greeks understood, the relation between David and Jonathan or between Achilles and Patroclus. This Sacred Band formed the front of the left wing. Further, whereas the whole Spartan line was drawn up as usual with a uniform depth of twelve spears, Epaminondas made his left fifty deep and flung it forward in the attack. The extra weight of this deep wing broke the Spartan right. King Cleombrotus and four hundred out of seven hundred Spartans were slain. The loss of men was serious for a little state like Sparta, but the loss in prestige was even worse. This, in Xenophon's story, is how the news came to Sparta: "It chanced to be the last day of the Boys' Gymnastic Festival, and the choir of men was therefore at home. When the Ephors heard of the disaster they were sorely grieved, as in my opinion was bound to be the case, but they did not send the men's choir out or stop the games. They communicated the names of the fallen to their relatives, but they warned the women to bear their loss in silence and not to make lamentation. So next day you could see the families of the slain going about in public with cheerful, smiling faces, but as for those whose men-folk had been announced as living, they went about in gloom and shame." So Lacedaemon set itself with dogged resolution to endure what the gods might send.

Epaminondas with true insight determined to raise up a counter-balancing power in the Peloponnesus, to hang upon the flank of Sparta if she should ever again try to tyrannise over Greece, and to pen her in. His plan was to form city-states among the Arcadians and Messenians, who, oppressed or enserfed by Sparta, were ready-made enemies. Besides, if Sparta lost her Messenian helots her military system must fail. Mantinea was restored to the organisation of a *polis*, Messenia was given a new capital, and a new and splendid city was specially constructed to unite several scattered Arcadian villages in one interesting federal constitution. But the Great City, as she was proudly named, was not a great success. Perhaps the Arcadians were too little arcadian in their habits to fulfil the scheme of Epaminondas. Some had dreams of grandeur, and in any case Arcadia developed too large an army which inevitably sought employment and glory. It is very characteristic of the Greek mind that the news of the Theban triumph was very ill received in the city of her ally Athens. Athens might cherish a respectable hereditary feud with Sparta, but Thebes she had always detested. Thebes was her next-door neighbour. Though you might have to fight a Spartan, you couldn't avoid a certain liking and sympathy for him. Besides the Thebans not the Spartans had wanted to destroy Athens at the end of the Peloponnesian War. Once again the orators drew upon that inexhaustible precedent of the Persian wars, when Sparta and Athens had stood together against Thebes and Persia. So Athens was persuaded to draw away from Thebes and form an alliance upon equal terms with Sparta. But her action was not very vigorous.

The nine years between the battles of Leuctra and Mantinea are commonly described by historians as a period of Theban hegemony. It is true that Thebes was probably on land the most powerful state in Greece, and that Epaminondas played the foremost part in the diplomacy of that period, but she had no great following of states, and as Athens, Sparta, and Corinth were among those who declined to follow she can hardly be said to have led Greece. Also it is interesting to notice that the liberal-minded Epaminondas found it just as impossible as Athens and Sparta had done to hold a Greek alliance together without interference in internal politics and the use of garrisons. He sent governors into Achaia and Sicyon. We can understand Sparta, with her aristocratic habits, showing a prejudice for oligarchy, or Athens, the city of liberty and free speech, encouraging democracy. But that Thebes, herself only recently democratic and normally oligarchically disposed, should now enforce democracy upon her allies seemed only to be a piece of cold-blooded diplomacy due to the knowledge that oligarchies were generally committed to the Spartan side. Nor can Thebes be acquitted of trafficking with the old enemy. For Pelopidas was sent to Susa to plead the ancient alliance of Thebes and Persia at the battle of Plataea! In these three respects all the hegemonies of Greece are alike, all tarred with the same brush.

Thebes tried to kill the snake she had scotched at Leuctra. Several times she started to smoke out the Spartan nest. Twice she penetrated the inviolable precincts of Sparta, but each time when she looked into the streets of the unwalled city and saw the Spartan warriors standing at arms before their temples and hearths, she only looked— and found more pressing business elsewhere. Let one chronicler at least decline to quit that sinking ship. The foolish Arcadians might brag of their ancient descent as children of the soil; but the Spartans, under their old lion Agesilaus, could still scatter Arcadians with the wind of their spears in a "Tearless Battle", wherein not a single Spartan perished.

So we come to the last great fight of this epoch—that of Mantinea. Here Spartans and Athenians fought on the same side against Thebes. The Theban tactics were the same precisely as at Leuctra, and the Spartans had learnt nothing by the experience: They saw the line advancing *en echelon*, they saw the deepened left wing, and they took no steps to counteract it. As before, they were broken and routed. But in the hour of defeat a chance spear found its billet in the body of Epaminondas, and, like Wolfe on the Heights of Abraham, that hero fell in the hour of victory. When he heard that the two men he had hoped for as his successors had also fallen he cried to his followers to make peace with Sparta, and so expired. The star of Thebes waned with his death; and, indeed, all the fires of the Greek firmament soon paled before the rising sun of Macedonia—and Philip had learnt warfare from Epaminondas.

FOURTH-CENTURY CULTURE

In the fourth century—or rather in that earlier half of it which forms the theme of the present chapter—Greek art pursues its inevitable course of development. Perhaps the wasting influence of the Peloponnesian War, that most wasteful and unsatisfactory contest, had brought a touch of disillusionment upon the high ideals and youthful hopes with which the Grand Century had set forth. It may be simply the working of some law of Nature that all arts pass from the phase of earnest endeavour to that sense of triumphant mastery which so fatally entices into luxuriance and facility. In sculpture I think we shall see that it was thus with Greece. There is in the fourth century, some would say, a slackening of purpose, some loss of ideals, some tendency in the direction of prettiness and sentiment. Certainly with the triumph won and perfect mastery secured there was the opportunity only for individualism and the rendering of emotion and real not ideal appearance. The austere moralist finds much to castigate.

But we must not yet begin to speak of degeneration. The Mausoleum and the *Republic* of Plato are not yet works of decadence. Some modern historians are rather vulture-like in their scent for decay. They show an unseemly gusto in tracing the causes of decline and fall of states, so that they begin the post-mortem long before the breath is out of their patient. Greece of the fourth century is still very active and vigorous, still improving the old arts and inventing new ones. Fourth-century Athens is far too like earlier twentieth-century England for an Englishman to feel quite comfortable in using the term "degeneration" of her.

In politics, for example, she was beginning to make things much less comfortable for the rich. With levies upon capital, both inefficient and inequitable, she was beginning to drive capital into concealment, so that rich men could no longer be made to undertake single-handed the "liturgy" of equipping a battleship, but had to be grouped in companies for the purpose. The system, in effect, can have been helpful neither to agricultural nor to mercantile enterprise. It went back to ancient times and the haphazard conduct of public finances, which even "experts" failed to reform. Statesmen, too, were throwing off the dignified reticence of the old regime, to parade the most sordid financial considerations, and to set class against class, by reminding the poor how much nicer it would be if they were rich. Even more was done for the poor now than formerly; they were taught to look to the state for cheap food, and even free education. The principle of payment of members of the Assembly had been introduced. Conservatives were alarmed by the growing numbers of state functionaries openly drawing salaries from the Treasury for the duties which they performed, instead of leaving those duties to be neglected, or expecting the rich to perform them in their spare time and recoup themselves in less odiously public fashions. In international relations there was some abatement of nationalist frenzy; in governmental systems there was a marked advance in the direction of federalism, accompanied by a devolutionary process towards local government. In the theatre there was a movement towards lighter entertainments and highly elaborate performances, with lavish display in the matter of dress and scenery. The price of flute-girls was controlled but favourite courtesans made large incomes, and sometimes married very respectably indeed. In sport, too, there was a growing tendency to professionalism, much deplored by old-fashioned people. Boxers and wrestlers no longer considered the grace of their movements, because they found that victory was apt to follow more consistently upon hard training and an animal diet. In literature, as we shall presently see more fully, poetry was beginning to yield to prose, and prose was becoming more businesslike and scientific. In social life thinkers were beginning to raise the problem of sex, and even women themselves may have joined in the agitation for some measure of justice for their sex. Euripides, indeed, who was rather apt to go further than conservatives approved in his treatment of social problems, had actually made his Medea utter these audacious words: "I would rather stand thrice in the line of battle than bear a child once."

If we had to sum up the new characteristic of the fourth century under a single phrase, we should perhaps be justified in saying that the professional spirit was making itself felt in all directions. We see it in the military art, where the citizen hoplites, with their extremely simple tactics and strategy, are yielding to mercenaries under professional captains. The statesmen are now no longer the famous generals of the day, nor men marked out by birth and wealth for high position, but trained speakers, and often professional speech-writers. Literature is no longer in the hands of men like Aeschylus and Sophocles, who were soldiers or generals as well, though Xenophon is of course a notable example of the writer who takes literature among his other activities. But now there are professional sophists teaching oratory and various literary arts. Books circulate freely, schools of professional philosophers arise, as in Plato's garden of the Academy. This specialisation naturally involves an increased attention to technical processes, a more scientific and less human outlook, and a growth of self-consciousness. For example, it is now that constitutional histories begin to be written. While people are young and strong they are apt to take their constitutions for granted. Greece is now grown to full stature, and beginning to grow introspective and emotional.

The public taste has changed somewhat in matters of art. The impoverished states of the fourth century no longer lavish their wealth to the same degree upon glorious temples, and sumptuous statues in ivory and gold. Private dedications occupy more of the artist's time, and though the subjects are still of a religious and ideal character, yet the gods have become a great deal more human. Herein we may probably see the influence of Euripides. The heroes of the epic cycle no longer possessed much interest for their own sake. Jason and Medea only raised for Euripides an absorbing problem in matrimonial relations. So the Apollos and Aphrodites of the fourth century are as human as the Madonnas and St Sebastians of the sixteenth. Psychology intrudes upon art. Allegorical impersonations begin to be popular among the subjects of statuary. Human portraiture also begins, though slowly, to be practised with some realism. Nudity in sculpture, which had hitherto been mainly confined to athletic works, where it is obviously appropriate and necessary, is now extended even to images of deities, and under the chisel of Praxiteles Aphrodite uncovers her loveliness and modesty. Eros, too, her son and tormentor, becomes a popular type, not yet as the chubby babe of Graeco-Roman times, but as a youth, almost fullgrown, with long wings upon his shoulders. Nevertheless this growing worship of human grace has not yet suffered any overwhelming tendency to sensuality, nor yet has Greek art as a whole lost its reticence and dignity.

SCULPTURE

Meanwhile the artist has improved enormously in the technical details of craftsmanship. It was now only a foreign potentate who could give commissions for statues in such splendid materials as were at the disposal of Phidias. Bronze was still the ordinary material for important works, but marble, which had formerly been chiefly used for ornament in architecture, was not uncommonly employed for statues even by the great masters. With more serviceable tools for drilling, sawing, and pointing (where that rather mechanical process was employed), the great artists of the fourth century could play upon marble as if it were wax or clay. This emerges clearly in what are mostly copies of the masters. They could represent textures and surfaces by the degree of their finish, so that the leather of the shoe is of a surface distinct from the skin of the foot in the Hermes "of Praxiteles". There is an extremely subtle contrast between the leopard-skin and the flesh of the young satyr by the same artist in the admirable torso copy which is in the Louvre, though much is owed to the techniques of copyists in a later tradition. Whereas earlier artists had tried to represent hair by grooves gouged out upon the surface of the head or by rendering each tress as a separate thread, Praxiteles discovered the marvellous impression of curls that could be produced by roughly blocking out several masses and leaving the play of light and deep shadow to indicate a surface movable and alive. New secrets of sculptural anatomy were now at command. Praxiteles discovered the value of that groove which runs vertically down the front of the body between the pectoral and abdominal muscles on each side. He discovered also the anatomical distinction between the male and female brow in that ridge of flesh, known to artists as the bar of Michelangelo, which overhangs the eyebrows. By setting the eyeballs deeper under the brow, and emphasising the long drooping curve of the upper eyelid, the fourth-century artists greatly enhanced their command of expression and emotion, transient qualities after which the fifth century had not greatly cared to strive. Scopas, indeed, carried this discovery to the verge of the legitimate, for the few incomplete fragments of his work which survive are almost theatrical in the intensity of their gaze. Marble, of course, demands methods of its own distinct from those of metal. It is true that the conversion of works of bronze into marble by later copyists necessitated the use of supports not present in the original, but it is also due to the material of originals, in a large measure, that various supports, such as tree-trunks, pillars, and urns, have to be introduced into marble statues in the round. Thus it became inevitable to make the figure lean frankly upon his support, and so we get those graceful reclining attitudes which are often cast in the teeth of Praxiteles as symptomatic of decadence.

Phidias and Praxiteles are as pre-eminent among the names of ancient sculptors as are Polygnotus, Zeuxis, and Apelles among the painters, Of the two, Praxiteles was the most praised, and his works had the highest value in the Roman market. This being so, it is remarkable how little we know of his personality—practically nothing except that he was an Athenian, and was the son or brother of another famous sculptor called Cephisodotus. Plausible stories are told of his relations with Phryne, who is said to have been his model for the Cnidian Aphrodite. She is said further to have cajoled him into giving her the Eros dedicated at Thespiae, by first making him promise her the best of all his statues, and then discovering which he thought the best by raising a false report of fire at his studio. His period of activity seems to have extended from about 370 to 330 B.C.

His three masterpieces were the Cnidian Aphrodite, the young Satyr, and the Eros of Thespiae, but we have a long list of his other works. Of the first, Pliny tells us that it was the finest statue not only of Praxiteles, but of the whole world, and that many had made the voyage to Cnidos expressly to see it. He adds a story that Praxiteles had made two figures of Aphrodite and offered them to the people of Cos at the same price. One was draped, the other nude, and the Coans preferred the former, "thinking it more austere and modest". We must remember that naked goddesses were novelties. The other was purchased by Cnidos, and there were bitter regrets at Cos when they found how much more celebrated was the naked Aphrodite. King Nicomedes of Bithynia subsequently offered to liquidate the entire national debt of Cnidos, "which was immense", if they would only sell him the statue, but one is glad to learn that the little island preferred to keep both its debts and its goddess. Apparently it was in her capacity as a marine goddess, a "Notre Dame de Bon Secours" (Euploia), that these islanders chose Aphrodite, the foam-born, for their patroness.

Coins of Cnidos indicate the pose of the statue with sufficient clearness for us to identify a Venus in the Vatican as a copy of the Cnidian Aphrodite. Papal decency saw fit to encase her legs, beginning just below the hips, with drapery constructed of tin (Plate 89, *b*). This would, if anything could, impair the aspect of perfect modesty which shows in every line of her pose and expression. She is not aware of human spectators; there is no self-conscious prudery, as in the abominable Medici Venus, which was an attempt by a later and baser generation to imitate the same type. She has left her robe to hang over the tall water-jar, and is stepping from or towards the bath, not without shrinking, and not in ignorance of her beauty. Even in this imperfect copy we recognise the qualities which made Lucian admire the statue—"the design of the hair and forehead, the finely pencilled eyebrows, and the look of the eyes, so tender, yet so bright and joyful". He adds elsewhere that "a proud smile plays over her lips". A lovely girl's head in Parian marble, now in the Glyptothek at Munich, appears to me so clearly to resemble a younger sister of the same goddess that it must bear some relation to an original by Praxiteles (Plate 89, *c*).

The Capitoline Gallery also possesses a copy of the "Young Satyr" of Praxiteles, "called by the Greeks περιβόητος"—that is, world-famed (Plate 91, *b*). Readers of Hawthorne will remember his eloquent description of the "Marble Faun", and though we, better supplied with ancient originals, can recognise that this is only *after* (and not very near) Praxiteles, yet even as it stands the statue has a peculiar charm and fascination. The sculptor has conveyed the impression of a young creature of the woods, only half human, shy and wild as an animal, and as careless and happy. His smile is as lazy as his attitude. Yet we notice the reserve with which his animal characteristics are indicated merely in the shape of his pointed ear and the "unclassical" profile of his face. Not only is his weight thrown upon one leg, as in all the statues of Praxiteles, but the other foot is gracefully curled round it. This is the only complete ancient copy of the Satyr, but there is a mutilated torso in the Louvre, so fine in its finish and texture that critics once wondered whether it were not an original.

Of the Eros which Phryne dedicated at Thespiae we have no certain copies. But it is evident that many of the Erotes in our galleries were inspired by that masterpiece, and the prettiest is the Eros of Centocelle, a three-quarters figure of admirable design, though of rather slack execution.

Then there is the Hermes. A minor work in the eyes of Antiquity, the object of unqualified admiration by so many in modern times who make the pilgrimage to Olympia. It is also the foremost problem among the sculptures of the fourth century and later (when problems abound). Is it an original or a copy? The problem is not likely to be solved to every one's satisfaction. It is in any case an outstanding example of ancient sculpture and a yardstick of each successive generation's taste. This Hermes was found more than thirty years ago by the German excavators in the very temple of Hera where Pausanias had seen him. No copy or cast or photograph can do more than faintly shadow the incomparable beauty of the marble. In photographs, however, we may appreciate the delicacy of the whole design, in which dignity so marvellously blends with grace and strength with charm. It is Hermes the young Arcadian shepherd's patron deity, Hermes the musician of the tortoise-lyre, the weaver of guile, the bringer of luck, and the kindly escort of souls on their last ferrying. He is playing in careless indulgence with a baby boy, the infant god of wine, but his eyes and his gentle smile (Plate 92) are for someone farther off—not the human spectator. It may be noted, as proving that the technical triumphs of Greek art were gained, not by inspiration, but by hard work at established types, that the child is not very successfully rendered. Greek sculptors could not even yet sufficiently detach themselves from convention to copy the round contours of a baby's face. Critics are divided in their attempts to reconstruct the motive of the raised right shoulder. Evidently the right hand held some object charming to the infant Dionysus, a bunch of grapes, perhaps, or the serpent-wreathed wand proper to Hermes. As it stands in a photograph we can perhaps recognise the loveliest statue in existence, but we cannot see the craft with which the surfaces and textures are rendered. We do not know for certain whether Greek sculptors of the fourth century habitually worked their own statues from start to finish with their own hands. We do know that the surface-finish was regarded as a very important part of the work, and that there were various devices, such as wax-polishing, employed to get the fullest value out of the grain of the

marble for flesh parts.   Praxiteles is especialy named as employing
a painter to tint his marble.

In addition to the Hermes, we have direct literary evidence as to
a great group of Artemis and Apollo, the work of Praxiteles, at
Mantinea.   We are told also the subject of certain reliefs on the
architectural base of it, and reliefs of very fine workmanship corres-
ponding in subject have been excavated at Mantinea.   There is thus
a very fair presumption that these panels were designed, if not executed,
by the master who made the group.   One slab, here illustrated
(Plate 93, c) shows the contest between Apollo the harper and Marsyas
the semi-bestial player of that barbarous instrument the flute.   Marsyas
had challenged Apollo to a contest, and being quite inevitably defeated
was flayed alive as a punishment for his presumption.   The penalty is
delicately indicated by the Phrygian slave who holds the knife in the
centre.   The fourth century artists seldom missed a psychological
point, and Praxiteles has emphasised the contrast between the dignified
god in his majestic harper's robes and the naked, violent Satyr distending
his cheeks as flute-playing barbarians were not ashamed to do.   It is
evident that the Marsyas is a quotation by Praxiteles of the celebrated
figure by Myron.   We note, as a technical point in the history of
relief sculpture, the effect produced by the wide spacing of the figures.
On the other slabs are beautiful though mutilated figures of the Muses,
who acted as umpires in the contest.

We have copies also of another Praxitelean original, Apollo
Sauroktonos (the Lizard-slayer) (Plate 91, a), but the copyist has
evidently exaggerated almost to caricature the elegant slimness of the
young god.   But on the basis of our knowledge of the Hermes I
think we can reconstruct in imagination an exquisite statue even out
of the effeminate Vatican copy.   The true Apollo would not lean all
his weight upon the tree; consequently the tilt of his hips would be
less violent.   His face would be much more carefully modelled, with
less of that womanish smoothness of contour.   But the copyist has
noted and tried to express the lovely brow which Praxiteles gave to
all his heads.   The careless grace, the impression of youth and playful
strength belong to the original, and are highly characteristic of the
artist.   The motive of the statue seems to have been a new and rather
bold invention; we know of no cult of a lizard-slaying Apollo.   It
is true that Apollo was the deity commonly invoked in cases of
natural plagues, such as invasions of field-mice or locusts, but it seems

more probable that Praxiteles, desiring to represent Apollo in a new guise, deliberately chose to portray him as a boy at play. It is clear that Praxiteles was a strongly original and inventive genius, who was not afraid to give his own impression of established types. Out of the gross and bestial Satyr he made a delightful elf of the woods, and he turned the vigorous athlete Apollo into a slender stripling.

Of Scopas the Parian, the second great sculptor of the fourth century, we have fewer certain traces. Some mutilated heads found on the site of the temple of Tegea (Plate 93, *b*), where he made his great pedimental scene of the Calydonian boar-hunt, indicate the new note of pathos and emotion which he introduced into the carving of the human head, and a battered statuette in Dresden (Plate 94, *a*) represents the type of his Maenad in a posture of wild abandon. We know that Scopas was engaged on the Mausoleum and on one of the thirty-six sculptured columns of the great temple at Ephesus, but nothing that remains from either of those buildings can be ascribed to him with certainty. Perhaps the most famous work of Scopas was an Apollo which for long adorned a temple on the Palatine at Rome. The Ludovisi Ares has been considered to be a reduced copy of a colossal statue by him, which also found its way to Rome, and the resting attitude of the handsome war-god, so free from any trace of ferocity, is characteristic of the manner in which the fourth century civilised and humanised all its subjects.

The third is Lysippus of Sicyon, an extraordinarily prolific artist, of whose style we may form a very clear conception, although we have no originals. Athletic types were his favourite work, and his favourite technique was bronze-casting. His discovery was the added grace and beauty which could result from decreasing the proportion of the head to the body. Wherever we find small curly heads very lightly poised upon a strong, vigorous body we may trace the influence to Lysippus. His most famous statue was the young athlete scraping off the oil from his arm with the strigil. The emperor Tiberius fell in love with this "Apoxyomenus", as it is called, and removed it from the front of the baths of Agrippa to his own bed-chamber, but the people of Rome raised such an outcry that he had to restore it. A statue in the Vatican has long been recognised as a marble copy of this work (Plate 90, *b*). In 1894 the French excavators of Delphi found a marble statue of an athlete Agias, which for some years was proclaimed a contemporary copy of a Lysippian work. It is an earlier and less characteristic work than the "Apoxyomenus", and its connexion with Lysippus is not universally accepted. Lysippus was also the sculptor-in-ordinary to Alexander the Great, and we may trace to Lysippian originals many of the numerous portraits of the Macedonian conqueror (Plate 97, *a*). Lysippus was a theorist as well as a practical sculptor, and, like Polycleitus, produced his own theoretical "Canon" of sculptural proportions. He was (with the possible exception of the Devil) the first professed impressionist, for Pliny records a saying of his: "Other sculptors had represented men as they were, while he portrayed them as they appeared to be." We have also certain fine works of sculpture of unknown authorship, and, it must be admitted, in some cases, of disputed date. For while the general concensus of opinion ascribes some of them to the mid-fourth century, cogent arguments have been put forward to place them in the second as Hellenistic works of art. First there is the Demeter of Cnidus in the British Museum (Plate 99, *b*). This is the Mother, Our Lady of Sorrows, mourning with sad eyes, but not in despair, for her daughter Persephone. The influence of Praxiteles may be traced in her brow and lips. The workmanship of this statue, as being, with the exception of temple reliefs, the finest Greek original in our Museum, deserves careful study. And perhaps we should look at the drapery rather than the head to determine its date, which some would give as the second century B.C. Very beautiful also is that sculptured drum from one of the thirty-six columns of the great temple of "Diana of the Ephesians", another of the treasures of our Museum (Plate 94, *b*). It is scarcely probable that time should have spared the one column which Scopas himself designed, but we may trace some of his influence in the emotional character of the faces, and much of Praxiteles in the grace of the attitudes and the poetry of the concept. The application of relief to a rounded surface is in itself a work of great difficulty, and we have seen how boldly it had been attempted in the same temple by artists of a much earlier day. This is a funeral scene such as might be represented on an Attic tombstone. In the centre is a matronly figure, headless, alas! fastening her mantle on her shoulder preparatory to the journey; on her left is Hermes, very young and boyish, extending his caduceus as if pointing downwards, but looking upwards to a point above the woman's head. On her right is another figure, whom from his long wings and boyish form we should take, perhaps, for Love, were it not that his sad eyes and heavy sword mark him out as Death. Some think that the woman is Alcestis, and it is scarcely likely that any but a heroine, at least, would occupy such a place in such a building. To make both these emissaries of death so young and charming is an idea typical of the fourth century, and especially of Praxiteles.

An outstanding work, perhaps an original of the first quarter of the fourth century is the figure of a youth (Plate 90, *a*) dredged up under romantic circumstances off the island of Cythera (Cerigo), which lies at the extreme southerly point of Laconia. This was part of a cargo of spoils from Greece looted by the Roman general Sulla and ship-wrecked off Cape Matapan. No satisfactory guess has yet been made as to the name of the statue or the motive of its attitude. In my opinion the upstretched arm suggests that the man is playing "yo-yo", a pastime for the antiquity of which there is independent evidence. More important, it is a link in the development between the Doryphorus and the later tradition of Lysippus. Again the lovely winged head, which originally belonged to a full-length statue of Hypnos (Sleep), is one of the most striking bronzes in the British Museum (Plate 93, *a*). It is of the Praxitelean period, but not by Praxiteles. It is clearly related to the period which produced that figure of Death, "the brother of Sleep", on the Ephesian column. This example has been covered by exposure to the air with a beautiful green patina, often imitated with the application of acids by modern bronze-workers. But the Herculaneum bronzes, which had been preserved for eighteen centuries in an airproof casing of lava, are today in much the same condition as when they left the studio. Though they were made, no doubt, in Roman times as reproductions of earlier (third century?) originals, Lysippus is the artist whose influence is most clearly visible, as, for example, in the vivid Pair of Wrestlers, or the Seated Hermes. I have already said that the old cities of Greece were mostly too impoverished to undertake great architectural works in this period. Ephesus, however, had her great temple of Artemis burned down by an enterprising individual with the very modern ambition of getting his name before the public. For fear of increasing his success I will not repeat it here, but when Alexander the Great offered to rebuild the temple out of his own pocket the Ephesians declined, possibly on the ground that their temple had already advertised a malefactor and they did not desire it to be a further advertisement for a benefactor. So they rebuilt it themselves with such splendour that it became one of the Seven Wonders of the World.

Advertisement, you see, was in the air. The almost extreme self-repression of the individual was passing, and in the same spirit a wealthy ruler of Caria who in Greek eyes was a tyrant and in Persian eyes a satrap determined to raise a tomb for himself and his wife which should also be a wonder of the world. His name was Maussollus, and the Mausoleum he built consisted (so it has been suggested) of a columned shrine raised upon a lofty pedestal and surmounted with a pyramidal structure of ever-narrowing square courses of masonry, the whole crowned by a colossal chariot with four horses, the work of Pythis. Considerable remains were found by Sir Charles Newton at Halicarnassus, and are now in the British Museum. We know that Scopas and other famous artists were employed upon the work. The most important relic is the colossal statue of Maussollus (unless it represents a later and relatively unknown ruler of the same state in the second century B.C., for there is strong evidence that it was not mounted on a chariot), which, considering the fragmentary state of the other remains, is in remarkably fine preservation (Plate 99, a). Here we have a realistic portrait. The face of the prince is not in the least conventional, has, in fact, a distinctly barbarian profile, yet preserves a dignity and worth of its own, and visibly suggests a foreign dynast. The reliefs (Plate 95) which adorned the pedestal are also distinctive and interesting. We observe, as on the Mantinean basis, that the figures are widely spaced. Their poses are visibly contrived for decorative effect on a system of correspondences much less subtle, and therefore much less effective, than on the Parthenon frieze. The designer has not shrunk from portraying violent action in the battle of Amazons; yet there is beauty in every figure, and remarkable technical skill; and the charioteer (Plate 95, a), leaning forward in his ardour, his robes swept back by the wind, is deservedly famous. Here, surely, is a great work of art in small compass. The story goes that four of the most famous artists of Greece, one of them Scopas himself, were employed on the work, and that on the death of their royal patron they completed their task without pay for the honour of their art.

THE OTHER ARTS

Nothing has been said here about painting, because Greek painting is essentially a matter for the historian of art who can study what Pliny and others said about it and try to find some intelligent meaning in it by reference to pottery and sculpture. Of course the influence of Polygnotus, Parrhasius, Zeuxis, and Apelles should be traceable even in the humble decorators of pitcher, pot, and pipkin. But we have no relics of the original work of any of those artists, and the ancient art critic is an obscure and uncertain guide. He seems to have had the most ridiculous canons of art, and to have considered it the greatest triumph of painting when birds came to peck at the grapes in a picture. The only Greek pictures that we have are the mural frescoes and mosaics of Pompeii, which belong properly to the Roman department, and a few Egyptian mummy-cases painted by Greek artists. Therefore, if you please, we will leave Greek painting to the connoisseurs, with the remark that Apelles of the fourth century was considered the greatest of all Greek masters. Perhaps the Alexander-mosaic of Pompeii (Plate 97, *b*) is the best extant production of a painting of the fourth century. That the colouring of the original is satisfactorily reproduced on this would be hazardous to maintain, but it is likely that the mosaic does give some idea of the extent to which problems of foreshortening, grouping, and shadows had been solved.

Nor can the ordinary student of culture get much satisfaction out of Greek music. It is rather cheering to reflect that after all they did not know everything down in Athens, but left one or two things for us to discover. One of them was harmony. We have heard accomplished savants give curious and not wholly unpleasant renderings of Greek music, and distinguished composers like Sir Hubert Parry have written very beautiful airs which are said to be Greek. Broadly speaking, we may divide modern reproductions of Greek music into two classes: those that are Greek, and those that are music. It is certain that the Greeks attached very great importance to music, far more, in fact, than we do generally. It was for a gentleman, who must be able to perform at a social gathering, the foremost instrument of ancient education, and, because of its relationship to mathematics, philosophers from Pythagoras to Plato insisted very seriously upon its moral and spiritual efficacy. The Greeks divided music into three principal modes and four subordinate ones, according to the key employed. The Dorian Mode was the lowest in pitch. It was the music of the seven- or eight-stringed cithara used in martial songs and dances. The Spartans were so conservative in matters of music, as in all else, that when the famous Timotheus of Miletus appeared in their city with his new twelve-stringed harp the Ephors ordered the strings to be broken. The Phrygian Mode was based on the minor scale with a flat seventh (G to G), and the Lydian on the major with a sharp fourth (F to F). The Lydian was the music of the "soft, complaining flute", and its high-pitched sounds were condemned by the austere critics of the mainland as too sensuous and emotional. Wind music was, as we have seen on the monuments, originally regarded as a barbarian monstrosity, but a fourth century dinner-party would scarcely have been complete without at least one turn on the double pipe by a pretty *auletris*. A sort of double pipe is still used by Greek shepherd-boys, and in the modern example which I have seen one pipe was used as a "drone", as in the bagpipes. This instrument is probably a humble survivor of the "syrinx" played by Arcadian shepherds in antiquity. The superior instrument played by the *auletris* would be really a double clarinet. The flute, as we have it, was not known in antiquity.

The Greek potter never made any legitimate advance beyond the Red-figured style of the fifth century. In the latter part of the fifth century vase-painting at Athens became more sentimental or flamboyant, in its representation of the life of the womens' quarters, or of mythology ultimately rendered in terms of the stage (Plates 84, *a*; 83, *a*). The vases of this age are not without a certain soft charm or lush attractiveness (Plate 83), but we miss the assurance of an earlier period. The technique was transferred to Italy where the influence of the stage, comic and tragic, was even more apparent. The series of Panathenaic amphorae (those large jars painted with figures of Athena and athletic subjects intended for prizes at the Panathenaic Games) continues unbroken, and their design changes little because they have to correspond with a conventional type. The custom was that they should have their figures in black, and accordingly the painter obeyed the custom by leaving parts of his vase in the red of the surface clay, and treating those parts as panels on which he painted his figures in black. Towards the end of the century—that is, in the days of Alexander—it appears that vases were more frequently made in metal; the wealth set circulating by the conquest of the East introduced a taste for vases of gold and silver, and the earthenware itself increasingly takes forms which can only be explained as imitation of metal. Thus the surface is often raised in relief, and vases are apparently cast in moulds.

Coins (Plate 96) and gems exhibit increased technical mastery. In general, surprisingly, coin types, though pre-eminently a matter of use and wont, responded very quickly to the artistic fashions of the day. An exception was Athenian coinage. The Athena type with owl and olive-branch on the reverse is always of a conventional and somewhat archaic character. Elsewhere the coins and gems of the fourth century reach their highest point of perfection, and that is a point which has never been surpassed. As usual, Syracuse is in the forefront for beauty of design, and a new series, inspired by the Syracusan victory over Athens, revives the glorious types of Gelo and Hiero and improves them. The decadrachms of this period, representing the head of the nymph Arethusa surrounded with dolphins and bearing on the reverse a four-horse chariot at full gallop, are regarded by numismatists as the most beautiful coins in existence. The best of these bear the signature of their engraver, Cimon. A gold coinage began here about the time of the repulse of the Athenian Armada. Corinthian coins with the flying Pegasus on the obverse and a head of Athena in a Corinthian helmet on the reverse also attain the summit of their beauty in this century. But even out-of-the-way places like Panticapaeum, the corn depot of Southern Russia, and some of the tiniest and remotest of states, employed engravers of consummate art. Just before the beginning of the century three cities of the island of Rhodes united to form one republic, which rapidly rose to wealth by way of commerce and good government. It produced a coinage of great excellence, the figure of the sungod Helios on the obverse and a rose (rhodon) as a punning emblem on the reverse. It is only with Alexander the Great's successors that the portraiture of mortal rulers begins to appear on Greek coinage. It is then rapidly developed, and some of the monarchs of the East are portrayed by Greek artists with great vigour and realism (Plate 103) a foretaste in miniature of later sculpture on a major scale (Plate 100).

Lastly, architecture exhibits similar tendencies towards technical facility and a less austere spirit in the use of ornament. To this period belong the new temple at Ephesus and the Mausoleum already mentioned; earlier than either, and in fact belonging to the late fifth century, is the kindred sepulchral monument from Lycia known as the Nereid Monument, from the graceful figures of sea-nymphs set between the columns on the tall basis of the shrine. In Athens, through the century, we have the new walls of the city and the Piraeus constructed with Persian help by Conon and improved by the statesman Lycurgus, the stadium for athletic contests, the little choregic monument of Lysicrates, and the stone theatre of Dionysus. The luxurious Corinthian order is now more popular than the staid Doric. The invention of this beautiful type, with its curling acanthus leaves and volutes is attributed to the Athenian sculptor Callimachus, a versatile artist of Periclean days. It was the discovery of a new drill for stone-cutting which made it possible. A legendary explanation of its origin was naturally provided. Callimachus had been struck with the beauty of a column on which a woman had placed a basket of flowers in memory of the maiden whose tomb it marked, and a live acanthus had sprung from the cracked stone below the basket. The earliest appearance of the Corinthian capital is, so far as we know, to be found in the temple at Bassae. It became increasingly popular, especially in Roman times. Owing to its slenderer shaft, Vitruvius compares the Corinthian order to a young girl, while he likens the Ionic to a matron and the Doric to a man.

In the terracotta statuettes which have been found in such large numbers at Tanagra and elsewhere we have some of the most delightful as well as the most characteristic examples of fourth- and third-century art. They are generally found in tombs, and seem to have been made largely for the purpose; but many must have been toys and ornaments for the living. They sometimes represent deities, and we have several examples of Eros, and Aphrodite. By far the commonest subject is a young girl draped in a mantle. Indeed, the maker of such ware is called in Greek Koroplastes—"Girl-modeller". Domestic scenes are common, girls talking, dancers, animals, and so forth. Some are jointed, and many of them were obviously designed as toys. Sometimes they were glazed, but far more often the colours were applied directly to the clay after it came from the mould. The colours have therefore in many cases entirely disappeared. Apart from their singular grace and charm, they give us extremely interesting examples of Greek costume. The British Museum has a very fine collection, which well deserves study. A few of them appear to be modelled from famous statues of the period.

LITERATURE AND PHILOSOPHY

This is, as we have noticed, an age predominantly of Prose. Poetry is for the time being (and for us) almost extinct, partly, perhaps, because the Athenian theatre was already so well supplied with material by the great masters of the previous generation, and partly because public recitation was no longer the sole means of publication for literature. It is true that Agathon, a member of the literary circle which included Socrates and Plato, was esteemed almost on a level with the three great tragedians, but all his work has been allowed to perish. The fourth century is the era of the "Middle Comedy", a stage of transition in which political references were being abandoned and the delineation of manners and social life was taking its place. There are sundry surviving fragments to represent this genre, quarried from the laborious works of Athenaeus and the like, and the latest plays of Aristophanes, such as the "Plutus". The New Comedy of manners, in which the great master was Menander, begins towards the end of the fourth century and fills the first half of the third.

Prose would naturally fall into three categories—History, including political and economic writings, Oratory, and Philosophy.

The fifth century had produced the two great historians Herodotus and Thucydides, both of whom treated their subject from a lofty standpoint with a distinctly ethical purpose. The typical historian of the fourth century has a much more restricted outlook. Instead of seeking to point a moral or to illustrate the larger aspects of life, he is contented with investigating and narrating the facts of the past for their own sake or for any purpose to which the reader may care to put them. Such were Ephorus and Theopompus, whose work, though lost to us, formed the base upon which such writers as Plutarch built their narratives. Undoubtedly, however, these historians often had causes of their own to serve. The constitutional history of Greece, which was originally compiled by various writers of this period, is full of contradictions which distinctly point to theories constructed under the influence of interested motives and in accordance with certain political tendencies. The venerable figures of Solon and Lycurgus, many biographical details concerning Miltiades and Themistocles, have been composed by persons whose motives seldom included any disinterested love of truth. Xenophon I have already described as one of the characteristic figures of the day. He always betrays a strong tendency in favour of Sparta, and especially his friend King Agesilaus.

Oratory as a branch of literature resting upon formal rules of rhetoric is a creation of this period. The Greeks had always been a rhetorical people. We have noted how, even in Homer, persuasion by the power of speech was a god-given attribute of kings and elders. The Greeks, and the Romans too, went into battle under the influence of oratory as our Highlanders are aroused to martial frenzy by the eloquence of the pibroch. No one doubts that all the speeches in Thucydides' history are his own invention, but if they bear any resemblance to the real thing we must believe that the Greek soldier was encouraged, in the fifth century, to fight by a very sober and logical style of speech, including a categorical estimate of the chances in his favour. The modern reader is frequently lulled to sleep by the words of Brasidas or Nicias encouraging his men to battle. Thucydides was, it seems, influenced in his peculiarly austere style of rhetoric by Antiphon, who was the first professional rhetorician to engage in politics. But even Antiphon was content to direct operations through his pupils and clients. In the fourth century the trained professional orator comes forward on the Pnyx or in the theatre as a public states-man, and gives orders to the professional soldiers who now command armies and fleets. The profession of the pleader had grown inevitably out of the legal system in vogue in Athens. Where suits were decided by juries numbering hundreds, a rather violent style of pleading had naturally arisen. Although it was necessary by law for the litigants to conduct their own case, it became customary for them to apply to speech-writers like Lysias, Isaeus, and Demosthenes for a speech to be learnt and recited as dramatically as possible. We should expect such performances to be highly emotional and to consist largely of oratorical claptrap. That, on the contrary, they are for the most part severely logical, that purple passages are carefully eschewed and references to national feeling kept within limits, is the clearest possible proof of the high intellectual standard (or the cynicism) of the average Athenian citizen who sat upon the jury. It is true that defendants did dress in mourning and produce wives and families in rags and tears to move the sympathies of their judges, but their arguments must be sensible and must include copious reference to the letter of the law. From the so-called "Private Orations" of Demosthenes we obtain rare glimpses of social life at Athens in the fourth century, the banker Phormio who rises to affluence from slavery, who is liberated and marries his master's daughter, the elegant hooliganism of rich young men who quarrel in camp and assault one another in the Athenian market-place, the extraordinary luxury of Meidias, who rode on a silver-plated saddle, or the quarrels of neighbours in the country about watercourses and rights of way. In a later chapter we shall have to consider the public orations of Demosthenes as the opponent of the Macedonian conquerors. He is unquestionably for European literature the father of oratory. Cicero learnt his art from Demosthenes, and Burke from Cicero. Cleverness is the distinguishing mark of Demosthenes; his style is restrained and logical. I do not think he was morally great, or even more than tolerably honest, but he was so subtle a pleader that I for one always have an instinctive desire to take the other side.

Isocrates, "the old man eloquent", who died about 338 B.C., is an interesting figure, very typical of his day. He became a professor of rhetoric, and kept a school in which he had a hundred pupils, each of whom paid him one thousand drachmae for the course. He received as much as thirty talents for writing a single speech. But he was a pure theorist; he scarcely ever delivered his orations, which were written for private reading, and carefully polished for that purpose. Some modern historians discern in him a statesman of wide and lofty views. It is true that he advocated peace, retrenchment, and reform for Athens. It is true also that he spoke in his great Panegyric Oration, a work which had taken him ten years to write, in favour of concerted action by Hellas against the Persians. But I fear that Isocrates as a Panhellenist is a fraud. Panhellenic orations on the text of the Persian wars were a standing dish at the Olympic festival. Gorgias of Leontini, among others, had delivered a similar oration in past years. It is surely a proof of the deadness of Panhellenic feeling in Greece that the assembled Greeks could both applaud such orations and sign the peace which the Great King had sent down from Susa. Moreover, the Panegyric itself is written in a very curious tone for a genuine internationalist. He begins very happily: "Athens and Sparta united, shoulder to shoulder, as they stood at Plataea, Athens and Sparta . . . yes, but in that order, mind you . . . Athens must come first . . . Sparta is, and always has been, a bully and a sneak . . . don't you remember . . . ?" That is the spirit of the Panegyric. Nor is the style really comparable to that of Demosthenes. Carefully constructed

7. (a) *right*
Head of Alexander in the British Museum.

(b) *below*
The "Alexander Mosaic" in the National Museum, Naples, from Pompeii.

98.　The "Alexander Sarcophagus" from Sidon, in Istanbul.

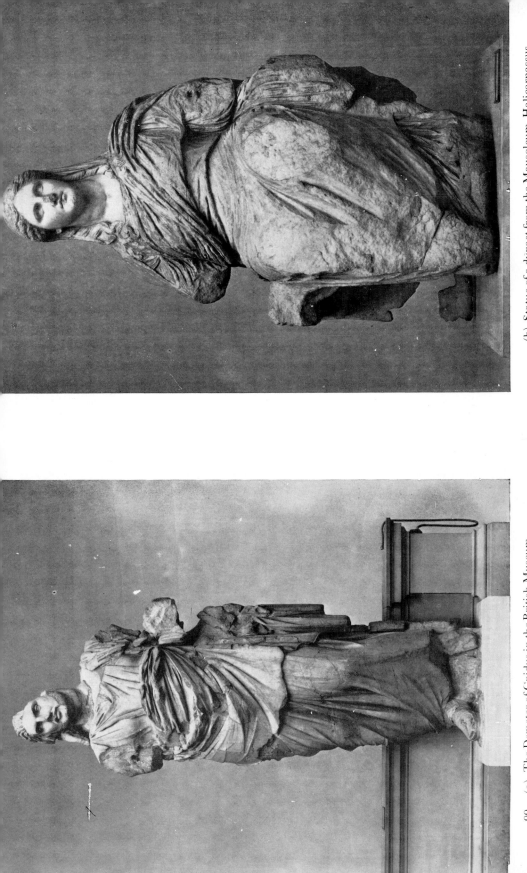

99. (a) The Demeter of Cnidus in the British Museum.

(b) Statue of a dynast from the Mausoleum, Halicarnassus.

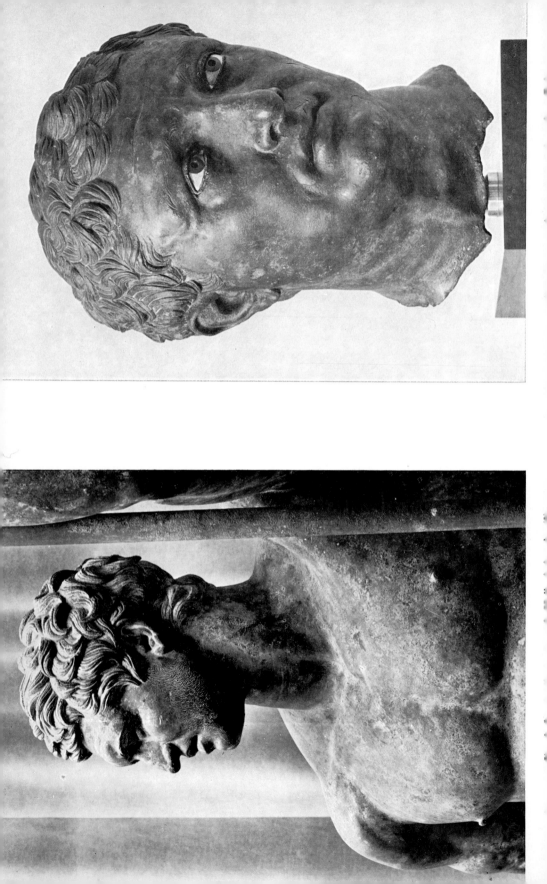

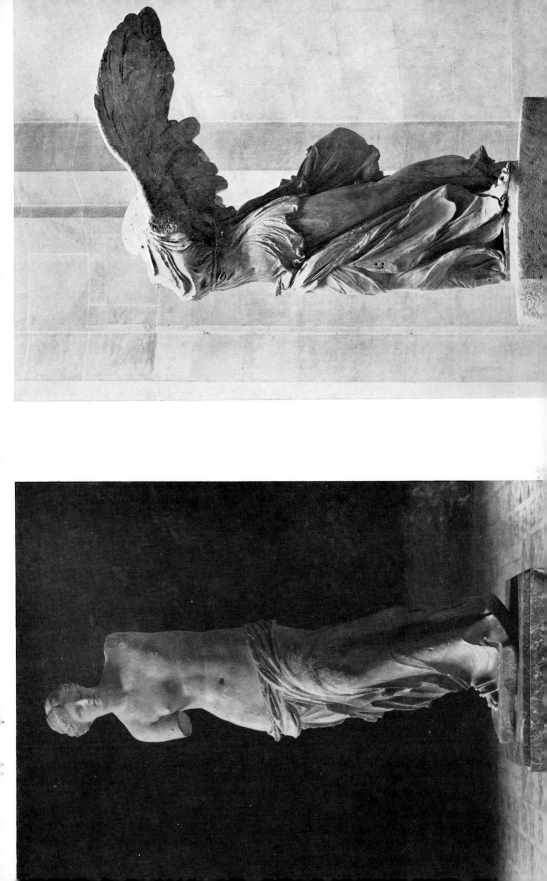

102. Part of the major frieze of the Great Altar of Pergamon, with the Battle of the Gods and Giants, in Berlin.

103. Portrait coins of Hellenistic rulers.

as it is, it smells of the lamp; there is a wearisome mellifluousness in its cadences, and a certain odour of self-consciousness and self-righteousness in its tone.

Turning now to philosophy, we are confronted at once with the problem of Socrates and his real personality. The sage himself wrote nothing, but he has been written of by two immediate disciples, Xenophon and Plato. Between the two we must form our idea of the man. It is likely that Xenophon missed a great deal of the inner meaning of his master's teaching, but it is certain that Plato used Socrates as a mouthpiece for his own ideas with a freedom which could only be tolerated in a country where portraiture was seldom as yet practised as an art. Socrates may be shortly described as a man who went about asking "Why?". It is a habit that we are too apt to repress in children: the Athenians put Socrates to death for it. Remember that it was the age when sophistry—that is, formal profession of superior wisdom—was beginning to be rife, when professors of this, that, and the other were abroad in the streets of Athens. You may reduce any professor to tears by asking him "Why?" with sufficient persistence, especially if you are followed by a train of admiring young men of good family. Socrates was very pertinacious and absolutely fearless. So a jury of Athenian citizens condemned him to drink hemlock on the charges of corrupting the youth with atheistical doctrines. He was certainly not an atheist. He was deeply religious in the highest sense. The goodness of God and the immortality of the soul were two of the fundamental dogmas to Socrates. He objected, or at least Plato did, to the theology of Homer as undignified, in that it exhibited gods laughing and weeping. But he used constantly to speak of "the God", "the divine principle", and even of a "Daimonion", or divine spirit in his own breast.

In the main, there is no doubt but that the condemnation of Socrates was, like that of Christ, a political move. Both Critias and Theramenes, the foremost leaders of the oligarchic revolution, were among the disciples of Socrates. Both Anytus and Melitus, his accusers, belonged to the democratic reactionaries who had overthrown them. If we may judge by Plato and Xenophon, Socrates was unquestionably a keen critic of the innumerable sophistries upon which democracy was built. With all that, Socrates was a good citizen and patriot. He had fought in many Athenian battles, the soldiers marvelled at his contempt for cold and danger, he had done his best to prevent the unjust sentence upon the generals of Arginusae, he had incurred the hostility of the Thirty Tyrants.

The trial and death of Socrates presents a scene which for pathos and nobility stands, with one other, alone in history. At the first trial he was condemned only by a majority of six. Athenian law permitted him under such circumstances to propose an alternative penalty. He proposed, accordingly, that he should be entertained for the rest of his life at the public expense, along with the officers and benefactors of the state, in the Presidential Hall. This Socratic irony was treated by the judges as contumacy, and at the second hearing he was condemned to death by a large plurality of votes. Plato has written of his end in three great dialogues—the "Apology", the "Phaedo", and the "Crito". In the "Apology" Socrates concludes his address to the jury with these words: "This only I ask of you. When my sons grow up, gentlemen, if they seem to be concerned about wealth or anything rather than virtue, punish them, I pray you, with the same affliction as that with which I have afflicted you, and if they pretend to be something when they are nothing, make it a reproach to them, as I have made it to you. If you will do that, we shall have received justice at your hands, I and my sons. Ah, I see it is now time for us all to go hence, me to my death, you to your life. But which of us is going on a better errand—that none can say, but only God alone."

The dialogue of the "Phaedo" is perhaps the sublimest thing in literature. It purports to be the last discourse of Socrates to the friends who have come to share his last moments. He preaches the immortality of the soul, the unimportance of death, nay, the urgent necessity of that release from the hampering and deluding trammels of the body, if a philosopher is to see things as they are and enjoy the knowledge of reality. He puts it as a "myth", using the current Greek mythology of Styx and Hades and Tartarus to enforce his doctrine of Hell, Paradise, and Purgatory. His friend Crito asks for instructions as to his burial.

"Bury me any way you like," answered Socrates, "if you get hold of me and I don't escape you." He looked at us with a quiet smile and proceeded: "No, sirs, I can't convince Crito that I am this Socrates who is now conversing with you. He thinks I am that one whom he will presently see dead, and he asks, if you please, how he is to bury me. I have been making a long speech to prove that when I have drunk the poison I shall not be with you any more, but shall have gone away to enjoy whatever blessings await the departed; only I am afraid it is all lost upon Crito, with all my consolations for myself and you. So you must be my sureties with Crito in a pledge just contrary to that which he gave to my judges. He went bail that I would remain here. You must go bail that I shall certainly not remain, but abscond and vanish. Then Crito will be less afflicted, and when he sees my body being burnt or buried he won't grieve for me as if something unpleasant was happening to me, and he won't say at the funeral that it is Socrates he is laying out or burying."

Then the story of his painful and courageous death is told in language of extraordinary simplicity and dignified restraint. "Such, Echecrates, was the last end of our companion, as we should say, the best, the wisest, and the justest man of all we had ever known."

Socrates had done much towards giving Greek philosophy its new trend. The earlier philosophers had been much concerned with the physical universe, trying to discover its origin, and thereby its "principle"; this had been apt to degenerate into that paltry inquisitiveness about mere phenomena which many people are still apt to dignify with the name of "natural science". Socrates sought not so much the origin as the end of things; he made philosophy concern herself with the nature of reality and incidentally with ethics and conduct.

The development of ideal philosophy may probably be ascribed, in the main, to Plato rather than Socrates. The general English reader will find a Christianised version of the Platonic theory of Ideas in Wordsworth's "Ode on Intimations of Immortality". Put very briefly, it is that the material world apprehended by the human senses is only a copy or pale shadow of the realities "laid up in heaven". The soul comes into this world

> Not in entire forgetfulness
> And not in utter nakedness.

We recognise the forms of things by their likeness to the patterns apprehended by the soul elsewhere. Thus, as Plato says in the "Meno", all learning is a process of recollection. Knowledge is virtue. The words of St Paul to the Corinthians are almost a verbal echo of this teaching of Socrates: "For now we see in a mirror, darkly;

but then face to face: now I know in part; but then shall I know even as also I am known."

The doctrines of Plato about Love have been strangely perverted in the popular mind by a singular freak of language in the use of the word "platonic". They are expounded in two very different dialogues, the almost boisterous "Symposium", where Socrates and his friends agree to diversify the drinking with a series of discourses on Love, and that most exquisite composition called the "Phaedrus", in which Socrates and his friend converse on the same topic as they lie in the shade of a spreading plane-tree upon the grassy banks of the Ilissus.

The human soul, coming from eternity into life, has not forgotten altogether "the sea of beauty" of which it had once enjoyed the vision. All beautiful things remind us of it, and (once more to quote Wordsworth):

> Hence in a season of calm weather,
>   Though inland far we be,
> Our souls have sight of that immortal sea
>   Which brought us hither.

Thus all men possess a natural yearning for beauty, however much their glimpses of it may have been darkened and distorted by their earthly experiences, and in their beloved they are seeing the reflection of the reality of beauty. The procreant impulse is part of man's yearning for immortality; it is out of goodness and beauty that the immortal is to be begotten.

With Plato's political views as expressed especially in the "Republic" we shall be able to deal more fully in the next chapter, when we come to consider the political theories which arose out of the conditions of the city-state. It is clear that in the hands of men like Socrates and Plato philosophy was usurping the place which according to the ideas of some religion ought to occupy in the minds of men. Greek religion, or at least the official Olympian worship as defined by Homer, Hesiod, and the Tragic Poets, had never attained much influence over the morality of its worshippers. But now philosophy was definitely claiming to teach virtue. Not only sophists like Protagoras and Hippias, but even philosophers like Socrates and Plato, claimed to put right conduct on a basis of knowledge, and therefore of education. Hence followed the arguable conclusion that virtue was to be for the rich and well-born. Philosophy looked snobbish from the start; it tended to exclude all but the select few from any chance of salvation, and, if it had had its way, would have excluded them from any political rights whatever. The strength of Greek philosophy is in its earnest opposition to materialism, its proper scorn of base, trivial, and temporary pursuits. But therewith it felt and inculcated a contempt of honest labour, and thereby it drifted farther and farther apart from practical life. For that, of course, the institution of slavery is largely responsible.

VI

THE MACEDONIAN WORLD

εἴπερ ἴσην ῥώμην γνώμῃ, Δημόσθενες, εἶχες
οὔποτ' ἂν Ἑλλήνων ἦρξεν Ἄρης Μακεδών.
PLUTARCH

ALEXANDER AND HIS WORK

THE fate of that old god Cronos, supplanted by his own children whom he had tried in vain to devour, is more or less the common lot of all parents of vigorous offspring. The Athenians had a nocturnal festival in which young men ran in relays, each member of the team handing his torch to another, and, as Aeschylus says in a fine metaphor, "the first is the victor, even though he be last in the running". So at this point of our history we begin to be aware of new forces arising, or shortly to arise, in the Greek world, new powers on the fringe of the Hellenic circle now stepping into the light and taking their places in the torch-race of civilisation. Such were Rhodes (the new commercial republic), Caria under Maussollus, Thessaly under Jason, Cyprus under Evagoras, Pergamum under Attalus, the two Leagues (Aetolian and Achaean), and above all Macedon under Philip and Alexander. The stream of culture and intelligence that emanated from Athens and the other ancient cities was now pulsing in the finger-tips of Greece. Many of these new powers are more than half barbarian. They are either monarchies or confederations. What generally happens is that leaders arise who are themselves sufficiently endowed with civilised intelligence to utilise the latent force in a race of untamed and uncivilised warriors. In the military sense the case is that the old powers had grown into the habit of replacing their citizen militias by paid professional soldiers, and their citizens accordingly had grown slack and unwarlike. Rulers like Philip of Macedon were able to raise much larger native levies and to drill them into the professional tactics of the day. Economically it was wealth that told. The old cities were, partly, no doubt, through their own lack of foresight, in a state of financial exhaustion, while Philip, by his control of the gold-mines, Attalus and Evagoras by their private wealth, and the Phocians by their sacrilegious seizure of the treasures of Delphi, were still able to bring large forces into the field. The old powers were thus left behind in the race through the force of circumstances beyond their control. In fact, the day of the city-state seemed for a time to be drawing to a close, and larger units, either kingdoms or confederacies, to be taking its place according to their natural superiority.

It is possible, then, to argue that the old city states were degenerate. This is a proposition that deserves examination. In some respects it is false. If it be the mark of historical decadence that the motive power of a race is in some mysterious way paralysed so that invention ceases and no more new experiments are made in culture or politics, then we may assert with some confidence that Greece was not yet in the fourth nor even in the third century in such a condition. We shall see something of her new inventions in literature, philosophy, and art in this chapter. In politics the federal systems of Western Greece were distinctly novel and promising. Even in warfare she fought bravely enough at Chaeronea, as she did much later against the invading Gauls. Even Athens, when her dark hour came and she had to submit to garrisons and alien governors, never acquiesced, but rose again and again in rebellion against them. Sparta for a short time in the third century performed the most difficult of all political feats, namely, a reformation and regeneration of herself from within. At Sellasia under Cleomenes III in 222 B.C. the few Spartans who remained fought against tremendous odds with all their ancient sublime devotion, and died to a man as their ancestors had done under Leonidas. So true is it that moral and spiritual qualities in a people do not come to the sudden end that often befalls a state when it depends for its greatness on material prosperity or physical force.

But the most serious symptom of later Greece was a real physical decline, for which history has no remedy and no mercy, a decline of population. The Spartiate race of Lacedaemon, for example, became almost extinct. There were no more than fifteen hundred of them at the date of the battle of Leuctra, and after that we hear of expeditions containing no more than thirty genuine Spartiates. In a less degree it was the same all over old Greece, and whether it was due to malarial fever or to economic distress, it made the political decline of these states inevitable.

Now it is necessary to go back a little into the earlier part of the fourth century to glance at the rise of Macedon and its conquerors. At the opening of the century Macedon was still almost uncivilised; it was ruled by a monarchy surrounded with an aristocracy of knights very much after the Homeric model. At that time its kings had begun to acquire enough education to mingle a little in Greek politics, and Archelaus in particular had the good taste to invite Euripides and Agathon to his court. Philip II obtained the throne by suppressing his young ward, the rightful king. At that time Macedon was overrun by wilder barbarians from the west, and it was long before Philip could make head against them. He did so at last by the organising genius which he displayed in remodelling his army, the astute statesmanship with which he made and broke treaties, and still more by the wealth he secured and the use he made of it in bribing his enemies. Philip was, in short, the organiser who occasionally precedes the conqueror and grows the laurels for his successor to wear. Expansion to the west would be difficult and unprofitable. To the east lay the important cities of the Chalcidian peninsulas, the gold-mines of Mount Pangaeus, protected by the city of Amphipolis, the rather decrepit kingdom of Thrace, and then the way was clear to the Black Sea and to Asia. Now this was the life-line of Athens' food supply, and the main artery of the sea-borne traffic which made the Piraeus a great port. A conflict was therefore inevitable.

The statesman who led the anti-Macedonian party at Athens was the orator Demosthenes. His brilliant series of Philippic and Olynthiac Orations are full of denunciations of the crafty monarch, full of trumpet-calls to the ancient valour of Athens which sometimes ring rather hollow to modern ears. Demosthenes was not exceptionally honest, but there is no warrant for suspecting the purity of his patriotism. He himself set the example of bearing a shield personally in the ranks, and he must have been conscious throughout his public career that he was in danger of assassination or of execution if the enemy triumphed. The wisdom of his opposition to Philip has also been questioned. Events were to prove that these Macedonian kings were not barbarians; on the contrary, their warmest aspiration was to be counted as Greeks, and they had, as they frequently testified, a great love of Greek culture and a deep veneration for Athens as the home of it. This the future was to prove; the present only showed a foreign monarch devouring piecemeal the interests of Athens in the north. Perhaps Demosthenes ought to have realised that Macedon was too strong for Athens, but no one could seriously expect old Greece to succumb to this upstart without a struggle. For one thing, Macedon had not and never acquired a really strong fleet. But her army was certainly irresistible.

Philip had learnt strategy at the feet of the Theban Epaminondas. The army he created included a *corps d'élite* of noble horse-guards, the Companions of the King. These were the earliest first-rate mounted troops in history, and it was by their means that the dashing exploits of Alexander were subsequently achieved. For the infantry his great invention was the phalanx. This was clearly a modification of the deep formation invented by Epaminondas. It consisted of sixteen ranks armed with a spear 21 feet long. They stood in close order so that the points of the first five ranks projected from the front to present a bristling hedge of spears. The remaining eleven ranks, we are gravely informed, held their spears obliquely in the air to ward off missiles! Let the military reader find a military justification for this extraordinary arrangement. To me it seems a further confirmation of my civilian view that Greek tactics were primarily designed to prevent armies from running away. We observe that when Alexander took Persian troops into his phalanx he put twelve ranks of Persians into the lines, with a row of Macedonians *at their rear*. In any case troops standing in close formation armed with weapons seven yards long must have been useless for any but defensive purposes; and, as a matter of fact, the victories of Alexander were generally gained by the lightning charge of the king at the head of his knights.

We need not touch upon the shabby "Sacred Wars" which caused Philip to enter Greece on the invitation of Thebes. It was at Chaeronea in 338 that Philip defeated a mixed Greek army in whose ranks Demosthenes was fighting as a hoplite. Philip was generous to the Greeks, and especially to Athens. Next year the darling wish of his heart was obtained, for he was elected president of a Panhellenic union destined to fulfil his great scheme of avenging the Persian invasions of Greece by a march into Asia, or at any rate by the freeing of the Greek cities of Asia Minor. In the next year he was murdered, and his brilliant son Alexander has been suspected of complicity in the plot.

The grand idea of Philip's, begotten perhaps from the study of Isocrates, was certainly inspired by the examples of Cyrus and

Agesilaus. Unfortunately it was far from arousing any enthusiasm in Greece. Persia itself was a long way off and money could be had from the Great King without fighting for it. There was a sordid scramble for bribes among the Greek statesmen. As soon as they heard of Philip's death they broke into unseemly jubilation, and voted compliments to his murderers; they hoped that things would return to their old routine, and that there would be no more talk of crusades. They had reckoned without Alexander, for it is seldom that a Philip is succeeded by an Alexander.

This young man who conquered the world and died at the age of thirty-three has quite naturally captivated the imagination of posterity and formed a model for ambitious generals of later days. Julius Caesar sighed to think of his inferiority in achievement. Augustus paid a visit to his tomb, and wore his portrait on a ring. Napoleon consciously imitated him. As a soldier he was not only an organiser of victory, though of course he owed a great deal to his father in this respect, and a strategist with an eye for a battlefield, but also a dashing cavalry leader, the sort of man to ride straight for the enemy's king, to be the first in the breach, and to leap down alone into the enemy's town. He did this sort of thing with impunity; he never lost a battle. He was chivalrous to ladies. He married a beautiful Eastern princess called Roxana, he rode a beautiful war-horse called Bucephalus. If Lysippus and Apelles may be trusted, he had the face of a Greek god. He had just that touch of dissipation which somehow rounds off the conception of a popular hero. He had the good fortune to die young, in the hour of victory.

And what is to be the sober historian's estimate of this dazzling person? We may minimise his triumphs by suggesting that the Persian empire was helpless before him, like ripe fruit waiting to be gathered. We may suggest with reason that he strove by the most ruthless means to free himself from the tutelage of the great Macedonian nobles who were his commanders. We may certainly charge him with conquering insanely without stopping to organise, and with neglecting his own kingdom and failing to deal adequately with the political condition of old Greece. We may point to the extraordinarily rapid collapse of his empire. But then he died suddenly in the midst of his work, and left no grown heir to succeed him. In some respects I think we must all admit that he showed very remarkable gifts of statesmanship. Though half a barbarian by origin, he was an enthusiast for Hellenism, and his plan, it can be argued, was to spread it at the point of the spear all over the civilised world. When he destroyed Thebes he spared one house—the house of Pindar. When he marched over the burning deserts of Asia, he took poets and artists in his train. He would stop his march every now and then to exhibit Greek athletics and Greek arts to the wondering Orientals. He planted Greek cities wherever he had time to stop, from Alexandria at the mouth of the Nile to Candahar (another version of his name). He had the art which makes a successful apostle, the gift of being all things to all men except, perhaps, to the Greeks of Greece; but these he left behind him. In Egypt, the land of religion and mystery, he made a solemn pilgrimage into the desert, and got himself accepted as the son of the god called by the Greeks Ammon. In Persia he recognised the merits of the Persian provincial system, and appointed his own satraps, or even retained the existing ones. He treated Persian women with the deference to which they were accustomed, and added one to his household in the manner to which they were also accustomed. His Macedonians murmured at his Oriental dress and manners, but Alexander was still a Greek at heart, the lines of Homer always rang in his ears, and he fancied himself a reincarnation of Achilles pursuing his Phrygian Hectors over the dusty plains of Troy. He was mad, no doubt, to march so far over those weary deserts into Turkestan, through those dreadful defiles of the Hindu Kush. Only the mutiny of his army turned him back when he reached the farthest of the Five Rivers of the Punjab. And then it was frantic lunacy, or a ruthless resolve to punish the men who had failed him, to lead his army home along the burning coasts of the Persian Gulf. When he died he was projecting a naval expedition along the coasts of Africa. Most conquerors have a touch of insanity, no doubt. The sanest of them was Julius Caesar, and the maddest was Charles XII. But Alexander the Great had lucid intervals of imaginative statesmanship. It is in this respect that he differs from the vulgar type of adventurer and stands among civilising conquerors like William the Norman with his Domesday Book, Napoleon with his Code, and Julius Caesar with his Julian Laws and his calendar. This intellectual suppleness was the mark of Alexander's Greek education, though it still remains a difficulty to trace in his career the influence of Aristotle, his tutor.

On his death at Babylon in 323 the whole empire fell to pieces. After a brief space and a pretence of unity his various generals, themselves men of the greatest brilliance, sought their own advantage. Most of them naturally desired to emulate their master and secure as much of his empire as they could for themselves. Out of the confusing struggles of the next generation three great kingdoms gradually emerged: that of Macedonia, warlike and turbulent under various shortlived dynasties, that of Asia, huge and wealthy under a line of Seleucids, and that of Egypt under a long family of Ptolemies. The subjects were alien, except for some city communities, the rulers Greek. In the country, no doubt, Oriental life and language continued, but in the newly-founded towns and for purposes of government both the language and the civilisation were Greek. Thus Alexander had done his work. It can be variously described: either he had added a good deal of the eastern Mediterranean and the Middle East to the Greek world, or he had linked Greece firmly to the East. Curious traces of Hellenism are found even in distant India.

In this world of "the Successors", as they are called, the ancient states of Greece are not altogether negligible. Rhodes continued to be free and rich. Athens, as I have remarked, was occasionally oppressed and sometimes enslaved by the Macedonian rulers to the north, but for the most part she continued as a lively community, conducting her own affairs as vehemently as ever, pretending an independent policy, which, however, could not exist except by playing off one dynast against another. Sparta stood sullenly aloof, joining no confederacies, but dreadfully shrunken in population. I have alluded to her notable experiments at reform in the third century under Agis and Cleomenes. It was ended by the crushing defeat at Sellasia from the Achaan League and the Macedonians. Towns like Argos and Corinth preserved their liberties by joining the Leagues. Epirus was a new Power rising to fame by the same road as Macedon under an adventurous king called Pyrrhus. He unfortunately turned west instead of east in his search for worlds to conquer, and there met another rising power, a race of real soldiers who made short work of the Greek phalanx, even when supported by heavy cavalry in the form of Indian elephants. It was these Romans who, when they came in due course to return his visit, put "Finis" to this chapter of Greek history, and proceeded themselves to undertake the task of writing the next.

ALEXANDER IN ART

We have numerous works of art which portray Alexander the Great, and as he is said to have granted the sole right of depicting his royal form to Lysippus the sculptor, and to have commissioned Apelles as his royal painter, we may presume that most of the portraits go back to an original by one of these artists (Plate 97, *a*). We have enough description of the pictures by Apelles to show that he treated his model with all the obsequiousness of a court painter. There was Alexander in the guise of Zeus wielding the thunderbolt, Alexander in the company of Nike and the Heavenly Twins, Alexander leading the god of war in triumph, Alexander mounted on Bucephalus. The only relic which may give us an idea of the treatment of such subjects in pictorial art is a very fine mosaic floor at Pompeii (Plate 97, *b*). It represents the conqueror charging bareheaded into the press of the Persian bodyguard to win his greatest victory. You see Darius in his Oriental "mitre" anxious and terrified, just turning his chariot out of the battle. The scene is represented with great spirit, and Alexander's face is happily preserved. The horses in particular are most faithfully rendered. The mosaic is probably copied at second or third hand from a painting by one of the great artists of tradition, Philoxenus of Eretria.

The same scene is depicted with greater brilliance on the famous sarcophagus from Sidon. On one side of it Alexander and Parmenio are fighting the Persian hosts, and on the other side they are engaged in a lion-hunt (Plate 98). Few works of art can compare with this monument in magnificence or in historical interest. It is especially interesting in the history of art because it gives us a good example of the application of colour to sculpture. It also affords fine specimens of Greek mouldings and designs. The material is Pentelic marble imported from Athens. This sarcophagus is now in the museum at Constantinople.

Of the many busts and heads of Alexander, none gives us a very favourable example of the work of Lysippus. A head in Paris, the identity of which is assured by an inscription, may be taken as the best extant copy of what must have been one of the most popular portraits of Alexander; several other versions have come down to us (Plate 97, *a*). We are told that Lysippus alone was permitted to make portraits of Alexander, because "others desiring to represent the bend of his neck and the emotional glance of his eyes, failed to render his manly and leonine aspect". It should be noted that Lysippus made a famous group of Alexander's hunting, of which a little copy may be recognised in a bronze at Naples, and another of Alexander's troop of horse; but it is doubtful whether the Constantinople reliefs go back to Lysippian originals.

Alexander was worshipped even in his lifetime as a god. He claimed, among other divine claims, to be a son of Ammon. In this character he is represented with the ram's horns of that Egyptian deity on a coin of Thrace struck by Lysimachus, one of his generals and successors (Plate 103, *a*). Alexander was the first of mortals to have his portrait on Greek coins, and it is only in virtue of the divine honours paid to him that this is conceded even to the Conqueror of the world. Many of the later kings followed his example, and portraiture on the coins now becomes common, so that we possess in this medium the veristic portraits of some of these makers of the world (Plate 103).

ALEXANDRIA

In studying the early civilisation of Europe, which means the history of the Mediterranean peninsulas, one must not forget that economically Egypt is the key to the whole position. In natural resources it is by far the richest country in that region. Hitherto, however, it had been shut off from the rest of the world by its own peculiar civilisation and religion, though the Greeks had occasionally borrowed ideas from it and sometimes interfered in its historical course. Now Alexander gives it a Greek government and a Greek capital. In order to crush the Phoenician fleet which had been the principal naval support of the Persian Empire, he had been compelled to destroy the city of Tyre. But it was more than a strategic move. He intended the commerce and sea-power of the Levant to be henceforth in Greek hands. He succeeded brilliantly in his purpose. Phoenicia passed away from the stage of history, and only survived in her great colony of Carthage.

The city of Alexandria was laid out on a mathematical plan by Greek architects. Its situation near the delta of the Nile was exceedingly favourable to commerce, especially as the difficult navigation of its waters was mitigated by the construction of a great lighthouse, one of the Seven Wonders of the World. In the division of the empire Egypt had the good fortune to fall to the share of Ptolemy, a ruthless and skilful dynast. He and his successors pursued a policy of commerce and expansion. There was brisk traffic between Alexandria, Rhodes, Pergamum, Athens, and Syracuse, and Alexandria grew to be the greatest city in the world. It was pre-eminently Greek, but tinctured also with some of the Orientalism of its environment.

Along with commerce the Ptolemies cultivated literature by founding a sort of university or college called the Museum. It consisted of a temple of the Muses, rooms for its members, a common dining-hall, cloistered walks for the peripatetic teacher, and above all a magnificent library, for which the kings of Egypt made it their ambition to collect all the books of the world. Half a million MSS. were gathered there in the third century. The chief librarian was the master of the whole institution, which was a place of research and literary production rather than of education. At the same time Ptolemy made a point of attracting all the foremost literary men of the Greek world to his court. It cannot be denied that the Alexandrian culture was rich and vigorous. Great strides were made in science and mathematics, new and promising forms of literature were invented, but at the same time the sheltered air of the Museum tended to produce, as is inevitably the case with collegiate institutions, a rather frigid and academic type of work. At Alexandria, for instance, the first critics arose, and the first literary scholars, whose task was mainly to elucidate and comment upon the works of Homer. One of these scholars invented the Greek system of breathings and accents to help in the recital of verse. The most famous of all of them was Aristarchus, the Father of Criticism. In science and mathematics we must mention our old friend Euclid, who reigned in the hearts of schoolboys until the day before yesterday. Here for a time worked Archimedes, the great engineer of Syracuse and founder of mechanics, statics, and dynamics. Wondrous stories are told of his inventions and of his absent-mindedness. Once as he was entering the bath the overflowing of the water gave him a valuable scientific hint. He was so pleased that he forgot to dress, but ran home through the streets crying, "Heureka! Heureka! (I have found it)". At Alexandria, too, lived Eratosthenes, who first measured the circumference of the earth, and worked out a system of chronology for history. There were many other historians of lesser repute at the Museum.

In poetry Alexandria is connected with some important developments, chiefly literary revivals of ancient modes. Thus Apollonius the Rhodian attempted to revive the epic, and wrote a long peom in hexameter verse on the Argonautic expedition of Jason. It is of course rather cold and formal, it is a long way from Homer, but it is of considerable merit in the field of poetry. Alexandria revived also the elegiac couplet, chiefly for short epigrams, some of which have the beauty and colour of a Greek gem. We may see for an example that epigram of Callimachus from which I have taken the couplet at the head of my Introduction, and which was so charmingly translated by William Johnson Cory. I quote another elegiac epigram of Meleager's to show how modern in tone and subject these dainty lyrics had become in the first century B.C.:

Poor foolish heart, I cried "Beware",
    I vowed thou wouldst be captured,
So fondly hovering round the snare.
    With thy false love enraptured.

I cried, and thou art caught at last,
    All vainly flutterest in the toils.
Lord Love himself that bound thee fast
    And meshed thy pinions in his coils.

And he hath set thee on his fire,
    In drugs thy swooning soul immersed,
In stifling perfumes of desire,
    With scalding tears to quench thy thirst.

So far it is mainly a record of revivals, but in Theocritus, who, though Sicilian by birth, passed most of his active career at Alexandria, we have the inventor of a new and most important branch of literature. With him pastoral poetry was a fresh and genuine creation. His Idylls are, as their name implies, a series of cameo pictures of shepherd life in Sicily. We have found no space here to speak of the later developments of Sicilian history, which in the fourth and third centuries became once more a desperate battleground between Carthaginian invaders and clever Syracusan tyrants like Dionysius and Agathocles. It is strange to think that the beautiful rustic life depicted by Theocritus could exist among the hills and glens of Sicily in spite of all the turmoil of history. Andrew Lang completely vindicated Theocritus from the charge of artificiality by pointing out that the shepherds of modern Greece sing in language of refined and impassioned poetry that is perfectly natural and spontaneous. Large parts of the Idylls sound like quotations of such songs of Nature. Theocritus was, of course, the source of that pastoral convention which has produced so much that is artificial in art and literature amid much of supreme beauty. We think at once of Vergil, Spenser, Sidney, Milton, Watteau, and the Dresden Shepherdess. Theocritus is the literary father of all these. In his famous Fifteenth Idyll, which describes with exquisite humour the conversation of a pair of Sicilian dames going to see a festival of Adonis at Alexandria, we have the characteristics of another literary form—the mime. This is a rudimentary style of drama which seeks to portray little genre scenes of life with no attempt at a plot. Herodas of Cos was the principal master of this art.

Two pupils of Theocritus were Bion and Moschus, both accomplished elegiac poets. Bion's dirge for Daphnis and Moschus' lament for Bion have provided the type for Vergil's lament for Daphnis, for Milton's "Lycidas" for Shelley's "Adonais", and Matthew Arnold's "Thyrsis".

ATHENS AND HER PHILOSOPHERS

In Alexandria, then, the Hellenic genius was as fruitful as ever. But it was growing under glass there, and it was not pure Occidental culture. We have to think of the Greek Ptolemies, descended from Macedonian generals, as on the one hand writing Greek poetry and inviting Greek scholars to criticise it, but on the other hand accepting homage and adulation as Eastern potentates, and actually marrying their sisters after the customary manner of Pharaohs. In Egypt Father Zeus took over the horns of Amen-Ra and became Zeus Ammon. Aphrodite, the foam-born goddess, assumed her Oriental nature once more and was mated with young Adonis in weird and wanton Eastern ritual. Adonis was no Grecian youth, but a mystic personification of the spring, and his worshippers tore their hair and made lamentation for him with the same frenzy as made the priests of Carmel cut themselves with knives in honour of Baal. All over Asia Minor Hellenism had to mingle with Asiatic elements, losing in the contact all its fine austerity and sweet reasonableness. From Asia came the worship of Cybele, an Oriental Great Mother, with horrid mysteries performed by priestly eunuchs. Even the sculpture with which the wealthy Attalids adorned their great altar of Zeus at Pergamum, hard by their splendid theatre (Plate 104), though Greek in plot and execution, is of almost Asiatic luxuriance and violent beauty (Plate 102). Passion and effort replace calm and dignity even as they do in the new Asiatic schools of oratory. Alexander's violent battering at the gates which separate East from West had produced a strange hybrid in many of the cities of Eastern Greece.

But in some quarters the Greek spirit still produced lovely and reasonable work in art and literature alike. There is not degeneracy in the Aphrodite of Melos known to the public as the Venus of Milo (Plate 101, a). Some, maybe, would prefer the Aphrodite of Cyrene, a later Roman copy of a bronze of the third quarter of the third century B.C., as being more "feminine" (Plate 89, a). But the Aphrodite of Melos is worthy to stand with the Cnidian of Praxiteles, though differently conceived. While she displays the Late Hellenistic type of female beauty she also possesses the dignity and force of Phidias. Unless you follow the pedants who make some point of the arrangement of her drapery, there is not a trait of vulgarity in her aspect. All the archaeological indications seem to suggest that her author lived during the latest second century B.C. in the Asiatic city of Antioch on the Maeander. She was found in a cavern on the little island of Melos, hidden there by who knows what devout worshipper or terrified pirate? She is, in fact, surrounded with mystery. No one has succeeded in restoring her missing arms, though by far the most plausible theory is that which would make her hold a shield for a mirror in the same manner as a type of Aphrodite of the second half of the fourth century known from a marble copy of an original bronze. With much else she proves that you cannot close the history of Greek art with Praxiteles and Lysippus.

One of the most interesting figures among the warriors who followed Alexander was Demetrius the Besieger of Cities, who gained his title from a celebrated but unsuccessful siege of Rhodes. He gained the kingdom of Macedonia and took over Athens. In celebration of a naval victory gained by him over Ptolemy I in 306 B.C. he set up a wonderful statue of Victory standing on the prow of a warship. Her wings are outspread, her drapery is blown back by the wind, she is all life and motion. This statue is reproduced on his coins. Along with the Venus of Milo the chief glory of the Louvre is a magnificent marble figure (Plate 101, *b*) found in the island of Samothrace, embodying much the same general idea as the figure on the coins. This was long held to be the original of Demetrius; but it can hardly be so, for Demetrius would not have set up his memorial in Samothrace, on ground belonging to a rival. The statue in the Louvre is a later work, probably commemorating a victory of the Rhodians over Antiochus III (222-187 B.C.). The Late Hellenistic dynamics and structure of the figure are different from those of Demetrius's monument which was in the classical tradition. Also the Nike did not blow a trumpet but held a victor's ribbon in her hand. The reader should compare it with that earlier Victory fashioned by Paeonius (Plate 75, *a*). He will see that the drapery is much richer and the whole conception far more sensational.

In all this period the dear city of Pallas had not suffered any material change. She had lost her maritime possessions, and in external politics she was but a pawn among the kings of Macedon and Egypt. But for the most part she remained a free community, governed by her Assembly. The Piraeus still remained an important centre of commerce. Intellectually Athens still ruled the world not only in virtue of her past achievements, but by the continuing pre-eminence of her philosophers. Her principal literary product of these days was the New Comedy of Menander and his school. Menander's work was taken over more or less bodily by the Roman poets Plautus and Terence, who sometimes weave two of them together into one play, a process known by the not inappropriate technical name "contamination". From the Roman comedians they passed almost direct to the Elizabethan age, so that in the history of the drama Shakespeare's "Measure for Measure" begins almost where Menander left off. The sands of Egypt have yielded large fragments of this dramatist, and lately a whole play, the *Dyskolos*, or "Angry Old Man", has been discovered, to shed more light on a poet so highly regarded by the Romans.

If we turn now to philosophy we find the great name of Aristotle overshadowing everything else. If we have a true sense of historical proportion, we shall probably admit that the words of Aristotle have conquered the world in far truer sense than the spears of his great pupil. For Aristotle is the father of the inductive method, the patron saint of all those who observe and verify facts in order to discover the laws that control them. He was born at Stagira, in eastern Macedonia, but he came to Athens to be a disciple in the Academy, that pleasant olive-grove where Plato was the master. Twenty years he spent thus in study, and then he was commissioned by Philip to teach Alexander and other noble youths of Macedon. As soon as this task was completed he returned to Athens, and there founded his famous Peripatetic school of philosophy, so called because his lectures were delivered in the shady walks or the covered court that surrounded the Lyceum. In the morning he would discuss abstruse questions with an inner circle of adepts, and in the cool of the evening deliver polished lectures to a wider circle. The fame of his teaching was spread throughout the world, and all the ablest intellects of Greece gathered to hear him. All his life he received the most generous support from Alexander, who made a point of collecting strange beasts from all quarters to enrich his zoological studies and augment the first of all learned collections in what can be called the first residential university. The attitude of the monarch towards learning was in striking contrast to the behaviour of the Athenian democracy. On the death of Alexander some wretched hierophant instituted a prosecution for impiety against Aristotle, just as they had done against Socrates, and forced him to withdraw from Athens for the closing year of his life. It is perhaps significant that the year 322 B.C. saw not only the deaths of Demosthenes and Aristotle, of the champion of democracy and of the philosopher of the polis, but also the end for a time of Athenian freedom.

Aristotle took all knowledge as his province and proceeded to map it out for further investigation. It is impossible even to enumerate all his extant writings here, and they are only a small part of what he wrote. For scientific method he wrote on Logic and Dialectic, and here he was the discoverer of the syllogism and distinguished the inductive and deductive methods of reasoning. For literature he dissected Poetry and Rhetoric, laying down principles which have exercised a profound influence since. In his Ethics he defines the nature of virtue in a sense that is truly Hellenic. Virtues are the mean between two vices. Thus liberality is the virtue of which prodigality and parsimony are the extremes; courage is the mean between foolhardiness and cowardice. For Natural Science he wrote the first treatise on zoology, enumerating about five hundred different species. It was the first time in the history of the world when men had thought it worth while to observe the world around them. Most of this scientific work was beyond the reach of mankind, and remained so for two thousand years. The Romans studied him, but scarcely advanced a step. In the Dark Ages Europe lost even the power to follow him, and much of his teaching was recovered from the wise men of Arabia. The mediaeval schoolmen were content with abridged translations for their "scientific" knowledge and made him a strait-jacket for their ideas. It was not until the fifteenth and sixteenth centuries that Europe came again to be able to study and understand him, and later to supplement observation and classification by experiment.

Plato had treated Political Science in three great dialogues, the greatest of which is the *Republic*. The ostensible object of this work is to define the nature of Justice, and in order to do so Socrates and his friends set out to construct an Ideal Republic. Before they have gone very far it is evident, and indeed it is admitted, that such a state as they envisage cannot exist upon earth, though it may be laid up in the heavens for an example. It is a small Greek city-state. Plato discerns three elements in every state, the producers, the warriors, and the thinking element. Of these he makes three rigid classes, though education, upon the importance of which Plato everywhere insists, is to provide the means of rising for all. Music and gymnastics are the twofold base of Platonic education. The thinking part of the community are to have the sole title to government. They are to live a simple communistic life, rather like the nobles of Sparta, but without their military activity. In order that nothing may disturb their absolute unity, Plato decrees that wives and children are to be held in common, as well as all property. These strange doctrines have caused Plato to be held as the father of Socialism, but it is to be observed that in Plato communism is only advocated for a restricted circle of aristocrats, and that it is based not upon economic considerations, but on ethics in a spirit of asceticism. In a later dialogue Plato regretfully admits that laws are necessary to a state, seeing that you cannot keep your philosophers on the throne when you have got them there. This admission may be occasioned by the failure of Plato to realise his ideals in actual practice. He had an extraordinary chance. He was invited over to Syracuse to mould the character and policy of the young tyrant Dionysius II. He argued that it was useless to place an ideal system of government before a young man who was not of sufficient education to appreciate it. He therefore determined to begin with the education of the prince and began it with geometry. The issue may be easily guessed.

Aristotle approached Politics from a more practical standpoint. True to his inductive method, he first collected accounts of all the existing forms of government in the Greek world, more than a hundred in number. Unfortunately, the *Polity of Athens*, discovered in 1891, is the only surviving example. Then in his great treatise called the *Politics* he attempted to criticise practical statesmanship from a scientific standpoint, and in his turn also constructed something like an ideal state. For him, as for all Greek thinkers, politics was only a branch of ethics. The state came into existence for the sake of enabling men to live; it survives for the purpose of enabling men to live well. The object, therefore, of the statesman is to get the right kind of people at the head of affairs—and that means Aristocracy. Viewing all Greek society from the philosopher's standpoint, he regarded all those whose economic position required them to be mainly interested in gaining a livelihood as too much preoccupied with sordid cares to possess political virtue or to be fit to govern. His governing class is therefore necessarily the rich class, just as it was with Plato, though neither philosopher would admit wealth as the sole or even the main criterion. Aristotle regards Monarchy as a good form of government also, if you could secure that the monarch should be better than the people he rules, and should rule for their advantage, not his own. There is also a good form of Republic or Free Constitution, in which the whole body of the citizens take their turn in office. But each of these three sound forms of government has its own special danger—Aristocracy degenerates into Oligarchy when the few rule for their own advantage, Monarchy into Tyranny, and the Free Constitution into Democracy, or, rather, the rule of the Mob.

It is evident in all his writings that he regards the Athenian government as a bad one, but we must remember that he only saw it in its decline. The most valuable part of his teaching is that wherein he defines the state as a partnership, not in all things, but only in those things which concern its *telos* or end—the good life. Also, it is made up, not of individuals, but of smaller partnerships such as the family. It is on these grounds that he criticises the doctrine of communism. Since the whole object of political life is to secure moral completeness, it is obvious that the citizen does not surrender his whole being to the state. Thus both philosophers are alike in putting aside the claims of the working classes in the commonly accepted sense of this term. Both are therefore aristocratic. Both look upon the state as existing for moral rather than economic ends. Both regard the laws and constitution as something sacred and clearly beyond the reach of the citizens. Neither of them has conceived the idea of political progress, which, indeed, is an idea of very modern origin. Such was the philosophic ideal of the city-state, in some respects worse than our own.

Aristotle summed up the experience of the polis, but stood on the threshold of a wider world. After Aristotle Greek political thinkers took up and developed the hints he drops as to the Mixed Constitution, in which the three elements Monarchic, Aristocratic, and Democratic are to be subtly mingled as they were in Sparta and Rome.

Other schools of philosophy arose at Athens which from their more vital influence upon the lives and actions of ordinary men are quite as important in the history of human civilisation. Zeno, a native of Citium in Cyprus, united East and West, Semite and Greek and founded in the Stoa Poikilé of Athens the Stoic philosophy, and Epicurus taught the doctrines which bore his name, at the same time when Aristotle was lecturing in the Lyceum and the successor of Plato in the Academy. Both were largely concerned with the rules for right conduct in life and a life in the world (*oikoumene*) not necessarily in the polis. The Stoics taught that wisdom and virtue are the true goal of man. Virtue consists in living according to Nature, and it becomes the business of the wise man to discover what is essential and distinguish it from what is merely accidental and ephemeral. Pleasure, praise, even life itself, are among things accidental. At its best Stoicism insisted very sternly upon duty, and the contempt of pain and death. In this way it seized upon all that was noblest in the Roman character and raised up under the Empire a series of martyrs who alone withstood the tyrants because they were not afraid of death. It approaches the sublime in the mouths of Marcus Aurelius and Epictetus. Filtering through the Asiatic temperament and mingling in its course with the higher teaching of Pharisaism, it did much to form the philosophy of a certain Jew of Tarsus, and through him has vitally influenced Christianity. In another sphere its insistence upon Natural Law bore fruit in Roman jurisprudence and lies at the base of all the legal systems of Europe.

Epicurus, on the other hand, made pleasure the end of life, not the mere bodily pleasure with which his name has been associated, but that which in the sum of its moments goes to form what we call happiness. It was necessary to happiness that men should cast off all the degrading fears born of superstition and know that the gods—if indeed gods exist—are too much occupied themselves in enjoying celestial happiness to condescend to punish and afflict the mortals under their feet. So the Epicureans accepted a material theory, largely due to Democritus, which explained the universe on atomic principles. Death was merely the resolution of body and soul into their primordial atoms. The less noble spirits among them undoubtedly taught the maxim "Let us eat and drink for tomorrow we die", but in such a mind as that of the Roman poet Lucretius Epicureanism is a fine and lofty thing, with its fearless spirit of inquiry and its bitter scorn of superstition.

We should mention also the Cynics, whose chief teacher was Diogenes, for they inculcated a contempt for pleasure and an asceticism which led some of them to live a hermit life, or, like mendicant friars, to carry neither staff nor scrip and to take no thought for their raiment. Among the common folk, as critics and opponents of established authority, they had their long-lasting importance.

It is evident, then, that intellectual life was still in full vigour at Athens in the third century. But there was a weakening already visible. These Greeks could still think clearly, even nobly, but it was not until they made Roman converts that noble thoughts could be translated into noble action. As for the Greeks, their restless tongues and subtle brains carried them away into logic-chopping and childish love of paradox. There was a day when Athens sent on an embassy to Rome the three heads of her chief schools of philosophy. Their brilliant discourses charmed and amazed the simple Romans. Carneades proved that virtue was profitable, and the Romans were delighted. On the next day he proved that it was unprofitable, and the Romans were astonished. Cato, however, the truest Roman of them all, thought that Rome was better without such brilliant visitors. And he was probably right.

VII

EPILOGUE

ἡ πόλις ἡμῶν ... τὸ τῶν Ἑλλήνων ὄνομα πεποίηκε
μηκέτι τοῦ γένους ἀλλὰ τῆς διανοίας δοκεῖν εἶναι.
ISOCRATES

IT was, according to Isocrates, the fruit of the activity of Athens, that Hellas had ceased to be a geographical expression and had become the definition of an intellectual standpoint. In that very true sense Greek history cannot close. It falls into chapters which are ever to be continued as soon as man begins to think again. Whosoever from the beginning of his action already contemplates its final end and adapts his means thereto in earnest simplicity, whosoever knows that pride and vain ostentation will assuredly bring its own punishment, of whatever land or age he may be, he is a Greek. In that sense we cannot close Greek history. Greece, as Horace said in a very hackneyed phrase, vanquished the Roman, her barbarian conqueror, and the Roman took up the mission of extending Hellenism over the West. The history of Roman civilisation only begins in the second century, when Rome was first brought into contact with Greece. Elsewhere* we shall see how Greek culture permeated everything at Rome after that, supplied her with art and literature, taught her philosophy, overlaid and almost destroyed her native religion, and even wrote her history. Losing Hellas, Europe sank into ages of darkness: recovering her, the European nations began to think again. Shakespeare we trace through the Latins to Menander, Milton through Vergil to Homer and Theocritus, Bacon to Aristotle, Sir Thomas More to Plato, and so with the others. So that everyone who reads books or enjoys art in Europe today is indirectly borrowing from Greece.

Moreover, it is fairly obvious that Greece has not ceased to exist as a geographical expression. The more we study modern Greece, the more we are convinced that the Hellenic race is by no means extinct. Greece was, it is true, conquered by the Romans in 146 B.C.

*The Grandeur that was Rome, by the same author.

237

The latter had been forced partly by the aggression of Pyrrhus and partly by the expansion of their own empire to take some action in the Eastern Mediterranean.   There they found themselves physically as men among children, intellectually as children among men.   Nothing is more striking than the almost reverent spirit in which the Roman soldiers first moved about among the old cities of Greece.   But the Greeks were impossible neighbours, and at last, after infinite forbearance, the Romans were compelled by their masculine sense of order to take the responsibility of controlling Greece.   Corinth was destroyed for a warning, Macedonia made a province.   But cities like Athens and Sparta were left to govern themselves, though, of course, their foreign policy was subject to Roman control.   Athens still continued to talk and write and teach.   She became a sort of university town to which noble Romans were sent for their studies. Even when Achaea was added to the list of Roman provinces in the days of Augustus it did not mean that Athens ceased to be a free city. In the days of the Empire the more cultured emperors, like Nero and Hadrian, loved to pass their time in Greece, in the attempt to share in her intellectual prestige.   So we have Nero performing in the Olympic Games, and Hadrian rebuilding a large part of Athens. It was Hadrian who attempted to complete the gigantic temple of Olympian Zeus begun by Pisistratus.   The Athenian schools of philosophy continued to attract strangers from all parts of the world, until Christianity began to see its bitterest foe in the Stoics, who taught many of its doctrines.   Julian the Apostate dreamed for a moment of reviving Greek philosophy, so as to overcome Christianity by borrowing many of its doctrines, but at last a decree of Justinian closed the Athenian schools of Philosophy in A.D. 529.   Meanwhile clouds of barbarian invaders were continually passing over the land. The Goths under Alaric ravaged Greece.   The Slavs conquered and peopled a great part of it without, in the long run, materially altering its nationality.   Norman invaders conquered it, and not long before our own conquest Harold Hardrada entered Athens in triumph. Then came the Latin crusaders and Venetians.   All through the thirteenth and fourteenth centuries there were Frankish Dukes of Athens.   In 1456 Mohammed II conquered her, and thenceforth, with a temporary period of Venetian triumph, the Turks ruled Greece with a heavy hand until the glorious War of Independence, in which Lord Byron sought to play a part of prophet and warrior.   In 1830 Greece was declared an independent kingdom, and shortly afterwards provided with a youthful European king from Bavaria. The experiment was not a success. The Greeks succeeded in getting rid of one king, and Europe obligingly furnished another from her inexhaustible stock of younger sons. In 1897 the little kingdom plunged into a war with her big neighbour, Turkey, for which she lacked resources and organisation. Since then the victorious wars of 1912 and 1913 completely restored the prestige of Greek arms and greatly increased her territory and resources. The part played by Greece during the First Great War, her sufferings in the Second, and economic and political problems since are fresh in the memory and need not be recounted here.

We have already seen that Greek art still crops out in occasional masterpieces down to imperial times. With literature this is still more the case. Long after the best of Roman literature was over and done with, Greece kept putting forth new products. The Greek novel, for example, in Lucian and Heliodorus is something entirely fresh and of great importance in literary history. The biographies of Plutarch are a new departure; so are the guide-books of such writers as Pausanias. The case of Lucian, in particular, shows that a Syrian of the second century A.D. could write in pure Attic Greek. In him we have the prototype of Swift and Sterne, a brilliant mocker and a creative genius. Throughout the Byzantine and mediaeval periods, if the torch of Greek letters sometimes flickered low, it was never wholly extinguished, and Greek literature may claim in some form or other to be continuous from classical times to modern days.

The story of Greek art is not substantially different. The Greeks continued to influence the Romans and to participate in the adaptation of their achievements to Roman uses; so much so that it is difficult in the Late Hellenistic and Imperial Roman periods to distinguish with any certainty or satisfaction in many cases between "Greek Art" and "Roman Art", for example in the supposedly "Roman" art of portraiture (cf. Plate 100, *b*). There are numerous problems of date, artist and location of centres of production, which included Athens as well as cities of Asia Minor. It was natural for the Greeks, at the decline of the Hellenistic world, to turn their eyes to the new patrons from the west. We must try to understand their attitude, and beware of speaking too often of the "starveling" and obliging Greek after the manner of Juvenal, or of criticising the taste of late Greek sculptors (where "Greek" in effect means East Mediterranean). We must remember the part played by the Roman patron, and *his* influence on taste.   From the time of Rome's first triumphant entry into the eastern Mediterranean the inexhaustible stores of archaic and classical art of Greece, Asia and Sicily were plundered for the benefit of Rome and Roman individuals: Cicero was in it as well as Verres. It meant the multiplication of copies for those not lucky enough to obtain originals, and copies of various quality according to the purse of the patron.   To these copies and to contemporary critics such as Pliny we owe our knowledge, such as it is, of great works of art otherwise lost. But there was more than this, and more than the applications of Greek art to works of luxury on a minor scale, such as the Portland Vase in two-coloured glass—one of the best-known objects in the British Museum thanks in part to Wedgewood—or the splendid precious metalwork of which scant examples survive. The Greeks continued also in the main current of artistic development and application. Here again it must be stressed that "Greek", largely though not wholly, means "Eastern Mediterranean", and of the period after the conquests of Alexander the Great. It was natural when so much had been achieved earlier that sculptors became mannered and archaistic, or exuberant and tasteless, as in the Laocoon, or brutal like those they portrayed (Plate 100, *a*)—but who shall talk of taste when it varies so much from generation to generation? It is also important to realise the part the Greeks played in, for instance, the late Republican coinage of Rome, in great works like the Ara Pacis Augustae and the Market of Trajan, or in the great carved sarcophagi; and in periods such as the Hadrianic and even before. Again later, if Septimius Severus was a Roman and an African, it was through Greek artists of the school of Aphrodisias in Caria that he embellished his native town of Sabrata. As in much else the story of Greece becomes that of Rome.

BIBLIOGRAPHY

The following Bibliography is divided into two sections: (A) Popular or semi-popular works intended to supplement the present book; (B) Standard works (also containing bibliographical lists) which will provide the basis for more detailed study.

(A)

General

H. D. F. KITTO, The Greeks (Penguin Books, 1957).

M. I. FINLEY, The Ancient Greeks (Chatto and Windus, 1963).

R. M. COOK, The Greeks till Alexander (Thames and Hudson, 1961).

J. M. COOK, The Greeks in Ionia and the East (Thames and Hudson, 1962).

A. G. WOODHEAD, The Greeks in the West (Thames and Hudson, 1963).

C. M. BOWRA, The Greek Experience (Weidenfeld and Nicolson, 1957).

J. BOARDMAN, The Greeks Overseas (Penguin Books, 1964).

Archaeology and Art

R. W. HUTCHINSON, Prehistoric Crete (Penguin Books, 1962).

C. W. BLEGEN, Troy and the Trojans (Thames and Hudson, 1963).

J. D. BEAZLEY and B. ASHMOLE, Greek Sculpture and Vase Painting (Cambridge, 1932).

PIERRE DEVAMBEZ, Greek Painting (Weidenfeld and Nicolson, 1962).

A. LANE, Greek Pottery (Faber and Faber, 1948).

J. CHARBONNEUX, Greek Bronzes (London, 1961).

G. M. A. RICHTER, Greek Art (Phaidon, 1959).

This latter outstandingly well illustrated and written work leads on to a series of splendidly illustrated books on aspects of art, with first rate Intro-, duction and Notes:

S. MARINATOS and M. HIRMER, Crete and Mycenae (Thames and Hudson 1960).

H. BERVE, G. GRUBEN and M. HIRMER, Greek Temples and Shrines (Thames and Hudson, 1962).

R. Lullies and M. Hirmer, Greek Sculpture² (Thames and Hudson, 1960).

M. Robertson, Greek Painting (Skira, 1959).

P. E. Arias and M. Hirmer, A History of Greek Vase Painting (London, 1961).

There are attractive British Museum publications such as:

D. E. L. Haynes, An Historical Guide to the Sculpture of the Parthenon (1962).

R. A. Higgins, Greek Terracotta Figures (1963).

Also publications of the American School of Classical Studies in Athens obtainable in the U.K.:

Guides to the American excavations at Athens (Agora), Corinth and Pylos.

Works based on the Agora Museum exhibits: Pots and Pans of Classical Athens. Amphoras and the Ancient Wine Trade. The Athenian Citizen.

(B)

More advanced or standard works arranged in categories and alphabetic order of author:

General History

J. B. Bury, History of Greece³, revised by R. Meiggs (Macmillan, 1952).

N. G. L. Hammond, History of Greece to 322 B.C. (Oxford, 1959).

Prehistoric and Early History. (a) *The Bronze Age.*

J. Chadwick, The Decipherment of Linear B (Cambridge, 1958).

G. E. Mylonas, Ancient Mycenae (Routledge, 1957).

M. P. Nilsson, Homer and Mycenae (Methuen, 1933).

D. Page, History and the Homeric Iliad (California, 1959).

L. R. Palmer, The Interpretation of Mycenaean Greek Texts (Oxford, 1963).

J. D. S. Pendlebury, The Archaeology of Crete (Methuen, 1939).

A. J. B. Wace, Mycenae (Princeton, 1949).

A. J. B. Wace and F. Stubbings, A Companion to Homer (Macmillan, 1962).

T. B. L. Webster, From Mycenae to Homer (Methuen, 1958).

There are the following fascicules published (to January 1964) of the revision of the Cambridge Ancient History:

(1) C. W. Blegen, Troy.

(2) W. K. C. Guthrie, The Religion and Mythology of the Greeks.

(12) F. Matz, Minoan Civilisation. Maturity and Zenith.

(15) JOHN CHADWICK, The Prehistory of the Greek Language.
(18) F. H. STUBBINGS, The Rise of Mycenaean Civilisation.

Prehistory and Early History. (b) *The Fall of Mycenaean Civilisation ; Iron Age Recovery and Early Greek History.*
NILSSON (1933), Wace-Stubbings (1962), Webster (1958) as above.
A. ANDREWES, The Greek Tyrants (Hutchinson, 1960).
V. R. d'A. DESBOROUGH, The Last Mycenaeans and their Successors (Oxford, 1964).
T. J. DUNBABIN, The Western Greeks (Oxford, 1948).
T. J. DUNBABIN, The Greeks and Their Eastern Neighbours (Hellenic Society, London, 1957).
M. I. FINLEY, The World of Odysseus (Chatto and Windus, 1956).
J. FORSDYKE, Greece before Homer, i. (Max Parrish, 1956).
G. L. HUXLEY, Early Sparta (Faber and Faber, 1962).
C. ROEBUCK, Ionian Trade and Colonisation (New York, 1959)
C. G. STARR, The Origins of Greek Civilisation (Cape, 1962).

The following fascicules of the revision of the Cambridge Ancient History:
(7) J. M. COOK, Greek Settlement in the Eastern Aegean and Asia Minor.
(13) V. R. d'A. DESBOROUGH and N. G. L. HAMMOND, The End of Mycenaean Civilisation and the Dark Age.

Economic and Social History
F. E. ADCOCK, The Greek and Macedonian Art of War (California, 1957).
V. EHRENBERG, The People of Aristophanes[2] (Blackwell, 1951).
G. GLOTZ, Ancient Greece at Work (London, 1926).
J. HASEBROEK, Trade and Politics in Ancient Greece (London, 1933).
A. ZIMMERN, The Greek Commonwealth[5] (Oxford, 1931).

Political Thought and Institutions
V. EHRENBERG, The Greek State (Blackwell, 1960).
A. H. M. JONES, Athenian Democracy (Blackwell, 1957).
T. A. SINCLAIR, History of Greek Political Thought (Routledge, 1951).

Philosophy and Science
E. BARKER, Plato and his Predecessors (Methuen, 1925).
W. K. C. GUTHRIE, A History of Greek Philosophy i, Earlier Presocratics and Pythagoreans (Cambridge, 1962).
W. JAEGER, Aristotle[2] (Oxford, 1948).
G. S. KIRK and J. E. RAVEN, The Presocratic Philosophers (Cambridge, 1957).
S. SAMBURSKY, The Physical World of the Greeks (Routledge, 1956).
G. SARTON, Ancient Science through the Golden Age of Greece (Oxford, 1953).

B. SNELL, The Discovery of the Mind (Blackwell, 1953).

(22) G. S. KIRK, The Homeric Poems as History.

(24) T. C. CASKEY, Greece, Crete and the Aegean Islands in the Early Bronze Age.

Religion and Mythology

E. R. DODDS, The Greeks and the Irrational (California, 1951).

ANDRÉ-JEAN FESTUGIÈRE, Personal Religion among the Greeks (California, 1954).

W. K. C. GUTHRIE, The Greeks and their Gods (Methuen, 1950).

M. P. NILSSON, Greek Piety (Oxford, 1948).

H. J. ROSE, A Handbook of Greek Mythology[6] (Methuen, 1958).

Poetic Literature and the Drama

Works on the historians and orators are inseparable from History and have been omitted here.

C. M. BOWRA, Greek Lyric Poetry[2] (Oxford, 1961).

G. S. KIRK, The Lays of Homer (Cambridge, 1962).

H. D. F. KITTO, Greek Tragedy[2] (Methuen, 1950).

D. W. LUCAS, The Greek Tragic Poets[2] (London, 1959).

D. PAGE, History and the Homeric Iliad (California, 1959).

A. PICKARD-CAMBRIDGE, The Dramatic Festivals of Athens (Oxford, 1953).

A. J. B. WACE and F. STUBBINGS, A Companion to Homer (Macmillan, 1962).

T. B. L. Webster, Greek Theatre Production (Methuen, 1956).

Art and Archaeology

Publications of sites, except Athens, are omitted. References to them will be found in the Bibliographies of the main works listed below.

Architecture

A. W. LAWRENCE, Greek Architecture (Penguin Books, 1957).

A. PLOMMER, Simpson's History of Arch. Development, i, Ancient and Classical Architecture (Longmans, 1956).

Sculpture

RHYS CARPENTER, Greek Sculpture (Chicago, 1960).

A. W. LAWRENCE, Classical Sculpture (Cape, 1929).

A. W. LAWRENCE, Later Greek Sculpture (Cape, 1927).

G. M. A. RICHTER, The Sculpture and Sculptors of the Greeks[3] (Oxford, 1950).

G. M. A. RICHTER, The Archaic Grave Stones of Attica (Phaidon, 1961).

G. M. A. RICHTER, Kouroi. Archaic Greek Youths (Phaidon, 1960).

Vase Painting
R. M. COOK, Greek Painted Pottery (Methuen, 1960). With an excellent
bibliography.

Coins
A Guide to the Principal Coins of the Greeks (British Museum, London,
1932).
C. T. SELTMAN, Greek Coins^2 (Methuen, 1955).

Gems and Seals
J. D. BEAZLEY, The Lewes House Collection of Ancient Gems (Oxford,
1920).
J. BOARDMAN, Island Gems (Hellenic Society, London, 1963).
V. E. G. KENNA, Cretan Seals (Oxford, 1960).
G. M. A. RICHTER, Metropolitan Museum of New York, Catalogue of
Engraved Gems (Rome, 1956).

Jewellery
R. A. HIGGINS, Greek and Roman Jewellery (Methuen, 1961).

Town Planning and Topography
I. T. HILL, The Ancient City of Athens (Methuen, 1953).
R. E. WYCHERLEY, How the Greeks built Cities^2 (Macmillan).

Inscriptions
A. G. WOODHEAD, The Study of Greek Inscriptions (Cambridge, 1959)

INDEX